Information Structures:
Implementing Imagination

Information Structures: Implementing Imagination

Dave Clay
FLORIDA INSTITUTE OF TECHNOLOGY

WEST PUBLISHING COMPANY
ST. PAUL   NEW YORK   LOS ANGELES   SAN FRANCISCO

Cover: "Revolution of the Viaduct" by Paul Klee.
© COSMOPRESS, Geneva/A.D.A.G.P., Paris/V.A.G.A.,
New York 1986

Design by Paula Schlosser

© 1986 By WEST PUBLISHING COMPANY
50 West Kellogg Boulevard
P.O. Box 64526
St. Paul, MN 55164-1003

Printed in the United States of America

Library of Congress Cataloging-in-Publication Data

Clay, David.
Information structures.

Includes index.
1. Data structures (Computer science)   I. Title.
QA76.9.D35C56   1985   005.7'3   85-20321
ISBN 0-314-93163-5

CONTENTS

Dedicated to

HAREMHAB
  an ancient Egyptian
VITTORIO
  a modern Italian
and the ZEN
  in us all.

PREFACE

During the time that I was preparing myself for writing this book, people who learned of my intentions curiously asked what the book was about. My early response was, "It's about computers." This elicited a variety of humorous and perplexed facial responses which I came to enjoy. Then one day on a train from Florence to Rome, a German woman posed the question. This time, my response came out as "information." Pressed for more details about the book, I described it with the word "imagination." Thus, the focus of my book began to emerge. In its final form this book presents imaginative ways of arranging data into relationship-capturing entities, called information structures, and methods for creatively implementing these structures in a program environment.

Let me describe who I think you are and where you may be in your computer science training. You are a student, officially or independently, of computer programming, in particular, and computer science, in general. Your backround includes academic courses or self study in basic computer organization, a higher level language (particularly PASCAL), and possibly assembly language. In working with the higher level language, you have written programs dealing with lists and tables of data using one- and two-dimensional arrays. From either the basic computer organization course or the assembly language course, you have developed the awareness that the nature of a computer's memory organization is an ordered set of *contiguous* storage locations and that ultimately all references to data exist by way of the numeric address of one of these storage locations. These two requisite skills, a megabit of imagination, and the guidance of this book, compose a bag of magical programming tricks which will enable you to dazzle any monolithic Merlin.

Magical feats are always comprehensible after the details of the illusion are revealed. This book seeks to fulfill the following aims:

1. To inform you about various Information Structures, how they can be implemented in a programming language, and the likely program environments in which they can be useful;

2. To increase your imagination quotient in the realm of problem solving via computer programming; and,

3. To entertain you so that we can accomplish our pedagogical partnership in a light and enlightening manner.

Our success in achieving these aims will provide you with a new perspective of the field of computer programming.

This can be called a "novel textbook" because, at times, it reads like an enjoyable novel. Although entertaining, this book is also seriously dedicated to helping you learn about information structures. The conscientious reader will emerge a more enthusiastic computer programmer, able to approach problem solving creatively. Therefore, enjoy the light-hearted approach but do not take the topics lightly. Learning is the plot; smiling while you learn is the intent.

To clarify my use of the term *information structures*, let me contrast it to *data structures*, a term that other authors write about. Although we describe the same beasts, I envision them with slightly different characters. The term data structure connotes a collection of raw data waiting for someone to sort through it and come up with some useful information. The term information structure, on the other hand, suggests a collection of data elements in a carefully planned arrangement, patterned according to the relationships among the data elements. In this imagined structure, the relationships between data elements are formed by certain guidewires. Given the necessary accessing tools, the information in the structure can easily traverse these guidewires and be extracted. (Hence, building logical informational interrelationships into the initial information structure is vital.) As you encounter the term Information Structure throughout the text, visualize this image of data elements connected by guidewires.

This book strives to describe rather than to define information structures; a definition limits but a description frees your imagination to mold structures to suit various needs. These new creative additions to your repertoire of programming skills will be presented in four ways: information structure as an abstract concept; graphical representation of the structure (a graphic display is worth more than 2^{10} words); physical implementation of the structure within a program; and algorithms that are helpful in using the information structure. You will do well to keep a clear focus on which of these four distinct but connected entities is being dealt with in your readings.

The implementation of an information structure and the information structures suggested for the problem solutions are useful approaches but they are not definitive ones. I encourage you to exercise your imagination to create other approaches. However, you must always consider what ramifications a "new and improved" approach may have on your problem solution or information structure. The trade-offs between two approaches include such questions as: Does one approach require more memory space? Does it reduce execution time? Does it entail considerably more program development time? These three criteria can be used to judge the relative efficiency of any algorithm or implementation. Such "Trade-Offs" are presented as special features throughout the text. They are devoted to efficiency considerations of various algorithms and implementations. Our aim is to increase your awareness of the art of making trade-offs.

Another feature designed to help you explore various information structures is "Insights with Dr. Digital." These dialogues between the fictitious Dr. Digital and his friendly students, Wilma and Waldo, are designed to provide you with skills and insights on improving your creative problem solving and imagination. Each dialogue deals with a specific concept concerning the creative problem solving process. (The book *Experiences in Visual Thinking* by R. McKim (Brooks/Cole Publishers) is also helpful for this purpose.)

Additionally, "Imagination Challenges" are scattered throughout the chapters. The "ICs" ("I sees") pose problems whose solutions require you to exercise your imagination rather than just your reasoning skills. They are built-in study breaks, in a sense. Both the ICs and the Insights with Dr. Digital enhance the main theme of this book. They do not contain any information upon which other materials depend. Their value to you, the reader, is in the chance that they offer to expand your awareness of the binary aspects of your being: analytic vs. imaginative, rational vs. intuitive.

In the years I have taught these topics, I have felt that they occupy a pivotal position in the career of a computer science student. With insight, imagination and skills gained from an information structures course, the student can be transformed from a language implementor to a creative information processor. Since information structures inhabit so many niches of the computer science environment and support so many commercial application packages, all efforts to find keys that unlock the doors of your imagination will be abundantly rewarded in future courses and career endeavors. So together let us journey into the new, helpful, and friendly lands of information structures.

Many people contributed to the completion of this four year long endeavor, and to them I offer my thanks. A responsive corps of reviewers encouraged my continuance, fine tuned my approach and pinpointed weaknesses in early versions of the manuscript. To these kind critics I offer mega-thanks for your suggestions and comments: Andrew Bernat, University of Texas, El Paso; Yechezkel Zalcstein, Memphis State University; Robert Sterling, Tidewater Community College; Dominic Magno, William Rainey Harper College; Donald Smith, Rutgers University; Robert Crawford, Western Kentucky University; Morteza Anvari, California State University–Fullertown; William Bruce Croft, University of Massachusetts–Amherst; Stephen Huang, University of Houston; John Leeson, University of Central Florida. Other people in various capacities also put their energy into the project. The following tree of acknowledge is dedicated to them.

TREE OF ACKNOWLEDGE

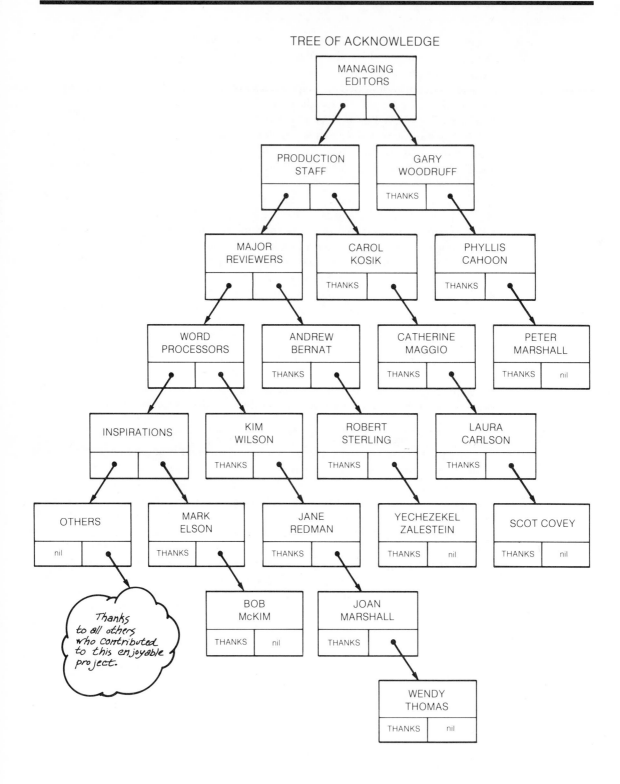

1

Information, Structures, Implementation

A skilled carpenter masters many tools and masters the matching of the tool to the task.

—R. McKim

1.1 Information

1.1.1 BREAKING THE ICE

When I was in college, I had a professor who gave an unannounced hour-long test on differential equations the day after the Christmas holidays. I have never forgotten this test, though differential equations have long since reached a vanishing point within my memory. I believe this is an effective educational technique. Let us therefore, begin with a quiz about this book.

1. Name two colors used on the cover of the book.
2. How much, in grams, does the book weigh?
3. How many pages are between pages 35 and 82, inclusive?
4. Which color on the cover is the most attention grabbing?
5. Will this book alter your perceptions about computer programming?
6. Did you pass the quiz?

1.1.2 ARRIVING IN THE LAP OF KNOWLEDGE

If my theory is correct, after this ice-breaking shock you will never forget this book—and I can only hope that the information it contains will fare better than differential equations did with me.

Now for the real purpose of the quiz. How did you arrive at the point of knowing the answers to these questions? You used different methods of collecting the necessary information; as Webster's dictionary suggests, "to have information is to have knowledge." Let us consider the process you probably used to answer each question.

To determine the colors on the cover, you most likely relied on your senses to convey information like "red, yellow, or green." The second question—the book's weight in grams—is generally beyond the capabilities of the senses; for an accurate answer, you would depend upon a measuring device. A second process—mental computation—might also have been needed to convert an English measure into metric units. For question 3—the inclusive pages between 35 and 82—there are two possible approaches. The first requires input from the sense of touch and the mental computation of counting. The more elegant approach is entirely mental and relies on the computation that $82 - 35 + 1$ (for inclusiveness) $= 48$. A quick summary indicates that we can determine information by using our senses, measuring devices, and reasoning. How are you doing so far—have you correctly answered three out of three?

After the first three questions we leave solid ground. With question 4 (which color grabs your attention?) you may have an idea of which color affects you the most, just as the next person may know what the answer is for him.* What we have here is subjective information, which comprises a large part of the information we carry around. It has its realm of validity. The next question—whether the book will alter your perceptions—might be considered in the same category of subjective information. There is one important difference, though: the question asks about your future state of being, but your feelings and impressions are more a gauge of your present state. Arriving at an answer thus requires a slightly different approach. From my perspective as textual sculptor, my intuition tells me that the book will definitely refine and deepen your perceptions of programming. You probably also relied on your intuition to arrive at an answer. Intuition comes into play in situations where you know an answer but do not know how you know it. The last question—whether you passed the quiz—completes our survey of methods of obtaining information. Since no criteria have been set for passing, no process for collecting information can yield an answer that could be validated now or in the future.

These questions offer a glimpse of the multifaceted nature of information. It ranges from being at your fingertips to being nonexistent.

In trying to reveal some of the characteristics of information as it occurs in our everyday world, I have shown how you can access information through various human processes. From this standpoint, it could be said that information is what you have after checking with *all* your senses: the physical senses, the sense of confidence in machines, the sense of reasoning, the sense of feeling, and the sense of intuition.

Since information can be derived from a wide range of processes, the term as used in everyday language has developed numerous connotations. Its use in the home as well as the business or scientific environment reflects different levels of precision and means of verification. Such a widely used term for an abstract concept

---

*In this book, a gender has been selected for each chapter and all personal pronouns in the chapter match the gender. Chapter 1 is masculine, not because men come first but because I believe men are the "odder" of the sexes. The even-numbered chapters will use feminine pronouns.

will undoubtedly refuse to be bound by the limits of any dictionary definition. This realization brings us to a crucial question: how is it that computer science has made such tremendous advances in 40-odd years with such an elusive character as its life-blood?

1.1.3 INFORMATION AS A TECHNICAL TERM

Within the technical field of computer science, the term *information* has a more limited scope than it does in the world at large. Still, this does not mean that computer scientists or even authors of computer science texts are willing to define the creature that commands so much of their attention. A quick survey of four similar textbooks revealed that not one offered a definition of the term *information* or included it as an index entry. So, what is information in the field of computer science? In the apt words of A. Tenenbaum and M. Augenstein in *Data Structures Using PASCAL,* "Unfortunately, although the concept of information is the bedrock of the entire field, this question cannot be answered precisely. In this sense, the concept of information in computer science is similar to the concepts of point, line, and plane in geometry—they are all undefined terms about which statements can be made but which cannot be explained in terms of more elementary concepts."

I will adopt the same strategy, allowing that primitive creature, information, to remain unclad while sunning itself on the bedrock of computer science; we will be content in this book with snapshots of varied poses. Let us first see what can be said about information by eavesdropping on three individuals involved with computer science.

Dave, the computer engineer:
"The current state of this flip-flop at each clock cycle will provide the information needed for our decision."
"The information moving across this channel will be a bit stream."
"Bit, byte, and word are units of memory that can represent varied amounts of information."

Dee Dee, the computer programmer:
"A memory map is needed to see where the information is stored."
"Will the information about the cities be in numeric or character format?"
"Shall we arrange the information in a linked list or tree structure for our alphabetized output?"
"The information from this routine will be decorated with fancy frills ($, *, labels, what have you) and then outputted."

Brad, the data processing manager:
"This is our new procedure for ensuring that the information for input is valid and correctly coded."
"Garbage in, garbage out." [Editorial remark: This snapshot is a negative. It describes what information is not.]
"Mr. Big needs the information in these reports by noon today."

In which poses have we caught our friend information today? It seems that information can be in a flip-flop, in an area of memory, in a coded or structured format, or in a completed report. From these varied viewpoints you see that information can be quite physical; it can be manipulated and managed. From other viewpoints you would undoubtedly catch different glimpses of the nature of information in computer science. Rest assured that your portrait will continue to develop as you learn more about information science.

1.1.4   DATA OR INFORMATION

Another term in computer science that can easily be classified as indefinable is *data*. Data can be collected, coded, inputted, outputted, searched, sorted, and in general processed. It cannot, however, be delimited and defined. Constructing a definition is not my purpose in this section, nor will I describe ways of viewing data. I want instead to focus your awareness on the two terms—*data* and *information*.

Let us approach these terms by way of a short exercise. You will need to find another person familiar with computer science who will agree to spend 15 minutes working with you. For the first 5 minutes one member of the pair sits with eyes closed and describes what he sees when visualizing the entities of data and information. The other person takes notes of what is said. Then the pair switches roles and repeats the exercise for 5 more minutes. The final 5 minutes you can spend comparing notes and discussing the differences in your perceptions.

Various questions may develop from this exercise. Do these two terms really describe different entities? Are they just different manifestations or degrees of the same indefinable quantity? Would it be helpful to consider data as unrefined and information as refined through some algorithmic process? Is there a need in computer science to differentiate between the two terms? Or is data synonymous with information and therefore data structures with information structures?

It is my contention that it is useful if not necessary to establish a distinction and to build some extensions on this foundation. In the next section, I will describe the viewpoint I will take on this subject for the remainder of this book, in the hope that you will share the same frame of reference.

1.1.5   SYNCHRONIZING OUR IMAGES

Let us consider four terms that provide an important framework in which we will work.

The colors on the cover of this book, its weight, the number of pages between page 35 and page 82, the wholesale price of an inventory item, and your height and student number are all examples of **data**. These items are measured and recorded quantities that describe an object or situation.

Data are not higher or lower, better or worse—they just are. For our purpose data are raw, unrefined, isolated, recorded, coded, or inputted. They are waiting to be processed, analyzed, and molded into answers to questions that have been posed about objects. Thus data processing involves the transformation of recorded data into information, or answers to questions.

If more than one attribute of an object or situation is measured, recorded, and then grouped together for processing, the collection is then a **data element**. Whenever you fill out an application form, you are creating a data element. Your name, address, weight, height, and other attributes collectively become one. The application form is then placed in a file with other applications. A process like counting the number of applicants does not depend on your name or address, since the units of investigation are the data elements. Determining the number of male applicants, on the other hand, requires an individual field of data in each data element to be accessed. Therefore, the way the data element is viewed varies depending on the question being answered.

When I use the word **information** in this text the main characteristic that will be implied is a relationship. Information reflects some relationship among other pieces of information—between information and data elements, or among data elements. This relationship may be established by outside evaluation or by internal processing.

Your IQ (intelligence quotient) is information that is based on an external evaluation of your relationship to a hypothetical standard. You may fall above or below the norm: your score stands in a particular relationship to the others.

Consider the substances of pyruvic acid, acetic acid, and acetyl CoA. Entering these names into a software system would be an operation involving data. If you indicate how these three chemicals are related via a particular process, then information is present. For instance, in the Krebs energy cycle of the human body, pyruvic acid is converted to acetic acid, which is in turn transformed into acetyl CoA. The linear dependent relationship expressed in the above statement is the type of characteristic on which the concept of information is based. The most challenging part of problem solving and computer programming is recognizing the relationships involved and incorporating them into a computer program.

The term **information structure** will be used in two separate but connected ways. First, in the realm of thought, it will refer to an abstract concept, the fruit of imagination, that describes a particular pattern of relationships among data elements. The flowchart, used for years in computer science, is an information structure. It indicates the sequential and logical relationship of a series of activities. What happens before or after a given action? When a given condition exists, what alternate actions are appropriate? The flowchart is a useful concept, an information-bearing structure.

Second, in the realm of computer programming, when you solve a problem, the solution must accurately reflect the relationships involved while using the simple resources available—CPU (central processing unit) operations and memory space. Designing information structures in this sense is the main challenge tackled in this book. The information structures that we will create will consist of a collection of memory locations (variables, records, arrays), a set of coded routines (CPU operations), and, most important, a group of programmer-selected conventions ("assume that the first column stands for . . . "). These elements working together emulate the relationship pattern of a particular abstract information structure. This statement may seem somewhat vague so early in the discovery process. I urge you to return to this section after each chapter and notice how the picture is becoming clearer.

From here let us step into the backyard of our newly introduced friend—the information structure—and take a few snapshots of it relaxing before it gets busy working for us in later chapters.

- **"JUST FOR REFERENCE"**

Knowing occurs through—

- the physical senses
- the sense of confidence in machines
- the sense of reasoning
- the sense of intuition

Information as a technical term in computer science—

- is undefined like point, line, and plane in geometry
- may be described at various levels, from the physical bit level of the computer engineer to the contents of a report handed to the manager

Describing terms establishes a common frame of reference—

- **Data**—measured, recorded quality of an object or event
- **Data element**—one or more measured, recorded qualities of an object or event that are grouped together for processing
- **Information**—a relationship among a collection of data elements
- **Information structure**—in the abstract realm, a pattern of relationships among data elements; in the physical realm, a set of language elements, a group of programmer-selected conventions, and a collection of coded routines to emulate the relationship pattern

EXERCISES

1. During the quiz presented at the beginning of this chapter, what methods did you use to arrive at your answers?
2. Would your answers to the quiz change over time? What distinguishes the answers that change with time from those that do not?
3. List the various senses that can be used to help us arrive at the point of knowing something.
4. Why is it difficult to define the term information precisely?
5. Describe the range of meanings that the term information can take in the field of computer science.
6. Describe the main characteristics of the following terms: data; information.
7. Discuss your reaction to the exercise in subsection 1.1.4. What new aspects of data or information were added to your perception?
8. Give two everyday illustrations of the terms data, data elements, information, and information structures.
9. List the three components that constitute an information structure in the computer programming environment.
10. Create a six-question quiz about yourself that can be answered with just the five senses, measuring devices, and the sense of reason.

11. Create a six-question quiz about yourself that involves subjective information.

12. For the question below, record in detail the process that you use to arrive at the answer: Over the last 24-hour period, consider everything you have eaten. How many items fall into each of the four basic food groups (vegetables and fruit, bread-grains-cereal, milk and dairy products, and protein—fish, meat, or beans)?

1.2 *Structures*

1.2.1 BEYOND THE QUANTITATIVE

In most real-life situations that involve problem solving, it is necessary not only to collect data but also to identify the active factors that influence the situation. Once these factors are specified, their relationships must be determined. In approaching problem solving with the aid of a computer, it is the relationships among the active factors that are captured in information structures.

Let us illustrate the importance of relationships by way of an example—a problem called RUSTY'S Riddle.

FRED's mother LAURIE gave her daughter, TERRY, 41 mangoes to share equally between her sister, CAROLYN, and brother, JONATHON, while also giving some to her cousins PETE, RUSTY, DEBBIE, JUAN, and SUSAN. TERRY gave 16 mangoes to her uncle BILL and 11 to her aunt JOAN, with instructions on how to distribute them to their respective children. If PETE and his brother received the same amount and their sister DEBBIE received one more than they did; and if in LAURIE's sister's family RUSTY received one less than his cousin JUAN, while his sister received one more than her cousin DEBBIE—then how many mangoes did SUSAN receive?

Why SUSAN when it's RUSTY's riddle? Perhaps it should rightfully be called SUSAN's share. But wait—in analyzing the problem by sorting out the factors and relationships, what I end up needing to answer is, who is RUSTY's sister? When this is determined, I can answer the quantitative question with a little arithmetic.

Thus neither question can overlook the relationships of the individuals stated in the riddle. These relationships must be set straight before the quantities can be usefully applied. How can these relationships be represented in order to aid in solving the problem? Figure 1.1 is a natural choice, with each line representing a parent-child relationship. In this way, siblings as well as cousins can easily be identified.

Verify for yourself that Figure 1.1 does indeed capture the pattern of relationships in the riddle by rereading the riddle and focusing your attention on the stated kinships.

Now notice that in the graphic representation, called a family tree, each position in the tree has two areas for data to be recorded—one for name and the other for the number of mangoes received. Our tree is thus an information structure consisting of data elements. Parent-child, sibling-sibling and cousin-cousin relationships are all present in the structure. Instead of a dozen names in an unrelated list, we have a richer structure containing far more information—12 parent-child relations, 13 sibling-sibling relations, and numerous cousin-cousin relations. With this relationship

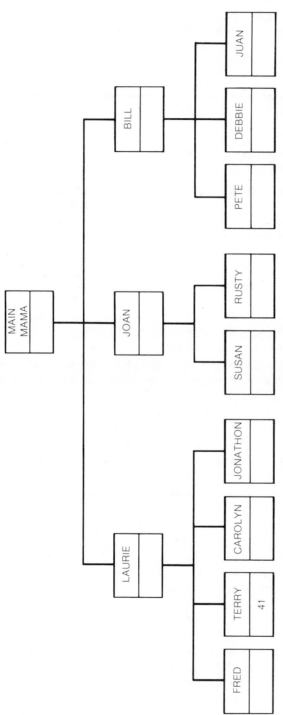

Relationships between cousins are indicated. Starting from Terry's box, distribute the mango around the family tree.

Figure 1.1

pattern, you can begin to tackle the algebraic portion of the problem. For each data element in Figure 1.1, write down the number of mangoes received. Who ended up with the smallest share?

To summarize—an information structure contains data elements and preserves the pattern in which the data elements are related. Let us look around the world we operate in and see what other patterns we can recognize.

1.2.2   LOOKING AT WHAT'S AROUND

We'll start our guided tour with some examples that are similar to the family tree. In a botany library where the plant classification system is computerized, the information must be arranged so that queries about plants that preceded, succeeded, or evolved parallel to a given plant can be easily answered. So you can see that much more than a list of plant names is needed.

Another field in which this branched pattern of relationships is also important is the analysis of languages, both natural and computer. Natural language analysis would appear in a voice recognition system where a sentence must be broken down into various phrases and then each phrase must be divided into its units, phonemes. For computer languages, a compiler evaluates each command for syntactic correctness by parsing its parts. This task can be approached with a set of tree structures similar to the family tree.

For instance, the parent can be called the WHILE command which has four children: the *WHILE* keyword, a *BOOLEAN* expression, the *DO* keyword, and a command to be performed. Both the *BOOLEAN* expression and the command have their own children, some of which also have children. A compiler takes your *WHILE* command and checks that it contains the relationships expressed in the tree structure for the legal *WHILE* command. If any relations are missing or if extra ones are included then you know the consequence—SYNTAX ERROR.

When you visit a metropolitan area and ride its public transportation system, you will be using a different pattern of relationships. Not only are the data concerning the time schedule of the bus important, but also such relationships as which bus routes intersect and where the interchange occurs are useful to have in hand to avoid spending too much time on foot. Changes in a particular bus schedule are not isolated data updates, but must be evaluated in the context of the relationships present. An arrangement of this nature is called a **network**. Notice that a network lacks the characteristic hierarchy of our first examples. Other sample networks include the U.S. Postal Service or the telephone system, which sometimes may route a call from Dallas to Atlanta through Chicago because normal routes are overloaded. On the space shuttle there are five computer systems, all of which must interact. The collection of relationships incorporated into this computer network must be able to monitor, record, analyze, and respond to numerous subsystems on board in real–time.

In the not-too-distant past of the computer, execution speed was fast enough and human programming sophistication was slow enough that the computer was waiting more than it was executing. To exploit the resources of computers more thoroughly, multiprogramming was developed. Under this scheme, scheduling algorithms are used to process multiple programs. As each program is submitted for execution it is assigned to an appropriate waiting list or **queue**. When the executing program enters a situation where it must wait for another component, such as the magnetic tape system, the multiprogramming computer system will suspend execution of the program. It will then select a program from the appropriate waiting list that matches the available resources of memory and time. The new program then begins execution and the computer system is not idle. Keeping track of these waiting programs and assigning available resources to the next program in the queue is the responsibility of the **operating system** of a computer system. In this environment, "first come, first served" may not be the best strategy, as more complicated relationships may be involved. This relationship pattern has a linear nature compared with the previous two. It would also experience more changes in the order of the data elements.

What other examples exhibit the characteristics of the queue information structure? Have you been to a bus stop, bank, supermarket, or burger factory lately? These clearly match the described pattern. If you have ever attended a "bus boarding event" in some places, then you might have second thoughts as to the existence of this pattern of relationships.

Now let us shift gears and think of any alphabetical list that frequently experiences changes at any point in the list. What did you think of? Your course schedule during registration time? The class roster the week after school begins? Your private address book with the names of the people you want to date? The Dow Jones top 20 stocks? By now you have the idea. An ordered list whose order is frequently updated. If you had a personal computer and decided to computerize your short but active address book then you would need to consider the problem of having an ordered list that needed to be rearranged at the ring of a telephone. Based on the tricks you have in your beginner's bag of programming skills, how would you pull this off? If you want a hint, either call the directory assistance operator (he should know) or take a peek at Chapter 4.

An extremely important area of computer science that uses all of these patterns of relationships is computer simulation—writing a program that simulates an actual situation.

In this case, the relationships are the main concern of the program. The output, being a reflection of the relationships and the initial conditions of the situation being simulated, is only a report of the final state of all factors involved.

Airline pilots train on computerized flight simulators to test their response to critical conditions on board. A flood control system for the Mississippi delta could be simulated to predict the results of a hypothetical hurricane from the south southwest with 165 mile-per-hour winds. A medical student could test various medications in a simulated emergency condition and receive a report of the body's projected response. Each example above involves a complex web of interrelationships. To perceive the workings of this web and to emulate it by using a simple binary computing engine is a feat worth reflecting upon and by the way, many simulations depend on differential equations, so don't forget them!

Well, our little tour of the world around us is ending. I hope that the outside view of the assorted information structures has been stimulating and enlightening. Later we will enter more deeply into the structures for a look at the details. I particularly enjoyed Rusty's family mango tree.

TRADE-OFFS

Let's look at where two of the factors used to select an information structure place us on the scales of decision.

Assume that we have an ordered list of data elements to implement. Two options are to implement the list as a tree structure or as a linked list. (The details are presented later.) How does the capacity for change affect our decision?

Adding a new data element to the ordered list involves finding the correct position and then storing the data in memory based on certain conventions. Now, the tree structure is more efficient for locating the correct position. Both structures are equally useful in terms of actually storing the data elements. So the scale is skewed toward the tree. But, to delete a data element is a very different story. The linked list is a much more efficient structure for this operation.

An application that has a static ordered list would thus be better suited by a tree structure. However, an application using a dynamic ordered list would fare much better with a linked list implementation.

Let's shift our attention to the matter of access. What options exist here?

Assume that the data elements consist of the name, address, and phone number of a chiropractor's clients. Consider the following requests:

Request A: Given a client's name, find his phone number.

Request B: Given a phone number, find the client's name.

The structure that you would design to answer request A is not well-suited to answer request B, and vice versa. If the chiropractor's assistant must be able to answer both requests frequently, then the information structure must provide access to both relationships. The trade-off depends on how often each request occurs.

You can see that it is quite important for you, the programmer, to know the set of questions that must be answered and the relative frequency of each question.

1.2.3 FACTORS IN DESIGNING A STRUCTURE

As you add various information structures to your bag of programming skills, you will have to decide which structure to use for a particular application. Let's look at some factors to consider before you reach in the bag and pick the first one that seems to fit.

Nature always comes first. By this I mean that the nature of the relationships to be implemented must be considered first. Does the relationship pattern appear to be linear, branched, or weblike? The first thing to determine is the relationship pattern, which dictates whether the appropriate structure is like a list, a family tree, or a computer network.

Next you should determine what capacity for change is required. From the previous examples, you can see that the family tree and botany classification system remain fixed for the duration of use, while the public transportation network must accommodate changing time schedules and services. You need to determine how static or dynamic the structure will be.

The last factor involves access to the information in the structure. Each type of structure provides some information that is easily accessible, as an inherent function of the structure itself—such as the number of children in a family tree. However, other information requests may require considerable processing. For instance, to determine how many cousins Rusty has from the tree of Figure 1.1 is more difficult. An algorithm can be developed but it is more complicated and consumes more time. It is thus important to determine the questions that will be most frequently asked, so that a structure can be designed to provide rapid access to the answers.

These three factors—the nature of the relationships, the capacity for change, and the expected information requests—will help you design more useful information structures.

■ "JUST FOR REFERENCE"

Information structures go beyond the quantitative, including not only the quantitative data within the data elements but also the relationship between the data elements.

Relationship patterns can be linear, branched, or weblike—

- linear—course schedules, class rosters, address books, Dow Jones most active stocks, waiting lines within an operating system
- branched—family tree, botany classification system, language analysis
- weblike—public transportation system, U.S. Postal Service, telephone system, space shuttle computer network

Factors important to the design of an information structure—

- the nature of the problem and its relationship patterns
- the capacity for change to the structure's
- the type of information requests to be provided

EXERCISES

1. Rusty's Riddle illustrated the importance of the relationship pattern within an information structure. State the relationship that was used in this problem to relate the various data elements to each other.

2. Both data elements and their relationships are important features in solving a problem. Use your imagination to describe another common situation that illustrates the interdependence of these two concepts. State precisely what the relationship is among the data elements.

3. Draw a family tree, beginning with your father's grandmother (or as far back as you know).

4. Give examples of other situations that resemble the relationship pattern illustrated by family trees.

5. Give examples of other situations that resemble the relationship pattern illustrated by an intercity bus network.

6. Explain why computer simulations of real-life events are prime candidates for the use of information structures.

7. List three factors to consider in selecting an appropriate information structure.

8. For each example mentioned in this section, use the relationship pattern as a basis to associate one of the following attributes with each example: linear pattern; branched pattern; weblike pattern.

9. Draw a diagram of a hypothetical situation that exhibits a weblike pattern.

1.3   Implementation

1.3.1   ABSTRACT TO PRACTICAL—LOGICAL TO PHYSICAL

In this section we will be concerned with constructing a bridge from the abstract world of concepts to the concrete world of computer programming. This is the area where your imagination plays a very important part. As you sit with the mental image of an information structure and slowly select a way to represent this structure in the computer's memory then carefully code the routines that will utilize the relationships within the structure, you are engaged in the creative process known as **implementation.**

When this process is complete the logical relationships that existed as mental abstractions are transformed into a physical memory representation and a set of practical routines. It is extremely important that you establish this distinction firmly and definitely, for it will enable you to have a definite direction in the implementation—you want to move from *there* to *here*. It is easier to accept the distinction when you know that the same information structure can be implemented differently on two different computers and even on the same computer by different programmers. And it is because of this choice of different means to an end that your imagination contributes significantly to the implementation process. It is also because of this same feature that each implementation must be evaluated in terms of its efficient use of computer resources and compared to any alternate method that may come to mind.

With the idea that implementation is the bridge that leads from a high plateau where information structures reside as abstractions to a fertile plain where information structures grow from practical routines and physical memory representation, we can now move on to the plain and consider this process in more detail.

1.3.2   PRACTICAL ROUTINES FOR SUPPORT AND ACCESS

As you visualize yourself walking up to an implemented information structure, you notice assorted auxiliary units clustered around the main building. Upon closer investigation you discover that they do not contain information within them. These auxiliary units turn out to be the software programs that were developed to maintain and access the information within the structure. They are grouped into three distinct categories.

One category is designed to aid in building the implemented information structure—by procuring the physical space for a new data element, installing the data in the proper area within the new space, and constructing the guide wires to all related data elements.

Another category is involved in the task of maintenance. As you remember, one factor in the design of an information structure was the capacity for change during the lifetime of the structure. Maintenance routines will preserve the faithful representation of the information structure. If a data element must be updated, then an auxiliary program will be used to follow the guide wires to the desired data element and perform the desired update. If a data element must be removed, then a different routine will cut the necessary guide wires, attach any new ones required, and indicate the storage space as vacant. The number and variety of such units will depend largely on the capacity for change, as mentioned earlier.

The last category has the most user-oriented function of the three. When information is desired then one of the access programs will be called to locate and transfer a copy of the information to the surrounding environment. It is within this category that you will notice substantial differences among the auxiliary units. Some of the smaller, simpler units are used when the information requested is designed into the implemented information structure; in such cases you will see the access programs scamper along the guide wires, record the information directly, and scamper back. The larger, more complex units seem to lumber over the structure, making copies of information in the structure, analyzing what it has collected, and finally providing information about the information within the structure. The programs in this category will vary widely from one application to another and will naturally be the last ones implemented around the structure itself.

As you walk away from the imagined information structure and its auxiliary units, it would be wise to look over your shoulder before you go on. Let the whole scene soak into your consciousness. Often in your career as a software engineer you will be responsible for developing and implementing similar structural systems. Before you depart, consider that the supporting and accessing routines are separate but integral components in the implementation of an information structure.

1.3.3 USING THE PHYSICAL TO EMULATE THE LOGICAL

As you continue your stroll away from the implemented information structure, stop on the connecting bridge. From this vantage point you can see the information structure in both its abstract and physical form. Though they appear the same in behavior, you notice that they do not look the same. Why is this?

The answer lies in the contrasting environments in which they reside. The abstract form rests in a limitless, nebulous, multidimensional space governed only by the constraints of imagination. The physical form, on the other hand, is part of a computer program. It resides within the confines of a computer memory and is governed by the organization of memory. Since any program is written in a particular computer language, the capabilities of the language impose additional constraints.

Let us consider an example. In subsection 1.2.2, the information structure called a network was introduced. Figure 1.2 depicts a network and a typical memory organization. The network does not really have a top or bottom, a first or last part, or an inside or an outside. It can be viewed from many directions and still retain the pattern of relationships. The memory, on the other hand, does have a rigid orientation. There is a first, second, next, and last word. Any physical representation of the network that resides there cannot escape the fact of contiguous memory locations.

Figure 1.2

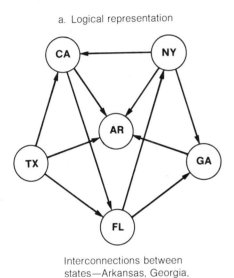

a. Logical representation

Interconnections between states—Arkansas, Georgia, Florida, Texas, California, New York

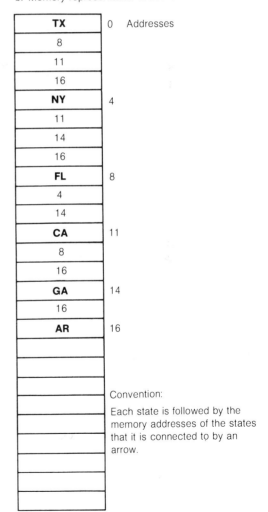

b. Memory representation of network

	Addresses
TX	0
8	
11	
16	
NY	4
11	
14	
16	
FL	8
4	
14	
CA	11
8	
16	
GA	14
16	
AR	16

Convention:

Each state is followed by the memory addresses of the states that it is connected to by an arrow.

What aspect of the implementation process accommodates this disparity? The programmer must establish some conventions for arranging individual items of data in memory. This is an extremely important first step and can determine the efficiency of everything that follows. The programmer then uses his knowledge of these conventions while writing the code to retrieve information from the memory representation of the structure. Unfortunately, these intangible though crucial assumptions appear explicitly only in the program comments and documentation (if the programmer is complete in his responsibilities). They are implicitly contained in the way that memory locations are referenced by individual lines of program code.

If you will allow me the poetic license to mix modes of data storage (numbers and characters in words), and if you will accept the convention that after each abbreviated state name appear the memory addresses of the states that it is connected to, then you will see that the contents of memory in Figure 1.2b are a first approximation for the network of Figure 1.2a. They are a first approximation because there are ways to improve on the representation in order to produce more efficient access routines—ways that do not require the magic wand of poetic license. Figure 1.2b does preserve the relationships between the states; although physically there is a first state, logically it is not possible to make such a classification.

For each of the other information structures presented in subsection 1.2.2, it would be necessary first to come up with a set of imaginative conventions for the memory representation of the information structure and then, using these conventions, write the auxiliary routines. This, in a nutshell, is the topic of the remaining chapters.

It was mentioned earlier that the programming language contributes to the climate of the physical implementation process. If you are familiar with the capabilities of more than one language (BASIC, FORTRAN, PASCAL, LISP, SNOBOL, etc.), then you know that certain operations or certain types of data are easier to handle in some languages than in others. Character data (also referred to as strings) are an obvious example, since each language provides such a different scheme for storing strings and different operations upon strings. The two factors that you will need to keep in mind concerning the language to be used in the implementation are the types of data that can be stored and processed (integer, real, complex, character, etc.) and how these types can be arranged (simple variables, vector arrays, tables, etc.). These are your building blocks—and where one language may provide you with bricks, another may generate prefabricated walls to your specifications.

As the sun begins to set on the last section of Chapter 1, and before we leave the bridge of implementation, we will soon overhear an evening dialog between Dr. Digital and his prize pupil, Waldo, underneath the blossoming mango tree.

■ **"JUST FOR REFERENCE"**

Implementation is—

- the transformation from abstract ideas to the physical environment of the computer
- an opportunity to exercise the imagination through alternative transformations
- composed of conventions for physical memory representation and auxiliary routines

INSIGHTS WITH DR. DIGITAL

Scene: *Dr. Digital is sitting on a blanket under a mango tree. Waldo is near the river, under the bridge, using a stick to run ripples across his reflection.*

Dr. Digital: Well, Waldo, on our walk today on the plane and plateau, what thoughts and images did you gather and bring with you?

Waldo: I mostly noticed nature. The nature of the information structures on the abstract side of the bridge was mostly multidimensional and able to occupy space in complex patterns. The nature of the implemented structures on the other side—since they reside in a computer's memory—was quite up and down, one-dimensional. You know, it is still kind of mystical to me that two entities so different in nature can behave so identically.

Dr. Digital: Do you remember what apparatus—*you* might call it an apparition—makes this possible?

Waldo: Ah, . . . I guess my memory takes second place to a computer's. No.

Dr. Digital: The set of conventions selected by the software engineer before the construction of the implemented information structure.

Waldo: Oh, yeah, I guess that slipped away because the conventions are an intangible component of the structure and I didn't see them in the memory representation of the structure. However, I did notice the building blocks that were used. Why was it again that some of those building blocks looked old and simple yet others looked modern and complex?

Dr. Digital: Mode of expression, Waldo. The computer language that is used to express the implementation provides for different types of data (the building blocks) and different ways of arranging the data. So one structure could have been built in BASIC and another in SNOBOL.

Waldo: Oh, I saw that one, the IGLOO—it was built with BASIC SNOBOL. Ha Ha Ha.

Dr. Digital: I've heard of artificial intelligence, Waldo, but I think you just invented artificial humor.

Auxiliary routines are used—

- to aid in building the information structure
- to maintain the relationships in an information structure during any changes
- to access the information stored within the structure

In physical memory representation, the contiguous nature of computer memory causes a disparity between the abstract idea and the physical implementation.

To evaluate the capabilities of a programming language—

- consider the basic types of data that are provided
- consider how these basic data types can be arranged

EXERCISES

1. Why is your imagination so important during the implementation process?

2. In what way is imagination related to the need to evaluate the efficiency of an implementation?

3. Describe the three categories of auxiliary routines that are found within an implementation of an information structure.

4. Which of the three categories of auxiliary routines is the most user-oriented?

5. Explain why auxiliary routines are separate but integral components of the implemented information structure.

6. Contrast the two forms of an information structure—abstract and physical.

7. What are the two main constraints in the physical form of an information structure?

8. What characteristic of the memory organization is most disparate from the abstract form of an information structure?

9. What method is used by the programmer to accommodate this difference?

10. Using the convention stated in this section for the network of states as a guide, develop a memory representation for the family tree of Section 1.2.1. State your conventions for memory usage.

11. What two features of a programming language are influential during the implementation process?

2

Stacks

The power of imagination makes us infinite.

— John Muir

2.1 Setting the Stage

2.1.1 DIRTY DISHES, KLEENEX, AND COMPUTER SCIENCE?

In this chapter the stack information structure makes its debut. As the curtain rises, we set the scene by presenting four objects and two situations that exhibit similar relationship patterns. This gives us a realistic stage on which to view the abstract form of a stack and to spotlight its traits. From here we will go backstage for the implementation process, meet the cast of supporting players, and see our main character disguised as an array. This is followed by three examples of applications in which the stack plays a leading role. For a finale we present some fancy footwork with a topic called recursion and a guest appearance by Dr. Digital. Please hold your applause until after the exercises. Now, on with the show.

Our first unlikely quartet consists of a pile of dirty dishes ready to be washed, a box of kleenex belonging to an indecisively allergic body, a set of serving trays at the beginning of the university cafeteria line, and the stack of pennies in front of you at the evening's penny ante poker game. What feature groups these four collections together and relates them to a topic in computer science? Certainly not the objects themselves, though they all have the attribute of flatness. What about the way that they are arranged? Each group has an order. One plate lies next to another, one kleenex will be used before the next. People waiting in a line are also next to each other, and each will be served before the next. However, I would not add the waiting line example to the four original examples in order to make a quintet. Perhaps the similarity lies not only in the arrangement but also in how the arrangement experiences change. If you need a kleenex or a serving tray, where does it come from? If you have a dirty plate to add to the pile where do you put it? If you have to add a penny to the poker pot, do you take one from the middle of the stack? If I wanted to be reincarnated as a rarely used object then I would become the bottom tray in the cafeteria of a small college with declining enrollment. It is indeed the arrangement of the objects, as well as how the arrangement experiences change, that forms the basis for their selection as examples and, as we shall see later, their relation to computer science. Now, let us move on to two situations that further develop our little plot.

2.1.2   WHO WILL GET THE TOP HAT?

In southern Wyoming, an imaginary collective community, named FOCUS, raises hay and grain for the cattle tended by the sons of each family. Since the group is a collective, all members handle all the varied jobs of the community. The members have listed all the separate job responsibilities and designed a hat for each job. In this way, if you need to talk to the COOK or FARMER or IRRIGATOR or CHILDREN'S SUPERVISOR, then you look for the person wearing the right hat. When lunch rolls around, the members come into the common dining room, takes off their hats, deposit them in the hat bucket next to the door, take their minds off work, and eat lunch, enjoying the uniqueness and individuality of the other people. As the people finish lunch, they go to the hat bucket, take the hat on the top, and assume the role associated with that hat. Since people are arriving for lunch and leaving the dining room at different times, the arrangement of the hats in the hat bucket fluctuates considerably.

What can be said about the characteristics of the hat bucket? When you walk up to the bucket after lunch, the only hat you can see is the top hat, and that is the one you're supposed to take. If you are not satisfied with the role of the top hat—say your hands are tired from kneading bread all morning and you can't see milking cows all afternoon—then what do you do? Since you can't see the other hats, you look around and see the morning's PHONE ANSWERER still enjoying lunch. You'd like that job, but you don't know how long it will be before the hat reaches the top. Then you realize that you don't even know whether the hat is in the bucket, although the previous wearer is still in the dining room. So you wander back, have another glass of milk, and wait.

What can you say about any two adjacent hats that are in the bucket? How are they related to each other logically? Let us take the PLOWER and the GARDENER hats and assume that the GARDENER hat is closer to the top of the bucket than the PLOWER one. Did they come in to lunch together? Maybe, but not necessarily. Two people may have come after the PLOWER and two others may have left before the GARDENER arrived. The relationship of the hats may be expressed in terms of time spent in the bucket. You can say the GARDENER hat is "younger" than the PLOWER hat, but not by how much.

What do you do about leftovers at the end of lunch—people without hats or hats without people, that is? Sit back and reflect on this problem. (And by the way, why do they call the collective FOCUS? Because that's where the sons raise meat [sun's rays meet]).

2.1.3   CHECK IT OUT

At a small college with declining enrollment in central Texas, called DATA U, the gymnasium has a check-out system for basketballs, illustrated in Figure 2.1. In the morning the rack is full of numbered basketballs; during the day students take ard

Figure 2.1

return them at irregular intervals. The rack has a sign that covers the opening when all the balls have been checked out. It also has an indicator on the other end that tells the supervisor when all the balls have been returned at the end of the day.

What can we say about the ball rack? Again, the only numbered ball that you can see is the one at the front of the rack—in the term of the last section, the youngest ball. What else can you see? You can tell whether the rack is empty, full, or in neither state. For any two adjacent balls, one is younger and one older in terms of the time spent in the rack since they were last used.

What operations will the supervisor be involved in when dealing with the rack of balls? When a ball is returned she will push it onto the front of the rack; when one is checked out she will remove it from the front of the rack; and at opening and closing time she will check the indicator to make sure it is full.*

*The gender of the pronouns in Chapter 2 and all other even-numbered chapters will be feminine, and now the sexes are "even."

2.1.4   WHAT IS BUT AIN'T

When I was enrolled in a college art history course, I was always shown examples of good Renaissance still lifes, beautiful impressionist landscapes, and exciting abstract paintings. I would always ask to see some bad Renaissance, impressionist, or abstract works so that I could see the differences and develop a better feel for the criteria used by art critics. In the same vein, here are some examples of situations that may be called stacks by common folk but not by us professional critics of such structures.

For example, anyone who counts a smokestack as a stack is full of hot air. To be sure, the smoke comes out the top, but it is generated at the bottom. Action occurs at both ends; thus this is not a stack. Another similar situation occurs when an airport has difficulty in accommodating a large number of arriving planes. The flight controller directs the pilot to enter a holding pattern and the airplane enters a "stack" of other planes above the airport. If this were a stack in our sense then the youngest plane would be the first to land and the pilot of the oldest would be hoping that her fuel would last since she would be the last to land. In actuality, the planes land in the order they arrived; entering and leaving occurs at two positions in the airplane "stack", which fails to meet our professional criteria.

Before the rest of the show begins, what do you say we leave here, jog over to the Data U cafeteria, take a serving tray from the stack, and grab a glass of milk and a stack of pancakes. But wait—is it really a *stack* of pancakes?

■ "JUST FOR REFERENCE"

Characteristics shared by a stack of dishes, kleenexes, and pennies include—

- the linear arrangement of the objects
- the way that the arrangement experiences change

Common attributes demonstrated by sample stacks top hat and ball rack—

- users have access only to the top element
- information about what lies below the top is unavailable
- ordering is based on a time criteria
- the youngest element is available first
- empty, full, and neither are the states of the ball rack

Operations that occur naturally include—

- adding new objects on top of older ones
- removing the youngest
- recognizing when no objects are present

EXERCISES

1. Design a scenario for the common dining room at FOCUS that enables you to come in before the GARDENER and become the GARDENER for the afternoon.
2. One day at the common dining room at FOCUS, a person is standing at the hat bucket

ready to leave but no hats are in the bucket. What does this imply? What about an empty dining room with one hat left?

3. In the gymnasium at Data U the basketball rack can have three different states, determined by the signals attached to the rack. What are these three states?

4. Name the two changes that the supervisor makes in the balls in the rack and the two checks she performs.

5. For each example in this section, describe how the terms *older* and *younger* relate to the objects involved.

6. Summarize the attributes of a stack that are illustrated by the examples in this section.

2.2 Formalizing the Structure

2.2.1 DESCRIPTION: COMPONENTS AND RELATIONSHIP PATTERN

With the stage set, we are ready for our leading character to display some of its special traits and abilities. Remember that we are viewing the stack through the soft and pliable lights of abstraction and it is only necessary to describe what we see.

The stack is a collection of data elements, arranged in an ordered list, in which changes in the arrangement can occur at only one location of the list. The location in the list where the two changes—insertion and deletion—occur needs to be indicated. This position is called the **FRONT** of the stack. Since changes are limited to the front of the stack, the stack exhibits a **last in–first out (LIFO)** behavior. The number of members in the collection of data elements will fluctuate during the lifetime of the stack. If the number of data elements in the collection is zero, then the stack is termed **EMPTY**. There is no upper limit to the number of data elements that may be members of the collection.

The LIFO behavior at the front of the stack has implications that cascade through the ordered data elements. A relationship can be described between all adjacent pairs of data elements that is a result of the LIFO behavior. Consider an adjacent pair over a given time period. If one of the pair eventually reaches the front of the stack and is then deleted, we can see which of the pair has been in the stack longer. With this ability to view the process over an expanse of time and to determine the direction of the front of the stack relative to the adjacent pair, we can say one of the pair is **older** and the other is **younger**. This is the pair's relationship pattern. This character trait of stacks was illustrated by the hats in the bucket of subsection 2.1.2.

If you are viewing the stack's performance from a different orientation—say from the balcony—then you will have a slightly different perspective. You might refer to the front of the stack as the **TOP** of the stack; the younger/older attribute becomes a higher/lower relationship instead. This is an equally valid way of describing stacks, and one used by other texts. If you do any supplementary reading it should be easy to exchange your front row seat for one in the balcony. I will use either term, *FRONT* or *TOP*, to indicate the same concept—the location in the stack at which changes can be made.

2.2.2   VIEWING A STACK

In both of the previous examples, one noteworthy feature was that access to elements in the stack is limited to the top hat and the front basketball. This is also true with the abstract model: all activity takes place at the front and hence we can view only the front data element. For purposes of explanation and demonstration, this presents a difficulty because at times I will want to show the entire collection of data elements. In order to accommodate these needs I have enlisted the aid of our resident illusionist. She has set up a series of mirrors, so that we not only have a natural view from the front but we also have the illusion of seeing the transparent stack from the side, as seen in Figure 2.2. It is to be held in mind that it is indeed an illusion—as a programmer you will not have a similar advantage.

In Figure 2.2 the stack was given particular orientations in space. These are only two of the 4 regular orientations that can be used. One orientation matches the way the stack of basketballs is viewed in subsection 2.1.3. The hat bucket example of subsection 2.1.2 provides a different orientation; it is from this direction that the terms *top*, *bottom*, *higher*, and *lower* preserve their natural connotations. Another orientation is the symmetric reflection of the hat bucket. As you will see later, this perspective turns out to be the most convenient during the actual implementation process. The particular orientation selected is not important to the abstract model. I would also like to point out that the relationship of younger/older holds regardless of the orientation, since the relationship is based on time and not space.

Let's observe the dynamic, changing nature of the stack by visiting the gym at Data U. I will describe the scene around the equipment room where the basketballs are kept and summarize the changes that take place by using the codes CKOUT for a ball being removed from the rack and RET#*n* for the return of ball number *n* to the rack.

Figure 2.2

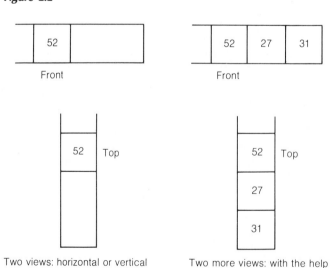

Two views: horizontal or vertical perspective, seeing only one data element

Two more views: with the help of illusionist, seeing all data elements

You can see the effects of each activity by looking at the stop-action shot of the stack to the right. The numbers refer to the numbers recorded on each ball. We zoom in on the action at 10:06 a.m.

Time	Activity	Code	Contents of Rack
			FRONT 5 6 2 9 7 1 4 3
10:06	Initial state of the ball rack		
10:08	Randy and Robert come in for some one-on-one	CKOUT	6 2 9 7 1 4 3
10:16	Joan and Liz show up for a game of seahorses	2 CKOUTS	9 7 1 4 3
10:21	Roy comes in to test his new pacemaker	CKOUT	7 1 4 3
10:24	Liz picks up her CS book and leaves	RET#2	2 7 1 4 3
10:28	The Wilson Dorm intramural team comes for practice	5 CKOUTS	empty
10:30	The Bruce brothers show up to shoot some hoop and leave		empty
10:37	The paramedic returns Roy's ball	RET#9	9
10:45	Randy and Robert hustle to class	RET#5	5 9
10:50	Two of the Dorm team head for the cafeteria	RET#4, RET#2	2 4 5 9
10:58	Carolyn and Laurie bounce in for a game or two	CKOUT	4 5 9
11:03	The Bruce brothers try again	CKOUT	5 9
11:09	The rest of the Dorm team check in, then check out	RET#1, RET#7, RET#3	3 7 1 5 9
11:13	Joan realizes that she is late for class and so goes to lunch	RET#?	FRONT ? 3 7 1 5 9

Based on the sequence of snapshots, what ball was checked in by tardy but talented Joan? Which balls are still on the court and who is giving them a workout?

Now that you have an intuitive feel for the operations of a stack, I would like to formalize these concepts.

2.2.3 NATURAL STACK OPERATIONS

The changes that you have seen in the last example illustrate the two main elementary operations with a stack. The primitive operation of inserting a data element at the front of the stack will henceforth be referred to as **PUSH.** There are two parameters that need to be specified to describe the operation. The value to be pushed and the stack to be used.

The primitive operation of deleting a data element from the front of the stack will be called **POP.** It also has two parameters: the value being removed and the stack. It is important to note that in the abstract model of a stack it is not logically possible to perform a POP upon an empty stack.

In order to check for this possibility, a signalling operation is natural. This operation checks to see whether the stack is empty, like the sign on the ball rack. This will be referred to as EMPTY and provides a boolean answer—true or false.

No similar safeguard is needed for PUSH in our abstract model, since we assume unlimited growth potential for insertions. However, when implementation is considered I think you can see the handwriting on the wall.

The last primitive operation does not change the stack. It provides direct information access. If it is necessary to know the value of the front data element without changing the stack then the LOOK operation can be used. Of course, using LOOK when the stack is empty is another illogical operation.

These four operations are the stage crew that keep our main character, the stack, functioning. More complicated operations can be developed by using these primitive ones; the exercises offer some examples. In Section 2.3 we will go backstage and see for ourselves how the physical stand-in for the abstract stack is developed.

▪ "JUST FOR REFERENCE"

In the abstract model, a stack is—

- a collection of data elements
- arranged in an ordered list
- capable of experiencing changes at only one end of the list

Behavior or relationship pattern is characterized by—

- last in – first out—LIFO structure
- younger/older relationship between each pair of data elements

States of the stack—empty and not empty

Orientation—FRONT view or TOP view are both used

Primitive operations on the stack include—

- PUSH—inserting a data element at the front
- POP—removing a data element from the front
- EMPTY—checking the state of the stack
- LOOK—providing a copy of the data element at the front

EXERCISES

1. By rearranging the following ordered list of words and by inserting new words, develop a description of the abstract model of the stack.
   . . . (arrangement, collection, elements, front, list, ordered, stack) . . .

2. In the example of the ball rack of subsection 2.2.2, which balls were still checked out and who was using them?

3. Redo the ball rack example, this time assuming that the Wilson Dorm intramural team skips practice and goes to the movies. How does this change the state of the stack from that point on?

4. List the operations that are performed on a stack.

5. Describe two situations in which a normally appropriate operation upon a stack is inappropriate.

6. Using the primitive operations—PUSH, POP, EMPTY, FULL and LOOK—design an algorithm to accomplish the following operations:

   a) Remove the first *n* elements from the stack.

   b) Determine whether *n* elements are in the stack without changing the order of the elements.

   c) Remove the *n*th element on the stack, if it exists, without changing the order of the other elements.

   d) Reverse the order of the top three elements on the stack.

   e) Reverse the order of all elements on the stack.

   f) Determine whether the top element equals the bottom element of the stack.
   Note: More than one stack may be needed for any of the above problems.

7. Write an algorithm that determines whether a given value, *X*, is on the stack.

INSIGHTS WITH DR. DIGITAL

Scene: *The school cafeteria in the afternoon, with Dr. Digital quietly reading a paper entitled "Approximating Pi and Why!"*

Wilma: Oh, hello, Dr. D! Mind if I share some space at the table?

Dr. D: Good p.m., Wilma! I'd gladly trade my reading for your company.

Wilma: Appears that you use the cafeteria space to feed yourself in two ways: a bit of pie for your body and a bit of pi for your mind.

Dr. D: An oddish perception but true indeed. These minds we carry around with our bodies, or vice versa, are always hungry for mental food to make sense of and for perceptions fed to us by our senses. Finding a congenial place to feed them is sometimes a problem.

Wilma: Yes, indeed. Unfortunately my mind seems to have gone on some sort of a diet lately. Dr. D, I'm having problems with problems. Lately, whenever I sit down to begin a problem-solving session with myself, it's like no one is there. My mind is a blank, no images float in front of my mind's eye.

Dr. D: Imagine that, a mind full of blanks waiting to be filled in! But, Wilma, I've seen your work. The solutions to the last two assignments were fine, so it is obvious that your mind wasn't without ideas and images then.

Wilma: That's right, Dr. D, but those

assignments were just extensions of what I had learned from the last course. I could easily see the solution because I had seen something similar before. But the next assignment is different, I think. I don't seem to have anything to compare it with. As you might say—"I don't have the right programming tool in my tool kit at this time".

Dr. D: Wilma, my dear, you are experiencing I-triple-S, information structures shock syndrome. You see, information structures are tools of a completely new dimension. They are ideas that you may have seen but have not yet noticed or formalized and hence have not seen with the mind's eye. You are at a point where your data bank of sense perceptions is not enough. When you encounter a problem for which you have no precedent experience, it's time to pull out the Big I.

Wilma: The Big I? I give up, Dr. D— what's up with this I thing?

Dr. D: Often, creative problem solving requires the use of our sleeping guru of wisdom—Imagination. It helps us create images that evolve into ideas when we have few or no experiential images or ideas to begin with. From a spark we can start a fire, but knowing how to strike that spark is sometimes the problem with problems.

Wilma: So, I need to look in a new way—not at what I have done but at what I am doing. How do I learn to look with imagination?

Dr. D: Unfortunately, Wilma, few classes are devoted to developing your imagination skills. It's too bad that I.Q. stands for intelligence quotient rather than imagination quotient—otherwise we educators could be involved in expanding young people's minds rather than extending their intelligence by feeding them more facts and principles. But there are ways that you can improve your ImQ, as I call your imagination quotient.

Wilma: Oh, that's fantastic! How and when can I start?

Dr. D: Right now—by simply thinking

visually. You have already begun the first phase of visual thinking by being a perceptual being. Your senses provide you with perceptual images or memories of past experiences. Each person has her own skill level in recreating these mental images, and this level can be improved by conscious effort. For instance, what flavor pie was I eating when you walked up?

Wilma: Wow—so much has occurred since then. I imagine, I mean, I recall—was it . . . blueberry?

Dr. D: You have just exercised your perceptual image recall system, strengthening its ability to work. Exercising your perceptual image recall system is the first phase of improving your ImQ.

The second phase is forming mental images. When you form mental images, you may or may not use perceptual images as a basis. The main idea here is to internally construct the image to your own design criteria. Your image may have parts or processes that you have never before experienced. For example, here's a little exercise for your mental imaging system. Describe a new flavor of pie that you would enjoy trying.

Wilma: Oh, Dr. D! Pies are my passion! Let's see, I mean, let's imagine a . . . peach—no—um—oh, yum! How about a banana and sweet potato pie?

Dr. D: Excellent. Now strengthen your mental image even more—fill in some details. What type of crust does it have? Does it have a topping? Are the bananas sliced on top or mashed with the sweet potatos? An important aspect of mental images is how clearly you "see" them.

Wilma: Oh, okay! [drooling with delight] It has whipped . . .

Dr. D: Whoa, Wilma—let's move on. You can practice improving the clarity of mental images in various ways. We just created a mental image of an object with a certain amount of detail and sharpness. You could also exercise your mental imaging system by "seeing" a person that you have never seen. For instance, close your eyes, rest your thinking mind, and let the image of your next boyfriend slowly begin to form. Notice the shape of his face, the shape of his nose, the color of his eyes, the color of his hair, and now the expression on his face. [Dr. D pauses for a sip of watermelon juice.] Okay Wilma, describe what you are seeing . . . Wilma . . . Wilma, are you awake?

Wilma: Oh, Dr. D. It is, I mean, it was—which is it?—so beautiful. He's handsome and we were going to the school dance and—

Dr. D: Well done, Wilma. You have stepped right on through phase 2 into phase 3. You are beginning to create a scenario, to imagine an event. You are controlling the mental image that you have created. You can do the same thing with other processes also, such as an information structure.

Wilma: So you're saying that when you were describing the stack yesterday in class, I could have gone through the same three phases of visual thinking—recalling similar perceptual images, creating a mental image of an abstract stack with some degree of detail, and then manipulating the image so that I could see stack operations.

Dr. D: That is correct. What's more, you can do that with all the information structures that you will encounter. And once you have developed the skill to "see" the structures as live entities, then you can manipulate them in the context of a problem that you are attempting to solve.

Wilma: So this is how I will be able to come up with a solution to a problem for which I have little or no precedent in my experience. I can create the experiences through visual thinking via my mental images and my control over them. Oh, wow! What a great tool, Dr. D. Thanks!

Dr. D: One last and very important piece of advice. Practice giving yourself permission to roam in the fields of imagination. By wandering freely through the airy spaces of imagination, you will build up confidence in the mental images that you will meet. It is necessary to give yourself permission because we all have received conditioning not to daydream, to quit "acting like a child." We need to loosen these constraints that have been placed upon us.

Wilma: That seems like sound advice, Dr. D. Can you give me some exercises that can help me on the road to an expanded ImQ?

Dr. D: Why sure, Wilma. Here's one for strengthing your perceptual image recall system. Borrow one of those digital watches that beep on the hour. Pick a day this week and wear the watch. Everytime it beeps, stop what you are doing and list the past hour's activities in as much detail as you care to. Choose one of the activities and then visualize it occurring slightly differently. Do this exercise for five to eight hours consecutively during the day.

You can use your computer for the next exercise. Write a program that accepts a list of object nouns (such as boat, horse, watermelon), a list of action verbs (such as eats, runs, types) and a list of adverbs (such as quickly, sadly, humorously). Your program should randomly select one word from each list and then print out the sentence in the form: noun   verb   adverb.
For example, it might output the sentence:
A watermelon types quickly.
For each sentence that you read, give your imagination permission to awake from its sleep and form the mental image suggested by the sentence. Once the mental image is clear, let a scenario develop and follow wherever it might lead you. You might want to wear that digital watch again and set it for some fixed time limit, just in case you get too comfortable in wanderland.

Wilma: Okay, Dr. D, these exercises sound like fun. How come you don't give us exercises like these in our regular courses? Good-bye!

2.3 Implementing the Structure

2.3.1 MEMORY REPRESENTATION AND CONVENTIONS

As the description of the implementation process for a stack begins it is important to clarify who the intended user(s) will be. If you are incorporating a stack into your own application program, then you will be able to take some shortcuts and perform some simplifications to tailor the implementation to your needs. If you are designing the implementation for use by others, then you will need to be complete and modular in your design and guard against potential misuses of the stack by the user. In the following implementation I will proceed from latter assumption, so that the finished product will be available for use by any programmer who has the need for the stack information structure.

In the past, when you needed to store a list of data elements you used an array for storage and subscripts as a means of access. To store an ordered list of varying length like the stack, you can also use an array for the memory representation. In order to keep track of where the front element of the stack is located in the array, it is sufficient to have the integer subscript of the location in which the front stack element is stored. So a simple integer-valued identifier needs to be set aside as an indicator of where the top of the stack resides within the array. **Therefore in terms of memory requirements, there are only two: an array or block of memory locations in which the dynamic stack can range during its fluctuating lifetime, and an identifier, which provides access to the stack by always pointing to the location of the front stack element within the array.**

Let me be quick to point out that the array is not the stack, but only a medium within which the stack can operate. Likewise, the simple identifier is not the front element of the stack, but a means of finding it.

Now that we have the floor plan laid out, it is time to make some decisions on how to arrange what we have. **Since the array will provide the space within which the stack will operate, it is necessary to decide how much space will be set aside.** This decision can be based on an estimate of the maximum number of data elements expected in the stack at any one time. This means the user of the stack must have a feel for the nature of the problem and the range of the data that will be entered. It is possible for the decision to be determined by the nature of the problem itself—for example, the maximum number of balls in the rack is a known, fixed quantity, as is the maximum number of hats that will ever be in the hat bucket. Regardless of how the maximum is determined, it must be one of the conventions incorporated into the implementation. This requirement for fixing the size of the array and therefore of the stack is a departure from the abstract stack model, but with a judicious estimate it should produce no practical restrictions.

We must also pick which end of the array will be considered the fixed end of the stack—that is, the bottom.

Figure 2.3 illustrates our two options. As you can see, it's a matter of orientation. You will also probably recognize the logic of the terms *top, bottom, higher,* and *lower* that are commonly used in speaking of stacks. Though the traditional choice has

Figure 2.3

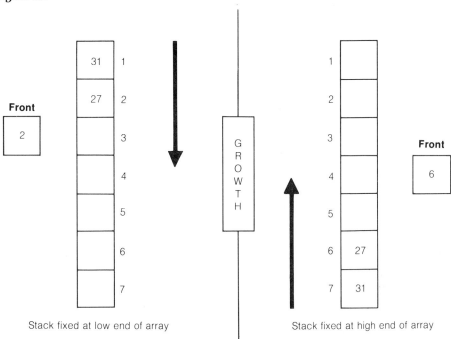

Stack fixed at low end of array | Stack fixed at high end of array

been the orientation on the left, the choice is yours and should be based on your particular programming style and the characteristics of the language you will use. Though neither orientation seems to produce any advantages over the other, once the selection is made it will effect the way the operations PUSH, POP, and EMPTY will be coded.

In Figure 2.3 a convention was used for the identifier indicating the front of the stack. How would you state this convention? **"The value of the identifier will be the subscript of the array location which presently holds the front element of the stack"** is what I seem to have heard you say. Though this seems like a natural choice, does it mean that we have no other avenues to consider? When some people park their car, they orient it so they can leave quickly rather than park quickly. Likewise, with the identifier that points the way to the stack, we could assume the identifier's value to be the subscript of the next available array location before the front stack element, in anticipation of the next PUSH operation. For instance, in Figure 2.3, the FRONT would equal 3 on the left array. This would affect the implementation of all operations. In particular, it would determine the initial value that our pointing identifier would have.

The previous three decisions dealt with the memory representation floor plan and how the data elements will be arranged and accessed within the array. The next decision concerns operations on the stack. **At each end of the array, we might encounter a subscript that is outside the range declared for the array.** Where does the responsibility belong for checking for these two special conditions? If you are preparing the implementation for your own use within an application program, there is no one else to rely on. If the implemented information structure is for general usage and all developed programs will be placed in a library, then the responsibility can lie with either the user or the implementor or both. As implementor, you will decide how and where to check for special cases and then clearly communicate this through the documentation and program comments.

Once this decision is made it immediately leads to another one: what response to make to each special case detected. The answer will depend on the language that you are using, the method of implementation, and, of course, the type of special case. Some options for handling this situation will be covered in subsection 2.3.3.

We have now described which assumptions must be made before coding the support and access routines that will give the dynamic traits of a stack to our memory representation, the array. In the next subsection, we will see what decisions the show's director has made in these areas and how they affect the procedures that follow.

2.3.2   SUPPORT AND ACCESS ROUTINES

In Chapter 1, when describing an implemented information structure, I referred to some utility buildings clustered around the structure. In this case, these support and access facilities provide the dynamic traits of the stack. I will now present the conventions and the code to implement the support and access routines.

These conventions will be used in expressing the routines:

1. The array will include a maximum of 100 locations.
2. The first location of the array will be considered the fixed end of the stack. Thus growth via the PUSH operation will occur from smaller to larger subscripts.
3. The value of the identifier that is used to access the stack will be the subscript of the current front element of the stack. It will be initialized to zero.
4. Checking for errors will be performed in the operations PUSH and POP.
5. The response to a detected error shall be through the utility routines RE-SPOND _ TO _ OVER and RESPOND _ TO _ UNDER, to be described later.
6. The data elements will be assumed to be integers.
7. The following identifier names stand for the following entities:
   a) STACK—the integer array within which a stack is stored.
   b) FTPTR—the subscript of the front data element of the stack.
   c) VALU—the value either inserted or deleted from the stack.
   d) ANSWER—the value TRUE or FALSE, depending on the condition tested.

All operations will be presented as Turbo PASCAL procedures in order to provide independent modules that can be adjusted to the individual differences of a particular computer system or dialect of PASCAL. As procedures they do not exist unattached, but are components of larger modules. When a larger module must possess some prerequisite feature before it can use one of the following procedures then it will be stated. For example, all larger procedures must declare a new type for passing integer arrays as arguments to these procedures. This requirement would be met by including the following definition in the declaration section of the encompassing procedure:

```
const MAX = 100 ;

type INTEGERARRAY = array[1..MAX] of integer ;
     POINTER = 0 ..   MAX ;
var  STACK : INTEGERARRAY ;
     FTPTR : POINTER ;
```

This declaration is a need of PASCAL and may not be required in other language implementations.

There will be six procedures presented: PUSH and POP, EMPTY and FULL, and RESPOND _ TO _ UNDER and RESPOND _ TO _ OVER.

The first operation to be presented is PUSH. Given the three parameters, VALU (value to be inserted), STACK (the array), and FTPTR (the subscript of the location of the front data element), it will check to see if the operation is permissible by using another module—FULL (given later). It will then either respond to the special case via the procedure RESPOND _ TO _ OVER or insert the value into the stack and change the value of the subscript identifier, FTPTR. Here is the procedure for the PUSH operation:

```
procedure PUSH(VALU:integer;var STACK:INTEGERARRAY;var FTPTR:POINTER);
begin (*DECLARATION OF PUSH ROUTINE *)
if FULL (FTPTR) then RESPOND_TO_OVER (* RESPONSE TO SPECIAL CASE*)
      else begin
              FTPTR := FTPTR + 1 ;
              STACK[FTPTR] := VALU
            end (* OF INSERTION OPERATION *)
end (* DECLARATION OF PUSH ROUTINE *);
```

Since this is the first PASCAL procedure that you have encountered in this text, let me point out a couple of important features. In the list of formal parameters in the first line the use of the keyword *"var"* before an identifier means that the identifier is considered a *reference* parameter; any changes made within the procedure will be effective outside the procedure. This is the case with the last two parameters, STACK and FTPTR. If the keyword *"var"* is omitted then the value of the parameter is useful within the procedure and changes are made only within the procedure. This is referred to as a value parameter. You can think of this option as involving either two-way or one-way communication capabilities among procedures.

The FULL function determines whether all locations within the array are occupied. This condition itself is not a problem, but when a PUSH operation is attempted and the FULL condition already exists, we have a situation called OVERFLOW. Some indication should be issued and some response taken. In our procedure, if an overflow occurs, execution will be suspended and control transferred to the procedure RESPOND _ TO _ OVER. The options that can be included in this procedure will be covered in Subsection 2.3.3. Since the user of these procedures will also have access to the FULL function, she can check the stack's condition before a PUSH operation and select her own response to the overflow problem. The PUSH procedure also conducts this test for those programmers who forget or refuse to take the responsibility themselves.

The function FULL follows:

```
function FULL (FTPTR:POINTER): boolean ;
(* GLOBAL IDENTIFIERS : MAX - number of array locations *)
begin   (* CHECK UPPER LIMIT OF ARRAY *)
  if FTPTR = MAX then FULL := true
               else FULL := false
end;
```

The simplicity of this function rests on two important subtleties that underline the synergistic character of every implementation. The very simply stated condition for a full array—FTPTR = MAX—depends on two conventions agreed on earlier. These conventions are summarized by the table below, which also presents the effects of two alternate conventions.

Convention	Alternate Convention	New Condition Defining FULL
The orientation of the stack in the array: growth is from low to high.	Growth is from high to low.	FTPTR = 1
Significance of FTPTR: parameter indicates exact location of front stack element.	Parameter indicates next location before front stack element.	FTPTR = MAX + 1

Changing either convention would greatly affect the implementation of the FULL procedure, so it is important for you to be aware of the ramifications of any changes within this network of interrelated conventions and procedures. It is important to notice that one of our conventions has been isolated from influencing the implementation. Because we have defined the maximum subscript as a constant, MAX, a change to this convention does not require a change to the defining condition of a full array. This type of isolation or independence is a desirable goal for all implementations.

The algorithm for POP follows the same story line as the one for PUSH. Let's jump right in and see what we find.

```
procedure POP(var VALU:integer;STACK:INTEGERARRAY;var FTPTR:POINTER);
begin
if EMPTY( FTPTR )  then RESPOND_TO_UNDER
                               (* RESPONSE TO UNDERFLOW *)
               else begin
                       VALU  := STACK[FTPTR];
                       FTPTR := FTPTR - 1
                       end      (* OF DELETION OPERATION *)
end ;        (*DECLARATION OF POP PROCEDURE *)
```

As I said, POP is rather straightforward, given the model of the PUSH procedure. It should be noted that the parameters VALU and STACK have switched roles as far as the need for the *"var"* preceding them.

If you have done your morning exercise and are wide awake, then you may be questioning why the operation to delete an element from the stack leaves the array in which the stack lives unchanged. If you have also had that morning run to the computer center to pick up your output, you probably remember that it is because the array is not the stack but only its humble abode. Though the array did not change, FTPTR did, and it is FTPTR that provides access to the stack elements. This idea is worth a few minutes of reflective thought so you might put aside the book, lean back, and consider the relationship between the array and the stack for a while.

Now that you are back, how would you define UNDERFLOW, the special case tested for in the POP procedure? If you said UNDERFLOW occurs when the stack is empty or when FTPTR equals zero, then you are halfway correct. Again, it's the combination of the empty condition of the stack with the request for a POP operation that constitutes the special condition. In some applications, you want the stack to be empty—like the hat bucket after lunch—and so the user will also want access to the EMPTY procedure. The procedure for checking the empty status of the stack also depends entirely on the second and third conventions stated at the beginning of this section. Any changes in these two conventions will affect the validity of the test. The procedure is analogous to FULL and is coded as:

```
function EMPTY (FTPTR:POINTER ):boolean;
begin
EMPTY := FTPTR = 0
end ;
(* Notice the alternate way to express the test *)
```

It may be necessary for a user to access the front element of a stack without removing it. As an exercise, write the procedure LOOK, which returns the value of the front element of the stack and leaves the stack unchanged.

For debugging an application that uses a stack it can be helpful to follow the sequence of changes, as we did when we used the stop-action camera on the basketball rack. If you write a procedure called SNAPSHOT that prints the entire contents of the stack, then the user can obtain a series of snapshots and analyze the changes in order to track down a logical error that is producing an overflow or underflow condition. Such a procedure will more than pay for itself.

2.3.3   FLOW PROBLEMS AND RESPONSES

As indicated in the last section, the PUSH and POP operations can indicate two conditions that require special responses. The content of the response for a particular implementation is influenced by the intended use of the stack procedures. If they are for your sole use then you can develop the procedures RESPOND _ TO _ UNDER and RESPOND _ TO _ OVER to provide as much in the way of printed comments and debugging assistance as you deem necessary. If the procedures are being provided for general use, then it is not so easy to tailor the response routines.

Let's start from the top and consider overflow. The user needs to push another data element onto the stack, but the array has been filled by previously pushed data elements. The cause of this condition is either an underestimate in the original maximum for the array or a logical error in the program that produces an overabundance of PUSH requests. Let me offer two options for the response. First, RESPOND _ TO _ OVER can output a useful diagnostic message and then call it quits by returning control to the operating system. The user can then change the estimate

TRADE-OFFS

An algorithm that uses two stacks, both containing the same type of data elements, faces an interesting choice. Obviously, the declaration of two identifiers of type STACK provides the necessary information structures.

An alternate approach is to have a double stack structure—one storage area in which two stacks are managed. This is declared as:

```
type DOUBLE_STACK = record
                    STACK_AREA : array[1..200] of DATA_ELEMENT;
                    LOW_STACK : 0 . . 200 ;
                    HIGH_STACK : 1 . . 201 ;
                    end ;
var   STK_PAIR : DOUBLE_STACK ;
```

The crucial convention is that the low stack has a growth from the lowest subscript towards the highest subscript and the high stack grows from high to low.

What's on the plus side of the trade-off scale? Mainly greater growth potential—each stack can potentially have 200 data elements. Two independent stacks using the same amount of memory are each limited to 100 data elements. This extra flexibility is very attractive and can avoid an overflow situation in either or both stack.

However, the primitive stack operations require an additional argument indicating which stack to process. They also have extra logic, as a PUSH on one stack decrements a stack pointer while a PUSH on the other stack increments the other pointer. This added decision logic shows up as an increase in execution time of the primitive operations.

If the application requires the use of three stacks, then either two double stack structures can be used, with some underused memory space resulting, or a double stack and a single stack can be implemented. This uses memory more effectively; however, two sets of primitive stack operations are needed, one for each stack type.

The double stack structure involves a trade-off. In exchange for the asset of more effective and creative use of memory, the logic of the operations becomes more complicated and execution time is increased.

of the maximum size of the array and try again, or she can look for a logical error by analyzing a series of snapshots of the stack up until overflow occurs. The second option is system-dependent and is applicable in a system that allows for an array to be redimensioned during execution. In this option, RESPOND _ TO _ OVER could operate under the assumption that the cause was an underestimate; when the first overflow happens the array could be reallocated with a larger dimension and the user duly notified that such action was necessary. The control could then be returned to the user's procedure and normal processing continued. Such generosity should only be offered once: a second overflow condition should be assumed to result from a logical error and action similar to the first option can be taken. This approach has the attractive advantage of enabling logically sound but conservatively estimated procedures to execute without being rerun. It also allows the implementation to take another step toward properly emulating the idea of unlimited stack growth.

Although overflow is an effect of the implementation process, underflow is not. It results from either a faulty algorithm or invalid data, or it may simply be an indication that this phase of the processing is complete.

In the first two cases, the programmer expected a data element to be in the stack and was trying to access it either with POP or LOOK. The programmer's false expectation comes from faulty logic in the procedure using the stack or invalid data used by the procedure. (For instance, if a procedure assumes that parentheses are always balanced and the data presented don't contain them.) In this instance, an appropriate response to underflow is to produce diagnostics and terminate execution of the user's program. It then becomes the programmer's responsibility to verify the correctness of the data and the logic of the algorithm used.

In the third case, the user may wish to respond to this condition in her own way. To ensure that underflow is detected, the programmer must test the stack status explicitly with the EMPTY function before each use of the POP. The programmer's need to know when all the data elements have been removed from the stack can usually be solved by initially placing a special value on the stack. By looking for this value on the front of the stack, the condition of "empty stack, therefore finished processing" can be detected.

Another option is to add a boolean argument to both the POP and PUSH procedures. These indicate whether an underflow or overflow has occurred. Users can then select their responses, based on the particulars involved.

In this subsection, I have given you some possible responses to the overflow and underflow condition. Please remember, though, that each application is unique, and you may see an alternative approach that is better suited to that application. As implementor of the information structure you have the flexibility to exhibit your creativity.

■ "JUST FOR REFERENCE"

Implementation process requires setting conventions regarding—

- storage requirements (arrays and identifiers)
- orientation of the information structure in the storage space
- significance of values of special identifiers
- definition and response to special cases

Coding procedures using the stated conventions are also needed—

- Operations for access and checking
- Operations for change

All components combine in a synergistic fashion.

One possible set of conventions would include—

- an array of arbitrary size to hold stack and an integer identifier for identifying the location of the front of the stack
- bottom of the stack fixed at the low subscript end of the array
- integer identifier signifying the exact location of the front of the stack
- messages to the user announcing the special cases of underflow (subscript less than minimum allowed) and overflow (subscript greater than maximum allowed)

Procedures using the above conventions are coded as follows—

- EMPTY—check condition of FRONT identifier and set boolean value
- FULL—check condition of FRONT identifier and set boolean value
- PUSH—if no overflow condition exists then increment FRONT identifier and store data element in the array location indicated by FRONT
- POP—if no underflow condition exists then retrieve FRONT data element of stack, return value, and decrement the FRONT identifier

Synergistic combination of all components operates through the collection of conventions, expressed both in a mind space via program documentation and in a program space via coded procedures, plus the use of the coded access and support routines in the framework of an application program.

EXERCISES

1. List the areas in which conventions must be set in order to implement a stack.

2. Draw a diagram that represents a stack implementation using the following conventions and that already has three data elements in it:
   a) There will be a maximum of 12 array locations.
   b) Subscripts will range from 0 to 11.
   c) The growth of the stack will be from low to high subscript.
   d) The FRONT pointer will not be a part of the array.
   e) The FRONT pointer will contain the subscript of the first element in the stack.

3. Draw a diagram that represents a stack implementation using the following conventions and that already has four data elements in it:
   a) There will be a maximum of 15 array locations.
   b) The subscripts will range from 0 to 14.
   c) The growth will be from high to low subscript.
   d) The pointer to the first element on the stack is contained in the array and is found in the location with subscript 0.
   e) The FRONT pointer contains the subscript of the array location in front of the first element in the stack.

4. Write the condition that defines the empty stack and the condition that defines the full array for each set of conventions listed in exercises 2 and 3 above.

5. Given the following conventions as expressed in the diagrams, state the condition that indicates when the array is full and when the stack is empty.

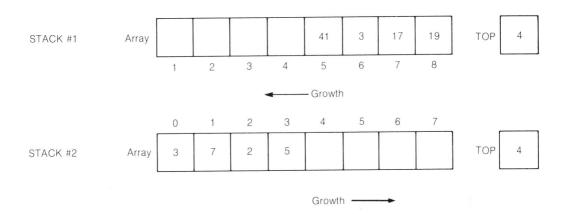

6. What condition can you state that will ensure that a stack will be empty after a sequence of POP and PUSH operations on an initially empty stack?

7. Which of the following sequences are possible outputs from a magic stack box that can do two things: input a single character at a time and push it onto a stack; and pop a character off the stack and output it? For each part assume that the input sequence is O R A N G E, that is, O first, R second, and so on.

   a) A R N G O E
   b) G E N A R O
   c) E G N A R O

8. Write the POP operation for a stack that uses the following conventions:
   a) There will be 50 locations in the array X.
   b) The subscripts will range from 0 to 49.
   c) The growth will be from high to low subscript.
   d) The FRONT pointer points to the location of the first data element in the stack.
   e) The data elements are integer values.

9. Using the first-generation operations EMPTY, POP, PUSH, and FULL as assumed procedures, write the following second-generation operations:
   a) MIXUP2—interchanges the top two stack elements.
   b) MIXUP3—reverses the order of the top three stack elements.
   c) GETDOWN—Returns the value of the bottom stack element and leaves the stack unchanged.
   d) MOVEUP—Interchanges the top and bottom stack elements;
   e) NEGOUT—Removes all negative numbers from the stack and leaves the order of the nonnegative numbers unchanged.

f) POPDOWN—Returns the value of the bottom stack element and removes it from the stack.

g) FLIPOUT—Removes all elements from the top of stack until a given value is found or the stack becomes empty.

Note: Some of these operations will require the use of an auxiliary stack as temporary storage in order to preserve the ordering.

10. Describe an implementation method for representing two distinct stacks in one array of 200 locations. State all conventions that you would use and write the first-generation operations for both stacks.

2.4 Applications

In the solution of various problems in programming languages, the use of the stack has been invaluable. Though the problems vary in nature, their solutions require the special LIFO behavior exhibited by the stack. The stack has been used for nested procedures and syntactical analysis in compilers and assemblers. So integral to the solution of these problems is the stack that some computers have been designed with stack capabilities as part of the hardware. The characteristic of the solutions that requires the qualities of a stack is the ability to suspend the action, to stop in your tracks, to take off on a new path but remember from whence you came, and to begin again at the same point on the original path. Stacks permit a kind of suspended animation, like leaving one sphere of existence and entering a similar but new one. A chronological recording of events, a history which you intend to return to but in reverse chronological order—these are the traits which the solutions share. Let us now look at a couple of the solutions in which the stack stars.

2.4.1 NESTED PROCEDURES

You have probably written a large program in which one procedure or subroutine calls another procedure, which calls another. When this happens the process of the first procedure is suspended and a new path in the second procedure is followed—but with the certainty that the execution will eventually backtrack to the first procedure. As you write more complicated programs and develop structured programming skills, the depth of the path will increase but your confidence will not have to be stretched. How does the computer find its way back? Has the computer taken a cue from Hansel and Gretel and left little bits of data along the path? Its wizardry in this area (actually it is deviously devised by the compiler) is illustrated in Figure 2.4 and explained below.

Using PASCAL as an example of nested procedures enables me to add a little twist and emphasize the suspended animation feature. Since a PASCAL procedure can define within itself another procedure with duplicate identifier names, the identifier references must be unambiguously handled. In Figure 2.4 you see four procedures—MAIN, which contains FIRST, which contains SECOND, which contains

Figure 2.4

```
        procedure MAIN ;
         var A,B,C:integer;

        procedure FIRST ;
         var X : integer;

        procedure SECOND
         var X,Y : real ;

            procedure THIRD ;
             var  A,B : real;
                   X : integer;
            begin (* procedure THIRD  *)
               .
               .
            end;

        begin  (* procedure SECOND *)
          .
    3→   THIRD;
          .
        end;

        begin (* procedure FIRST *)
          .
          .
    2→   SECOND ;
          .
        end;

        begin  (* procedure MAIN *)
          .
          .
    1→   FIRST ;
          .
          .
          .
        end;
```

THIRD. Procedures FIRST, SECOND, and THIRD all contain an identifier denoted X. References to X in procedure SECOND must not affect the value of the identifier X in FIRST, which must retain its current value while both SECOND and THIRD are in operation. Take some time to look at the arrangement of the procedures and the diagram before reading any further.

The explanation that follows is a model of how a PASCAL compiler might handle nested procedures. Each compiler has its own method. This model will convey the general idea.

As each procedure is called by an encompassing procedure, an environment is created within which the called procedure will operate. The environment of the calling procedure (created when it was originally called) is temporarily suspended. The steps in this process are outlined below. Upon a call to a procedure:

1. Calling environment is suspended by—
   a) Saving all identifiers on the stack,
   b) Saving the location of the next instruction after the procedure call on the stack.

2. Called environment is created by—
   a) Creating the storage block for all identifiers and parameters in the environment,*
   b) Transferring execution control to the *begin* block of the called procedure.

The sequence of diagrams in Figure 2.5 demonstrates this dynamic process. It begins with the environment for procedure MAIN, which is already in existence because of the original call to that procedure. The sequence of calls are those indicated in Figure 2.4. In Figure 2.5a you can see the nesting of environment FIRST in environment MAIN. The calling environment has been suspended and the stack is used to preserve it while it is inactive. The called environment is created and activity can occur within this environment. As this activity progresses until another event occurs, the calling of procedure SECOND.

The results of this event are recorded in Figure 2.5b. The steps in the process outlined earlier are again applied. The identifier X of procedure FIRST is saved on the stack. The location $2\rightarrow$ of the next instruction after the call to procedure SECOND is pushed onto the stack. These two steps effect the suspension of procedure FIRST and pave the way for the transfer to procedure SECOND. The environment for procedure SECOND is created within the newly suspended environment by setting up the storage block for identifiers X and Y. Finally, execution control is transferred to the *begin* block of the active environment.

The stack has enabled the identifiers of all suspended procedures to be protected. The problem of an ambiguous reference—for instance to identifier X—is solved by accessing the identifier that is in the storage block of the active environment only. This explains how different PASCAL procedures can declare local identifiers that have the same name. The local attribute means that only the identifier in the storage block of the active environment will be accessed, while any synonym identifier is cozily tucked away on the stack. However, the question of global identifiers is not answered by this model. For example, how is a reference to identifier A in environment SECOND handled? This is an important question which I shall leave unanswered in this text. By using your imagination, resources in the library, and people in your educational environment, you may discover the solution before you take a formal compiler design course. Thus I'll leave this topic as an imagination challenge for you.

What would the environments and the stack look like after procedure SECOND calls procedure THIRD? The same steps are applied as in the previous two calls. As an exercise, draw the nested environments and the current stack before procedure THIRD ends.

As you can visualize, the level of nested procedure calls can progressively continue as procedure THIRD calls FOURTH, which calls FIFTH, and so on. The depth to

---

*Some compilers create this storage block in a special memory area, which I am referring to as the storage block, while others utilize the stack itself to contain the identifiers of all suspended environments *and* of the currently active environment.

Figure 2.5

a. Event: procedure MAIN calls procedure FIRST at 1 → of Figure 2.4.

Result:

Stack

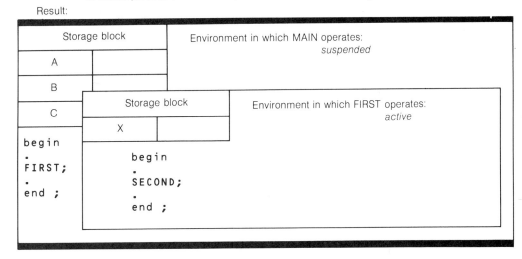

b. Event: procedure FIRST calls procedure SECOND at 2 → of Figure 2.4.

Result:

Stack

Storage block		Environment in which MAIN operates: *suspended*
A		
B		

Storage block — Environment in which FIRST operates: *suspended*

X	

```
begin ;
.
FIRST;
.
end ;
```

```
begin
.
SECOND;
.
end ;
```

Storage block — Environment for SECOND: *active*

X	
Y	

```
begin
.
THIRD;
.
end ;
```

Stack (b):

```
2 →
X
1 →
C
B
A
```

which this can continue is limited only by—what? Imagination? No, not imagination, but implementation. The maximum size of the stack will limit the number of suspended environments that can be accommodated. Since this depends on how many identifiers must be saved for each environment, the level at which overflow will occur depends on the sequence of calls and not on the number of nested procedures.

The preceding explanation illustrates how to move deeper into nested procedures. It is also necessary to have a process which returns from the depths, so to speak. What will occur when the *begin-end* block of the currently active environment completes? At this point the active environment does not need to be suspended, for it has completed its defined task. Instead, we must bid farewell to the called environment and resume the most recently suspended task. For example, when the active procedure SECOND completes, then the environments must revert to Figure 2.5a, with execution resuming at $2\rightarrow$. Not by luck but by design, this environment sits on the top of the stack, so a POP operation will help us return to the most recently suspended environment. To revive the environment entirely, the identifiers in the newly activated environment must be restored. Again by design, these identifiers and their values are easily reinstated by POP operations upon the stack. Now the environment for procedure FIRST is prepared to resume its defined task, having waited for procedure SECOND to complete its duties. The same fate awaits procedure FIRST. When its *begin-end* block terminates, the environment within which it was created will be resumed and we will have merrily climbed out of the nest of procedure calls, each time depending on a stack to help us out.

I would summarize the steps of the return process as follows:

1. Revive the calling environment by
   a) Removing the location of the next instruction from the stack.
   b) Restoring identifiers to the storage block by removing them from the stack.
2. Begin execution at the indicated location in the newly activated environment.

This return process, in combination with the process for handling a call to a procedure, defines a simple model for how a computer system provides for the important programming technique of nested procedures. It also illustrates why local identifiers lose their values upon exit from a procedure: the environment in which they existed is deallocated. To be sure, we have minimized or avoided certain aspects here (like global references and parameter references). But let's not forget who the star of the show is—the stack!

One powerful possibility that the stack provides in this area is that of a procedure calling itself until some termination condition is reached. This process, called **recursion**, is used to solve a variety of problems.

The classical example is the factorial. The factorial operation is denoted by the ! symbol (exclamation point). The factorial of 15, expressed as 15!, is calculated by multiplying 15 by 14!; 14! is calculated by multiplying 14 by 13!, and so on. When the terminal condition is encountered—calculating 1!—the factorial is defined as equal to 1 rather than as reapplication of the factorial operation.

A procedure to calculate the factorial would call itself. This would result in a sequence of procedure calls, resulting in the pushing of data onto the stack. Eventually the stack is used to move back through the sequence of calls.

Recursive procedures have the drawback of being expensive by using memory and time. Also, it is possible for a stack overflow to occur, if a sequence of calls uses the entire space of the array housing the stack.

This very important case of recursive procedure calls deserves much more attention. Therefore, subsection 3.5 will cover varied aspects of recursion and the importance of the stack in its implementation.

I hope that seeing how the simple stack provides a solution in an important area of computer science—nested procedures—gives you an appreciation of our first information structure and arouses your imagination as to what other feats can be in store for the stack in particular and information structures in general.

■ "JUST FOR REFERENCE"

Nested procedures require the ability to call procedures in sequence and then to return through the sequence.

Algorithm for processing a procedure call involves two steps—

- suspension of calling environment via pushing identifiers and pushing return address onto the stack
- creation of called environment

In the algorithm for processing a procedure return, the calling environment is revived by popping the return address and popping the identifiers from the stack.

Recursion—a collection of nested procedure calls in which a procedure calls itself until a terminal condition occurs. The stack serves to keep track of parameters and the nesting depth.

EXERCISES

1. Describe the role of the stack during a procedure call.
2. How can three nested procedures all declare an identifier SUM and preserve the integrity of the procedures when SUM is referenced?
3. Using the notation of subsection 2.4.1, assume that the following sequence of procedure calls have occurred: FIRST is called, next SECOND is called, and then THIRD is called. Show the contents of the stack at this point. Draw the suspended and active environments.
4. Describe the process involving the stack when the *begin-end* block of a procedure ends.
5. How many POP operations will be invoked between the call of procedure THIRD and after procedure FIRST has returned to the main program? (Assume the same sequence of calls stated in question 3.)
6. Assume the following skeleton procedure.

```
procedure MAIN
var A, B , C : real ;
  procedure A_PART ;
  var B , C : integer ;
  begin
    .
    .
  end;
  procedure B_PART ;
  var A , C : real ;
  begin
    .
    .
  end ;
  begin
  A_PART ;
  B_PART ;
  end ;
```

Draw the environments each time a new procedure is called. Begin when procedure MAIN is called and continue through the serial calls to A _ PART and B _ PART.

7. Given the following statement and procedure, draw the sequence of environments.

```
FACTORIAL (4 , F_VALUE ).
    procedure FACTORIAL ( N: integer ; var FACT : integer );
    var T : integer;
    begin
    if N = 1 then FACT := 1
            else begin
                FACTORIAL ( N - 1 , T ) ;
                FACT := N * T ;
                end ;
    end ;
```

2.4.2 BUILDING A MIGHTIER MOUSE

Each year a contest is staged for computer-controlled robotic mice in which the mighty mice struggle against the combined elements of geometry and time to be the fastest computer rodent through this year's amazing maze. Each robot must have the necessary mechanical systems to make turns and a perception system to sense corners, intersections, and dead ends. A computer program is used to make these distinctions and, more importantly, to make decisions at intersections and to remember where it made the last poor choice of paths. In developing the strategy for finding that "best" path to the exit of the maze, the stack once again takes the cake (cheese, of course) for contributing the most to the effort. We will now look at how it contributes to this problem in particular and to others that have a similar framework. This problem illustrates the classical backtracking algorithm used in various artificial intelligence problems.

The maze is a generalization of the floor plan of any building in which the rooms have all shrunk to zero dimension and all that is left are the halls. Figure 2.6a shows a hypothetical floor plan with numerous rooms off the hallways. This floor plan could be incorporated into the robot butler that is being marketed by the designer of last year's mightiest mechanical mouse. It could also be used to develop another electronic game where the player travels the halls, opening doors to find adventure and treasures. Whatever the need, some way of implementing the information of the floor plan and accessing the information would be required. Figure 2.6d gives a possible way of representing the floor plan as a matrix.

The following conventions explain the representation. The zero represents open hall space and 1, 2, 3, 4 represent space that can be entered only from the west, north, east, or south, respectively. The 5 means the space cannot be entered from the outside. With these conventions as a starting point, algorithms can be developed to walk the halls, finding doors with adventure hiding behind them.

If only the halls, not the rooms, are of interest then you might design the floor plan in Figure 2.6b. This representation is simpler, with only ones and zeros representing where one can and cannot walk. If you would rather see the paths than the limiting walls then you can use the visualization given in Figure 2.6c. If your pride will allow your imagination this much stretching, imagine yourself to be a robot mouse, hungry for some electrical gratification. Your foresight is very limited and you rely on your hindsight and your perserverance. How would you follow the little spots in Figure 2.6c to reach that quantum of electric cheese?

The algorithm that I will present uses Figure 2.6c as a basis, with Figure 2.6e representing the maze. The algorithm assumes that no circular paths exist in the maze. It is helpful to classify each spot in Figure 2.6c according to the number of paths that can be taken from the spot. Figure 2.6f shows the five classifications used. However, remember our foresight can see ahead only one spot, and we can only classify a spot when we reach it.

The strategy of the robot mouse is as follows:

```
FROM THE ENTRANCE SPOT, CONTINUE WALKING UNTIL REACHING:
        1. AN INTERSECTION AND
                THEN SELECT A PATH FROM THE INTERSECTION,
                    REMEMBER THE INTERSECTION AND THE PATH
                    SELECTED,
                    BEGIN WALKING AGAIN.
    OR
        2. A DEAD-END AND
                THEN BACK UP TO THE LAST INTERSECTION,
                    TAKE ANOTHER PATH NOT YET TAKEN,
                    BEGIN WALKING AGAIN.
    OR
        3. THE EXIT SPOT WHERE THE MOUSE IS ELECTRIFIED.
```

At this point in the chapter I am confident that you see where the stack will be used—remembering the sequence of recently visited intersection spots. The stack is also used to save the direction taken from these spots. In case the current path becomes a dead end, the mouse can return to the first spot on this path, blocking the path off to prevent retracing its steps. This is a *very important* part of the strategy because it is by blocking all dead-end paths that a path leading to the exit is discovered.

It is important to notice how the solution is developed. I am using the modular approach, describing procedures that will be used and assuming their existence

Figure 2.6

a.
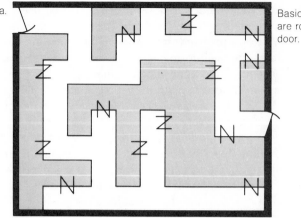

Basic floor plan: shaded areas are rooms; -N- symbol indicates door.

b.
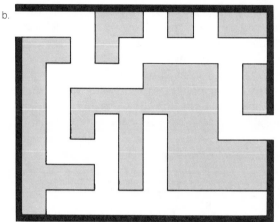

Floor plan as a maze

c.

Floor plan viewed as a pathway: a box with a circle can be occupied; a box without a circle is a solid space, i.e. a wall.

d.

0	0	0	5	4	0	3	0	5	4
5	5	0	5	0	0	0	0	0	0
3	0	0	0	0	5	5	3	0	2
5	0	5	4	5	5	5	5	0	5
5	0	5	0	5	0	1	5	0	0
3	0	0	0	3	0	5	5	2	5
5	4	5	0	5	0	5	5	5	4
5	0	0	0	0	0	0	0	0	0

Floor plan as a coded array of integers

0   Aisle space

5   Solid space

1   Door facing west

2   Door facing north

3   Door facing east

4   Door facing south

e.

0	0	0	1	1	0	1	0	1	1
1	1	0	1	0	0	0	0	0	0
1	0	0	0	0	1	1	1	0	1
1	0	1	1	1	1	1	1	0	1
1	0	1	0	1	0	1	1	0	0
1	0	0	0	1	0	1	1	1	1
1	1	1	0	1	0	1	1	1	1
1	0	0	0	0	0	0	0	0	0

Maze as a coded array

0   Path space

1   Solid space

f.

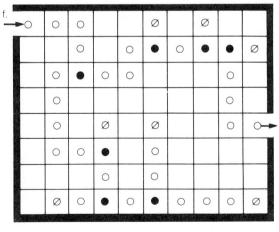

Pathway with classified spots

○   One way in/ one way out

∅   One way in/ no way out

●   One way in/two or three ways out

→○   Entrance

○→   Exit

without presenting the details of how they produce their results. The following preliminary assumptions are made:

1. The maze is represented as a two-dimensional integer array, as in Figure 2.6e, with 1 and 0 as values except for the exit spot.

2. The exit spot of the maze will be represented by a value other than 0 or 1.

3. The lowest and highest row and column of the maze array will contain all 1's, except for the entrance and exit spots. Hence all other spots have four neighbors and the procedure for classifying and selecting paths described below is simplified.

4. The stack will be implemented as an array of data elements where each data element is a record containing three fields: the row and column of the spot in the maze array and the direction from which the spot was entered (left side, top, right side, or bottom).

5. A list of all spots visited, from the entrance spot directly to the present spot, will be kept, added to when movement is made and erased when a path is found to be a dead-end. When the process finishes this list will provide a path of spots to the exit spot.

6. These procedures exist:

   a) INITIALIZE (MAZE, ENTRANCE)—to initialize the MAZE array, to set the exit spot, and indicate which spot is the ENTRANCE spot.

   b) CLASSIFY (MAZE, SPOT, CLASS)—to classify the SPOT by looking at its three neighbor spots (excluding the neighbor spot in the direction from which the SPOT was entered) and assign the value 0, 1, 2, 3 to CLASS for a dead-end, continuation, intersection, or exit spot respectively.

   c) SELECT _ PATH (MAZE, SPOT, NEXT _ SPOT)—to select the NEXT _ SPOT on a path from the given SPOT. Any strategy of selection can be used as long as the path by which this SPOT was entered is not chosen. For example, a clockwise rotation from N to E to S to W may be used.

   d) BLOCK _ PATH (MAZE, SPOT)—to change the value in the MAZE array corresponding to SPOT from 0 to 1, which effectively blocks the paths starting at this SPOT.

   e) ADD _ SPOT _ TO _ LIST (SPOT, LIST)—to add a SPOT to a LIST of visited spots.

   f) ERASE _ PATH (SPOT, LIST)—to delete from the LIST the spots from the last one added to the given SPOT when a dead-end path is found.

   g) PUSH (SPOT, STACK)—to push a data element SPOT onto the STACK.

   h) POP (SPOT, STACK)—to pop a data element SPOT from the STACK and return its value.

   i) PRINT _ PATH (LIST)—to print the path of spots from the entrance to the exit spot.

Having stated these assumptions, here is the controlling strategy that will be implanted into the robot mouse's brain:

```
program CHEESEHUNT;

type SPOTS = record
                  ROW:0..20;
                  COL:0..20;
                  ENTRYDIRECTION:1..4;
             end;
     STACK_MODEL = record
                      STACK: array [1..100] of SPOTS;
                      TOP: 0..100
                   end;
(* Declaration of variables *)
(*      arrays : STACK - the stack will operate out of this structure *)
(*               MAZE  - the configuration of the maze resides here *)
(*               LIST  - used to store the list of spots visited *)

var      ENTRANCE, SPOT, NEXT_SPOT, FIRST_OF_PATH:SPOTS;
         STACK:STACK_MODEL;
         CLASS:0...3;
         LIST:array[1..2,1..100] of SPOTS;
         MAZE:array[0..20,0..20] of integer;

(* Program begins to unfold *)
begin
(*   Set up the maze and the co-ordinates of the entrance spot *)
(*   Classify the entrance spot as continuation, intersection, dead-end*)
(*   Set current spot being considered to the entrance spot *)

    INITIALIZE (MAZE, ENTRANCE);
    CLASSIFY (MAZE, ENTRANCE, CLASS);
    SPOT:=ENTRANCE;

(* Until the exit spot is found apply the strategy *)

repeat
   case CLASS of
      (*if continuation spot is encountered, select sole path out *)

      1:begin       (* move to the next spot available and *)
                    (* add the current spot to the list of spots on the path *)
           SELECT_PATH (MAZE, SPOT, NEXT_SPOT);

           ADD_SPOT_TO_LIST (NEXT_SPOT, LIST);
        end;    (* of case for a continuation spot *)

      (* if intersection spot is encountered, save spot on stack *)

      2:begin       (* select a path out and save next spot on stack *)

          PUSH (SPOT, STACK);

          SELECT_PATH (MAZE, SPOT, NEXT_SPOT);

          PUSH (NEXT_SPOT, STACK);

          ADD_SPOT_TO_LIST (NEXT_SPOT, LIST);
        end;    (* of case for intersection spot *)
```

```
(* if dead-end spot is encountered, POP first spot on dead-end path,*)

0:begin (* block the dead-end path, erase the path from the list*)
        (* and begin again at the most recent intersection spot *)
        (* found on top of the stack *)

    POP (FIRST_OF_PATH, STACK);

    BLOCK_PATH (MAZE, FIRST_OF_PATH);

    ERASE_PATH (FIRST_OF_PATH, LIST);

            POP (NEXT_SPOT, STACK);
    end; (* of case for a dead-end spot *)

    end; (* of all possible cases *)

    (* set current spot being considered to next spot moved to *)
    (* and classify the current spot being considered *)

    SPOT:=NEXTSPOT;

    CLASSIFY (MAZE, SPOT, CLASS );

    (* until the exit spot is encountered *)
    until CLASS = 3;

  (* when exit spot has been found then print the spots on the path *)

    PRINT_PATH (LIST);

end;  (* of the CHEESEHUNT program *)
```

The mouse is now ready to meet the challenge of the maze. Using the maze in Figure 2.6e as the challenge maze, work through the procedure. Keep the status of the stack and the list, classifying spots, selecting paths yourself, and substituting 1's for 0's when a path is blocked. In this way, you will attain a better understanding of why the algorithm works and how the exit spot is found. The crucial feature of the algorithm is that for each intersection spot encountered the outgoing paths are investigated and blocked until the intersection spot becomes a continuation spot, a dead-end spot, or a spot along the path to the cheese.

As you work through the maze journey, consider how to implement the list of visited spots. Where are changes to the list made and what kind of changes are they? Attempt to write the two procedures ADD _ SPOT _ TO _ LIST and ERASE _ PATH, remembering to state any conventions that you use.

The maze problem has provided me with a vehicle with which to illustrate briefly the concept of modular program design and stepwise refinement. I began by describing the strategy in a structured English form. Each step was rather broad and lacked the polish of details. The next step was to set some conventions on the memory representation of the maze and how some of the broad steps would be implemented. The next refinement of the solution was to describe some functional units called modules. These modules aided in the expression of the general strategy. Once again, only a certain degree of detail is necessary at this stage. Each module was presented with a module name, a list of parameters, and a brief functional description.

The combining of the original strategy, the stated conventions, and the functional modules produced the main program CHEESEHUNT. The final refinement is the coding of the actual steps involved in each functional module. These details have been unspecified until this point. For example, the procedure BLOCK _ PATH can easily be implemented as follows :

```
procedure BLOCK_PATH (var MAZE:INTEGERARRAY; SPOT : SPOTS ) ;
begin

with SPOT do

MAZE [ ROW , COL ] := 1

end ;
```

You can now finish this last refining step by supplying the final details for each module that remains.

The approach has allowed us to design the solution from the top level, a general strategy, to the bottom line, the coding of the functional modules. Thus, the maze solution for Rich, the robotic mouse, has also illustrated a problem-solving strategy for programmers.

This completes another stage appearance of this chapter's star, the stack. We have seen stacks used by the compiler designer for nested procedures and now by Rich, the robot rodent. These different problems share a characteristic that enables the stack to play a role in the solution of each. The next application for the stack is right at your fingertips.

■ "JUST FOR REFERENCE"

Maze strategy: continue walking until either—

- case 1: an intersection spot is encountered; then push the spot on the stack, select a new direction path, push first spot of new path on stack, and continue walking

- case 2: a dead-end spot is encountered; then pop spot at beginning of path, block the dead-end path, pop the spot that was an intersection, and continue walking

- case 3: an exit spot is encountered; then maze is traversed

For problem solving using modular design and stepwise refinement—

- describe the general algorithm, using large steps

- describe each large step in terms of smaller substeps until each substep is simple to design

- describe appropriate substeps of the general algorithm with smaller single-function modules

- describe a set of conventions for memory representation and other areas of concern
- using the general algorithm, substeps, and conventions, design the top level procedure
- describe a set of conventions for each module
- using the functional descriptions and the conventions, design each module
- code the details of each module at the bottom level

EXERCISES

1. Describe what important capabilities are provided by the stack in the maze algorithm.
2. Explain why the LIFO behavior of the stack is appropriate to the maze algorithm.
3. Write the two procedures ADD _ SPOT _ TO _ LIST and ERASE _ PATH. Use another stack information structure to accomplish the function of each module.
4. Complete the maze algorithm by coding all procedures that have not been coded.
5. You want to know how your robot mouse threaded its way through the maze. Determine what changes or additions are necessary to print the maze, with asterisks indicating spots used by the mouse to find the exit spot. Write the module to perform this added function and indicate where it belongs in the main program CHEESEHUNT.
6. What if no path to the exit spot exists? How does the CHEESEHUNT fare? Describe what happens and suggest a solution.

2.4.3   A STACK AT YOUR FINGERTIPS

Besides the electronic game, which has found its spot in all sorts of places in our modern society, another influential electronic gadget is the electronic calculator. It was actually the development of the handheld calculator that lead to the develop-

Figure 2.7

Photo Courtesy of Hewlett Packard, Inc.

ment of the "computer on a chip," the microcomputer. The microcomputer enables electronic games to tick and click, to flash and crash, to zing and zap, to snap, crackle, and pop and even to talk with a Texas drawl. To add and subtract, to multiply and divide are the feats of the electronic calculator. Let's look at one peculiar model.

You can choose from numerous models with various ranges of applications and special features. One stands out as different from most of the others. The calculators produced by Hewlett-Packard (HP) seem odd to many people at first. A picture of the keyboard of a simple model is shown in Figure 2.7. It's not the layout of the keyboard that attracts people's attention but the method of evaluating expressions.

To calculate a simple addition expression, such as 35 + 20, the sequence of keys depressed is

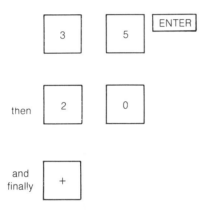

The two operands, 35 and 20, are entered before the operation—in this case addition—is indicated. For more complicated arithmetic expressions, the same concept is followed—the operator after the operands. It was this feature that required a new viewpoint from HP owners. So why did HP design a operational feature that was new to most of the buying public?

Part of the answer comes from looking at the arithmetic expression:
$$18 - 6 \times 46.$$
This expression can be interpreted two ways:
$$(18 - 6) \times 46 \quad \text{or} \quad 18 - (6 \times 46).$$
On calculators that use the conventional keying sequence, the user does some rearranging of terms, depending on the interpretation intended. How would we enter the two interpretations of this expression on the HP? For the first one, $(18 - 6) \times 46$, we would use the key sequence:

and for the second expression, $18 - (6 \times 46)$

In this way the key sequences are unique and cannot be misinterpreted. The user does some preprocessing by scanning the expression and mentally rearranging it to fit the HP pattern of expression. Thus, one reason for the feature is to eliminate the ambiguity of arithmetic expressions.

For more complicated expressions, the same pattern holds: **operator after operands.** The expression $(18 - 6) \times 46/(3 - 79)$ would be entered as:

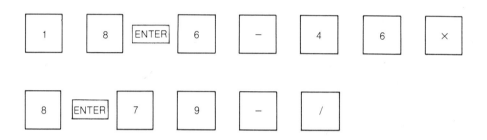

How does the HP calculator remember the operands of an operator? For example, the numerator for the division operator above has two operands and another operator entered before the division operator is indicated. How does it keep straight which operands that are waiting are associated with which operators that are entered?

A stack, of course! Consider the key sequence for $18 - (6 \times 46)$:

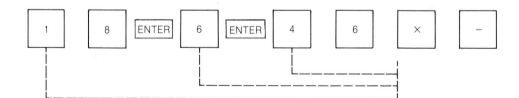

oldest, younger, youngest operand entered

The operands follow the relationship pattern for which the stack is most useful—last entered, first used. And so the HP calculator has a stack feature built into the hardware design.

How will the HP calculator use the stack as operands and operators are keyed in? Using the expression $(18 - 6) \times 46$ as an example, the chart below shows the process followed by the HP calculator. The contents of the HP stack are on the right.

Key Sequence	Action	Stack
		EMPTY
1. 18 ENTER	PUSH 18	18
2. 6	PUSH 6	6 18
3. −	POP 6	18
	POP 18	EMPTY
	OPERATE USING −	
	PUSH 12	12
4. 46	PUSH 46	46 12
5. ×	POP 46	12
	POP 12	EMPTY
	OPERATE USING ×	
	PUSH 552	522

The same process works for the expression $18 - (6 \times 46)$.

When an operand is entered, it is pushed onto the stack; when an operator is entered, a PPOpP (what I call a pee-pop) is performed:

> *p*op an operand from the stack,
> *p*op another,
> *op*erate using the entered operator,
> and *p*ush the result on the stack.

This algorithm is a very simple one for evaluating all entered arithmetic expressions unambiguously.

In the last paragraph, I said that *all* entered arithmetic expressions are evaluated unambiguously. Do you believe this, without any qualifiers? What about incorrectly entered arithmetic expressions? With the stack it is possible to correctly evaluate some as "incorrect." For instance, if we give the HP calculator a key sequence like:

for the arithmetic expression $(43 - 6) \times (45 - 7)$, having forgotten to enter the operand 7, then our old friend UNDERFLOW occurs in disguise. The HP can indicate that an error has occurred. On the other hand, if an expression is entered and one of the operators is forgotten, then there no indication is given that more than one value is still on the stack, so the problem goes undetected. With these two cases as qualifications, the previous statement now stands as "electronically" sound.

Another situation needs some further clarification. What about unary operators? We have learned that PPOpP is the process for binary operators. When a unary operator is detected then the four step process is reduced to three steps:

> pop the operand;
> operate with the unary operator;
> push the result on the stack.

Since the response is different for unary operators, it is necessary to distinguish somehow between a unary minus and a binary subtraction. How is this accomplished on the HP calculator?

The method for expressing arithmetic expressions on the HP is referred to as postfix notation or reverse Polish notation (RPN). The notation that is used in standard algebra is called infix notation, since the operator falls in between the operands. As you may recall, this is how arithmetic expressions in FORTRAN, BASIC, COBOL, and PASCAL are coded. It is by imposing the rules of precedence of operators that compilers can correctly analyze, interpret, and set up the code for evaluating the coded expression. Since the method for evaluating postfix expressions is so simple, compiler designers decided to take advantage of this feature to speed up the execution of the compiled program. During the compilation of your program, the compiler checks the arithmetic expressions for syntactical errors, then translates the infix notation to postfix notation and sets up code for evaluating the expression in its postfix form. In the infix-to-postfix translation, the stack once again plays an important part. (See exercise 6 at the end of this subsection for the algorithm.)

Sounds inefficient, doesn't it? Remember that in a working environment a program is compiled a lot less frequently than it is executed. Therefore, a savings in execution time offsets a little extra expense in compilation. Did I hear you say, "How clever!"? As they might say at HP, "How Polish!"

In summary, the stack aids programmers considerably. Each time the compiler is called, the stack is instrumental. The compiler uses the stack to analyze the infix notation for syntax errors and to translate the expressions to postfix notation. Also, each time the compiled program is executed then the stack is integrally involved in the evaluation of the postfix notation.

In order to take advantage of these features and for other important reasons, computer designers have included stacks in the architectural design of various computer systems. One of the earliest companies to invest money and effort in the stack was the Burroughs Corporation. They developed and marketed the B-5000, a highly stack-based computer architecture. Another computer, the PDP-11 minicomputer, uses a system stack for automatic processing of subroutine calls and returns. All system programs can use the stack for their own purposes. Newly developed computers, both microcomputers and larger systems, are designed with stack operations as part of their basic machine language instruction set. You should now have a feeling for the broad range of influence that the stack information structure holds in computer science.

▪ "JUST FOR REFERENCE"

Evaluation of postfix expressions

Case 1: If operand is entered then push operand on the stack.
Case 2: If operator is entered then—

- case 2a: if unary operator is entered,
      then Pop operand from stack,
          Operator using operator,
          Push result onto stack.

- case 2b: if binary operator is entered,
                       then Pop operand from stack,
                               Pop operand from stack,
                               Operate using operator,
                               Push result onto stack.

EXERCISES

1. Assume your PASCAL compiler has a module called the POSTFIXER, which accepts standard PASCAL expressions and produces the expression in postfix notation. If the input to the module is the following expression, what is the output of POSTFIXER?
   a) X * Y ^ 2 − 6 * X
   b) − A + B * C / 3
   c) − B + (B ^ 2 − 4 * A * C) ^ 0.5

2. For each of the postfix expressions below, show the contents of the stack as the expression is being evaluated. Draw a diagram of the stack after each operand and each operator is processed. (For notational purposes, the symbol ~ represents a unary minus operator.)

   a) 41   82 52 − +
   b) 21 78 − 85 46 + *
   c) 44 32 − 22 80 + ~ 3 + *
   d) 20 ~ 9 35 − + 8 * 7 + −
   e) 6 40 * 8 / 7 13 6 + +

3. Explain how you can detect two kinds of errors in the expression of postfix expressions during the evaluation phase. Is there a general rule involving the number of operands and operators that can be used to define the error conditions?

4. What advantage does a postfix notation have for the task of expressing and evaluating arithmetic expressions?

5. Another mode of expression is prefix notation, in which the operators precede the operands. Write a procedure that accepts an expression in postfix notation and produces an expression in prefix notation. Is it helpful to use two stacks for this project?

6. As part of a compiler project you must write a procedure which translates infix expressions to postfix ones. The algorithm for the translation uses a stack to hold the operators. By ranking the operators hierarchically, a strategy for ordering the operations can be derived. As a real challenge to your imagination, write this POSTFIXER procedure.

   Assume the following conditions exist for the expression:
   a) The operators consist of *, /, +, − in their normal hierarchy of precedence (no unary operators).
   b) Parentheses are used to influence the order of operators.
   c) The symbol := is the end of expression delimiter and is considered lower than + or − in the ordering.

   Follow the algorithm below to convert an infix to a postfix expression:
   a) Push := onto an empty stack.
   b) Get the next entity from IN _ STRING: [:=, (,), operand, operator]

c) Case entity of

:=   Move top stack operator to POST _ STRING, pop stack, and repeat until stack is empty.

(Push (onto stack.

)   Move top stack operator to POST _ STRING;
Pop stack until (is encountered;
Pop (off stack.

operand   Move operand from IN _ STRING to POST _ STRING.

operator   while level of operator is less than level of operator on stack do
        Move operator on stack to POST _ STRING and pop stack.
Push IN _ STRING operator on stack.

d) Repeat steps b and c until := is encountered.

7. Write an interactive PPOpP program that emulates the workings of an elementary HP calculator. Set up all the conventions for delimiters and special symbols for unary operators.

2.5 Curses—Again and Again and Again

2.5.1 BOTTOM-UP AND TOP-DOWN RECURSIVE DEFINITIONS

When programmers are struggling late into the night attempting and reattempting to debug a recursively written algorithm, they may be tempted to define recursion as the act of cursing again and again and again, ad infinitum. Though the art of program debugging is at times a recursive process (slowly narrowing down the suspected problem area into smaller and smaller areas until the bug is found and terminated), the concept of recursion has a more general appeal and application.

The appeal of recursion in mathematics was originally in the definition of formulas. Because recursion involves precise and succinct descriptions, it found an appropriate niche. Computer science has extended the application of recursion by adapting the essential idea to the task of designing algorithms. Now recursion is used to describe entire processes as well as mathematical formulas.

The concept of a recursive definition or algorithm has two components: (1) an explicitly expressed definition or algorithm when a special condition exists; (2) a circular definition or algorithm for all other conditions. In the latter case, the definition or algorithm is used as a functional part at least once within the definition or algorithm.

What characteristics give recursion its appeal? There are two complementary perspectives that can assist our understanding of one of programming's most enigmatic tools. We can look at this conceptual tool either from the bottom up or from the top down.

Let us start at the bottom and work up. The first step in developing a bottom-up recursive definition is to determine the simplest cases of what is being defined. These simplest cases are then defined explicitly. The next step of the definition process is the most subtle and crucial. It resembles a induction in mathematical reasoning, which basically says that if you can reach the first step of a staircase (the simplest case), and if from the nth step of the staircase it is proved possible to get to the next step, the $(n + 1)$th step (the induction case), then you can climb the entire infinitely rising staircase. For recursion, the induction step says that more complicated cases can be built from the simplest cases that are explicitly defined, and that from the newly constructed cases even more complicated cases can be built, recursively and infinitely.

Let's look at a quick example that demonstrates how the bottom-up recursive process provides us with a powerful defining tool. We will pick a familiar concept to define, the concept of power—taking a positive integer and raising it to a given power. In computer science we depend on the power of 2, so let this be our example. How would you define the function of raising 2 to the power of *n*? Automatically, you probably hear the statement, "2 times itself *n* times". Recursively, though, you need to visualize the process differently.

First, let us focus our attention on the simplest case. For notational purposes let me refer to our power function by POWER _ OF _ 2(N). For positive integers, then, the simplest case is POWER _ OF _ 2(1). This is indeed simple—2 times itself 1 time equals 2. So our ability to step onto that first step of the staircase is ensured by the statement:

```
POWER_OF_2(1) = 2
```

How do we recursively arrive at the second step? We must use the simple case as defined to construct more complicated cases. We could say:

```
POWER_OF_2(2) = 2 * POWER_OF_2(1)
```

Now we would have two cases defined—a simple case and a constructed case:

```
POWER_OF_2(1) = 2
POWER_OF_2(2) = 2 * POWER_OF_2(1)
```

We could continue to construct the definitions for the power of 2 for all positive integers, but as you can see it would be a never-ending task. We need some way of defining the process without defining each individual case.

The main feature of recursive definitions meets this requirement. We will define the POWER _ OF _ 2 function in terms of itself. This will give us the ability to generate all possible cases except the simplest case, which is defined explicitly. Try this recursive definition on for size:

```
POWER_OF_2(N)=2              N=1 (simplest case)
POWER_OF_2(N+1)=2 * POWER_OF_2(N)    N>1 (inductive case)
```

This definition suits our needs. Each power of 2 is constructed from a simpler case of the POWER _ OF _ 2 function and a simple multiplication. Eventually this continuous descent through simpler cases brings us to the simplest case. Since the simplest case is not defined in terms of the function itself, the descent ends (saving us from the depths of depression due to recursion overdose). The value of the function is therefore recursively and—most important—well defined.

In summary, the two important features of the recursive definition from the bottom-up perspective are:

1. Defining the simplest cases explicitly.

2. Defining additional cases in terms of simpler cases by referring to the function itself with a simpler (or smaller) argument.

As you can see, this method parallels the inductive process of mathematics. By starting out simply and at the bottom step and constructing a way to reach the next step, you cover all of the steps.

Another mathematical formula that has an intriguing history and is recursively defined generates the sequence of integers known as the Fibonacci sequence. The Fibonacci sequence begins as follows:

$$0, 1, 1, 2, 3, 5, 8, 13, \ldots$$

Each new integer is the sum of the previous two integers. Thus 21 (8 + 13) is the next entry in the sequence. As a challenge, try to write a mathematical formula that correctly predicts the nth integer in the sequence.

Recursively, it is elegantly simple. We start with the simple cases:

$$FIBO(0) = 0 \qquad \text{0th integer in the sequence}$$
$$FIBO(1) = 1 \qquad \text{1st integer in the sequence}$$

Now, the constructed cases:

$$FIBO(2) = FIBO(0) + FIBO(1) = 0 + 1 = 1 \qquad \text{2nd in sequence}$$
$$FIBO(3) = FIBO(1) + FIBO(2) = 1 + 1 = 2 \qquad \text{3rd in sequence}$$

And now the general recursive case:

$$FIBO(N) = FIBO(N - 2) + FIBO\ (N - 1) \qquad \text{for all } N > 1$$

This formula has two explicitly defined simple cases; all other cases depend on the previous cases in the sequence. The Fibonacci formula is an excellent application of the recursive principle because no simpler formula can express the relationship between a value—say, 21—and its position in the sequence, the eighth. These two examples of recursive definitions should provide a starting point in your journey toward understanding this intriguing concept.

We will soon look at recursion from another perspective. But first, as a challenge to your imagination, try to discover a real-world application of the Fibonacci sequence. Open up your vision and look at the world in a new way.

Now, back to recursion. When you are faced with a difficult or complex problem, one strategy is to tackle one part of it at a time. A set of simpler tasks is performed in order to complete the main task. This is the basic idea with recursion of the top-down variety. This approach works well when you are describing recursive processes rather than formulas, as we shall soon see. The top-down perspective on recursion takes the following approach: First, take a problem and break it into similar subproblems (usually by describing the same general process on a smaller set of data). Second, solve the subproblems and join the results together to find the solution for the larger problem.

Each subproblem can be approached in the same way—that is, it can be subdivided into smaller subproblems and the solutions combined. This process digs deeper and deeper, the subproblems growing smaller and smaller until each becomes simple enough to have a simple solution. Once this condition of simplicity is reached the recursive decomposition is terminated and the successive solutions are combined to form the overall solution.

This basic divide-and-conquer strategy may seem a bit (or even very) overwhelming at first, especially if you limit your vision to the type of computers and programs you are already familiar with. Imagining a single computer working on multiple subproblems simultaneously requires a stretch of the imagination. Even one computer working under a multitasking operating system may be difficult to envision, although it at least seems more feasible. But remember not to limit your choices. The advent of today's multiprocessors, systems with multiple central processing units at the disposal of one algorithm, opens up tremendous new vistas of program capabilities. One such capability is the handling of divide-and-conquer style recursive algorithms. Let us look at one fairly easy and fairly important example of this type of recursive algorithm.

The problem of arranging a list of numbers into ascending or descending order is a favorite assignment of many teachers of introductory programming courses. Beside this function, the function of sorting numbers is important to many applications in business and science programming alike. To sort an inventory list of 8765 items would be an expensive activity if done inefficiently. So the study of sorting algorithms has received considerable attention. This problem shall now receive our attention, focusing on designing a sort of the divide-and-conquer variety.

The following algorithm is an inefficient application of the divide-and-conquer method. It would be found in organizations that have a strict chain of command, such as the military (and some academic environments). I call it the General Pass deBuck sort. It seems that General deBuck has to arrange the serial numbers of the battalion in descending order. So she scans the list, finds the largest serial number on the list, writes it down on the desk, then crosses off the largest number and calls in the second-in-command, Colonel Sort deRest. General deBuck commands the colonel to "Sort the rest!" Well, Colonel deRest learned everything she knows from General deBuck, so she finds the largest number, writes it on the desk, marks it off the list, then calls in the next-in-command and issues the same command, "Sort the rest!" As we pass down the chain of command, where does the buck finally stop? Naturally, with Buck Private Simple Case. When Private Case receives a list with only one number and the command to "Sort the rest," she is dumbfounded that someone would give her such a simple task—especially since it's her serial number. Nonetheless, she stamps SORTED on her list of one and returns it to the person who gave it to her. As each person in the chain of command receives a sorted list, she appends the number written on her desk to the top of the list, stamps it SORTED, and returns it to the next higher up. Finally, General deBuck receives a list from Colonel deRest and immediately appends the largest number to the top of the list. The General Pass deBuck Sort is accomplished as General deBuck attaches her stamp of approval.

How would we write down this novel sorting method (or is it a short sorting novel)? General deBuck has passed us a copy through the chain of command.

General Pass deBuck Sort Algorithm for N Elements

If list has one element then

        list is sorted

else

        Find the largest in list, record it, mark it off.
        Sort the list of N − 1 elements.
        Append largest element to sorted list.

Mission accomplished.

This algorithm illustrates the important components of a recursive algorithm. It subdivides the problem into three steps, one of which repeats the same process on a smaller set of data. It eventually arrives at a case which is simple enough not to require the recursive use of the process. The final step combines the results of the other two steps to form the solution of a larger problem.

So why did I characterize this algorithm as an inefficient application of the divide-and-conquer recursive method? Mainly because the splitting of the larger problem into two subproblems is not balanced. In each step the data are divided into two groups—a group of one that contains the largest element in the data set and a group containing the rest of the data set. This approach leaves a heavy burden on the next in command. In a less hierarchical organization we might divide the data into two almost equal sets and give them to two teams to sort, incorporating the attribute of balance into the solution. This method will be illustrated next.

Our new algorithm contains the same three components:

1. A terminal condition with a simple nonrecursive solution.
2. A recursive call to the algorithm with a smaller data set.
3. A merging of the solutions to two similar problems.

The problem is the same but the solution is different. Instead of dividing the list of numbers into two quite unequal parts, the largest and the rest, let us divide the list into two almost equal parts and sort each half-list. Once both half-lists are sorted then they are merged together in descending order. The sorting of each half-list can be handled the same way: the list can be halved, each half sorted, and then the two merged together. When do we arrive at a condition that is simple enough to solve in a nonrecursive way? Well, Private Case knew the answer in the last algorithm—when the list has only a single element in it. A list with two elements is also fairly simple to sort since, it only requires a single comparison and a possible interchange of the two elements. So there are two terminal conditions in this algorithm. This algorithm is particularly well suited to a multiprocessor computer system.

Merge-Sort Algorithm for a List of N Elements

The algorithm for a MERGE-SORT would go something like this:

```
if N = 1 then list is sorted
        else if N = 2 then if first element < second element then
                                interchange them;
                        list is sorted
        else
                MERGE-SORT top half-list,
                MERGE-SORT bottom half-list,
                merge top and bottom half-lists.
```

This algorithm has a feeling of refined subtlety. It seems too slick, but all the ingredients of the divide-and-conquer strategy are present. One factor that may give you the feeling of masked subtlety is the handling of the list as if it were a basic information structure. For example, half-lists are formed as if it were as simple as halving an integer. The details of how the half-lists are formed, manipulated, and merged are quite important to the actual implementation of the algorithm. For our purpose of becoming familiar with the elegance of recursion we can exercise a little poetic license by simply assuming the details have all been worked out.

In comparing the two algorithms, what indicates that the MERGE _ SORT is more efficient? The step that deals the loser's award to the General Pass deBuck Sort is hidden in what appears to be a simple statement of a task: finding the largest item in the list. This is indeed a simple task. But how many times is it performed and how many comparisons does it require? By General deBuck's approach, it is necessary to look through the entire list every time to perform this step, except for the list with one element. Even though the merge operation also requires a large number of comparisons (at most one fewer than the sum of the lengths of the two half-lists), the overall comparison of the two algorithms is in MERGE _ SORT's favor.

We have now seen two examples of recursive algorithms developed top down and two functions whose recursive definitions have been illustrated from the bottom up. Regardless of the method, the prime aspects of recursion must still be present. These two aspects—the definition expressed in terms of itself and the explicit terminal case—are the pillars of recursion. Whether you begin with the terminal condition and its explicit definition and progress to the definition in terms of itself, or you begin by dividing the problem into parts that are solved by further subdivision until the simple terminal condition is reached, the essential nature of recursion is the same, the pillars are in place.

This new programming tool provides us with the ability to express complex solutions in an unusually succinct and precise way. It has been shown that all recursive algorithms can be rewritten in a nonrecursive way, implementing a stack to capture the workings of the recursive element. As problem solvers, we can develop elegant recursive solutions; as computer programmers, we can develop efficient, nonrecursive programs to simulate our recursive solutions. This transformation process from the recursive to the nonrecursive solution is covered in detail in subsection 2.5.3. The next section will show how the recursive procedure calling itself is handled in a computer system, illustrating the overhead costs that make the use of recursive procedures an expensive programming tool.

2.5.2 RECURSIVE PROCEDURES: A MODEL OF IMPLEMENTATION

Does a computer language that supports recursion have some special techniques built into the compiler? As it turns out, the techniques presented in subsection 2.4.1, Nested Procedures, are sufficient to handle recursive procedures. This becomes clear when you consider that a procedure calling itself is a form of nested procedure calls. Therefore, each time that a procedure calls itself, the steps in the procedure call process are activated. In this case, you might say that the calling and called procedures are the same, but this is not actually the case. The important difference is that the data that are actively processed by the calling procedure differ from those available to the called procedure.

By using the environment notation of subsection 2.4.1 and adding a couple of enhancements, I will demonstrate a model for implementing recursive procedure calls.

TRADE-OFFS

The fascinating tool of recursion is like the proverbial double-edged sword. This aspect is highlighted in compiler writing. The trade-offs concern the amount of time needed to design the compiler program compared to the effectiveness of its results.

One task of the compiler is to check the syntax of *if*-statements. The basic pattern that the *if*-statement module of the compiler program searches for is :

if (*boolean expression*) then (*statement*) else (*statement*);

When checking to see whether the statement after the *then* or the *else* is valid, the module may call itself—the case of a nested *if*-statement. Therefore, the recursive nature of PASCAL statements lends itself to analysis by a recursively written compiler.

The style of compiler writing which uses this approach is called *recursive descent*. It is straightforward, based on the precise definition of the language's grammar, and therefore requires less design time.

On the other hand, a compiler is a system program that is used frequently during the operating day. Since recursive descent compilers generally use more time during compilation, over a week's operation a significant time factor is involved. This affects overall system performance and the user's feelings about the system.

Thus, the compiler writing team strives to design a compiler in which both their time and the user's is used effectively. A compromise approach is to use recursion in the design phase and to implement the modules nonrecursively.

Recall that each procedure has an environment within which it operates. This was indicated by a box containing the procedure name, its status—suspended or active—and the storage block of data available directly to the procedure when it is active. A sample environment box is provided below to refresh your memory. A quick survey of subsection 2.4.1 may be a refreshing review at this point.

There are two enhancements to the notational model, presented in Figure 2.8. The first addition is to the storage block. As we trace the steps of a recursive procedure, it will be useful to know more details about the data stored in an active environment. So the storage block will show the identifier name, the type of the identifier (local, parameter, or function name), and the identifier's current value. These new categories are included by means of headings in the storage block. The second addition is useful in walking through the statements of a procedure. Let us call it a statement pointer, abbreviated SP. The SP indicates the statement currently being executed. With these two enhancements and your mental environment recently refreshed from subsection 2.4.1, let us recurse.

Let's start with a problem, possibly called the Reverse Polish Rotation (RPR for short), posed ages ago by Madam Azza Ikswokkowski. It seems that Madam Ikswokkowski, or Madam I for short, was a famous Polish linguist who was interested in linguistic rotations of words. She was ever so happy to find words and phrases that

Figure 2.8

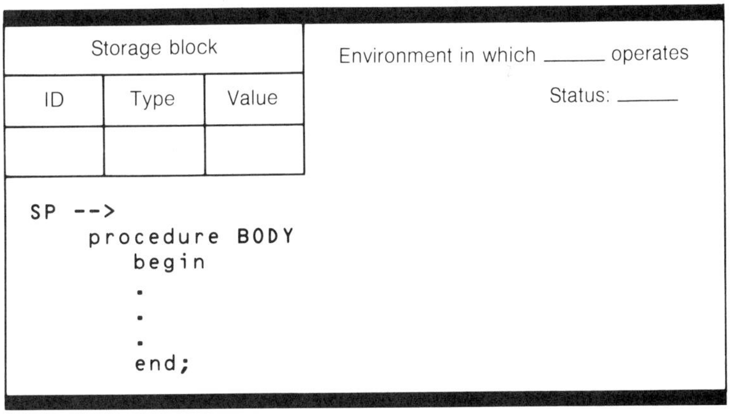

```
┌─────────────────────────────┬───────────────────────────────────────┐
│        Storage block        │   Environment in which _____ operates │
│   ┌──────┬──────┬────────┐   │                                        │
│   │  ID  │ Type │ Value  │   │               Status: _____           │
│   ├──────┼──────┼────────┤   │                                        │
│   │      │      │        │   │                                        │
│   └──────┴──────┴────────┘   │                                        │
│                              │                                        │
│   SP  -->                    │                                        │
│        procedure  BODY       │                                        │
│           begin              │                                        │
│             .                │                                        │
│             .                │                                        │
│             .                │                                        │
│           end;               │                                        │
└──────────────────────────────────────────────────────────────────────┘
```

"SP" stands for statement pointer.
Storage block contains the identifier name, type, and value.

were the same forwards and backwards. Thus lunch at NOON was Madam I's favorite meal, Christmas EVE her favorite holiday and, of course, OTTO, who always called her MOM, was her favorite son. This little pastime brought Madam I much renown for her pursuit of clever RPRs.

Alas, the days of Madam I have passed; as with time and all beneath its umbrella, change has occurred. Today, character strings like noon, eve, Mom, Otto, and Ikswokkowski are called palindromes. Instead of the simple statement used by Madam I to define RPRs, we find a recursive definition of a palindrome that goes like this:

A palindrome is a character string
    whose first and last character are equal
    and whose midsection is a palindrome.

The task is to write a recursive PASCAL procedure which can identify Madam I's favorite character strings, palindromes. I will now present such a procedure as a boolean function; two changes will be suggested later. But first I must state some assumptions that will facilitate my task:

1. A data type of STRING has been declared (or is available in your PASCAL dialect).
2. A function LENGTH returns the length of the string, that is, the number of characters in the string. (**Note:** NIL string is of length 0)
3. A function LEFTMOST returns the first character of the string.
4. A function RIGHTMOST returns the last character of the string.
5. A function MID returns the string remaining after deleting the first and last character of the argument string (possibly the NIL string).

With these assumptions and the recursive definition of a palindrome to start with, the procedure AZZA is dedicated to Madam Ikswokkowski and all you other palindromists.

```
function AZZA(STR : STRING) : boolean ;
(* AZZA   is a boolean function which tests a string STR         *)
             to determine if the string is a palindrome.         *)
(* STR   is a value parameter signifying the string to be tested *)
(*FIRST  is a local identifier whose value is the leftmost        *)
(*          character of the input string STR                     *)
(*LAST   is a local identifier whose value is the rightmost       *)
(*          character of the input string STR                     *)
(* FUNCTIONS USED :                                               *)
(*              LENGTH        - length of the string              *)
(*              LEFTMOST      - first character of string         *)
(*              RIGHTMOST     - last character of string          *)
(*              MID           - mid-section of string             *)
(*                                                                *)

var FIRST , LAST : char ;
    begin
     (*  test for terminal condition - a NIL or 1 character string  *)

(*1*)    if LENGTH(STR) < 2 then AZZA := true

                  else                    (* recursive definition  part *)

                  begin

(*2*)                FIRST := LEFTMOST(STR) ;

(*3*)                LAST  := RIGHTMOST(STR) ;

                     (* test for invalid palindrome *)
(*4*)                if FIRST <> LAST   then
                              AZZA := false

                     (* test mid-section for a palindrome *)

                              else

(*5*)                         AZZA := AZZA(MID(STR))
(*6*)                end
(*7*) end ;
```

The procedure follows the general guidelines for recursion presented earlier in this section. It tests for the simple cases first, those not needing a recursive call to solve them. The simplest case of a string with one or no characters is an obvious palindrome. Next, the procedure reduces the problem to a simpler problem by dividing the string into parts and checking to ensure that the parts satisfy the definition for a palindrome.

Let's work through a sample sequence of procedure calls to see that the procedure does indeed work and to see how the recursive calls are handled in our environmental setting. We can begin with a call to the palindrome function from some main procedure. This could be through a statement such as:

```
PAL := AZZA('MADAM');
```

This causes an environment for AZZA to be created and for the SP (statement pointer) to be set to 1. The number 1 refers to the number next to the first statement in the body of the procedure. This will be the convention for associating specific statements of AZZA with different snapshots of the environment.

Our initial snapshot would be:

Storage Block			Environment in which AZZA operates
Identifier	Type	Value	status: ACTIVE
AZZA	function name		
STR	value parameter	MADAM	
FIRST	local		
LAST	local		
SP → 1			begin . . body of procedure . end

Our next snapshot is after statement 1 has been evaluated and the two statements 2 and 3 have been executed. This snapshot shows the situation before the first recursive call to AZZA.

Storage Block			Environment in which AZZA operates
Identifier	Type	Value	status: ACTIVE
AZZA	function name		
STR	value parameter	MADAM	
FIRST	local	M	
LAST	local	M	
SP → 4			begin . . body of procedure . end

In executing the *if*-statement, the currently available values for FIRST and LAST are fetched from the storage block of the active environment. When the two values are compared, the *else* branch is taken and we encounter the call to the function AZZA. This causes the standard procedure call protocol to occur and we have a new snapshot to consider.

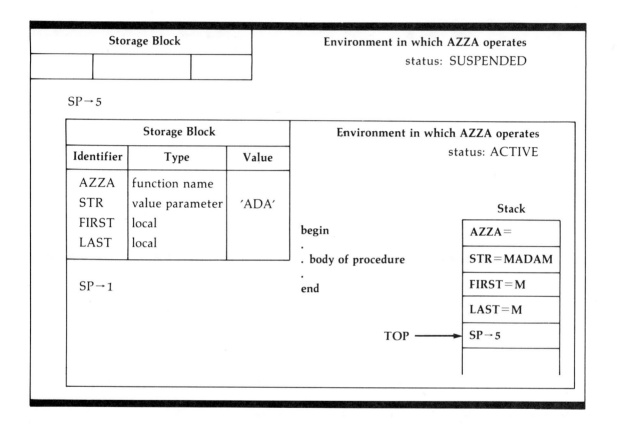

The first environment in which AZZA was operating is suspended. The storage block information is saved on the stack, along with the current value of the statement pointer. Another environment for AZZA is created within the suspended one. This has a new storage block of identifiers. Notice that the value of the identifier STR has changed because of the call that activated these changes: AZZA (MID(STR)). We will use the same procedure body but with a smaller string as data. This is the benefit of designating STR as a value parameter instead of a reference parameter.

From this new starting point, the statements in the body of AZZA are performed with the storage block in the active environment used for identifier references. As an exercise, draw snapshots that show the results of statements 1, 2, 3, and 4. Since the length of the string, STR="ADA", is not less than 2 and the value of FIRST is equal to the value of LAST, we arrive again at the recursive call to AZZA at statement 5. This time the argument being passed equals "D"; our next snapshot looks like this:

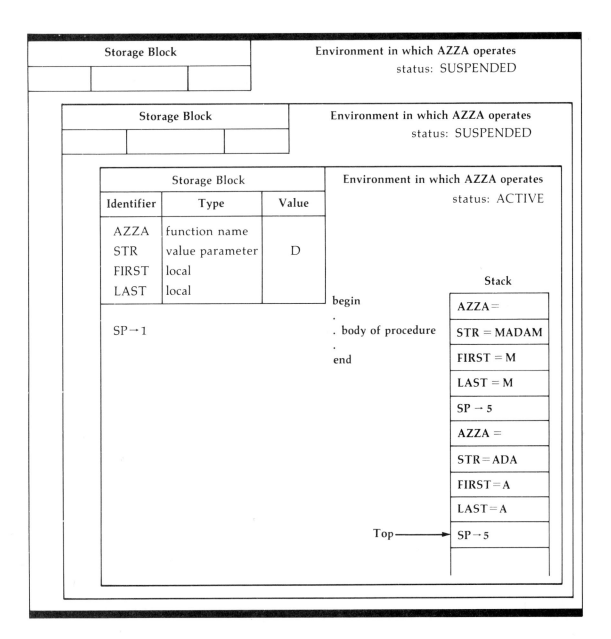

At this point, the task has been reduced to the simple case. The string is small enough to answer the question of whether it is a palindrome without resorting to recursion. Therefore, statement 1 assigns the function name its value, *true*, and the protocol for a return from a procedure call is initiated. The calling environment is restored by setting the SP to the value on top of the stack and the storage block is reestablished via the top four entries on the stack. This collection of five data elements, SP plus four identifiers, is sometimes referred to as an **activation record.** From the present situation you can see how the activation record is crucial to the faithful reinstatement of a suspended environment. With the calling environment restored, the function value returned and statement 5 executed, the next snapshot appears as follows:

	Storage Block			Environment in which AZZA operates status: SUSPENDED

Storage Block			Environment in which AZZA operates status: ACTIVE
Identifier	Type	Value	
AZZA	function name	true	
STR	value parameter	ADA	
FIRST	local	A	
LAST	local	A	

SP→6

begin
. body of procedure
.
end

Stack

AZZA =
STR = MADAM
FIRST = M
LAST = M
TOP ——→ SP→5

The next statement to be executed is the *end* for the procedure body. The return protocol is followed again. The suspended environment is awakened by popping the activation record that is perched on top of the stack. The function value of *true* is returned for the function name in statement 5 and this is assigned to the identifier AZZA in the newly activated environment. Here's the final snapshot before the last environment is also dissolved:

Storage Block			Environment in which AZZA operates status: ACTIVE
Identifier	Type	Value	
AZZA	function name	true	
STR	value parameter	MADAM	
FIRST	local	M	
LAST	local	M	

SP→7

begin
.
. body of procedure
.
end

Stack
EMPTY

The execution of the *end* statement causes control to be transferred back to the main procedure, which originally contained the statement PAL:= AZZA('MADAM'). This procedure, previously suspended, now returns to active status. Therefore, the recursive sequence of procedure calls and returns have run their course. The stack was very helpful in preserving the time sequence of activation records. The only limitation on how deep the course is travelled is the amount of memory available for the stack implementation. Thus, a stack overflow error with a recursive procedure is not an unknown event.

As you see, recursive procedure calls are a special case of the nested procedures implementation. Nothing new was added to accommodate procedure AZZA calling itself. It was handled in the same manner as procedure A calling procedure Z.

There is, in fact, another way in which recursion can occur. If procedure A calls procedure Z and procedure Z calls itself, this is referred to as direct recursion. If procedure Z then calls procedure A we have the sequence. A $\rightarrow$ Z $\rightarrow$ Z $\rightarrow$ A. This method of A calling itself after some intermediate steps is called indirect recursion. It provides no additional problem for the procedure call/return mechanism.

The vision of recursive procedures will open up your imagination to an immense pool of new methods of solving problems. With much happiness and a little concern, I am glad that this expansive and sometimes expensive tool is now in your programmer's tool kit.

To give a person a power tool and not caution her about its potential dangers is an act of irresponsibility. So lend me your ear for a bit of cautioning. The power of recursion lies in its succinctness and elegance. The danger is in its inefficiency of execution. The suspension of an active environment, the stacking of an activation record, the creation of a new environment, and the unstacking of an activation record to awaken a suspended environment are all time-consuming activities. Depending on the depth to which the recursion reaches, the overhead time for these actions can add up to a considerable amount of computer time. It may turn out that the overhead time for handling recursive calls plus the time to perform the steps in the procedure itself may be greater than the time needed by a nonrecursive procedure. Therefore, it is important to keep this cost factor in mind when you are coding solutions. Also, remember that it is always possible to convert a recursive algorithm into a nonrecursive procedure by clever use of your own implemented stack. In this way, you can use the tool's power and avoid its dangers.

Let's examine a subtle little change to our AZZA procedure that illustrates a pitfall of recursive procedures. The idea is also applicable to your general programming skills. By using the definition of a palindrome given earlier and the boolean nature of relational expressions in PASCAL, we arrive at the following expression:

```
A true          is one    whose first character   and    whose midsection is a
palindrome                equals its last                true palindrome
                          character
                or
AZZA            :=        (FIRST = LAST)    and      (AZZA(MID(STR));
```

This simple boolean-valued assignment statement can replace the entire *if* statement labeled 4 and 5 in the original procedure. By using careful consideration, you will be convinced that the two are logically equivalent. A fairly slick change!

Slick it may be, maybe even verging on elegant, but it is also inefficient. The crucial question is which operand of the boolean operator *and* is evaluated first? Does your PASCAL compiler check the relational expression (FIRST = LAST) before the function call AZZA(MID(STR))? Why is this important to know? Well, a lot of computer time could be wasted if the function call is evaluated first, a sequence of procedure calls is generated, and the sequence of recursive calls is retraced, only to find out that FIRST does not equal LAST. Walk through the changed procedure AZZA with the string EDCBABCDF and with a compiler that evaluates the boolean operator from right to left. Draw all the environments, change the stack, update identifier values, and so on. You will then sense the amount of time that can be wasted.

It is admittedly unorthodox for a compiler to work from right to left. However, some compilers evaluate all terms in a boolean expression. In such a case this slick assignment statement is better expressed as the original *if* statement. My concern here is to make you aware of this potential pitfall of recursion. The impact of "slick" code must be carefully considered from the standpoint that "logically equivalent" is not the same as "equivalent in terms of efficiency." This moral is easily proved by substituting

```
AZZA := AZZA(MID(STR)) and (FIRST = LAST)
```
for
```
AZZA := (FIRST = LAST) and AZZA(MID(STR));
```
for
```
if FIRST <> LAST then AZZA: = false else AZZA := AZZA(MID(STR));
```

So far two types of recursion have been mentioned, direct and indirect. With both methods, care must be taken to ensure efficiency. You must analyze the algorithm and determine whether a nonrecursive algorithm would yield more efficient performance during execution. Your skills of imagination can be combined with your analytical skills to provide a more finely tuned approach to problem solving.

2.5.3 TRANSFORMING RECURSIVE PROCEDURES

Now that we have this intriguing tool called recursion, why would we want to transform it? It seems to transform itself. As we move from problem statement to problem analysis to solution statement, we may find recursion a useful or even necessary tool. However, when we move to the program implementation of the recursive algorithim, we may want—or need—to remove the recursion.

When would we want to remove it? Compilers can be written by using a special approach called recursive descent. A compiler is a production tool. How many times do you think the PASCAL compiler program is used during one operating day? Frequently enough to have the overhead of recursive procedure calls become an economic factor. The compiler's recursive design would best be implemented in a nonrecursive way so that the overhead cost is not incurred.

"Okay," you might say, "that sounds like a legitimate argument, but when would I need to remove recursion?" The need comes in when your programming language does not support recursion. Let's say you have found a very quick recursive sort algorithm in the latest computer journal. With only FORTRAN and JOVIAL on the system, what are you going to do? By following the transformation process given below, you can write an even quicker program, simulating the recursive calls and returns by using a stack.

Here's the basic approach. We are going to act as a metacompiler. We will transform the recursive calls and returns into a set of metaprocedures and unconditional transfers. We will also transform the compact logic of recursion into an equivalent, though less elegant, pseudostructured version. Once the first iteration of this metacompilation is made, we will review the generated code and refine the structure to produce an optimized version.

There are four metaprocedures that are used. (By metaprocedure, I mean a PASCAL procedure that has a specific function for this transformation process and that is uniquely implemented for each recursive procedure.) Two are designed to manage the stack. Metaprocedure PRESERVE is responsible for pushing all the arguments onto the stack (or stacks if the data typing so dictates). RESTORE is the inverse of PRESERVE, popping the stack and restoring the identifiers to previous values. These two metaprocedures are used to stimulate the procedure's calls and returns to itself. When a new environment is entered, the old environment's values are preserved on the stack. They are then restored on returning to the old environment.

Which values in an environment are necessary to save? All value parameters, which may be assigned new values via the procedure call, and all local identifiers, which are reallocated in the new environment and will receive fresh local values. Don't forget that the return address is needed in order to know whence we came. Therefore the arguments to these metaprocedures consist of the list of value parameters, the list of local identifiers, and the address of the instruction after the call.

"What about the *var* type parameters?" is a question that may have surfaced in your mind. These are treated like the global identifiers—nothing special must be done. All references to these identifiers are directed back to the calling procedure, therefore no preserving or restoring is needed.

The next metaprocedure is SET _ ARGUMENTS. Its function is to prepare the new argument list for the simulated recursive call. Since no actual procedure call occurs, each argument in the call must be assigned its new value. Hence, statements like

```
NUM := NUM - 2 ;
N := N / 2 ;
LOW := MID + 1 ;
```

appear in SET _ ARGUMENTS. In this way, identifiers NUM, N, and LOW have the current argument values for the current simulated recursive call.

The last metaprocedure initializes the stack to empty. It is designated SET _ STACK _ EMPTY.

Let's start with the simplest recursive case. Assume that we have the following recursive procedure that performs a metaoperation (whatever is appropriate).

```
procedure RECURSE (A,B,C: real; var D:real);
var X,Y,Z: real;
begin
PRELIM_BLOCK; (* initialization, etc. *)
if not TERMINAL_CONDITION then
                begin
                BEFORE_BLOCK; (* prepare arguments, etc. *)
                RECURSE (A-3,B/2,C+1,D);
                AFTER_BLOCK; (* use results, etc. *)
                end
        else
                TERMINAL_BLOCK; (* process simple case *)
FINAL_BLOCK; (* output, tie loose strings, etc. *)
end;
```

This procedure is similar in format to both the General Pass de Buck sort algorithm and the function AZZA for palindromes.

It is helpful to trace the sequence of blocks that are executed during the execution of RECURSE. Assuming that the terminal condition is encountered on the third call to RECURSE, the following sequence is produced.

1.	PRELIM _ BLOCK	first call
2.	BEFORE _ BLOCK	
3.	PRELIM _ BLOCK	second call
4.	BEFORE _ BLOCK	
5.	PRELIM _ BLOCK	third call
6.	TERMINAL _ BLOCK	simple case processed
7.	FINAL _ BLOCK	return from third call
8.	AFTER _ BLOCK	
9.	FINAL _ BLOCK	return from second call
10.	AFTER _ BLOCK	
11.	FINAL _ BLOCK	return from first call

Take some time to step through the code, and the creation of the environments as we did in subsection 2.5.2 to verify that the sequence is correct.

Here are the steps in the transformation process.

1. Label the first instruction START.
2. Before the first instruction in the recursive procedure, set the stack to the empty state via SET _ STACK _ EMPTY.
3. Replace the call to RECURSE thusly:

```
PRESERVE (list of parameters,
           list of locals, NEXT);
SET_ARGUMENTS  (list of arguments);
go to START;
```

4. Label the instruction after the transformed procedure call as NEXT.
5. Replace the last *end* statement with:

```
if not EMPTY_STACK then
        begin
        RESTORE (list of parameters, list of
                        locals, LABEL1);
        goto LABEL1:
        end
end;
```

Applying these five steps to RECURSE, we have the first iteration in the transformation process.

```
        procedure RECURSE (A,B,C:real; var D:real);
        var X,Y,Z:real;
        begin
        SET_STACK_EMPTY;
START : PRELIM_BLOCK;
        if not TERMINAL_CONDITION then
                        begin
                        BEFORE_BLOCK;
                        PRESERVE(A,B,C,X,Y,Z,NEXT);
                        SET_ARGUMENTS(A,B,C);
                        go to START;
                  NEXT : AFTER_BLOCK;
                        end
                                else
                          TERMINAL_BLOCK;
        FINAL_BLOCK;
        if not EMPTY_STACK then begin
                          RESTORE(A,B,C,X,Y,Z,LABEL1);
                          goto LABEL1;
                          end
        end;
```

Reviewing this version, we find two small problems. First, it is not legal to branch into a block contained in an *if* statement. Therefore, AFTER _ BLOCK needs a new position and some accompanying logical adjustment.

Also, the statement that transfers control to AFTER _ BLOCK is not a legal PASCAL construct: there is no such thing as a LABEL variable. The label removed from the stack can not be assigned to the identifier LABEL1 and used in a variable *goto* statement. The solution to this problem is to notice that RECURSE calls itself from only one place and therefore only one place is returned to—the AFTER _ BLOCK.

So the two refinements are:

1. Move the AFTER _ BLOCK to directly after the RESTORE metaprocedure to simulate the return.

2. Label the FINAL _ BLOCK as LABEL1.

With these two refinements, the final nonrecursive version is given below.

```
        procedure RECURSE (A,B,C:real; var D:real);
        var X,Y,Z:real;
        begin
        SET_STACK_EMPTY;
START : PRELIM_BLOCK;
        if not TERMINAL_CONDITION then
                        begin
                        BEFORE_BLOCK;
                        PRESERVE(A,B,C,X,Y,Z,NEXT);
                            (*preserving NEXT is not
                            necessary*)
                        SET_ARGUMENTS(A,B,C);
                        go to START;
                        end
                else
                        TERMINAL_BLOCK;
```

```
LABEL1: FINAL_BLOCK;
        if not EMPTY_STACK then begin
                                 RESTORE(A,B,C,X,Y, Z,LABEL);
                                    (*not restoring LABEL is
                                    necessary*)
                                 AFTER_BLOCK;
                                 goto LABEL1;
                                 end
        end;
```

The procedure logic generates a sequence of: procedure calls to PRELIM _ BLOCK and BEFORE _ BLOCK; metaprocedure calls to PRESERVE, SET _ ARGUMENTS (saving the old environment and creating a new one) and unconditional transfers (recursive calls) to the start of the procedure. This stops when the terminal condition is encountered, where the TERMINAL _ BLOCK is executed. This is followed by a sequence of RESTORE calls (restoring old environments) and AFTER _ BLOCK and FINAL _ BLOCK executions until the stack is empty. By assuming a recursive depth of three as before, trace the execution of the blocks to verify that the two procedures are logically equivalent. Also check the special case of the first call satisfying the terminal condition.

Let's move to the next level of difficulty and transform a recursive procedure that calls itself from two places. The steps and refinements are similar. Consider the following procedure DOUBLE _ CURSE:

```
procedure DOUBLE_CURSE(A,B,C:real;var D:real);
var X,Y,Z:real;
begin
if not TERMINAL_CONDITION then
                begin
                PRE_BLOCK;
                DOUBLE_CURSE(A,C,B);
                MID_BLOCK;
                DOUBLE_CURSE(B,C,A);
                POST_BLOCK
                end
        else
                TERMINAL_BLOCK
end;
```

Applying the five-step transformation, we have our first attempt.

```
        procedure DOUBLE_CURSE(A,B,C:real;var D:real);
        var X,Y,Z:real;
        begin
        SET_STACK_EMPTY;
START:  if not TERMINAL_CONDITION then
                        begin
                        PRE_BLOCK;
                        PRESERVE(X,Y,Z,A,B,C,NEXT1);
                        SET_ARGUMENTS (A,B,C,CALL1);
                        goto START;
                NEXT1:  MID_BLOCK;
                        PRESERVE(X,Y,Z,A,B,C,NEXT2);
                        SET_ARGUMENTS (A,B,C,CALL2);
                        goto START;
```

```
              NEXT2: POST_BLOCK
                     end
        else

                     TERMINAL_BLOCK;
                     if not EMPTY_STACK then
                              begin
                              RESTORE(X,Y,Z,A,B,C LABEL1);
                              goto LABEL1
                              end
        end;
```

What difference do you notice? Right—each transformed procedure call needs to generate a new label, NEXT1 and NEXT2. This is necessary since there are two places to return . . . This feature causes a new problem when we begin to refine our prototype procedure.

When we move the blocks following each call to directly after the RESTORE metaprocedure (remembering to retain the ordering), the problem of which block is being returned to arises. After the environment is restored, do we execute the MID _ BLOCK or the POST _ BLOCK? This information was just made available by RESTORE via the argument LABEL1. But how do we use it? Since this is no simple case, the PASCAL case structure will do nicely. By performing the two refinement steps and embedding the shifted blocks in a case statement, we will effectively and efficiently de-curse DOUBLE _ CURSE.

```
        procedure DOUBLE_CURSE(A,B,C,:real;var D:real);
        var X,Y,Z:real;
        begin
        SET_STACK_EMPTY;
START: if not TERMINAL_CONDITION then
                begin
                PRE_BLOCK;
                PRESERVE(X,Y,Z,A,B,C,NEXT1);
                SET_ARGUMENTS (A,B,C,CALL1);
                goto START;
                end
        else
                TERMINAL_BLOCK;
  LABEL1: if not EMPTY_STACK then
                     begin
                     RESTORE (X,Y,Z,A,B,C,LABEL 1);
                     case LABEL1 of
                  NEXT1: MID_BLOCK;
                        PRESERVE(X,Y,Z,A,B,C,NEXT2);
                        SET_ARGUMENTS (A,B,C,CALL2);
                        goto START;
                  NEXT2: POST_BLOCK
                     end ; (* two cases of procedure returns *)
                     go to LABEL1
                     end
        end;
```

There are a couple of loose strings to complete the transformation. First, all labels must be added to the declaration area. Second, instead of pushing the actual labels onto the stack, for each call push an integer that corresponds to the number of the procedure call. For example, for the first call, push a 1, for the second a 2, and so on.

In the case statement, the restored integer value can be used to select the block to return to.

The third loose string involves the metaprocedure SET _ ARGUMENTS. Since there are two recursive calls, the arguments must be set up twice. In order to know which argument set-up to use, we need to pass the number of the procedure call in addition to the list of arguments. So in general, this metaprocedure would be called by SET _ ARGUMENTS (list of arguments, call number).

Finally, one additional refinement can be considered. In some cases, one or more local variables or value parameters do not need to be preserved on the stack. This is because they are not involved in any code after the procedure calls itself. Therefore, the procedure's efficiency is improved by not pushing and popping them. It will take a careful analysis of the particular recursive procedure to benefit from this refinement with confidence. So use this hint carefully.

Let's summarize the transformation process for a recursive procedure with one or more calling statements:

1. Label the first instruction with START.

2. Place the metaprocedure SET _ STACK _ EMPTY before the first instruction.

3. Replace each recursive call with the metaprocedures

```
PRESERVE (list of parameters,list of locals,call number i);
SET_ARGUMENTS  (list of arguments,call number i);
GO TO START;
```

4. Label the instruction after the transformed procedure call with NEXTi.

5. Replace the last *end* statement with

```
if not EMPTY_STACK then
      begin
      RESTORE(list of parameters, list of locals, call number i
      goto LABEL1;
      end;
  end;
```

6. As a refinement, move the blocks after each call to directly after the RESTORE metaprocedure. Preserve the order. Embed the blocks in a *case* statement, based on the call number.

7. As another refinement, label the final block (if one is present) or the *if* of step 5 with LABEL1.

With the above set of rules and you as the metacompiler, any recursive procedure can be transformed, losing both its strength and its weakness—elegance and expense.

■ **"JUST FOR REFERENCE"**

To use the bottom-up perspective on recursion—

● define the simplest case explicitly first

- define more complicated cases in terms of simpler cases and other simple operations
- for example: 1. POWER _ OF _ 2(1) = 2
             2. POWER _ OF _ 2(N+1) = 2 * POWER _ OF _ 2(N), N $\geq$ 1

To use the top-down perspective on recursion—

- divide the main task into smaller, similar subtasks
- divide each subtask into smaller, similar subtasks
- terminate the subdividing when the task is simple enough to solve, straightforwardly, without subdivision
- combine the solutions of the subtasks to form the solution of the main task
- for example: sorting algorithm

```
MERGE _ SORT a list of N elements
    if N = 1 then list is sorted
        else if N = 2 then
                        if 1st element < 2nd element then
                            interchange and list is sorted
                        else
                MERGE _ SORT top half-list of N/2 elements
                MERGE _ SORT bottom half-list of N/2 elements
                Merge top and bottom half-lists
```

Implementation of recursion using stacks—

- The stack is important in preserving the values of all identifiers when a procedure calls itself and a new environment is created.
- When the terminal condition of a recursive procedure is encountered the stack is used to revive the most recently suspended environment.

Steps for transforming recursive algorithms—

- Label the first instruction with START.
- Place the metaprocedure SET _ STACK _ EMPTY before the first instruction.
- For each recursive call to the procedure, replace it with the metaprocedures
  PRESERVE (list of parameters, list of locals, call number i)
  SET _ ARGUMENTS (list of arguments, call number i);
  goto START;
- Label the instruction after the transformed procedure call with NEXTi. (Increment i)
- Replace the last *end* statement with
  if not EMPTY _ STACK then
                    begin
              RESTORE(list of parameters,list of locals,call number i)

                    goto LABEL1;
                    end;

  end;

Refinements—

- Move the blocks after each call directly following the RESTORE metaprocedure. Preserve the order. Embed the blocks in a case statement based on the call number.
- Label the final block (if one is present) or the *if* with LABEL1.

EXERCISES

1. Describe the bottom-up method for specifying a recursive definition.
2. Develop a recursive definition for the factorial of a nonnegative integer. The factorial of N is the product of the integers 1, 2, 3, . . . ,N. The notation for the factorial of N is N!, that is, 4! = 1 * 2 * 3 * 4. For the recursive definition the special case of 0! can be defined explicitly as equal to 1.
3. Describe the top-down method for specifying a recursive definition.
4. Using a list of six numbers,—45, 26, 83, 37, 29, 57,—work through the General Pass de Buck Sort algorithm. How many times does the algorithm call itself?
5. Using the same list of numbers above and the MERGE-SORT algorithm written as a PAS-CAL procedure, draw the sequence of environments that are generated by the sequence of recursive calls to the MERGE-SORT procedure.
6. Another important operation on lists is to search them for a particular value. Design a recursive algorithm to perform a binary search on an ordered list. The idea is to look at the number in the middle of the list to determine if it is the number being searched for. If no match then decide whether to search the top half or the bottom half of the list for the number.
7. How many suspended environments will be in existence during the following calls to procedure AZZA?
   a) AZZA("DAD")
   b) AZZA("IKSWOKKOWSKI")
   c) AZZA("LOOOOOONGNOOOOOL")
8. Draw the sequence of snapshots for the following calls to procedure AZZA:
   a) AZZA("I SAW I WAS I")
   b) AZZA("ABCDEBA")
9. Write the AZZA procedure using the subtle change mentioned in subsection 2.5.2 and determine which way your compiler executes the statement in question. Reverse the order of the statement and see if there is any difference in execution time or results. Use an argument for the procedure call like "EDCBABCDF."
10. Describe the two reasons for transforming a recursive procedure.
11. Explain how the implemented versions of PRESERVE and RESTORE would differ when you are transforming two distinct recursive procedures.
12. Given the following function, called ACKERMANN's function, transform it to a nonrecursive version.

```
function ACKERMANN (X, Y : integer) :integer ;
var T : integer ;
```

```
begin
if X = 0 then ACKERMANN := Y + 1

    else if Y = 0 then ACKERMANN := ACKERMANN ( X - 1, 1)
              else begin
                      T := ACKERMANN (X , Y - 1);
                      ACKERMANN := ACKERMANN (X - 1, T)
                   end
end ;
```

Note: Interpret each function call as a procedure call with a reference parameter receiving the function's value. The reference parameter's value can be assigned to the function name when the last return is simulated.

Once you have transformed the recursive version, trace the call ACKERMANN(2,2) and show the stack contents after each metaprocedure PRESERVE is completed.

13. The following recursive procedure follows the form of the DOUBLE_CURSE model. Write the metaprocedures PRESERVE, RESTORE, and SET_ARGUMENTS for the transformation process.

    The procedure solves the classic Tower of Hanoi problem in which N disks of graduated diameters are moved from a source pole to a destination pole using one additional pole. The disk's movements are constrained by the following rules :

    a) Only one disk can be moved at a time.

    b) The ordering of the disks must remain intact, that is, the larger disks must remain below the smaller ones at all times.

```
procedure HANOI (NDISKS , SOURCE , DEST , EXTRA : integer);
begin
if NDISKS > 1 then
                    begin
                    HANOI (NDISKS - 1, SOURCE, EXTRA, DEST);
                    MOVE_DISK ( SOURCE, DEST) ;
                    HANOI (NDISKS - 1 , EXTRA, DEST, SOURCE) ;
                    end
                  else
                    MOVE_DISK ( SOURCE, DEST )
end ;
```

14. Transform the following recursive procedure. Notice that it has a different logical structure. Apply the rules given in section 5.3 and develop a set of refinements appropriate for this recursive structure.

```
procedure CURSES (A, B, C: real ; var D: real );
var X, Y, Z : real ;
begin
while not TERMINAL_CONDITION do
          begin
          PRE_BLOCK ;
          CURSES (B,C,A) ;
          MID_BLOCK ;
          CURSES (C,A,B) ;
          POST_BLOCK
          end
end ;
```

THE WORKOUT ROOM

PROJECT 1

You have developed a new way to order numbers for a mystical society, the Pystackoreans. The procedure for arranging an input sequence of numbers is as follows.

Initially, a largely positive number is placed on an empty stack, such as +9999. Thereafter, each number in the input sequence is compared to the number on top of the stack, and one of two actions is performed.

Case 1. If the number at the front of the stack is greater than or equal to the inputted number, the inputted number is pushed onto the stack.

Case 2. If the number at the front of the stack is less than the inputted number, the number at the front of the stack is to be printed and popped from the stack. This action continues until the number at the front of the stack is greater than or equal to the inputted number or until the number at the front of the stack is equal to +9999. When either condition occurs, the inputted number is then pushed onto the stack.

Finally, when no more numbers are available from the input sequence the numbers on the stack are to be printed in the order in which they appear in the stack. An illustrious example follows :

Input Sequence	Stack Contents	Output Sequence
	9999	
5	5 | 9999	
7	7 | 9999	5
9	9 | 9999	7
3	3 | 9 | 9999	
4	4 | 9 | 9999	3
8	8 | 9 | 9999	4
15	15 | 9999	8
		9
12	12 | 15 | 9999	
16	16 | 9999	12
		15
19	19 | 9999	16
10	10 | 19 | 9999	
14	14 | 19 | 9999	10
end	9999	14
		19
	front	end

Your first duty as the Grand Stack Master of the Pystackoreans is to write a PASCAL procedure to perform the ordering of numbers as dictated above by the father of the society, Pystackarus.

PROJECT 2

After many hours of wee-hours of work on your not-so-friendly personal computer, you are a little MIXED _ UP. You are so jumbled that you don't even want to know your own name so you decide to change it and mix it up a little. You envision the following description for a PASCAL procedure called MIX _ UP that should do the trick.

The program accepts your name as a character string and then prints out the vowels in your name in the order in which they occur in your name. It then prints the consonants in the reverse order in which they occur in your name. For example, if your name is DENISE then the program MIX _ UP would call you EIESND. Or if you are called AZZA then it would call you AAZZ.

As if you are not confused enough, a not-so-friendly friend shows up and suggests another PASCAL procedure for your consideration. Her suggestion for procedure UI _ PXM is given in the following description.

The program accepts your name as a character string and then prints out the vowels in your name in the reverse order in which they occur in your name. It then prints the consonants also in the reverse order in which they occur in your name.

For example, if your name is DOLORES, the program UI _ PXM would call you EOOSRLD. Or if you are called AZZA, it would call you AAZZ.

In your current state of micromania, you decide to write both programs on your microfriend so that you will have a choice of not-so-friendly names to hurl at it when the time is ripe (or the rime is tipe).

PROJECT 3

You have been secretly hired by the Cosmic Cryptology Collective to help decode messages that they suspect are being sent from an alien planetary world. In a dream, the collective head, Dr. Figital, has received a vision that she feels is the key to the decoding process.

First, she feels that the alleged alien messages are being broadcast as character strings with blanks separating suspected words. (Strange how the aliens use the same character set as our computer systems do!) Dr. Figital believes that the aliens' messages are being sent in reverse order so that the word SOUP would be sent as PUOS. But Dr. Figital's resident lingophysicist, Dr. Hoppler, has discovered that vowels travel slightly faster than consonants through stellar space. Therefore, a word like SANDWICH would be received as HICWDANS since it has been reversed and has experienced the so-called Hoppler effect of shifting vowels.

Your first job as part of the collective is to don the hat of resident software engineer and develop a PASCAL program to test the vision of the collective head and the research of the lingophysicist. Using the ideas that they have described, write a program to decipher the latest communication: EYH OMM ATHW IS ORF ERNIND?

PROJECT 4   *Curses! an assignment*

Your assignment, should you accept it (should you not accept it the curse will be upon you), is to write a PASCAL message mucker called CURSES.

The purpose of the program is to encode input messages using the following encryption strategy:

The message sender inputs a *four letter* word, $C_1C_2C_3C_4$, and another *four letter* word, $X_1X_2X_3X_4$. The message sender then inputs the message to be sent. The program CURSES scans the message one character at a time and each character is pushed on the stack until either the scanned character is in the word $C_1C_2C_3C_4$ or the end of the message is encountered. When the scanned character is one of the characters in $C_1C_2C_3C_4$, then print that character and continue to print the character on top of the stack until either the stack is empty or the character on top of the stack is one of the characters in $X_1X_2X_3X_4$. When the end of the message is encountered, print the character on top of the stack and pop the stack until the stack is empty.

Well here's hoping that the message mucking is successful, and all I can say to you is "GOOD" "LUCK" and "SOUNDS SIMPLE TO ME" or as CURSES might say, "OSDNOT EEM LPMIS SU."

PROJECT 5

You fear that your dorm mate has finally lost her marbles. She has set up an experiment in which five coffee cans have been placed on the floor. Now she intends to toss her 100 marbles into the air and then count the number of marbles that land in each coffee can. She will record the results and gather up the marbles from their assorted hiding places on the floor of your dorm room. She anticipates redoing the experiment five times before going to bed. You had anticipated going to bed long before you anticipate her finishing, so you come up with a less scattered idea.

You suggest that you will write a PASCAL program that will simulate the experiment and will provide her with additional information. You suggest the following program specifications.

The program will sequentially drop 100 balls numbered from 1 to 100. The location of the ball after it lands will be determined by generating a random number and using the following table:

Random number	1–15	16–30	31–50	51–70	71–85	86–100
Ball lands in	can 1	can 2	floor	can 3	can 4	can 5

The program will keep track of which ball falls in which can and also in what order they landed. After the last ball is dropped, the program will print the number of balls in each can and the order in which they landed in that particular can.

Your choice is whether to have five arrays for the five stacks that represent the cans or to implement the five stacks in one array with five distinct TOP pointers. Give it some consideration before you begin or you might be up later than you think.

Your dorm mate is thrilled by this idea and though she is not ungrateful for your concern for her health, she asks if it is possible for you to include the "bounce effect" into the simulation. It seems that when the cans get to be filled to 80% of their capacity, a ball landing in the can has a tendency (20% of the time) to bounce out onto the floor, and sometimes (30% of that time) its impact causes other balls to bounce out also.

You decide to include the "bounce effect" in the program and to report the number of times that a "one bounce" and a "double bounce" event has occurred.

You and your dorm mate are satisfied with this solution. You plan to write the program and run it five times in order to simulate the experiment five times. As you turn to your personal computer, your dorm mate puts away her marbles and serenely crawls into bed for some much needed rest.

3

Queues

*We would accomplish many more
things if we did not think of them
as impossible.*

— Chretien Malesherbes

3.1 Setting the Stage

3.1.1 THE ADVERTISEMENT: YOGURT, HONEY, NUTS, PEAS, AND QUEUES

In this section we visit a store as a means of illustrating the attributes of another information structure, the **queue.** You may suspect that we will be visiting a software store where you can choose information structures off the shelf. No, we could notice the same relationship pattern in any store. So, as we nourish our mind with these new concepts, we will also nourish our bodies in a natural food store, stocked with yogurt, nuts, peas, and queues. Open your shopping bag and your mind and fill them with sights and delights from the Q-Shop.

3.1.2 LOOKING AROUND THE FRONT OF THE STORE

As you enter the Q-Shop and look curiously around, on the left you see a dairy case with jars of yogurt, cartons of milk, and hunks of cheese. Scanning the store, you find the middle aisle stocked with open bags of flours, grains, beans, and peas. On the right wall, the shelves are lined with packaged dried fruits and nuts and rows of bottled honey.

Heading for the dairy case you remember that you want some yogurt and a half pound of Swiss cheese. As you stand in front of the dairy case, you see that there is a row for each flavor of yogurt. You want a strawberry yogurt, so you take the first one in the row. Then you reach for two banana yogurts and remove the first and second in that row. Finally, you remove the last pineapple yogurt, emptying the row. As you remove each jar, you check the expiration date.

As your attention shifts to cheese, you look at the bottom shelf and notice the Swiss cheese in a pile. Sorting through the pieces, you find the size you want. Here at the dairy case you have experienced two different organizations, the ordered rows of yogurt and the unordered pile of cheese. You have also changed both collections: with the yogurt you affected the front of each row; with the cheese you mixed up a random arrangement. Your experience with the yogurt was the first sample queue experienced in the Q-Shop.

Turning around, you walk to the middle aisle, looking for the peas. As you survey the open bags of whole wheat flour, barley, bulgar, millet, spiced almond granola, and mung beans, you finally find the split peas. As you scoop out a pound and a half of split peas, you realize that you will have to look elsewhere for your next queue. For a peculiar reason, an expression from last year's symbolic logic course flashes before your mind's eye and you see: Ps $\vee \sim$ Qs. You wonder what this statement is symbolic of.

Since the granola and peas are not queues, you head for the shelves on the far wall for some nuts and dried fruits. Suddenly, you notice a stock person filling the honey section next to you. Each new container of honey is entered at the rear of its particular row; therefore, the oldest jar of honey will be the first one purchased by the next customer. The stock person continues to place the honey containers at the rear of each row until it is full of honey. You now see the second way that the collection of items in a queue can be changed—adding to the rear.

The stock person enters items at the rear of the row and the customer removes them from the front. The relationship pattern between items is one of *closer to* and *farther from* the front, from the perspective of space, or *older* and *younger* from the perspective of time.

As in most U.S. business establishments, the check-out line is first come–first served. Remembering that in England a waiting line is called a queue; you enter the check-out queue.

Check-out queues can be organized in two ways. First, the line may be physically well defined, with people standing behind each other. The second method is illustrated by the take-a-number system used in many bakeries. When you enter, you take a number, thereby logically though not physically connecting yourself to the person ahead of you. People stand around randomly, waiting and enjoying the sweet aromas. It is not necessary to know who is before or after you: when your number is called, you are at the front of the queue. You wait your turn, independent of the physical or logical nature of the check-out queue, with your goods, patience, and money.

When you reach the front of the line, you notice the bills in the cash drawer. Since the $5 bills leave and enter from the same location, the top, you recall that this is just a stack of $5 bills, not a queue.

Being the last person in the check-out line, you strike up a conversation with Roland, the owner, and discover that he is a retired computer science professor. You mention that you are noticing various information structures in the store. He is surprised to have such a curious customer and invites you to visit the back of the store, where he will be glad to point out more attributes and examples of queues in the Q-Shop.

3.1.3 A TOUR OF THE BACK OF THE Q-SHOP

Striding down a hallway to the left of the cash register, Roland leads you to the store-room in the back. It is stocked with products that have been received but not yet processed. On each case, a date is written in red. You ask Roland what the dates signify, and he explains that each case is stamped with the date it is received. He uses this information to make sure that the first case received is the first case processed. For example, three cases of peas are dated Jan. 20, Feb. 16, and Mar. 29. Though they are physically located on different shelves, the access policy makes them a logical queue. Roland explains that the dates order the cases and that his policy that the first in the storeroom is the first out characterizes the queue structure. This helps you conceptualize the abstract qualities shared by the various queues in the Q-Shop. Roland next asks you to find the front case of Swiss cheese from the Swiss cheese queue so that he can cut it into hunks and place it in the dairy case.

Then Roland offers to show you the office, where he points out two small filing cabinets: bills payable and bills receivable. When Roland receives a bill from one of his suppliers, he puts it at the back of the bills payable file. He follows the policy of paying his bills in the order received. So when he feels like paying bills, he takes one from the front of the file cabinet, writes a check, and mails it. In this case, the bills payable queue is ordered both physically and logically, and his payment policy matches the characteristics of a queue. You begin to wonder how the bills receivable file is organized.

Before you can ask, Roland notices that some customers are waiting around the cash register, so together you return to the front. As you are gathering up your goods, you also gather up your thoughts about the queue information structure. These images surface: ordered rows of yogurt; taking the front bag of nuts; the stock person putting the honey bottles at the rear of each row until it is full. These phrases echo in your mind's ear—physically or logically ordered, first come–first served, first received is first processed, first in line is first out. As you leave you hear Roland ask, "who is first in line?" When three people each say "me!", Roland looks at you "queueriously" and you share a smile and a thought.

■ "JUST FOR REFERENCE"

In the Q-Shop's front section you—

- took jars of yogurt from the front of the yogurt row
- saw bottles of honey placed at the rear of each row
- took the last pinapple yogurt, thus emptying the row
- waited in a first come–first served check-out line
- saw the unordered collection of hunks of cheese
- searched through assorted but unsorted bags of grains, beans, and peas
- noticed the stack of $5 bills in the cash drawer

In the Q-Shop's back room you observed—

- dated cases forming a logical queue

- Roland's policy that the first in the back room is the first out
- the file for accounts labeled bills payable
- Roland's policy of looking at only the first and last bill in his bills payable file

EXERCISES

1. List the physical queues illustrated in the Q-Shop example.
2. The items in physical queues are related in both time and space. Describe the relationship between the items in terms of both of these dimensions.
3. Explain why the bag of peas in the front of the Q-Shop is not a queue but the dated cases of peas in the back are.
4. Using the check-out line at a local bakery as an example, describe the difference between a physical and a logical queue. How could the bakery ensure that it had a physical queue?
5. Explain why the file for bills receivable is not organized in the same way as the bills payable—that is, as a queue.
6. List two phrases that characterize the relationship pattern of the queues in the Q-Shop.
7. The sample queues mentioned in this section are examples of a class of queues called producer/consumer queues: the producer places items at the end of the queue while the consumer removes items from the front. For each situation below, indicate who is the producer, what it is producing, and who is the consumer.
   a) fast food store
   b) factory assembly substation
   c) automatic car wash
   d) computer terminal queue
   e) warehouse receiving room
   f) hospital emergency room

3.2   Formalizing the Structure

3.2.1   DESCRIPTION: COMPONENTS AND RELATIONSHIP PATTERN

Now that we have left the Q-Shop and its examples of some real-life queues, let us enter the realm of ideas and describe the queue in its abstract form. In this description you will detect the similarities to the real-life queues and notice the extensions allowable in the abstract realm.

The queue is composed of a linearly ordered collection of data elements where the collection may have zero or more members. In a collection with a nonzero amount of members, due to the ordered attribute of the collection, one data element is designated the first or **front element** of the queue and one data element is designated the last or **rear element** of the queue. In a collection with zero members, the queue is simply called empty. The queue may experience two changes to its ordering. A new data element may be added to the collection, following the rear element of the queue. The new data element then becomes the rear element. Or the front data element may be removed from the collection, in which case the next data element in the ordering becomes the new front data element. Thus the data elements, the ordering, and the two possible changes to the ordering are the three components composing the abstract queue.

The nature of the two changes on the ordered collection produces some special attributes of the queue. The queue exhibits a first in-first out (FIFO) behavior since a data element can only be removed after the data element in front of it has been removed. This is the same attribute that was exhibited in the check-out line in the Q-Shop—first come–first served. Thus data elements enter a queue in the same sequence as they leave it. This FIFO behavior constitutes the relationship pattern between the data elements in a queue. In terms of time, for any two elements, one has been in the queue longer than the other. In terms of orientation to the front and rear, one is nearer to the front and the other nearer to the rear.

The abstract queue can experience unlimited growth through new data elements entering at the rear. It can experience shrinkage until it is empty through removal of elements from the front. The attribute of unlimited growth is a luxury of the abstract model and can of course never be found in the Q-Shop, unless Roland stops paying his bills and all his creditors develop infinite patience.

Since the queue is changed at both ends, the fluctuations in size and "shape" give the queue an unattached, no-fixed-end, accordion-like image. In illustrating the queue, I face the same difficulties as with the abstract stack, and thus I will take the same liberties, remembering that the only data element we have direct access to is the front data element. We will see all data elements in the queue via a sideview and we will watch its growth and shrinkage through a sequence of stop-action shots.

To assist in illustrating the nature of an abstract queue I would like to introduce Karen, the caterpillar. If you have ever watched a caterpillar crawl you have noticed how it moves through two actions: it stretches forward with its head and then seems to shrink from its tail to its middle. With the aid of your visual thinking skills, this movement is seen to resemble the movement of a queue—with some important differences. Here now is Karen, coming on stage. This pretty but peculiar caterpillar always crawls backward, therefore stretching and growing at the tail (rear) and shrinking and losing part of herself at the head (front). She has the unusual ability to grow without limits, becoming as long as she wishes—and what is even more unusual, shrinking to nothing but remaining Karen. In Figure 3.1 you can see various snapshots of Karen at different stages of her life. Karen will visit us throughout the rest of the chapter.

The two abstract information structures, stack and queue, have some noticeable differences. The stack exhibits an up-and-down movement, since it is fixed at one end and changes at the other. The queue is not fixed at either end and tends to grow and shrink, since both ends change independently. The sequence of elements entering and then leaving the queue is straightforward, since the order is the same. In the stack, elements can leave in a different sequence than they entered. This is the difference between FIFO and LIFO structures.

Figure 3.1

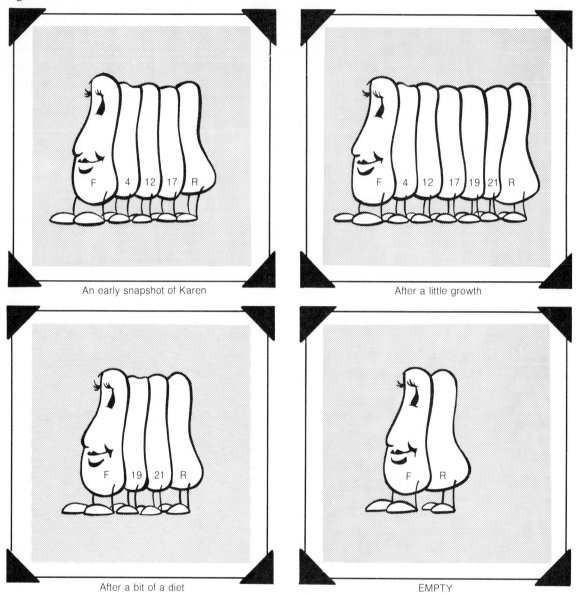

An early snapshot of Karen

After a little growth

After a bit of a diet

EMPTY

Stacks and queues do share some attributes: their data elements are linearly ordered; they have unlimited growth potential; they can be empty; and they are both useful in the field of computer science. As tools in both application programs—such as finding paths through a maze or simulating the assembly line process—and system programs—such as compilers and operating systems—these structures have found a role to play.

3.2.2 TYPICAL QUEUE OPERATIONS

As mentioned earlier, there are two primitive operations and one state natural to the queue structure. When a data element is added to the collection at the rear of the queue, then the operation of insertion or entering has occurred. Let us refer to this operation by the word ENTER. This abstract operation has no limits placed upon it. The second operation involves the removal of a data element from the front of the queue. Let me use the word LEAVE to refer to this operation. When the queue is empty then this operation has no meaning and produces no result. To avoid the above situation, it is convenient to sample the "emptiness" attribute of a queue. For this purpose, the boolean operation EMPTY returns a response of true or false, depending on the presence or absence of members in the collection.

3.2.3 TYPICAL OCCURRENCES OF THE QUEUE

With the queue's description and operations fresh in your mind, let me present the general areas where queues are likely. When an ordered group of entities (customers, computer programs, or products) arrive at irregular intervals at a processing station (cash register, operating system, or factory assembly line station) and must wait until the entities that arrived earlier are processed, then a queue can be utilized. This situation is particularly common when an entire process is to be simulated. For example, if a factory that assembles electronic calculators is to be built, the arrangement of the various processing stations can be simulated to determine the best arrangement in terms of time, productivity, and expense.

So let us gather up our thoughts, summon up our visual thinking skills, and begin to envision the process of implementing the abstract queue. Before going on to the next section, which presents two typical approaches to the implementation, play with the following Imagination Challenge. Additional challenges to your imagination will be scattered through the remainder of the text. They are intended to exercise your imagination, enhancing your ImQ—remember this?—your imagination quotient. How? By presenting problems that are difficult or impossible to solve with just the rational aspect of the mind.

■ **"JUST FOR REFERENCE"**

A queue may be described as a linearly ordered collection of data elements that experiences insertion changes at one end of the ordering, the rear, and deletion changes at the other end, the front.

The relationship pattern of the queue is FIFO—first in/first out.

Primitive operations of the queue include—

- ENTER—entering a new data element to the ordered collection at the end of the ordering
- LEAVE—removing a data element from the ordered collection from the beginning of the ordering

IMAGINATION CHALLENGE

Close your eyes and begin to visualize the objects that will be used in the implementation. Move them around with your mind's eye, then begin to manipulate them. Imagine a queue of video games being processed in a computerized assembly line by a union of happy robots. As your visual queue begins to change through the natural operations of ENTER and LEAVE, hear, watch, and feel each part interact. Continue to play with the image for a while. When you are ready then read on and discover what someone else has envisioned for the implementation of a queue.

- EMPTY—determining the presence or absence of data elements in the collection

Queues and stacks are similar in that—

- data elements are linearly ordered
- both have unlimited growth
- they can be empty
- they are useful in both system and application programs

Queues and stacks differ in that—

- stacks are fixed at one end while queues are fixed at neither
- the sequence of data elements entering a stack is potentially different than the sequence leaving, whereas both sequences are the same for queues
- stacks exhibit LIFO behavior while queues exhibit FIFO behavior

EXERCISES

1. Describe the abstract queue information structure.
2. Explain what is meant by the queue having a FIFO structure.
3. Describe the three primitive operations that can be performed on the abstract model of the queue.
4. Describe a situation in which one of the operations upon a queue would be illogical based on the current state of the queue.
5. Using the primitive operations, write algorithms to accomplish the following. Assume the data elements in the queue are integers.
   a.) Remove N elements from the queue.
   b.) Determine if more than N elements are in the queue without changing the queue.

c.) Remove N elements from the queue and replace all data elements that have values less than X at the end of the queue.

d.) In honor of National Deviant Day, you have decided to process the queue using the "underdog" policy. Reverse the order of the data elements in the queue.

e.) Reverse the order of the first N elements, leaving the remainder unchanged.

Note: Most of these exercises will require the use of one or more auxiliary queues (maybe even a stack).

6. List some ways in which the stack and the queue are similar information structures.

7. Describe how a queue could be emulated by using two stacks. Describe the queue operations ENTER and LEAVE in terms of PUSH, EMPTY, and POP.

3.3 Implementing the Structure

3.3.1 MEMORY REPRESENTATION AND CONVENTIONS TO CONSIDER

Now that you have the idea of the queue, you will undoubtly find a place to use it within a program. What will it cost you to get Karen, the queutie caterpillar, to crawl backward through your coded algorithm? Well, if you went to the software store then you would only have to acquire one array and two identifiers for your storage requirements, at most, you might be able to get by with just one array.

Since the queue is linearly ordered and the array is a contiguous block of storage locations, the choice of an array as a space for the crawling queue to roam is a rather natural selection. (With the use of an iota of imagination and some PASCAL power, the next chapter introduces a method that does not depend on the *contiguous* attribute of memory—linked queues.) Since the front and rear elements of the queue must be easily accessible, the need for the two identifiers is obvious. One identifier contains a subscript that will direct you to the location in the array where the rear element of the queue is stored. The other does likewise for the front element of the queue. So with the storage arrangements for the queue prepared, let's consider some conventions that will help bring Karen to life.

Your first consideration was really made back at the software store when you selected the array. You had to specify the size of the array needed. This maximum limit is determined by the demands of the problem being solved. In the software store, the sales clerk asked whether you wanted an array with subscripts from 1 to maximum or from 0 to maximum less one. As you will see later, the latter array model is quite helpful.

Once this decision is made then the question of orientation arises. What direction shall the queue crawl along the array? Figure 3.2 shows the two options. There are no outstanding advantages to either and the choice is based on your preference and the programming language's capabilities. Though the orientation is insignificant to the abstract queue, the decision will be reflected in the code of all the support and access routines discussed later.

Figure 3.2

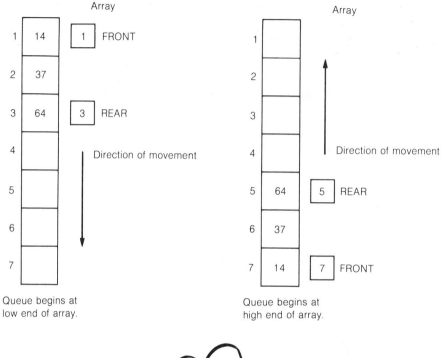

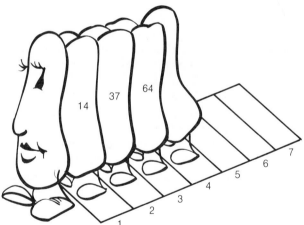

In Figure 3.2, the identifiers for the front and rear elements of the queue are as-sumed to point directly to the location where the front and rear elements are stored. This is an obvious convention with which to start. You will see later that a different convention—the front identifier directing you to the location before the front ele-ment—will become not a choice but a necessity.

The identifiers for the front and rear element can either be individual identifiers or they can be incorporated into a record containing the array and the front and rear identifiers. This will have the advantage of making the front and rear pointers transparent to the user of the queue. These two options are illustrated below:

```
type RANGE: 0..MAX;
     INTEGERARRAY : array[1..MAX] of integer;
var QUE: INTEGERARRAY ;
    FRONT, REAR : RANGE ;

type QMODEL = record
                 FRONT: 0..MAX;
                 REAR : 0..MAX;
                 QSTORE : array[0..MAX] of integer;
              end ;
var QUE : QMODEL ;
```

We will use the record structure approach, QMODEL, in subsection 3.3.4 and the other method in subsection 3.3.3. This gives you exposure to both approaches. From this vantage point, you will be better qualified to select between them.

With decisions made in these areas—maximum size of the array, range of subscripts, direction of movement, meaning of subscripts in the front and rear identifiers, and whether the identifiers are part of a record—we have set up a logic space within which the queue can operate. Your next step is to decide what operations to develop in order to put the queue into motion.

3.3.2   SUPPORT AND ACCESS ROUTINES

The procedures you will need to design include the primitive operations for an abstract queue, an operation due to the implementation process, and an operation for the convenience of the user of the queue. There will also be two auxilliary procedures to handle two special situations that might occur.

The procedures LEAVE, EMPTY, and ENTER will have the same functions as described in subsection 3.2.2. Because the implemented array has a limited size while the abstract queue does not, it is necessary to include a boolean operation FULL, which checks to see whether all array locations are being utilized. The procedure is more complicated than the analogous one used with stacks because of the way that the queue moves along within the array. Since two implementation approaches are presented, the code for these procedures is postponed until the next two sections.

The EMPTY and FULL routines will be provided so that the user can check for an empty queue before he uses LEAVE and for a full array before he calls ENTER. If the user forgets to perform these checks then the possibility of underflow and overflow, respectively, arises. Some response to these situations must be developed. The response options are similar to those given for the stack.

If the user wishes to see the data element on the front of the queue before deciding to remove it, it is necessary to develop an access routine that does not change the queue, only returning the value of the front data element. For this purpose, an access procedure, called UP _ FRONT, can be provided as part of the implementation package. This routine also checks for a request to access the front element of an empty queue. (If the user wants to access the rear element of the queue—even though not a legitimate abstract queue operation—a similar routine will have to be provided, though I am quite hesitant to suggest a name that is apropos.)

The list below summarizes the support and access routines needed.

Procedure	Purpose
LEAVE	remove front DATA element from QUE
ENTER	enter new DATA element into QUE
EMPTY	check QUE for the empty state
FULL	check the array for available space
UP _ FRONT	access the value of the front DATA element of the QUE
RESPOND _ TO _ OVER	respond to overflow
RESPOND _ TO _ UNDER	respond to underflow

Thus with our memory representation mapped out, our convention considerations listed, and the procedures LEAVE, ENTER, EMPTY, FULL, and UP _ FRONT described, we are ready to bring our caterpillar to life. In subsection 3.3.3 we will see Karen backed out onto a limb and we must figure out how to get her back. In subsection 3.3.4, we will set up a way for Karen to back up in circles to her tail's content.

3.3.3 A FIRST APPROACH: OUR CATERPILLAR BACKS OUT ON A LIMB

This first implementation takes a simple and straightforward approach. It will provide an adequate solution to the implementation process. We will need all of the support and access routines mentioned in the previous section and one additional one to rescue Karen, the crawling queue, from falling off of the limb that she has backed onto.

The following conventions will be used in this approach:

1. The array has subscripts from 1 to 6, is integer-valued, and is called QUE.
2. The direction of movement of the queue in the array is from low to high subscripts.
3. FRONT and REAR, the identifiers that contain the subscripts that indicate where the front and rear elements of the queue are stored, are not part of a record.
4. FRONT will contain the actual subscript of the front element and REAR will contain the actual subscript of the rear element.
5. Initially, FRONT = 1 and REAR = 0.

The three parts of Figure 3.3 show the queue at three different stages. In Figure 3.3a, the queue is in its initial empty state. After a sequence of ENTER and LEAVE operations—an ENTER followed by two occurences of an ENTER then LEAVE pair—there is only one data element in the queue (Figure 3.3b). If the next operation on the queue is a LEAVE, then once again the queue is empty, as shown in Figure 3.3c. From this figure we can state a condition that defines the empty queue. When

Figure 3.3

a. Initial condition—EMPTY

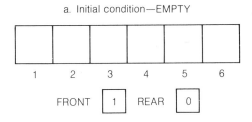

b. After the operations ENTER, ENTER, LEAVE, ENTER, LEAVE

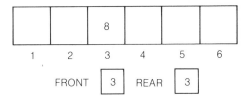

c. After the operation LEAVE—EMPTY again

FRONT is greater than REAR, then the queue can be considered empty. This condition is one of the features that gives Karen, our crawling queue, such a peculiar character. When her front is ahead of her rear then she is empty. This is because she always crawls backwards in the array, since additions to the queue are performed at the rear.

With the condition for the empty queue at hand the boolean function EMPTY can easily be written. It is given below:

```
function EMPTY (FRONT: RANGE ; REAR: RANGE): boolean ;
    (* Is front pointer of queue ahead of rear pointer? *)
begin
        if FRONT > REAR then EMPTY := true
                        else EMPTY := false
end ;
```

You can see that it is not necessary for the array to be an argument to test the emptiness attribute of the queue.

The transition from Figure 3.3b to 3.3c hints at the content of the LEAVE procedure. It is necessary to check for an underflow condition before allowing the LEAVE operation to take place. I will assume another procedure, RE-SPOND _ TO _ UNDER, is available to respond to the underflow condition if detected. With this is mind, the LEAVE procedure is coded as follows:

```
procedure LEAVE (QUE: INTEGERARRAY; var FRONT: RANGE ;
                                        REAR: RANGE ;
                                    var DATA :integer );
begin      (* Operation to remove data element from a queue *)
        if EMPTY (FRONT, REAR) then RESPOND_TO_UNDER
                            else begin
                                DATA   : = QUE[FRONT];
                                (* Return front element *)
                                FRONT := FRONT + 1
                                (* Remove from que
                                    by adjusting pointer *)
                            end
end ;
```

Again, as with the stack, the array is left unchanged even though the queue, which resides in the array, experiences a change. By changing the identifier FRONT, the previous front element of the queue is no longer accessible.

As we follow Karen and her backward crawl across the array, we next consider the function FULL; however, this procedure puts a little hurdle in our path. Figure 3.4 shows three possible snapshots of Karen on the limb. The three snapshots are not related to each other by a sequence of LEAVE and ENTER operations. They have been chosen to illustrate the three possible situations when the FULL function is called.

Figure 3.4

a. Not FULL, ENTER operation allowed

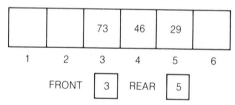

b. FULL, ENTER operation not allowed

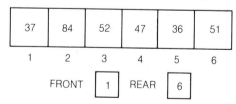

c. Not FULL. ENTER operation allowed or not?

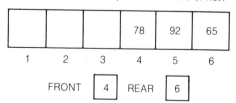

In Figure 3.4a, an array location is available for an ENTER operation, so the queue is not yet full and the function FULL should return the value *false* when this situation is encountered. Figure 3.4b illustrates the state when the entire array is occupied by the queue. Another ENTER operation would cause an overflow condition, therefore the function should return the value *true*. It is Figure 3.4c that provides us with a little challenge. The entire array is not being occupied by the queue, but Karen has crawled out to the end of the limb. Adding another data element to her rear would be indeed precarious if it were not impossible. In what way should the FULL function respond to this state of affairs? The array is not full but an ENTER operation is not possible. What can we do?

We could take the easy way out—leave Karen out on her limb and consider the queue to be full. This also would leave the user out on a limb, because he wouldn't know whether the estimate for the maximum array size was too small or whether the queue had crawled to the edge of the array.

With a little imagination, we can make the implementation a lot more accommodating and humane, for both Karen and the user. Suppose that when we test for fullness, if we notice Karen out on a limb like this, we bring her back to a more stable foothold (or should I say feethold?). In other words, we can shift all the data elements to the beginning of the array—the low end with subscripts 1, 2,. ... This will give the queue room for more insertions. Well, that's a simple solution, and in our example it is not very expensive, for the worst case is having to shift five data elements. We will need another auxiliary procedure to perform the shifting, and it will be quite simple to code. So with a little extra programming effort and a spot of imagination we are able to let the computer system adapt to the needs of the users rather than forcing the user to adapt to the constraints of the computer system. I hope you will incorporate this attitude into all aspects of your career in computer science, for then the computer is being used as a tool and an aide to humankind, rather than people becoming public servants in a computer kingdom.

What conditions can we use to distinguish the three cases we encountered? The REAR identifier is the central factor because when the REAR is not equal to the maximum subscript value then the array is not full. When the REAR is equal to the maximum subscript then the FRONT identifier indicates whether there is a full state or an end-of-the-array state. These conditions are clearly expressed in the function FULL below:

```
function FULL (var QUE:INTEGERARRAY; var FRONT:RANGE  ;
                         var REAR: RANGE ):boolean;
  begin        (*Procedure to check status of queue*)
      if REAR <> 6 then FULL := false
                                     (*CASE 1 NOT FULL*)
          else if FRONT=1 then FULL := true
                                     (*CASE 2 FULL*)
                   else
                                     (*CASE 3 END OF ARRAY
                                            BUT NOT FULL*)
                      begin
                       FULL := false ;
                       SHIFT_QUEUE (QUE,FRONT,REAR);
                      end ;

   end ;
```

It is necessary to use the *var* keyword on all arguments, in case the queue must be shifted. The procedure SHIFT_QUEUE will simply determine the number of data elements to be shifted and move them one at a time, shifting the one in location FRONT to location 1, the one in location (FRONT + 1) to location 2, and so on. In Figure 3.5, the queue in Figure 3.4c is shown before and after the procedure SHIFT_QUEUE is called. The code for this procedure looks like this:

```
procedure SHIFT_QUEUE(var QUE:INTEGERARRAY; var FRONT: RANGE ;
                                 var REAR: RANGE );
var NUMBER_TO_SHIFT, K :integer;
begin           (*Procedure to move queue to beginning of the array*)
   NUMBER_TO_SHIFT := (REAR - FRONT) + 1;   (*Determine number of data
                                                elements to be moved*)
   for K:=1 to NUMBER_TO_SHIFT do
        QUE[K]:=QUE[FRONT + (K - 1)];
   FRONT:=1;                           (*Adjust front and
   REAR := NUMBER_TO_SHIFT;               rear pointers*)
end ;
```

It is satisfying to know that the shifting process is completely transparent. The user is not aware of how the implementation is handled and has confidence in the magic that you have placed at his disposal.

I mentioned earlier that the shifting process is rather inexpensive, in our case. This was due to the shortness of the queue. When the maximum size of the array increases or the number of fields in each data element increase, then this shifting process can become a rather expensive use of computer time. In this case, another approach that does not require data movement should be developed. There is no exact formula that I can give you to determine when the shifting process becomes too expensive, but it is an aspect of this approach you should be aware of.

With this hurdle cleared and Karen out of jeopardy, we can now turn our attention to the last two procedures, ENTER and UP_FRONT. Without breaking stride, the procedure for ENTER is as follows:

```
procedure      ENTER(var QUE: INTEGERARRAY;var FRONT: RANGE ;
                        var REAR: RANGE ; DATA :integer) ;
begin
   if FULL(QUE, FRONT, REAR) then RESPOND_TO_OVER
                          else begin
                                 REAR := REAR + 1;
                                 QUE[REAR] := DATA
                               end
end ;
```

Once again arguments are all treated as reference parameters, since the queue may be shifted in the array.

The last procedure is UP_FRONT. With the stage so well set, it is your turn to star. Write the function that accesses the front of the queue without changing it.

With this first implementation, once again you see that consideration must be given to possible overflow and underflow. The status of the queue must be tested before you perform a LEAVE, ENTER, or UP_FRONT operation, with the flow situation responded to appropriately.

Figure 3.5

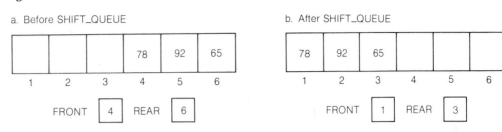

a. Before SHIFT_QUEUE

			78	92	65

1   2   3   4   5   6

FRONT 4   REAR 6

b. After SHIFT_QUEUE

78	92	65			

1   2   3   4   5   6

FRONT 1   REAR 3

The FULL procedure needed to distinguish between the entire array being occupied by the queue and the queue resting at the end of the array. It was also here that the implementation shows a spot of imagination and accommodation by using the rescue procedure SHIFT _ QUEUE.

This implementation sufficiently emulates the behavior of the abstract queue. Its main potential drawback is the time necessary to shift the queue—which depends on the number of data elements, the number of fields per data element, and the frequency that SHIFT _ QUEUE is called. By being aware of this weak spot you can decide more adequately when to use this approach.

Presently, even if you decide SHIFT _ QUE would be too expensive, you have no alternative. In subsection 3.3.4 I will describe another approach that eliminates the shortcoming of the linear approach with little change to the procedures. The changes will be reflected more in the conventions that are used. Our alternative approach also shows how the imagination can produce some interesting results. Before turning to subsection 3.3.4, click in your ImQ module and create an idea picture of how our crawling caterpillar can walk on the array without needing to be rescued from falling

 IMAGINATION CHALLENGE

An important attribute of your developing imagination is the fluency and flexibility with which you generate ideas. Fluency is involved with how many ideas you can produce, while flexibility involves how conventional or unconventional the ideas are. So sharpen these two important skills with the following exercise:

As a consultant to an advertising agency you are asked to come up with new uses for a product. For five minutes think of marketable and conventional ideas for the product—5$\frac{1}{4}$ inch diskettes. Write the ideas down and make sure that you come up with at least four uses. Now, for the same product, suspend your judgment of the conventionality of your ideas, let your imagination loose, and for five minutes compile a second, wilder list.

Repeat the exercise with another product and a friend of your choice. Compare lists and ImQs!

over the edge. When you have spent as much time as you wish exercising your powers of imagination, then read on.

3.3.4   A SECOND APPROACH: RUNNING AROUND WITH KAREN

In the last section, we had our backward-crawling caterpillar strolling down a dead-end street—the linear array. When Karen came to the end of the street, we would pull her back to the beginning before continuing with any more movements. This was acceptable as long as Karen had not stretched so much that it took a lot of effort to pull all of her back to the beginning of the street. Now let's see how we can eliminate the need for relocating the caterpillar.

The solution is quite simple. What if we take away the end and beginning of the street? What if we consider the array to be like a jogging track rather than a street? Karen can then back contentedly around the track without ever coming to an edge from which she needs to be rescued. If we consider the array to be circular, with the first storage location coming after the last, then we have eliminated the end of the array.

How shall we do this? How can we make the first subscript of the array follow the last one? There are two methods for turning the corner and having the array appear circular. Figure 3.6a shows the queue of Figure 3.4c, using the linear approach of the previous section. Figure 3.6b shows the array as we can visualize it using the circular approach.

Figure 3.6

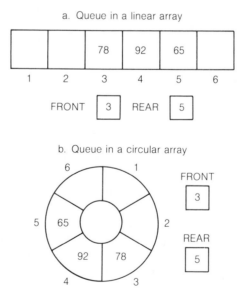

a. Queue in a linear array

b. Queue in a circular array

Convention: Location 6 is followed by location 1.
(Modulo arithmetic or a conditional statement can be used to accomplish the convention.)

The identifiers that indicate the front and rear elements of the queue are changed in two procedures, LEAVE and ENTER. In the linear model, the instruction in LEAVE looks like this:

```
FRONT  := FRONT + 1
```

To achieve a circular effect we change this instruction to:

```
if FRONT = 6 then FRONT := 1 else FRONT := FRONT + 1
```

Now the first subscript, 1, comes after the last subscript, 6, and we have walked our queue around the corner. The same replacement is made in ENTER to ensure that the subscript for the rear element also makes the turn after it reaches a value of 6. Clearly this example can easily be generalized for whatever subscript range you are using.

The second method for achieving circular behavior for our array is easier to use when the subscript range is specified as 0 to (MAX − 1). (Recall that this situation was referred to earlier in subsection 3.3.1, in regard to choosing the subscript range.) In mathematics is a concept called modulo arithmetic, the results of all addition and subtraction operations are divided by an integer, and the result for the operation is the remainder from the division. For example, (15 + 3) mod 7 (read "modulo 7") equals 4, since the remainder of (15 + 3)/7 is 4. Likewise (23 − 9) mod 7 equals 0, since the remainder of 14/7 is 0. The possible answers that can result from modulo 7 arithmetic are 0, 1, 2, 3, 4, 5, or 6—the set of remainders after dividing by seven.

How can this help you in implementing a queue? Some computer languages, including PASCAL, provide a modulo arithmetic function. Let's assume you have an array with seven locations, with a subscript range from 0 to 6. The *if* statement in the LEAVE procedure would be replaced by:

```
FRONT := ( FRONT + 1 ) mod 7
```

When the identifier FRONT equals 6 it is incremented to 0, since (6 + 1) mod 7 is 0. Once again, we have the queue turning the corner. The analogous replacement is made with the REAR identifier in procedure ENTER.

Since the mod function produces integers from 0 to (MAX - 1), your choice of subscript range is obviously influenced. Of course, if your language does not allow 0 as a subscript then you can always add 1 to the results of the MOD function, yielding a subscript from 1 to MAX.

So here we have the main idea of the second approach—a circular array—and a method to accomplish the new turn of events, modulo arithmetic. Now let us see what the consequences are of this new approach.

For the conventions of this approach, I will make four changes, three now and one later. The first change is that the number of locations in the array will be ten instead of six. This is only for variability in the presentation and does not change the essence of the approach. The subscript range for the array is thus 0 to 9. This is the second change and it is made to facilitate the use of the mod function.

The third change involves the identifiers FRONT and REAR. Let us use an important feature of PASCAL to emulate the structure of an abstract queue. By defining a new data type using the PASCAL record structure, we will include the array for the queue and the identifiers FRONT and REAR in one structure. The following PASCAL declarations reflect this change:

```
const MAX = 9 ;
type
      QMODEL = record
                  FRONT : 0..MAX ;
                  REAR : 0..MAX ;
                  QSTORE : array[0..MAX] of integer;
               end ;
var QUE : QMODEL ;
```

We can now use the identifier QUE in our implementation of the queue. We can store the data elements of the queue in the array QUE.QSTORE. When we want to access the front data element then we can do so through the identifier QUE.FRONT. Notice how the use of the constant MAX generalizes the declaration. This allows a future change to the maximum size of the array to be localized in a single PASCAL statement, const MAX = 9 ; and saves us from changing every statement in which the upper bound of the subscript range is used.

This major change is made so that the different procedure calls can pass just the identifier QUE and all information needed will be present within this structured data type. Therefore, QMODEL becomes a new abstract data type available to the application program.

The other conventions remain unchanged. The direction of movement is from low to high subscripts. The front and rear pointers point directly to the front and rear elements of the queue. The initial values for the front and rear pointers are the same as in the linear approach. Figure 3.7 illustrates all of these conventions.

Figure 3.7

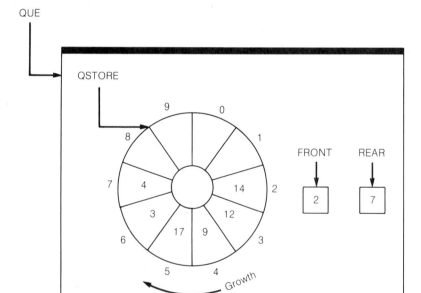

Snapshot of a queue in a circular array with pointers as part of the structured record

Another change to this set of conventions will be made later to solve a paradox that we shall encounter.

Let us begin by looking at the procedure ENTER. Notice the two changes, one in the argument list and the other resulting from the circular nature of the array. The procedure for this operation is as follows:

```
procedure ENTER (var QUE:QMODEL  ; DATA : integer);
begin
if FULL(QUE) then RESPOND_TO_OVER    (*Overflow condition*)
            else
              begin
                QUE.REAR := (QUE.REAR + 1) mod (MAX+1)
                QUE.QSTORE[QUE.REAR] := DATA
              end
end ;
```

With this procedure our caterpillar can jog backward around the array until her tail meets her head and the procedure FULL becomes true. What condition do you expect to find in the FULL procedure? When is her rear next to her front and her body stretched completely around the track? Consulting your visual image of the circular array and your internal PASCAL compiler, the condition is likely to appear as:

```
if FRONT = REAR + 1 then...
```

This expression is pretty good for 90% of the cases, but when FRONT = 0 and REAR = 9 then it doesn't hold true. If you remembered this possibility and altered the expression to read:

```
if FRONT = ( REAR + 1 ) mod (MAX + 1) then..
```

Then you have covered 100% of the cases. But actually, what you have now is one of the horns of a dilemma.

Let's look at Figure 3.8 and see what happens when ENTER and LEAVE operations happen in two special situations.

If we take the situation in Figure 3.8a and perform an ENTER operation on the queue, then the result is as demonstrated in Figure 3.8b. If the FULL function, with our stated condition, is applied to the situation in Figure 3.8b then it will respond with *"true,"* just as desired.

Now we take the queue in Figure 3.8c and perform a LEAVE operation. Figure 3.8d shows the result of this action.

If the FULL function is applied to the queue in Figure 3.8d, the function will also say that the array is full, when in fact it is empty. To say that an empty array is full is indeed a paradox. A similar approach from the other direction shows that the EMPTY function can give the value *true* with a full array. We thus have another paradox: the statement that a full array is empty. We have here a pair of paradoxes, which is worse than the original single horn of a dilemma. This situation is summarized in Figure 3.9.

It appears that the condition,

```
FRONT = ( REAR + 1) mod (MAX + 1)
```

defines both the FULL and EMPTY states—in which case, we cannot distinguish the

Figure 3.8

a. Before ENTER operation

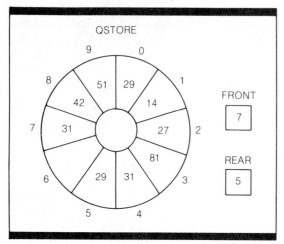

b. After ENTER operation

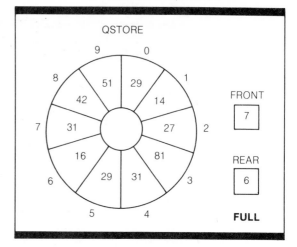

c. Before LEAVE operation

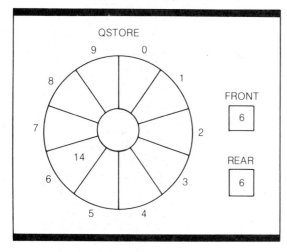

d. After LEAVE operation

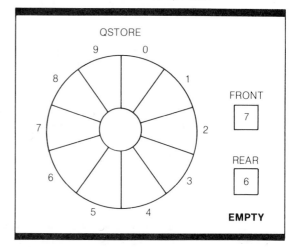

two states. This is quite unacceptable and some solution needs to be found if the circular approach is to become usable.

Here's a not-so-obvious solution that puts a tiny dent in the implementation's effectiveness. Most important, it does not increase the programming effort or execution time of the procedures relative to the linear approach. It involves changing one of the previously stated conventions and redefining what is meant by the array being full.

The new convention concerns the significance of the identifier FRONT. Previously it indicated the location of the front data element of the queue. Now, **let it indicate the location *before* the front data element of the queue.** Thus, if FRONT has a

Figure 3.9

EMPTY   \<or\>   FULL

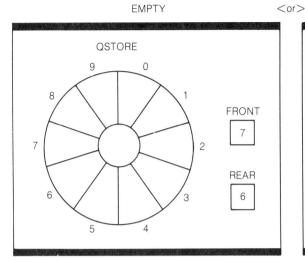 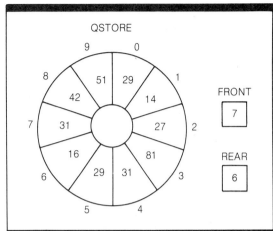

FRONT = (REAR + 1) mod (MAX + 1) is then true for both cases.

value of 6 then the front element of the queue is in location 7 of the array. If it has a value of 9 then the front element of the queue is in location 0. How does this change the condition for the EMPTY and FULL functions? How does it affect the initial condition for the identifier FRONT?

In Figure 3.10, you see a queue with one data element and then the empty queue after a LEAVE operation. Thus, the condition for an EMPTY queue is that the front and rear subscripts are equal. With this stated, function EMPTY can be given.

```
function EMPTY (QUE:QMODEL):boolean;
begin
     with QUE do
     if FRONT = REAR then EMPTY := true
                     else EMPTY := false
end ;
```

The new convention leaves the previously presented procedure ENTER unchanged because it deals with the rear of the queue only. It uses the function FULL, which will be described last, but this does not affect the performance of ENTER. Procedure LEAVE uses the front of the queue; because of the new significance of the value of FRONT, you will notice a small change in this procedure.

```
procedure LEAVE (var QUE:QMODEL; var DATA :integer);
begin
if EMPTY(QUE) then RESPOND_TO_UNDER    (*Underflow detect*)
          else with QUE do begin
                         FRONT := (FRONT + 1) mod (MAX + 1);
                         DATA  := QSTORE[FRONT]
                    end
     end ;
```

Figure 3.10

a. Before LEAVE operation

b. After LEAVE operation: EMPTY state

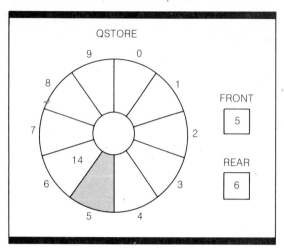

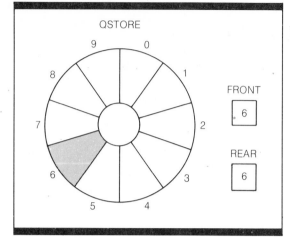

Queue with one element using the new convention for the front pointer

Condition for EMPTY state: FRONT = REAR.

The difference that appears in LEAVE is that the FRONT identifier is incremented before DATA is accessed. Because of the new convention, the operation functions appropriately.

All that is left is the function FULL, which is waiting for the condition of fullness to be determined. I mentioned earlier that the solution to the paradox requires a redefinition. Figure 3.11 illustrates the defining condition.

The three snapshots show an initial queue state (Figure 3.11a) and then the queue after two consecutive ENTER operations have been performed. The second snapshot, Figure 3.11b, will be defined as a full array—that is, no additional ENTER operations can be performed.

What is actually happening is that a **buffer location** is being adopted. This location will never be used to store a data element. Thus, the front and rear of the queue are always separated by at least one location. The buffer location is directly pointed to by the front pointer and is considered to be attached to the front element of the queue. This is why the significance of FRONT was changed. It's as if Karen, the caterpillar, was wearing a cushion on her nose so that she avoids backing into her own face.

With this redefinition, the maximum number of data elements that can be placed in the queue is reduced by one. We have reduced the efficiency of our implementation only slightly. This limitation can easily be alleviated by increasing the range of subscripts for the array by one.

What about Figure 3.11c? What would happen if one more ENTER operation was allowed and the buffer location was used to hold just one more data element? By

Figure 3.11

a. Initially

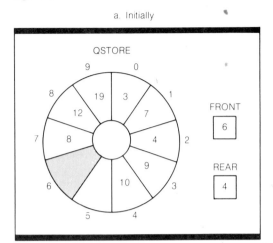

b. After an ENTER

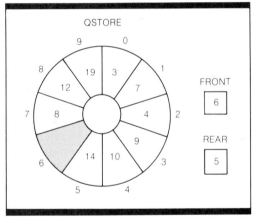

c. After an ENTER

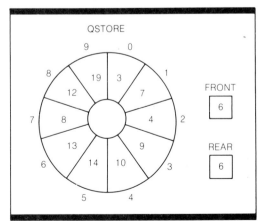

comparing this figure with Figure 3.10a, we see that we would end up back where we started. When FRONT and REAR are compared, the two situations appear identical, although they obviously are not. Therefore, by stopping with the queue as it is in Figure 3.11b, there are two unique conditions that allow us to distinguish the empty queue from the full array; the paradox no longer exists. The situation in Figure 3.11c is considered an overflow condition and is thus avoided.

What condition can be used to describe the situation found in Figure 3.11b? It turns out to be the one which brought out our dilemma:

```
if QUE.FRONT = ( QUE.REAR + 1) mod (MAX+1) then ...
```

What makes it valid now is that the condition for the empty queue,

```
if QUE.FRONT = QUE.REAR then ...
```

is different, and the empty and full states are defined by unique conditions. With the condition finally stated, the function FULL can easily be given as:

```
function FULL (QUE:QMODEL):boolean;
begin
   if QUE.FRONT = ( QUE.REAR + 1) mod (MAX+1) then
                            FULL := true
                   else FULL := false
end;
```

Now we have all the support and access routines necessary to activate the implementation of the queue by using a circular array. Since the presentation of this approach was through a combination of trial-and-error and discovery method, I would like to summarize the main components and conventions by the following table:

Conventions	Diagram Representing Convention
Memory space for queue: ten locations in an array with subscript range 0–9	
The array is to be considered circular	
The indicators of the front and rear are part of the queue model	

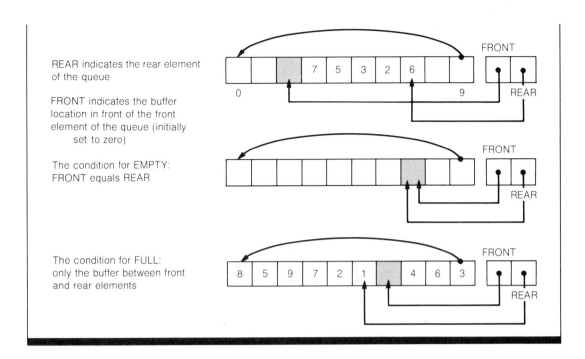

REAR indicates the rear element of the queue

FRONT indicates the buffer location in front of the front element of the queue (initially set to zero)

The condition for EMPTY: FRONT equals REAR

The condition for FULL: only the buffer between front and rear elements

The queue, in either the linear or the circular version, can now be added to your kit of programming tools. For the new benefits that the queue will bring, many thanks are due to Karen the peculiar caterpillar, who would rather see where she has been than where she is going and is not too proud to be rescued from precarious perches or to wear a cushion on her nose.

■ "JUST FOR REFERENCE"

General Queue Implementation Model

Considerations that must be addressed include—

- storage needs—two pointers and an array
- subscript range for the array
- direction of growth
- significance of pointer values

Routines are needed for—

- access: LEAVE, ENTER, UP _ FRONT
- support: EMPTY, FULL, RESPOND _ TO _ OVER, RESPOND _ TO _ UNDER

Implementation of Linear Model

Basic conventions include—

- growth from low to high subscript
- FRONT and REAR pointers that indicate exact location of front and rear element of the queue

States are defined as follows—

- Array is EMPTY when FRONT equals REAR plus 1
- Array is FULL when FRONT equals 1 and REAR equals maximum subscript
- Array is shifted when FRONT is not equal to 1 and REAR equals maximum subscript

Operations include—

- LEAVE: if not EMPTY then FRONT pointer equals FRONT pointer plus 1
- ENTER: if not FULL then REAR pointer equals REAR pointer plus 1
- SHIFT _ QUEUE: move queue elements to the beginning of the array

Implementation of Circular Model

Basic conventions include—

- growth from low to high subscript
- REAR pointer that indicates exact location of the rear element in the queue, while the FRONT pointer indicates the position of the buffer location in front of the front element of the queue
- queue that is implemented by using a defined structured data type consisting of the storage for the queue and the FRONT and REAR pointers

States are defined as follows—

- Array is EMPTY when QUE.FRONT equals QUE.REAR
- Array FULL when QUE.FRONT equals QUE.REAR plus 1 (modulo the number of array locations)

Circularization of the array is implemented by using modulo arithmetic based on the number of array locations to increment the pointers.

Operations include—

- LEAVE: if not EMPTY then QUE.FRONT equals QUE.FRONT plus 1 (modulo arithmetic)
- ENTER: if not FULL then QUE.REAR equals QUE.REAR plus 1 (modulo arithmetic)

Key features include—

- use of modulo arithmetic to give a linear array the appearance of a circular one
- use of a buffer location to uniquely define the EMPTY and FULL states

TRADE-OFFS

The implementation of the queue using a circular array leads to the use of a buffer location. The buffer location gave us an unambiguous interpretation of the empty and full states. What did it cost?

Since the buffer location is not used to store data, one record of the array structure is sacrificed. If the record is large (say, 256 bytes) then the unused space is a factor to the implementation.

One way to use the buffer location's space for another data element and retain the integrity of the implementation is to maintain a queue counter as part of the queue model. The new declaration is as follows:

```
type QMODEL = record
                FRONT : 0..MAX;
                REAR : 0..MAX;
                COUNT : 0..MAXPLUS1;
                QSTORE : array[0..MAX] of DATA_ELEMENT;
              end;
```

The empty and full states are still well defined, depending on the value of COUNT. All locations in QSTORE are available for data elements. And only one location (a byte or two) is added to the queue model.

Great, but what's on the other side of the coin? Execution time! Each ENTER operation must increment the COUNT, with LEAVE decrementing it. Therefore, extra coding — two instructions — must be added, with a consequential increment in execution time.

Once again, in computer programming nothing is free. The two QMODEL options exhibit the classic space versus time trade-off. Although in this example the amount of space and time appear minute, the idea is not.

EXERCISES

1. In addition to the natural operations of LEAVE, EMPTY, and ENTER, two additional operations, FULL and UP_FRONT, are used during the implementation. Describe the function of each of the five operations and state why it is important to the implementation.

2. In the linear approach to implementing a queue, another operation, SHIFT_QUEUE, was needed. State the condition that must exist before SHIFT_QUEUE would be invoked.

3. When does invoking SHIFT_QUEUE become an expensive process?

4. The circular approach saves the expense of any SHIFT_QUEUE operations. In order to implement this approach, what new features are added?

5. Given the following sequence of operations and the basic conventions below, show the contents of the pointers FRONT and REAR for each implementation approach:

Basic conventions: array of eight locations
data elements of type *char*
subscript range of 0 to 7
growth from low to high subscript

Initial state of queue:

0	1	2	3	4	5	6	7
		A	B				

Linear		Circular	
FRONT	REAR	FRONT	REAR
2	3	1;	3

```
ENTER(QUE,'C')
ENTER(QUE,'D')
ENTER(QUE,'E')
LEAVE(QUE,LET)
LEAVE(QUE,LET)
ENTER(QUE,'F')
ENTER(QUE,'G')
LEAVE(QUE,LET)
```

6. Assume that you have chosen to use a circular approach to implement a queue, that you intend to use modulo arithmetic to "turn the corner" of the array, and that the subscript range is from 1 to 25. Write the instruction to properly increment the FRONT pointer by one.

7. What is the advantage of including the FRONT and REAR pointers as part of the structured data type QMODEL that was defined in subsection 3.3.4?

8. Assume that you are implementing a queue in a language that cannot support the record structure. In order to achieve a similar advantage as indicated in question 7, you decide to let two locations in the array QSTORE, the next-to-the-last and the last location, be used

to store the FRONT and REAR pointers. In this way, the array QSTORE is the only parameter that needs to be passed to the various procedures. Using this new approach, write the procedures ENTER, FULL, LEAVE, and EMPTY. Use the same conventions as in the circular approach and state any new conventions that you adopt.

9. Change the procedure LEAVE to a function that returns the value of the data element at the front of the queue. What do you do if the queue is empty?

10. Change the procedure ENTER to a boolean function that returns a value of true if the operation was a success and a value of false if the queue is full.

11. How would you design the LEAVE procedure if you wanted to receive some indication of the success or failure of the operation?

12. One day while visualizing the circular approach to implementing a queue, you see a flag float into view and attach itself to the queue structure. While manipulating the queue with LEAVE and ENTER operations, you notice that the flag is down when the queue is not full and it is up when the queue is full. Now that your feet are back on solid ground, you decide to attempt this new approach by including a boolean identifier in the QMODEL structured data type and revising the LEAVE, FULL, and ENTER procedures. Does this imagined approach still require the use of a buffer location? What conditions now define the empty queue and the full array? Write the revised procedures and test them in an application program. Does the application program need to be changed because of this new implementation?

3.4 Applications

Many academic computer centers utilize a multiuser computer system where numerous users share the resources of the computer and its peripheral devices. The part of the computer system that handles the user's requests for service and allocates the resources available to satisfy the requests is the operating system (OS). The OS keeps a check on the status of all components of the computer system. When particular services are requested, the request is channelled by the OS to a special routine that accepts requests and allocates resources, if available.

The PDP-11 computer system operating under the RSTS/E operating system is an example of such a multiuser system. The computer system of the PDP-11 usually consists of the CPU, memory, disk drives, magnetic tape drives, a line printer, and numerous terminals for the user's interface with the PDP-11. When a user requests an action that involves the disk, the RSTS/E accepts the request and channels it to the special routine that handles this type of request. A different routine within RSTS/E is available for each peripheral device available.

The particular device that I wish to focus our attention on is the line printer. Each user's program will contain instructions that request information to be output. If this output is sent directly to the printer, the result would be a collection of interspersed lines of output from various users. Thus the resources of the line printer must be properly managed so that the output of a entire program is printed before the printer is reassigned to service another request.

In order to manage this affair properly, the program's output is channelled to a disk area reserved specifically for the user, instead of the line printer. In this way, a copy of the output of all programs is saved on the disk memory, in separate areas. When a program completes execution, the output generated is stored as a disk file.

The user then requests that the output file be transferred to the line printer. In RSTS/E the subsystem that handles requests to use the line printer is called QUEMAN.

The QUEMAN subsystem of routines has two primary responsibilities: (1) to keep a record of all requests for line printer services and (2) to assign the printer to service the next pending request when the OS indicates that the printer has just completed a request. In close communication with RSTS/E, QUEMAN keeps the waiting line of printer requests straight and the printer active. Figure 3.12 shows the relationships between the printer, the OS, and QUEMAN.

When a request is received, three possible cases can arise:

1. The printer is idle, it is not providing services to any user, and a request for the printer is received. In this case, the printer can provide service immediately.

2. The printer is busy, providing servicing to a previous request. The new request is added to the waiting list.

3. The printer is busy and the waiting list is full. In this case, the user is informed that the request must be resubmitted at a later time.

It is the nature and handling of the waiting list that is important to this chapter. The arrangement has all the characteristics of the queue information structure, particularly if the first request received is to be the first request served. I will assume that

Figure 3.12

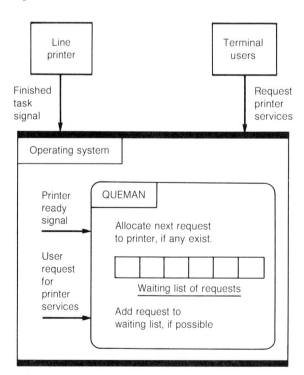

no priority system is available—all requests are of equal stature and will be handled when they reach the front of the queue. The actual QUEMAN subsystem is not so equitable or simple. What I will describe here is a hypothetical version of QUEMAN called QMAN.

The three phases to the presentation are (1) an outline of the strategy of the main parts of a hypothetical QMAN subsystem, (2) a description of the information structures used, and (3) the PASCAL code for each of the routines outlined. This will give you an idea of the usage and importance of the queue within an essential section of the computer system—the operating system.

The two routines correspond to the communications between the operating system and the QMAN subsystem, and QMAN's response to these communications. The first communication occurs when RSTS/E receives a signal from the printer that it has completed printing. RSTS/E then notifies QMAN, and QMAN responds by assigning the printer to the request on the front of the queue, if one exists. The strategy is given below:

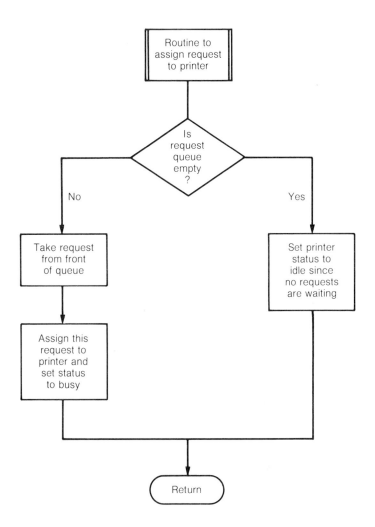

This strategy will keep the printer busy as long as requests are waiting in the queue. The only time that the printer will be idle is when the queue is empty and there is nothing waiting to be printed.

The second communication involves users' requests, which are passed to the QMAN subsystem by the operating system. The strategy must respond to all three cases mentioned previously. The strategy follows:

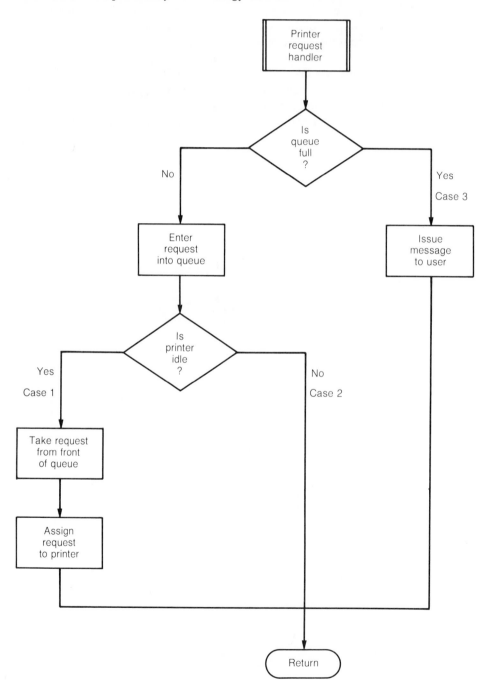

You will notice that for case 1, the request is placed in the queue; since the idle status implies an empty queue, the request is immediately removed from the queue and assigned to the printer. Notice also that the first routine described is used by this routine. These two strategies ensure that all accepted requests will be serviced either because they are made when the printer is idle or because they are at the front of the queue when the printer completes a request and new one is assigned.

The information structures that I shall describe for implementing QMAN are not the same as those used by the QUEMAN of RSTS/E. They are selected to give you the idea of the kind of information that would be used.

A queue will be needed; I will assume it is one that can handle data elements with three fields. The FRONT and REAR pointers of the queue are part of the structure (as in the approach of subsection 3.3.4). The queue would be defined by the following declarations in PASCAL:

```
const  MAX = 50 ;
type REQUEST = record
               ACCOUNT_NAME:string[10];        (*User ID*)

               DISK_ADDRESS:integer;       (*Location of
                                              output file*)

               LENGTH:integer            (*Number of
               end;                          blocks long*)

     QMODEL   = record
                  FRONT :0..MAX;
                  REAR  :0..MAX;
                  QSTORE:array[0..MAX] of REQUEST;
                  end;

     PCBLK    = record      (* printer control block*)
                  BUSY: boolean ;  (* BUSY = true ,idle = false*)
                  ACCT_NAME:  string[10]; (* user id of active
                                             job assigned to the
                                             printer*)

                  DISK_ADD: integer ;

                  BLK_LENGTH: integer
                  end;
var  QUE : QMODEL ;

     PRINTER : PCBLK ;
```

Another information structure is needed to keep track of the printer's idle/busy status and to assign the output file of a particular account to the printer. For this purpose, the record structure declared above, PCBLK—the printer control block—will be used. It will contain a boolean flag to indicate whether the printer is idle or busy and the specific parameters of each job—the account name, disk address of the file, and its length in blocks.

For the two procedures that will be presented in PASCAL, five procedures or functions will be assumed to exist: the support and access routines for the queue, EMPTY, FULL, LEAVE, and ENTER, and a routine ISSUE _ MESSAGE, which issues a message to the user when the queue is full and no additional requests can be accepted.

The first procedure will assign a request to the printer, if any exist. The code for this routine is:

```
procedure ASSIGN_REQUEST (var QUE:QMODEL; var PRINTER:PCBLK);
var ACTIVE_REQUEST:REQUEST;
      (*printer has just finished a request and is ready for another*)
begin
   if EMPTY (QUE) then PRINTER.BUSY := false      (*printer is idle*)
               else begin
                        (*remove front request and
                          assign it to the printer*)
                        LEAVE (QUE,ACTIVE_REQUEST);
                        with PRINTER do begin
                        ACCT_NAME := ACTIVE_REQUEST.ACCOUNT _NAME;
                        DISK_ADD := ACTIVE_REQUEST. DISK_ADDRESS;
                        BLK_LENGTH := ACTIVE_REQUEST.LENGTH;
                        BUSY:=true      (*printer is now
                                                set to busy status*)
                          end
               end
      end;
```

In this procedure, the state of the queue is checked and the printer is assigned the idle status if no requests are pending. If the queue is not empty then the printer is assigned the request on the front of the queue, the printer control block is filled with the necessary parameters, and the printer is set to the busy status.

The next procedure is the request handler. The OS provides the request that it has received. The code follows the strategy given before.

```
procedure REQUEST_HANDLER (var QUE:QMODEL ; var PRINTER:PCBLK ;
                           var NEW_REQUEST:REQUEST);
begin      (*the new request can be handled in 3 possible ways*)
   if FULL(QUE) then ISSUE_MESSAGE(NEW_REQUEST) (*CASE 3*)
                                             (*not accepted*)
            else begin
                     ENTER(QUE, NEW_REQUEST);    (*CASE 2*)
                                             (*enter only*)
                     if not ( PRINTER.BUSY ) then
                         ASSIGN_REQUEST(QUE,PRINTER);(*CASE 1*)
                                             (*assign  to printer *)
               end
end;
```

This routine either does not accept the request or accepts the request by placing it in the queue, where it either waits or is assigned to the idle printer immediately. The simple way in which this procedure is written is quite amazing if you read it over and temporarily forget all that resides behind the words FULL, ENTER, LEAVE, and QUE. Once the information structure and its support and access routines are implemented, they become elements of an extended language set and you are able to write code in a richer, more powerful, and more concise style.

The queue provides a simple and efficient tool for solving a problem that is quite important in computer science. The use of one computer by many users over the same time period is an efficient and economical way to use the powerful speed of calculation that the computer possesses. The challenge of how to manage this processing power and the resources of the peripheral devices was solved with sophisticated operating systems using various information structures, one of which is our friend the queue.

IMAGINATION CHALLENGE

Once upon a time, relative to now, people imagined that the earth was flat. Later, for many years, we humans believed that we lived in a three-dimensional universe. But with Albert Einstein's creative theory of relativity, we have theorized that we exist in a universe of four dimensions. There are the three dimensions of space, which surrounds us, and the fourth dimension of time with its subtle nature.

From your current four-coordinate vantage point in space-time, try to visualize an object that has dimension 2.5 (two and a half!). If this doesn't rattle and jog your imagination then try to "see" an object whose dimension is 1.34.

After struggling with this challenge, you might be interested in looking at a current book on computer graphics for the topic called fractal geometry to discover in what type of universe these objects *do* exist. Next imagine a universe with 11 dimensions! Look at the March 1985 *Scientific American*, for a peek.

■ "JUST FOR REFERENCE"

```
const   MAX = 50 ;
type REQUEST = record
                 ACCOUNT_NAME:string;         (*User ID*)
                 DISK_ADDRESS:integer;    (*Location of output file*)
                 LENGTH:integer;     (*Number of blocks long*)
               end;
     QMODEL    = record
                   FRONT:0..MAX;
                   REAR :0..MAX;
                   QSTORE:array[0..MAX] of REQUEST;
                 end;
     PCBLK     = record          (* printer control block*)
                   BUSY: boolean ;  (* BUSY = true ,idle = false*)
                   ACCT_NAME:        string; (* user id of active
                                              job assigned to the
                                              printer*)

                   DISK_ADD: integer ;
                   BLK_LENGTH: integer ;
                 end;
      var  QUE : QMODEL ;
           PRINTER : PCBLK ;
procedure ASSIGN_REQUEST (var QUE:QMODEL; var PRINTER:PCBLK);
var ACTIVE_REQUEST:REQUEST
         (*printer has just finished a request and is ready for another*)
begin
   if EMPTY (QUE) then PRINTER.BUSY := false      (*printer is idle*)
```

```
              else begin
                    (* remove front request and
                       assign it to the printer*)
                    LEAVE (QUE,ACTIVE_REQUEST) ;
                    PRINTER.ACCT_NAME := ACTIVE _REQUEST.ACCOUNT_NAME;
                    PRINTER.DISK_ADD := ACTIVE _REQUEST.DISK_ADDRESS;
                    PRINTER.BLK_LENGTH := ACTIVE_REQUEST.LENGTH;
                    PRINTER.BUSY := true;              (*printer is now
                                                       set to busy status*)
              end;
  end;
  procedure REQUEST_HANDLER (var QUE:QMODEL ; var PRINTER:PCBLK ;
                         var NEW_REQUEST:REQUEST);
  begin      (*the new request can be handled in 3 possible ways*)
     if FULL (QUE) then ISSUE_MESSAGE(NEW_REQUEST)    (*CASE 3*)
                                                 (*not accepted*)
              else begin
                    ENTER(QUE, NEW_REQUEST);    (*CASE 2*)
                                                 (*enter only*)
                   if not PRINTER.BUSY then
                           ASSIGN_REQUEST(QUE,PRINTER);(*CASE 1*)
                                                 (*assign to printer *)
              end;
  end;
```

EXERCISES

1. In an operating system on a multiuser computer system, what other peripheral devices, like the printer, would need a request handling subsystem like QMAN?

2. What three possible cases can occur when a request for the printer is received by the OS? What response does the OS make in each possible case?

3. If there were two printers of equal ability available in the computer system, how would this affect the strategy outlined for QMAN? Design an algorithm to benefit from the situation.

4. If there were two printers of very unequal ability then long files could be assigned to the faster printer and short files to the slower printer. In this case, QMAN might be organized to process two queues. Each request would be classified based on the number of blocks in the file and then placed in the appropriate queue. Develop a strategy for this new situation and describe the actions of both the request handler and the request assigning procedures. Answers may be in pseudocode.

3.5 Refinements and Extensions

This section presents the various refinements to the implementation of a queue and extensions to the basic queue structure. I will present the ideas and draw certain implications but leave the details of implementation to the reader.

3.5.1 POSTPONING A RESCUE

In subsection 3.3.3, when the queue was implemented as a linear array, we encountered the need to rescue the queue from the edge of the array and shift all the data elements of the queue to the beginning of the array. A very simple adjustment to the EMPTY function can possibly avoid or reduce the frequency of calls to SHIFT _ QUEUE.

When the queue is found in the empty state, the values of the front and rear pointers can be any value within the range of the array. For example, the queue could look like the one represented in Figure 3.13a. In this case, only three locations are left in the array before the SHIFT _ QUEUE routine will need to be called. What advantage is achieved if the EMPTY function resets the FRONT and REAR pointers to the initial conditions of an empty queue (Figure 3.13b) when the queue is found to be empty? From Figure 3.13b, you can see that the queue once again has the entire array in which to move, and the need for SHIFT _ QUEUE is less imminent. The most expensive part of the implementation may be avoided, depending on the sequence of LEAVE and ENTER calls that follow. As an exercise, rewrite the EMPTY function to perform this added maintenance operation.

3.5.2 WHEN FULL IS EMPTY AND EMPTY IS FULL

During the presentation of the second implementation approach in subsection 3.3.4, we encountered a pair of paradoxes that are due to the difficulty of distinguishing the empty state from the full state by relying on the values of the FRONT and REAR pointers. A solution based on the presence of a buffer location was presented. An alternate method exists that does not require introducing the buffer location or changing the convention concerning the FRONT pointer.

If the implementation introduced a queue counter that indicated the number of elements presently in the queue, then the empty state would be recognized when the counter equalled zero and the full state when it equalled the maximum number of

Figure 3.13

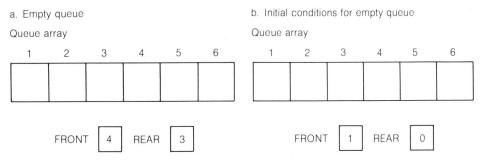

a. Empty queue

Queue array

b. Initial conditions for empty queue

Queue array

When the EMPTY function is true, reset the FRONT and REAR pointers to their initial conditions.

data elements allowed in the queue. The values of the FRONT and REAR pointers do not have to enter into the tests for the empty or full attribute.

The counter can be incorporated into the QMODEL data type that emulates the queue, just like the FRONT and REAR pointer. It will not really require an extra storage location because in exchange the buffer location is no longer needed as part of the queue. In fact, a savings in space may occur when the buffer location is not used, if the data elements are multifield records. The only added expense to the implementation is in execution time needed when the ENTER and LEAVE procedures must respectively increment and decrement the counter.

With this change, Karen the caterpillar can continue her circular crawl and never notice that the implementation is different. All the capabilities and potential flow problems are still present.

3.5.3   CATERPILLARS OUT ON A LIMB TOGETHER

If you had three Caribbean caterpillars and you wanted them to share the same limb then you would need a little more organization, a couple of new conventions, and a bit more storage space. With these new factors, you could easily have Ingrid, Carla, and Nicole, the Carib queue sisters, operating smoothly on the same limb.

The arrangement in Figure 3.14 suggests a way to organize memory so that our three sister queues have space to roam and the information to change them is readily at hand. The arrangement also opens up the possibility of one queue borrowing some space from a sister queue, should overflow be imminent.

With this declaration of a MULTI _ QMODEL data type, the respective queues can easily be accessed, even though it looks a bit awkward. To start with, the size of each queue must be set via the START pointer. The following statements achieve this (assuming an array of 70 locations).

```
QUE.START.Q1 := 10 ;
QUE.START.Q2 := 35 ;
QUE.START.Q3 := 50 ;
```

Hence Q1 has 25 locations to play with, Q2 has 15, and Q3 uses the last 21 locations. If you want to reference the data element on the front of the second queue, Q2, then this expression would be used:

```
QUE.QSTORE[QUE.FRONT.Q2]
```

Incrementing the REAR pointer of the first queue, Q1, is done by saying:

```
QUE.REAR.Q1 := QUE.REAR.Q1 + 1
```

The space reserved for each queue may be seen as either linear or circular storage areas.

For example, if Carla is known for running around in circles, then to make her area of the array behave like a circular array the following instructions would appear in the ENTER procedure:

				Queue storage area for		
Starting pointers			Front pointers	Rear pointers	Ingrid	Carla	Nicole

									....	....	....

10....... ·M..... N......MAX

Multiqueue model

START: subscript of where each storage area begins
FRONT: subscript of the front element of each queue
REAR: subscript of the rear element of each queue
QSTORE: array in which all three queues are stored

PASCAL structure of the multiqueue model

```
type
     QUEUE_SET = record
                      Q1:0..MAX;
                      Q2:0..MAX;
                      Q3:0..MAX;
                  end;
     MULTI_QMODEL = record
                      START: QUEUE_SET;
                      FRONT: QUEUE_SET;
                      REAR : QUEUE_SET;
                      QSTORE:  array[0..MAX] of DATA_ELEMENT ;

                  end;
     (* where DATA_ELEMENT is declared by user *)
     (* based on the particular application    *)
var QUE : MULTI_QMODEL ;
```

Figure 3.14

Example: Carib queues

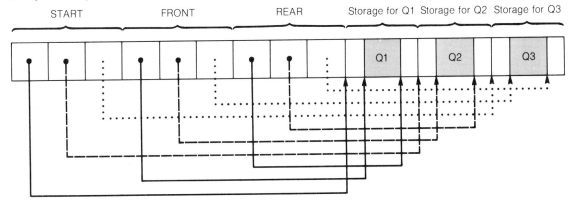

```
(* if queue 2 is about to run into the beginning of the    *)
(*   area reserved for queue 3 then wraparound to the       *)
(*   beginning of the area reserved for queue 2             *)
(*   else increment as usual                                *)
with QUE do
if REAR.Q2 + 1 = START.Q3 then
                          REAR.Q2 := START.Q2
                  else
                          REAR.Q2 := REAR.Q2 + 1;
```

As with multiple stacks, the advantage to this technique is that a FULL state can be accommodated by borrowing space from an adjacent queue, shifting the data elements and adjusting pointers. Once again you are able to accommodate the user and have the software bend to his needs rather than the other way around.

3.5.4 THE CATERPILLAR FAMILY

The queue presented in this chapter was the simplest of the species. Variations of the same idea can be useful and interesting. The basic four specimens of the queue species are presented in the list below:

Name	Description	Diagram
FIFO queue	ENTER at REAR only / LEAVE at FRONT only	QUEUE front rear
Input-restricted queue	ENTER at R only / LEAVE at F or R	QUEUE front rear
Output-restricted queue	LEAVE at F only / ENTER at F or R	QUEUE front rear
Double-ended queue (Deque)	ENTER at F or R / LEAVE at F or R	QUEUE front rear

Think of some real-life situations that exhibit the characteristics of the three new varieties. The implementation of these new specimens is similar to the FIFO queue of this chapter, except that for each new change to the structure another access procedure would be needed.

3.5.5 THE PRIORITY QUEUE

We have all been standing in a waiting line when someone enters the line ahead of us—because they have a friend holding their place or they are able to ignore the spoken or unspoken threats of those of us behind. In this case, the ordering that once defined the waiting queue is no longer valid and another system has taken its place.

The same type of queue is prevalent in computer systems, though the rules of the ordering are known to all. When jobs enter a computer system they are assigned a priority value, based on the nature of the job (memory requirements, output expected, etc.) or the person submitting the job (student, faculty, computer center personnel). The job's entry into the queue is based on its priority value and the priority values of those presently in the queue. Hence, it may go at the rear of the queue if it has no priority, at the front of the queue if it has the highest priority or somewhere in the middle.

The LEAVE operation still occurs at the front. The ENTER operation now follows a different strategy, with the ordering depending on the stated rules of the computer system.

Since the priority queue can experience changes anywhere in the ordering, the implementation must accommodate this new pattern. We will find that a general-purpose information structure, the linked list, is well suited to handle all the characteristics of the priority queue. This structure is the topic of Chapter 4.

■ "JUST FOR REFERENCE"

The implementation model may be refined by—

- resetting the FRONT and REAR pointers each time the EMPTY function is true (linear approach)
- including a queue counter to distinguish between the EMPTY and FULL states instead of using a buffer location and changing the convention for the FRONT pointer (circular approach)

The basic queue structure can be extended by—

- multiple queues sharing one common storage area so that an overflow situation can be avoided by borrowing space from an adjacent queue
- combinations of access to the endpoints, through input-restricted, output-restricted, or the double-ended (DEQUE) queues
- priority queues, which use an assigned priority value to determine at which position a new data element is to be entered into the ordering. Elements are removed through the standard position at the front of the queue

EXERCISES

1. Using an array of six locations and the linear approach described in subsection 3.3.3, develop a sequence of LEAVE and ENTER operations that shows the advantage of adopting the refinement of subsection 3.5.1—that is, resetting the pointers each time the queue is empty.

2. Write the EMPTY function to incorporate the refinement of subsection 3.5.1.

3. If the refinement of subsection 3.5.2 is included in the implementation of a queue, during which operation is the counter incremented and during which one is it decremented?

4. Revise the QMODEL declaration to include the queue counter and rewrite the procedures EMPTY, LEAVE, FULL, and ENTER to incorporate the counter.

5. When implementing multiple queues using one storage area, the LEAVE and ENTER operations must be changed to include the queue number as one of the parameters. Write the LEAVE and ENTER procedures for the MULTI _ QMODEL described in subsection 3.5.3.

TRADE-OFFS

The priority queue presents a challenge to our current implementation skills. To emulate a queue that experiences changes in various places, using the methods that we have seen, is not simple.

Assume we have a priority system with six categories. An implementation for a priority queue can enter the new data element either in the correct spot or at the rear of the queue. If the former option is taken, finding the highest priority data element is easy—it's at the front. However, the ENTER operation is more complicated and requires shifting of data elements, a potentially expensive task.

If the ENTER operation is made easy by using the second option of adding to the rear, then the LEAVE operation uses extra time to search for the highest priority data element. The entire queue must be accessed to accomplish this task.

The following diagram illustrates another creative approach. Let's use a different queue for each priority category. The ENTER operation places the data element at the rear of its corresponding queue, based on its priority. To find the data element with the highest priority, a polling process is used. Starting with the highest priority, each queue is checked for the empty state. When a nonempty state is found, the front data element is removed. Since the polling process checks a maximum of six queues, the time requirements for the ENTER and LEAVE operations are better than in the previous options. What's on the other side of the scale? The extra memory for six different queues.

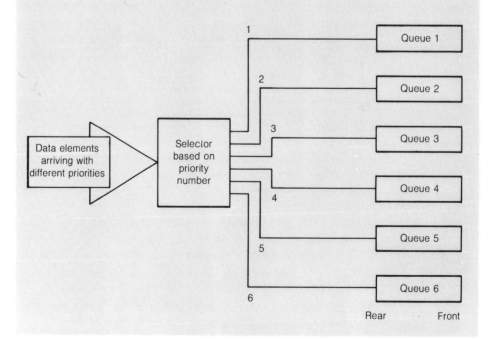

At this point in the text, therefore, we face trade-offs between (1) a slow ENTER operation and a fast LEAVE operation, (2) a fast ENTER operation and a slow LEAVE operation, or (3) a fast ENTER and LEAVE operation and extra memory for the queues.

One more option for the priority queue is waiting for us in the next chapter—linked lists.

6. Develop a strategy to use with the multiple queue implementation to handle the situation when the FULL function is true during an ENTER operation. This will involve a borrow-and-shift maintenance routine.

7. What operations would be needed to use a double-ended queue?

8. Explain how an output-restricted queue can be viewed as a combination stack and queue information structure.

THE WORKOUT ROOM

PROJECT 1: *QMAN, Rotund Robin, and the CPUs*

Though the title may sound like an electronic New Wave wonder band, it describes an important consideration for computer center directors. Jovial and rotund Robin, the local computer center director, has just purchased a dual processor computer system. It has two CPUs on its mother board and can process two jobs separately and simultaneously. To the pleasure, and sometimes dismay, of computer center directors, it has a tunable multiprocessing operating system.

The operating system has a QMAN subsystem that keeps a queue of jobs waiting for execution time on a CPU. Whenever either CPU has worked on a particular job for a predetermined time period, called a time slice, it suspends the processing of that job, returns it to the rear of the queue, and is assigned the next job at the front of the queue. This round robin system continues until a job runs to completion and leaves the QMAN subsystem. The question of selecting an appropriate time slice for each CPU is the main concern of rotund Robin at this time. In order to help him fine-tune the OS, he wants you to write the following simulation of the dual CPU scheduling system.

Starting with ten jobs in the system, each with randomly selected execution times between 30 and 120 seconds, initially assign one job to each of the CPUs and place the rest in the queue. Next, let Robin enter the time slice for each CPU.

Begin the simulation by graphically displaying the waiting queue in its initial state. Continue to update the display each time a change occurs to the waiting queue.

As each job completes execution, print the ratio of the actual execution time to the total time that the job spent in the QMAN subsystem. This will give an indication of the efficiency of the two time slices selected. When all jobs are completed, print the average of these ratios over all ten jobs.

Run the simulation program a few times using the same ten jobs with different time slices to see if a pattern is discernible.

PROJECT 2: *Cleaning Up!*

Your late Uncle Henry just left you a multilane automatic car wash outside Detroit. The layout of the car distribution system is below. As you can see, it is designed to handle the large cars that Detroit is so fond of, the medium-sized car owned by the average American father with 2.4 kids, and the rare small foreign car that is banned in Detroit.

You want to test two business policies. One is very straightforward: what happens if you let cars be serviced only in their respective wash areas? That is, they can go only into the wash area that matches their size.

Alternatively, suppose you let the medium car be serviced in either the medium or the large wash area, and the small car in the small, medium, or large area, as long as no other cars of the appropriate size are waiting. (You wouldn't want to let a small foreign car go before a waiting large-car-owning Detroitonian, now would you?)

Write two programs that simulate the car distribution system at Uncle Henry's Automatic Car Wash using the policies stated above. Using the same set of hypothetical consumers, compare the results, based on the time spent by each consumer and the total income from the consumers. You will have to set the parameters for how much time it takes to wash a small car as compared a large car, how much to charge a small car customer to have his car washed in the medium wash area, and whatever other factors you feel are important.

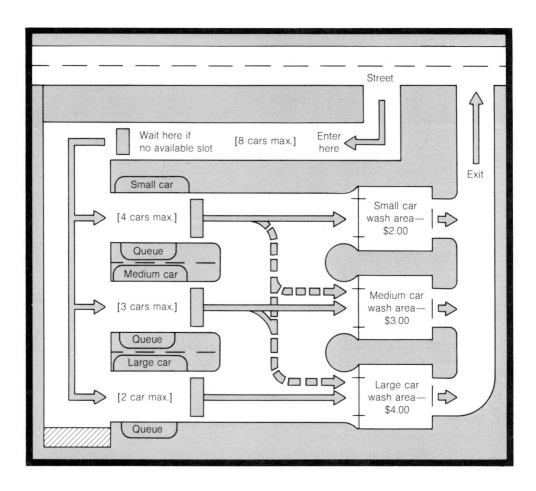

PROJECT 3: *QMAN to the Rescue*

Using the code found in the Just for Reference section as a starting point, develop a program that simulates the interaction among user requests, the operating system, the QMAN subsystem, and the line printer.

Assume eight users are randomly producing requests (these are the producers) to print files of random size (between two and 22 blocks). Assume the printer can process a file of n blocks in n time units (this is the consumer).

After each request has been satisfied, print out how many time units have elapsed since the request was made. Make whatever additional assumptions that you feel are necessary.

INSIGHTS WITH DR. DIGITAL

Scene: *Dr. Digital is walking by the school athletic field when Waldo, his student/friend, jogs towards him on the track.*

Dr. D: Hello there, Waldo! I see you're keeping fit on your feet.

Waldo (slowing down): Outdoor greetings, Dr. D. You must be finished for the day! I'm almost finished myself—only one more iteration to go on this for HEALTH = 1 to 8 do RUN loop. Can you wait on me?

Dr. D: It would be hard to wait *ON* you while you are running but I will wait for you. See ya later, looper.

[After a 440-yard pause, Dr. D and Waldo reunite.]

Waldo: Boy, am I glad that's over with. I wish I could think of eight different ways to run around that track in order to make the two miles more interesting.

Dr. D: Have you tried some unconventional approaches?

Waldo: What do you mean?

Dr. D: Well, you could imagine that the track is moving and you are leaping into the air so that it can move under you.

Waldo: Oh! Sort of a relativity of space rather than time. Or I could concentrate on feeling like an electron being pulled by the earth's magnetic poles around a nucleus at the center of the field.

Dr. D: That's the idea—flexibility in thought, the ability to flex that mental muscle of yours in different ways than you have before.

Waldo: We did something similar last week in our Information Structures class.

Dr. D: What do you mean, Waldo?

Waldo: By week's end we had come up with four different approaches to implementing the queue. That was pretty flexible, I would think.

Dr. D: Actually the four versions of the queue implementation show more the fluency of thought—the ability to come up with a group of ideas to solve the same problem. Each idea itself had its own level of flexibility, though.

Waldo: If I recall, the first version that we saw was the linear approach. That was very straightforward and I was able to anticipate how it was going to work.

Dr. D: Yes, that approach was fairly conventional, with the main area of flexibility being the SHIFT_QUEUE procedure that enabled the implementation to adjust to its own constraints.

Waldo: The day you asked the class to visualize an array as a ring of consecutive storage locations was definitely an unconventional day. I had used an array for many of my past programs and I had trouble seeing the array any other way but linear. So you would say that my concept of an array was inflexible.

Dr. D: If you don't mind, I do say so. What released the mental constraints that you placed on the concept?

Waldo: It was something that you said—"an idea is impossible if you judge it to be so, so just don't judge it."

Dr. D: Ah, yes! The greatest lock on imagination's door, humankind's incessant desire to judge objects, people, and ideas. It is most difficult to be aware when it is appropriate to use judgement and when it is better to lose it.

Waldo: I guess my prejudgment of how an array had to be was limiting my flexibility and fluency of ideas about the circular array. Once I let the judge go on vacation, the jail cell around my concept of an array dissolved and ideas began to emerge.

Dr. D: Yes, and once you could clearly "see" how an array could be circular, you were able to work with the image and see how the implementation evolved.

Waldo: Yeah, we began with our regular conventions, being real conventional, and then encountered our paradox—empty is full and vice versa. But by exercising a little flexibility, the buffer location was born.

Dr. D: By adopting the newly born buffer location and the necessary conventions, the parts of the implementation fell into place. In the minds of many, the conceptual surgeon had made a successful transplant.

Waldo: With this new idea so fresh in my mind, I was a bit amazed when Wilma suggested the use of the queue counter in place of the buffer location. I was able to visualize the necessary changes very quickly and could see, almost feel, how the new approach would work.

Dr. D: The atmosphere was rich with imagination! The judge was still on vacation. You were in a receptive and creative mental environment. With practice, as with your jogging, you can return to that environment whenever you want.

Waldo: Wow! That's a skill that sounds exciting and powerful. And you say it just takes practice?

Dr. D: Yes, at first you have to consciously send that internal judge on vacation. After you can feel the lock removed, then you can begin to concentrate on the fluent generation of flexible ideas. At times, the ideas seem to come to you rather than from you. Regardless how they arrive, greet them with receptive appreciation. Waldo, do you want a problem to practice on?

Waldo: Sure, Dr. D, lay it on me!

Dr. D: Now, you can visualize the array as either a block or a ring of contiguous locations, right?

Waldo: Yes, that's right.

Dr. D: Okay, send the judge to the crystal-clear Caribbean Sea and visualize an array as a pool of noncontiguous storage locations.

Waldo: Holy mackerel! Dr. D, what a challenge! I can't wait to dive into this one . . . but it sounds . . . pretty difficult.

Dr. D: Waldo—your judgement is still on-line. Remember—"Bon vogage, Judge!"

Waldo: Okay . . . but it may take a little magic to pull this off.

4

Linked Lists

The cycle is beginning to end.

– Dr. Digital

4.1 Setting the Stage

4.1.1 THE ORDER OF THE ARK

Once upon a time, far removed from now, a wise old man named Noah was given a job by a Personage Higher Up. A flood of changes was about to occur, and Noah was instructed to provide the link between the old world and a brave new one. Selected pairs of the earth's many creatures were to journey to the ancient seaport of Arkadelphia for a pending journey on Noah's newly built ark. Noah was to welcome each couple and house them comfortably on the ark until an obvious omen arrived, at which time the journey would begin.

A simple task it might seem, except for an additional memorandum passed down from Above. At the journey's end the ark's passengers would disembark in a pompous processional, with the animals leaving the ark in alphabetical order. This challenged Noah's imagination. Since the animals had travelled from different quarters and at different speeds, they would arrive at random times. If he tried to line them up on the ark, the arrival of the giraffe would require the gnats, lions, mastodons—in fact all the animals—to shift about on the deck. This wasn't a very practical solution. Besides, the placement of the alligators next to the ducks might be unfortunate, since the alligators would become both the predecessors and predators of the ducks.

Noah's 540 odd years had taught him a thing or two. With his spouse's aid he developed a solution to this challenging problem. When an animal arrived, Noah would determine its position in the logical alphabetical ordering, but he would choose its physical position based on the safety of the other animals and the ark. He would give the animal a card that indicated the next animal in the alphabetical order (with a strict command not to lose or eat the card and ruin his logical scheme). This provided the crucial link that would allow Noah to correctly order the animals as they arrived and to produce the processional as dictated.

But Noah had to decide which animal would lead the processional. He decided to keep a card in the back pocket of his tunic. On this card he would keep the name of

the animal then charted to lead the processional. Occasionally, he would update the card—for instance when the antelopes arrived and replaced the ants.

Later, when it was time to begin the processional, he would reach in his back pocket and call out the name of the first animal. As it left the ark, he would collect its card and call out the name of the next animal. This would continue until all the animals had merrily joined the processional. In this way, Noah could satisfy the requirements of the memorandum without depending on a physical arrangement.

With this plan in mind, Noah sat back with a stack of index cards and an indelible pen and watched the sky slowly fill with bulging, billowing clouds. While he waited for his guests, he ate an apple. What changes might he have envisioned with a modern day APPLE?

4.1.2 WHERE TO NEXT, MOM?

Your mother wants to go sightseeing in Europe. She has asked you to accompany her and to organize the itinerary for the three weeks abroad. She will give you specifications for the arrival and departure site and a list of cities that she wants to visit. You consider the offer for five nanoseconds and gladly accept.

As you begin to plan your method for organizing and keeping records for the trip, you realize that your mother will undoubtedly change her mind numerous times, so you design a system to handle the changes with minimal paper work. You begin with an information card for each city to be visited, with the format shown in Figure 4.1.

In the first phone conversation, your mother says that she has arranged a return flight into Frankfurt, Germany. She wants to visit Paris, Munich, Zurich, Geneva, and Salzburg. Using this information, you decide the following circuit would be a good route: Frankfurt to Paris to Zurich to Geneva to Salzburg to Munich to Frank-

Figure 4.1

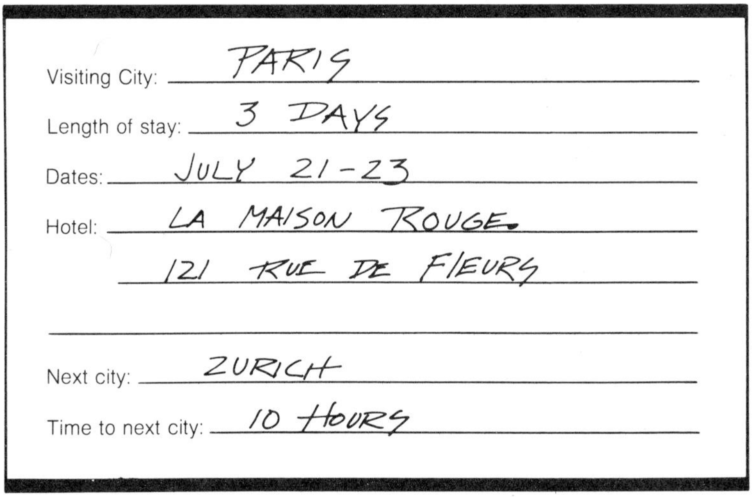

Visiting City: _PARIS_
Length of stay: _3 DAYS_
Dates: _JULY 21-23_
Hotel: _LA MAISON ROUGE._
121 RUE DE FLEURS

Next city: _ZURICH_
Time to next city: _10 HOURS_

furt. You draw a diagram to illustrate the path you plan to follow (Figure 4.2). You then fill out the six information cards and arrange them in order, with Frankfurt at the front. You are now ready to make any necessary changes.

What kinds of changes might you encounter before the trip begins? Your mother may want to stay more days in a particular city than you have allocated. If so, you will alter the Length of Stay and Dates information fields on all cards that are affected. She may decide to skip a city. In this case, you will delete a card and change the Next City field of the previous city. You will also distribute the days that had been planned for the skipped city among the other cities. If your mother adds a new city, the necessary adjustments must be made to various cards and a new card added to the file.

While you are considering these ideas, your mother calls. She has changed her mind about stopping in Zurich, and she is excited about going to Venice after seeing some photographs in a travel book.

To accommodate these two changes, you reconsider the planned route of Figure 4.2. You decide to spend the same number of days visiting Venice as Zurich and to

Figure 4.2

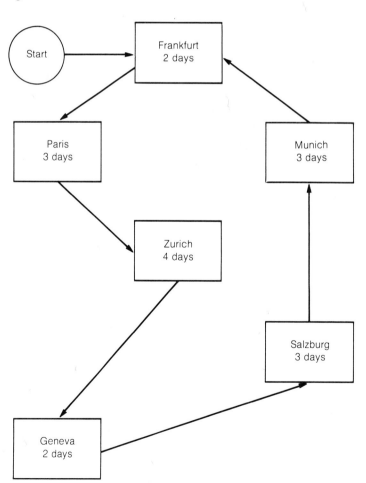

visit Venice after Geneva. To reflect your decisions in the card file you make the following changes (the diagrams reflect the effect of each card action):

1. Find Paris card and change Next City field to Geneva.

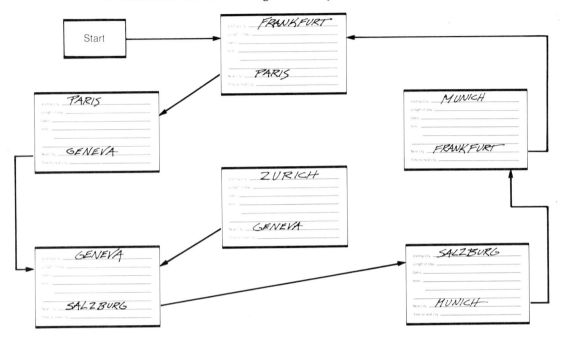

2. Remove Zurich card from the file.

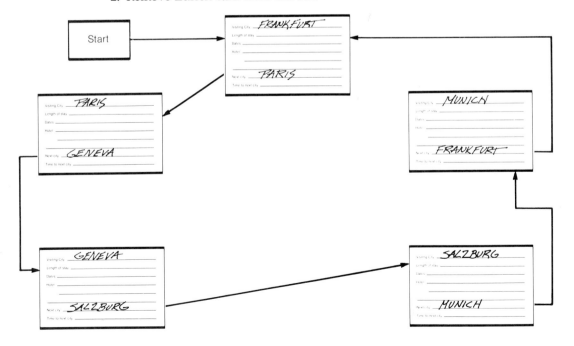

3. Find Geneva card and update the Dates field.

4. Fill out a new card for Venice.

5. Change Next City field of Geneva card to Venice.

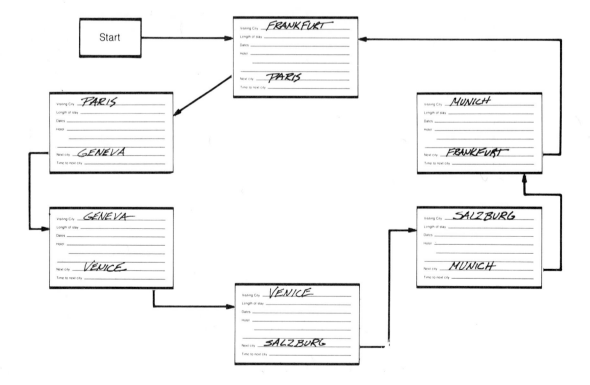

IMAGINATION CHALLENGE

A monk embarked on a mountain pathway at sunrise. After occasional stops to relax, her persistance was rewarded by a beautiful sunset as she reached a quaint cabin at the top. After a couple of days at the mountaintop refuge, she began the downward journey at sunrise. Enjoying the accelerated speed going down and various stops to appreciate the mountainside, she follows the same pathway as she had followed earlier.

Prove that she will pass a spot on the path, while descending, at precisely the same time of day as she did while ascending the mountain.

Two other changes could arise. If your mother finds a cheaper return flight from Paris, the starting point will be affected, though the order in which the cities are to be visited will not. The dates of the visits will need to reflect the change of starting point. You can easily reorder the cards to reflect this change.

If your mother found a special charter that arrived in Paris and left from Frankfurt, the circular nature of the route would be lost. But there would be no need to reorganize the route or your card file. You would simply update the last card so that it no longer pointed to the first card.

As you wait for the next ring of the phone, you begin to imagine a hand-held computer. It would keep track of this information for you and function as an English-to-French-German-Italian dictionary as well as calculate those difficult money exchange rates.

■ **"JUST FOR REFERENCE"**

Noah's Order of the Ark

Physically ordering the animals was impractical. The alternative, logical ordering, required—

- Noah to have a card
- each animal to have a card

To control processional process, Noah followed these steps—

- take card from pocket and find the first animal
- take card from animal and send down ramp
- find next animal
- repeat steps 2 and 3 until last animal joins the processional

European Circuit

Each city has its own information card. Each card indicates the next city in the circuit. Possible changes to the itinerary include—

- staying longer in one city (data update)
- cancelling a stopover (deletion)
- adding a stopover (insertion)
- choosing a new starting city (data update)
- booking arrival and departure from different cities (remove circuit attribute)

EXERCISES

1. In Noah's solution to the processional problem, two types of cards were used. Describe the function of each.

2. The last animal off the ark was a special case for Noah. Would the last animal receive a card? If so, what would it say?

3. Describe the process that Noah would use to locate the correct alphabetical position of a newly arrived animal pair.

4. Assume that three waves or quanta of animals arrived at the ark—a fast group, a medium group, and a slow group. Show the name that would appear on each animal's card after each quantum arrived.

Quantum 1:	cheetahs then
	foxes then
	antelopes
Quantum 2:	beavers then
	kangaroos then
	zebras
Quantum 3:	mastodons then
	anacondas then
	terrapins

5. Planning the European itinerary also involved cards. In this case, the cards were both physically and logically ordered. In Noah's case the cards were logically but not physically ordered. What characteristic of the itinerary planning problem enabled the cards to be physically ordered?

6. The original itinerary avoided the problem that Noah's scheme encountered—that is, whether the last animal had a card and what it would say. Why was this difficulty not encountered in the itinerary planning scheme? What suggested change would have brought this problem to the itinerary scheme?

7. List the various changes that could occur during the planning of the itinerary.

8. Assume that the first change that your mother wanted after the first planned itinerary of Figure 4.2 was to return to Zurich for two days after the visit to Salzburg to see a Swiss cheese festival. Explain the ramifications of implementing the change in your itinerary planning scheme.

9. List some other situations that might use a similar system of record keeping as the itinerary planning scheme.

4.2 Formalizing the Structure

4.2.1 PREVIEW OF TWO MODELS

The importance of this new information structure cannot be overemphasized. The linked list has come into bloom in various programming gardens. Both application programs and system programs, such as operating systems, assemblers, compilers, and data bases, provide fertile soil for the growth of the linked list. Hopefully, the models presented here will germinate some imaginative ideas of how the linked list might bear fruit for you.

In Chapter 1, I referred to some problems with shared characteristics that made them good candidates for a linked list structure. These included student's course schedules and class rosters during registration period. Both lists are ordered and can have data items added or deleted at any point in the list. The class rosters are very dynamic entities, growing and shrinking and experiencing changes at various positions. The linked list provides an imaginative solution to this type of problem.

The linked list's main feature is that **the ordering is explicitly expressed within the data elements themselves.** It is internal to the structure rather than implicitly provided by certain conventions, as with the queue and stack. Including the ordering within the elements produces two features for the linked list information structure. First, the linked list may experience changes at any point within the list without disturbing the ordering of the other elements. Second, access to elements within the list follows a different strategy than we have seen. This new strategy has both advantages and disadvantages.

Two models of the linked list will be presented in this section. Both will provide for the explicit ordering of the data elements. They differ, however, in a way that is analogous to the difference between one-way and two-way streets. Sometimes it is necessary to keep a list of numbers in ascending order and to access them only in that order. At other times the capability to access the numbers in either ascending or descending order is desired. Similarities exist between the models, but their algorithms have important differences. In Section 4.3, both models will be implemented, and a couple of helpful implementation surprises will be revealed.

Before leaving this preview, I would like to introduce Bruce, the merry magician. He will accompany us along our journey, and we will call upon his services at various times. Please accept his presence without question and appreciate his skills with amazement. Slowly his magical ways will be revealed to you, and in subsection 3.5 he will depart, leaving his magic to add to your bag of programming tricks.

4.2.2 SINGLY LINKED LINEAR LISTS

A singly linked linear list consists of an ordered collection of data elements where each data element contains one or more data fields and one link field. The link field indicates explicitly which data element of the collection is next in the logi-

Figure 4.3

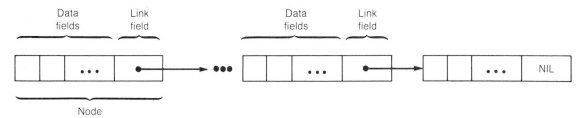

The nodes are logically ordered through the link field. The special value NIL is placed in the last node.

cal ordering of the list. The last data element of the ordering contains a special value in the link field to indicate its position. The singly linked linear list is represented graphically in Figure 4.3.

When used in linked lists, data elements are termed **nodes,** and the link field is the **pointer field.** The value of the pointer field of the last node of the list will be represented by the symbol NIL.

This model has two main characteristics. It has a single link between nodes, and the list is linear—that is, it has a first, second, and last node as a result of some ordering criterion.

The first node of the list must be identified in some way. This is done by creating a pointer field that indicates the first data element in the list. I will refer to this new component as the **external list pointer** to emphasize that it is not a part of the list, although it points to the list by pointing to the first node within it. This new component is the abstract version of the card that Noah kept in the back pocket of his tunic with the name of the first animal slated to leave the ark. Though Noah was not part of the procession, he possessed the necessary information to locate the first animal. The card held by each animal is the analog of the link field of our model. Figure 4.4 presents a graphic representation of an ascending list of integers with this new feature.

The strategy for accessing the data within a linked list is different from previous techniques you have used. **To access the data within the data fields of all the elements in the list, you would first use the external list pointer to locate the first data element, then access its data fields; then you would use its internal link**

Figure 4.4

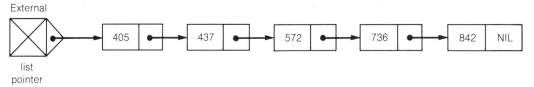

An ascending sequence of integers as a singly linked list

field to locate the second data element and access its data fields; and then you would use this element's internal link field, continuing this way until the NIL value is found. This access strategy should remind you of Noah's procession. Noah is the external list pointer, and he locates the first animal. The first animal gives Noah a card, the link field, as it leaves. Next, Noah finds the second animal, and the procession continues until all the animals have left the ark.

This feature of linked list processing can be a disadvantage because to access the data fields of a particular node, you must "pass through" all nodes before it. When the length of the list becomes quite long, the passing through process can become an expensive part of an algorithm. With this new structure we have traded the immediate access quality of stacks and queues for a sequential access feature.

In exchange, we have gained flexibility in changing the order of the list. For the stack and the queue, changes were restricted to specific locations. A linked list eliminates this restriction. Thus the linked list is most useful when frequent changes will be made to your list.

The most frequent changes involve inserting and deleting nodes from the list. These operations can be demonstrated by a sequence of diagrams. The first, insertion, is shown in Figure 4.5.

Figure 4.5

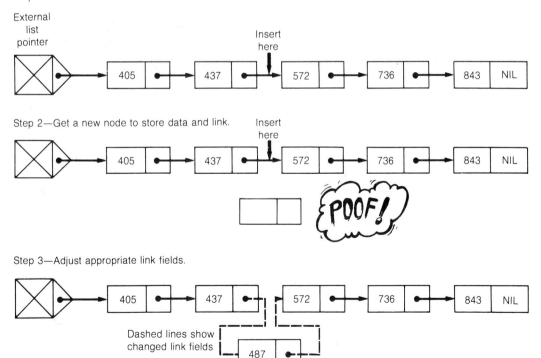

Step 1—Indicate where to insert new node.

Step 2—Get a new node to store data and link.

Step 3—Adjust appropriate link fields.

As you can see, only three fields are affected by this operation, two in the new node and the link field of the node before the spot at which the change occurs. And you saw Bruce in action for the first time. Whenever we need a new node to hold the data that are being inserted, we just ask Bruce to create one—and *poof!*, there it is. We won't concern ourselves with how he does it or where he gets the building materials yet—we'll just accept his magical talent with appreciative awe.

Deleting a node from a list is simpler than inserting one. It requires indicating which node is to be deleted and altering the link field of its predecessor node. Figure 4.6 illustrates this sequence.

Only one field is affected by the deletion operation. Once again, Bruce plays a part in this little drama. He's a thrifty sort of fellow, and he likes to recycle the building materials that he uses, so he takes back any node that we no longer need. His magic is amazing, and his concern for the computer environment is equally admirable.

Each operation contains a step that is more complicated in actual practice than the description may indicate. In the insertion operation, finding where to add the new node provides a little hurdle. In the deletion operation, the altering of the link field of the predecessor of the deleted node requires that we reach backward, while the list is set up only to reach forward. The step over this hurdle is not obvious. Think about these challenges; later we will see how to solve them.

Another type of change to a linked list is updating a data field of a particular node. This may require that you first find the location of the node and then change the value of the desired field. The process of finding a particular node is common in linked list processing, and it is helpful to think of it as an operation in its own right, even though the linked list is not changed in any way.

Figure 4.6

Step 1—Indicate node to be deleted: X marks the spot.

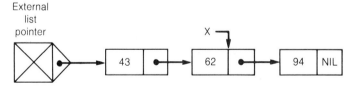

Step 2—Alter predecessor's link to skip over indicated node.

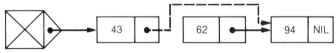

Step 3—Thanks, Bruce, for the use of the node.

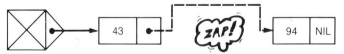

Algorithms that perform linked list processing must always test for and handle various special cases. For instance, when performed on the first node of a list, the deletion operation must change the external list pointer. Is the deletion operation on the last node handled differently? What about the insertion operation for both of these cases? As an exercise, draw the sequence of diagrams for performing the two operations, insertion and deletion, on the first and last nodes of a list.

Another special case is a singly linked linear list that has no data elements—an **empty list.** An empty linked list has the NIL value in the external list pointer. The frequent changes to a linked list mean that it is not uncommon for the list to become empty. What steps are necessary for adding a new node to an empty linked list? What should happen when an attempt is made to delete a node from the empty list? These considerations should be kept in mind when all algorithms are designed.

Singly linked linear lists can be useful in a number of areas. The class roster at registration time, for example, could be set up so that the node had two data fields, one for the student's name and the second for the student number. It would, of course, have a link field to provide the ordering among the registered students. This ordering could be either an alphabetical ordering of the names or a numerical ordering of the student ID numbers. The external list pointer would refer to the course name or number. Some snapshots of a typical class roster appear in Figure 4.7. We shall see more of this example later.

An optional feature may be added to the singly linked linear list model. The collection of data elements may have the extra attribute that all nodes are linked to exactly one other node. This would give the linked list a circular character. The itinerary of the European trip has this characteristic—a circular list of cities to be visited. This circular attribute is useful not only with a list that naturally has circular characteris-

Figure 4.7

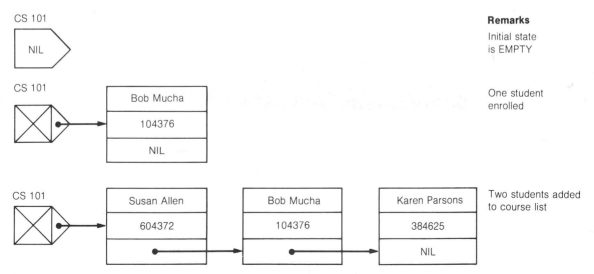

Nodes contain student's name and number and the link to the next student in alphabetical order.

tics. It is sometimes beneficial to make a strictly linear list—one having a definite first and last element—into a circular list. Examples will be presented shortly, but don't stop your imagination from wandering and wondering.

Two views can be taken when visualizing a singly linked list with the circular attribute. They are presented in Figure 4.8. The logical relationship among the data elements is the same for both orientations. The choice of the representation is more a matter of preference than of utility. But the two representations have different implications.

The upper representation suggests that there is an ordering among the data elements, but that none of the data elements can really be designated as the first. This is similar to the circular path the blood takes through the veins, arteries, and organs of the body. The other representation suggests that a linear ordering is present and that the last node is connected to the first node for some reason. This is reminiscent of the itinerary of the trip through Europe, where the first city visited is revisited for the return flight.

Once you choose to use the circular attribute, you are led directly to another choice that concerns the significance of the external list pointer. There are four alternatives, two for each of the two viewpoints noted above. These are illustrated in Figure 4.9.

When the list does not inherently have a first item, any data element may be chosen as the "first" node in the circular list. This approach was used in Figure 4.9a for the flow of blood through the body. The selection of the lungs as the starting point is no more natural than, for example, the left heart. The circuit as defined shows that the blood flows from the lungs to the left heart, to the intestines, then the liver, and next to the right heart and back to the lungs.

Another alternative, shown in Figure 4.9b, is to allow the external list pointer to

Figure 4.8

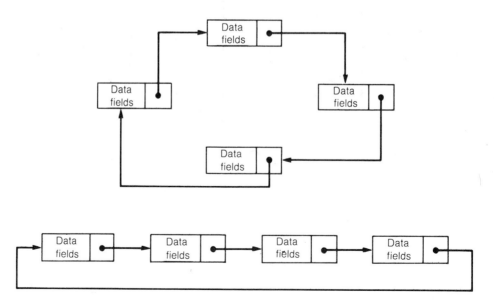

Figure 4.9

a. Blood flow through the body—arbitrary choice

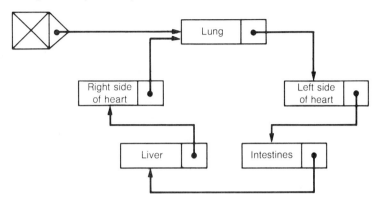

b. Blood flow through the body—pointer floats around

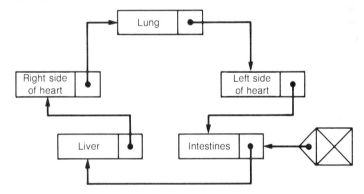

c. Cities in a round-trip excursion—pointer to the first node

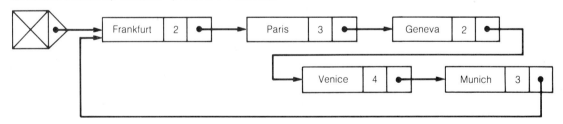

d. Job numbers in a priority queue—pointer to the last node

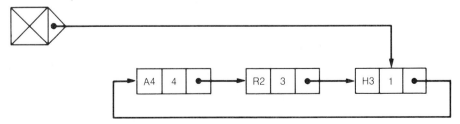

rotate around the circular list—that is, to assume that it points to the last node processed.

If the list is viewed as a linear list using the circular attribute as a convention, the external list pointer can point to the first data element in the linear ordering, as in Figure 4.9c. The final alternative is shown in Figure 4.9d, where the external list pointer is assumed to point to the last node in the ordering and to use the link field of this node to reach the first data element. This provides a more flexible approach, especially if changes occur primarily at the ends of the ordered list, such as with a queue. (This idea will be covered in more detail in subsection 4.4.)

The singly linked circular list shares certain characteristics with the singly linked linear list. Of course, the singly linked attribute provides both types with the ability to go forward through the list by way of the link field. Both lists can be empty, as indicated by an external list pointer that has NIL as a value. The access strategy for both models is similar, starting at the external list pointer and progressing through the internal link field of each node until the entire list is transversed.

The operations performed on the singly linked circular list are the same as for singly linked linear lists: insertion, deletion, finding nodes, and updating them. The algorithms for performing these operations are the same.

The special cases that must be considered are also the same for both lists. All the special cases involve changing the external list pointer. As an exercise, list the two special cases that can occur during an insertion and two that can occur during a deletion operation.

The main difference between the two models is the method of determining when the entire list has been traversed. Because the circular list does not contain the NIL value in any link field, the criterion used to indicate the completion of one circuit in linear lists cannot be used. Instead, the criterion will depend on the node at which the processing starts and the significance of the external list pointer. This topic will be illustrated more fully in subsection 4.3.2.

The main advantage of the circular attribute is the ability to start at any node of the linked list and process the entire list from that node. The algorithm is quite simple. You process the starting node, use its link field to reach the next node, process that node, use its link field to reach the next node, and continue in this fashion until the starting node is reached again.

The singly linked list thus provides an information structure that handles ordered lists of data that experience frequent changes to the ordering. **The singly linked list with its internal link field allows the logical ordering to be independent of the physical ordering.** Changes affect a minimum number of other data elements. Additionally, the circular attribute introduces extra flexibility in processing all the data elements in the list, regardless of the starting point.

You are probably looking forward to seeing how the implementation provides for the logical relationship among data elements to exist independently of the physical ordering of the array of records. With Bruce at our side, we have no worries now, and as your ImQ increases, success in this matter is definitely ahead.

Before we move to the implementation of the singly linked linear list, let's look at another version of the linked list information structure. This version, the doubly linked linear list, is analogous to a two-way street, on which you may travel both forward and backward. So—forward to the next section!

4.2.3 DOUBLY LINKED LINEAR LISTS

An ordered collection of data elements containing one or more data fields and two link fields is called a doubly linked list. One link field is used to indicate the next data element within the ordered list; the other is used to indicate the previous data element.

The link field to the next node is the NEXT pointer; the link field to the previous node is the PRIOR pointer. When the list is being processed by the NEXT pointer, the traversal is forward through the list; a traversal using the PRIOR pointer is a backward traversal.

Figure 4.10 is a graphic representation of a doubly linked linear list with four nodes, each of which has three data fields. The list represents an inventory list of cases of fruit juice, with the data fields being the juice type, the number of cases in stock, and the price per case.

Since the ordered list can be traversed in either a forward or backward direction, it will be useful to have two external pointers. One—the FORWARD pointer—will designate the first node encountered when the traversal proceeds in the forward direction; the other—the BACKWARD pointer—will indicate the first node encountered during a backward traversal.

Remember there is only one list and only one ordering of the list. The doubly linked linear list provides the ability to process the list in two directions and to move in either direction from a given node. The latter ability contributes to the simplification of algorithms for linked list operations.

When inserting and deleting a node, more link fields will be adjusted than in a

Figure 4.10

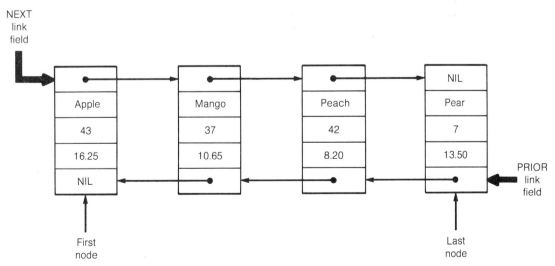

Nodes contain a NEXT link field, the fruit juice name, the number of cases in stock, the price per case, and a PRIOR link field. The nodes are alphabetically ordered by fruit juice name.

Figure 4.11

DIAGRAM	REMARKS

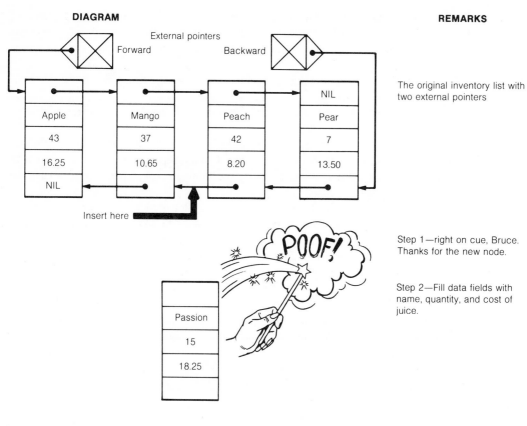

The original inventory list with two external pointers

Step 1—right on cue, Bruce. Thanks for the new node.

Step 2—Fill data fields with name, quantity, and cost of juice.

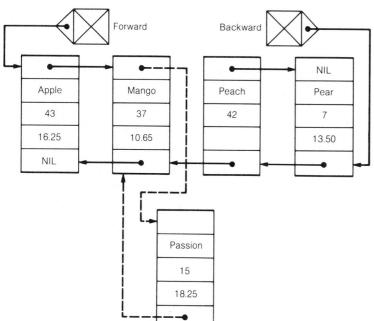

Step 3—Connect passion fruit node to mango node. Affected link fields: NEXT pointer of mango node; PRIOR pointer of passion fruit node.

Figure 4.11, continued

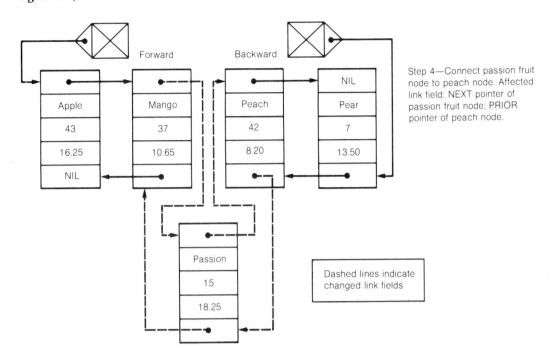

Step 4—Connect passion fruit node to peach node. Affected link field: NEXT pointer of passion fruit node; PRIOR pointer of peach node.

Dashed lines indicate changed link fields

singly linked list. This is illustrated in Figure 4.11, where the fruit juice inventory is altered to include the new shipment of 15 cases of passion fruit juice from Kenya at $18.25 per case.

As you can see, having twice as many link fields per node produced twice as many changed link fields during the insertion process as compared to the singly linked linear list. This does not particularly increase the complexity of the problem, since the alterations are analogous to those presented in subsection 4.2.2. But it does increase the amount of effort needed to complete the operation. When we arrive at the implementation phase, this added effort will translate into a small increase in execution time.

As an exercise, draw a sequence of diagrams for the deletion algorithm.

The special cases that can arise with a doubly linked list are also increased in number but not in complexity. Since we now have two external pointers that can be altered, insertions and deletions at either the beginning or the end of the list will require special attention. As another exercise, list the conditions that require special attention and include what special action must be performed in each case. An empty doubly linked list is also possible, and the presence of the NIL value in both external list pointers is the defining condition.

Since the doubly linked list requires a little extra effort in the insertion and deletion operations, you may be wondering how you can realize its cost-saving benefits. Obviously, an occasional need to process a linked list in reverse order would be served more efficiently by a doubly linked list—for example, if you sometimes must use a descending sequence of inventory part numbers rather than the normal ascending sequence.

The other main benefit of doubly linked lists is associated with the ability to access both the next and prior node from any given node. This is helpful in both the insertion and deletion operation. Figure 4.12 shows two linked lists of Dow Jones stocks, a singly linked list and doubly linked list. The data fields are the stock name, the high and low stock quote for the reporting period, today's change in price, and the number of reporting periods in which the stock has been in the top ten stocks. The stocks are descendingly ordered by the Change in Price field. Therefore, the external pointer for the singly linked list and the FORWARD pointer for the doubly linked list point to the stock that has experienced the greatest amount of positive change in today's trading.

Figure 4.12

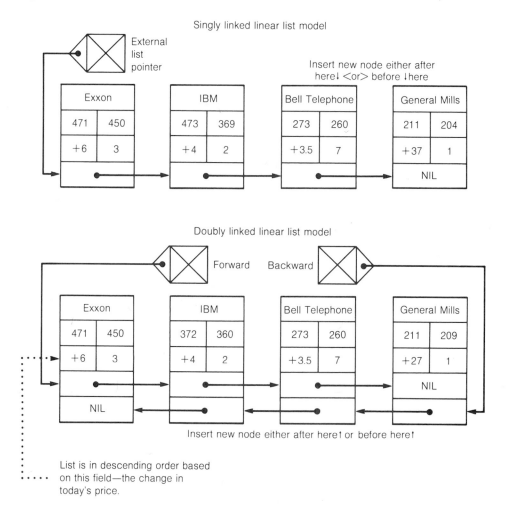

If a new stock is to be entered into the list in its proper sequence, the way in which its proper position in the list is designated is very important. If a stock named Mr. Juicy has increased its price quote by +3.0 points, the new node can be inserted either *after* Bell Telephone or *before* General Mills. For a singly linked list, the designation "after Bell Telephone" can easily be interpreted and the change easily implemented. But the designation "before General Mills" is insufficient by itself to accomplish the desired insertion operation, since the link field to be altered cannot be directly accessed from this spot.

With the doubly linked list, however, either designation is sufficient, since from either of the designated nodes, Bell Telephone or General Mills, it is possible to reach either the previous node or the next node in the sequence. Therefore, all link fields that need to be altered can be altered.

The same characteristic of doubly linked lists aids the deletion process, since the designation of which node is to be deleted can be given as "delete a given node," "delete the node after a given node," or "delete the node before a given node." All three of the requests require algorithms of equal complexity, since all affected link fields are easily accessed from the node given in the designation.

When an application requires frequent access and updates to a dynamically changing list, such as the Dow Jones daily top (or bottom) ten stocks, the doubly linked attribute becomes the best choice for the list design.

In some instances, the circular attribute, introduced in the previous section, can also be used with the doubly linked list information structure. To do this, the first node is linked to the last node through the PRIOR pointer, and the last node is linked to the first node through the NEXT pointer. In this way, both forward and backward traversal are circular and a criterion must be established to determine when a traversal of all nodes in the list is completed. The exact statement of the criterion will depend on the conventions set during implementation.

Adopting the circular attribute has one immediate effect. The doubly linked circular list now needs only one external list pointer. Since it is easy to move from the first node to the last node and vice versa (they are only one link apart), you need to specify only one or the other.

As before, the external list pointer can point to a naturally occurring first data element, a naturally occurring last data element, or an arbitrarily selected data element. Alternatively, it can float around the circular list.

When you are designing algorithms that process doubly linked circular lists, the same group of special cases must be considered. Any situation that requires the external list pointer to be changed must be handled in an atypical manner. As an exercise, for the doubly linked circular list, compose a list of situations that require that the external list pointer be updated. For each situation, indicate what special action must be taken.

You may be curious to know where this flexible information structure is found in everyday life. One example is quite close to home—in fact, it resides within each of us. The human body contains various cycles such as the blood flow cycle referred to in subsection 4.2.2. Another body cycle is the Krebs energy cycle, a sequence of chemical reactions, each of which is reversible. This cycle stores and releases energy whenever our bodies need to do so. If a medical university wished to provide some computerized tutorial programs, the Krebs cycle, with its reversible and cyclic attributes, would be an excellent candidate for the doubly linked circular list information structure. A diagram of the Krebs energy cycle is presented in Figure 4.13.

The reversible nature of the chemical reactions implies the use of the doubly linked attribute in an information structure to simulate the relationships in the Krebs energy cycle. Because it is a natural body cycle, the circular attribute is an appropriate addition to the information structure model. Therefore, from any point in the cycle, you can determine the next or prior chemical in either the anabolic or the catabolic

Figure 4.13

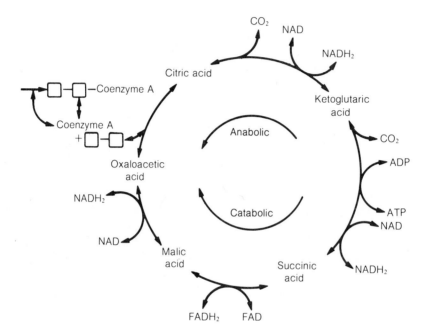

 IMAGINATION CHALLENGE

Imagine a green cube sitting on a table.

With your mind, slice the cube *vertically* into three equal parts. Rotate the three slices 90 degrees and with the same mental tool, cut the three parts vertically to form nine columns. Lay the cube of nine columns on its side so that the previous cuts are horizontal. Once again, vertically cut the cube with the mental tool, leaving a cube consisting of 27 mini-cubes.

By surveying the image with your mind's eye—How many of the mini-cubes are green on 3 sides, on 2 sides, on 1 side on no sides?

direction. The doubly linked circular list indeed provides a flexible model to use in a tutorial program on the Krebs energy cycle.

Now that you have seen both the singly linked and the doubly linked models of the linked list, it is time to shed our model-building clothes and to don the hard hat of the implementor.

■ "JUST FOR REFERENCE"

In the linked list model—

- the ordering is explicitly expressed within the structure through link fields
- frequent change is possible anywhere in the list, with little effect on the other data elements

Singly Linked Model

A singly linked list is an ordered collection of nodes, each containing one link field and one or more data fields.
An external list pointer is used to indicate the first node.
Operations include—

- inserting a new node
- deleting an existing node
- updating a data field of a node
- locating a node
- traversing all nodes in the list

Steps in the access strategy are—

- start at the node pointed to by the external list pointer and then process that node
- move to the next node via the link field
- repeat until NIL is found.

Special cases occur whenever the external list pointer must be changed—

- inserting a node in an empty list
- deleting the only node in a list
- inserting a node before the first node
- deleting the first node

Circular attribute—when the last node points to the first node—has several special characteristics—

- significance of the external list pointer is important
- processing can begin at any node and easily traverse the entire list
- the test for completion of a traversal is more complicated

Doubly Linked Model

A doubly linked list is an ordered collection of nodes, each containing two link fields and one or more data fields.
Two external list pointers may be used, one for each traversal direction of the ordering. The same operations exist as for the singly linked list.
Steps in the access strategy are—

- select a direction, either forward or backward
- use the appropriate external list pointer to locate the first node and then process that node
- use either the PRIOR or NEXT link field to locate the next node
- repeat until the NIL value is found

Special cases occur whenever either external list pointer is changed.
Circular attribute occurs when the last node points to the first node and the first points to the last; implications are similar to singly linked list.

EXERCISES

1. What is the important feature of a linked list regarding the method of ordering the data elements?
2. Describe three situations that have characteristics that make them good candidates for the linked list information structure.
3. Describe how each situation presented in Section 4.1 fits the model of a linked list structure. Associate the terms *nodes, pointer field,* and *external list pointer* with their counterparts in the situation. For example, the card in Noah's back pocket is the external list pointer of the animal linked list.
4. What are the two main characteristics of the singly linked linear list model?
5. For the singly linked linear list model, where is the special value NIL found?
6. Describe the access strategy for a singly linked linear list. Use Figure 4.4 as a sample.
7. Have all the possible special cases been accounted for in the access strategy for a singly linked linear list?
8. What are the five main operations performed on a singly linked linear list?
9. Draw the sequence of diagrams illustrating the two operations, insertion and deletion, on the first and last node of a singly linked linear list.
10. Describe what should happen when the two operations of insertion and deletion are performed on an empty singly linked list.
11. What two tasks does Bruce the magician perform for us?
12. What defines a singly linked list with the circular attribute?

13. What are the possible interpretations for the external list pointer for a singly linked list with the circular attribute?

14. List the two special cases that can occur during an insertion operation and the two that can occur during a deletion operation on a singly linked list with the circular attribute.

15. Using the singly linked list with circular attribute in Figure 4.9a, describe the algorithm for traversing the entire list, starting at the node for Geneva.

16. Describe the algorithm for circularly traversing a singly linked list without the circular attribute, starting at a node in the middle of the linked list.

17. What two advantages are achieved by using a doubly linked list instead of a singly linked list?

18. Using the doubly linked list in Figure 4.10, describe the steps for performing the following deletion operations:

   a. deleting the node after the PEACH node

   b. deleting the node before the PEACH node

   c. deleting the PEACH node itself

19. What condition is common to all special cases that occur with a doubly linked list?

20. List the special cases that can occur during the operations on a doubly linked list.

21. How does the access strategy for a singly linked list differ from that for a doubly linked list?

22. What new links are needed to give a doubly linked list the circular attribute?

23. Why does a doubly linked list with the circular attribute only need one external list pointer?

24. Draw a diagram of the Krebs energy cycle as a doubly linked list with the circular attribute.

4.3   Implementing the Structure

4.3.1   PREVIEW OF THE IMPLEMENTATION USING SPECIAL PASCAL FEATURES

Implementation of the linked list information structure is a challenge. The nature of the linked list is to have nodes deleted and inserted in an explicitly ordered collection of nodes. Conceptually, the nodes are individual units that are connected together (by the link field) to form the list structure. It is this individual but connectable character of nodes that presents the implementation challenge.

Simple PASCAL identifiers are individual units, but they cannot be connected to other PASCAL identifiers. Our steady ally, the array of records, consists of anything but individual units. In fact, we took advantage of the physically contiguous nature of the records during the implementation of the two previous linear structures—the stack and the queue. We must either search for a new storage entity or a new way of looking at the one that we have.

In this section, a new storage construct, special to PASCAL, is presented—dynamic allocation using pointer variables. In subsection 4.3.2, the singly linked list model will be implemented using this powerful PASCAL feature.

Since not all languages provide this capability, subsection 4.3.3 will present a new way of looking at and processing the array structure to implement a linked list. Subsection 4.3.4 will give the details of using this method to implement the doubly linked list. Bruce, the merry magician, will be back to help us manage this new perspective on arrays.

Now let's turn our attention to implementing linked lists using PASCAL's dynamic memory management system.

The first step in the implementation process is to decide on storage conventions for the data elements. Where will the linked list live and how are its nodes emulated?

The first question is answered automatically by the PASCAL system. The pool of available nodes will be simulated by the creation of a record structure where the allocation of memory for the record is provided by the special procedure *new*. Let's look at an example.

Assume we are using a linked list with a specific node structure—two data fields and a link field. To set the stage for the implementation, two type declarations are necessary. These are given below in the standard syntax for record structures and our new identifier construct—the pointer variable.

```
type NODEPTR =  ^NODE;        (* Pointer variable type *)
     NODE    =  record
                   DATA1 : real;
                   DATA2 : integer;
                   LINK : NODEPTR
                end;
```

The type declarations are somewhat circular: each is defined in terms of the other. The analogy that exists between the diagram of the linked list and the types declared is that the record structure is the node structure. It contains three fields—two data fields and one pointer field. The type NODEPTR is like the arrows between the nodes. The PASCAL compiler needs to know that NODEPTR is a pointer type (indicated by the ^ symbol) and what type of entity it points to (indicated by the NODE type). Hence the circular aspect of the typing.

If we have more than one node structure then we would have more than one pointer type declared. Also, we would declare one record structure for each distinct node structure.

Next, we set up the storage for all external pointers and auxiliary pointer variables we will need. This is accomplished by:

```
var EX_PTR1, EX_PTR2, PTR, HERE : NODEPTR;
```

where EX_PTR1 and EX_PTR2 are used as external pointers to the beginning of two distinct linked lists with the same node structure, and PTR and HERE are used respectively in walking through the list and indicating the node to operate upon. This instruction sets aside some memory for the four pointer variables. No initial values are stored there; this will be done during the execution of the program.

What values will be stored in these variables? Physical memory addresses—these variables will indicate where in memory the record structure for a node is stored. Knowing this permits the data fields and especially the link field to be accessed. The link field is represented by a pointer variable, so it also will contain a physical memory address—the address of the next record structure. In this way, the records are individual units that can be connected together to simulate the linked list structure.

How do you get a handle on one of these individual records? For instance, how do we set up a linked list with two elements?

This process occurs during the execution of the program and uses the dynamic memory management system of PASCAL. It is important to note that the previous two steps—type declaration and pointer variable allocation—were performed during compilation. Once the program begins, the dynamic nature of this method takes over.

The following procedure sets up a list with one node, using the type declarations from above.

```
procedure LIST_BUILD (var EXPTR : NODEPTR);
var PTR : NODEPTR;
begin
new (PTR);  (*allocate space for one record of type NODE*)
PTR^.DATA1 := 1.0; (*Fill data fields*)
PTR^.DATA2 := 0;
PTR^.LINK := nil;  (*set link field to NIL*)
EXPTR := PTR       (*set external pointer to first node*)
end;
```

Notice the following features of the procedure:

1. The special PASCAL procedure *new* allocates memory space to a record of type NODE and assigns the start address of the record to the pointer variable PTR. This is the equivalent of Bruce's POOF operation.
2. Access to a record is through the pointer variable that contains its address, using the expression PTR^.
3. Access to a field in a record is through the specification PTR^.DATA1.
4. The PASCAL keyword *nil* is used to indicate the end of the linked list.
5. The address stored in one pointer variable can be assigned to another pointer variable.

Therefore, in a linked list application, each time a node is needed, the *new* procedure provides the means to dip into the large pool of available memory locations and procure a block of memory that matches the node structure. The main advantage is that a considerable amount of memory is available for the linked list application. For instance, with a 512K work space and a 15K compiled image of the program, 497K of memory allows for a tremendously long linked list. If a node requires 256 bytes of memory, then 497K provides for a linked list with about 1988 nodes. Oh, what a task to find the last one!

Another built-in PASCAL procedure is important to linked list processing. When a node is being removed from a list and is no longer needed, the storage locations can be recycled—made available for use at a later execution time. The PASCAL procedure *dispose* is designed for this purpose. It has one argument, a pointer variable that contains the address of the record to be returned to the available memory space. (Bruce, being a comics fan, likes to call this operation ZAP.) It is important to note that some dialects of PASCAL implement this function as I have described it, while others ignore the ecological activity and either do not reclaim used record space or only reclaim the last records allocated. Early versions of Turbo PASCAL opt for the latter approach. It is important for you to investigate the method used to manage the dynamic allocation system for the version of PASCAL that you plan to use.

In summary, to implement a linked list using PASCAL, two phases of planning are necessary. First, the node structure is emulated with a record structure, through a type declaration. Pointer variables are allocated memory space through a *var* statement. Second, memory space for a new node is procured during execution through the built-in PASCAL procedure that manages this activity, *new*. The space may be reclaimed by another built-in procedure, *dispose*. These two operations are embedded in an application program that processes a linked list.

The next section will demonstrate how the three entities—application program, linked list processing procedures, and PASCAL memory management procedures—work together as an efficient team.

4.3.2 IMPLEMENTING THE SINGLY LINKED LINEAR LIST

To implement a singly linked linear list, we need an external list pointer (a pointer variable will serve the purpose), a supply of records (PASCAL's dynamic allocation system will supply these), and a set of conventions (which will be presented shortly).

In subsection 4.2.2, the list of students enrolled in a course during registration was identified as an application for this type of list. For this section, I will use this example, expanding the problem in one way and simplifying it in another. Previously, the nodes of the list contained two data fields, the student's name and identification number. In this section, the node will contain only the student number and the link field. To expand the usefulness of the procedures, the algorithms will be designed to handle an arbitrary linked list. Therefore a different linked list can exist for each course, with the external list pointer as the course number.

Let's start by looking at the conventions that can be established to aid our task. First, the record structure must be planned. The structure of the student record is simple since it consists of two fields—student number and link field. Let us assume that the student number is an integer between 1 and 50,000 and that the link field is a PASCAL pointer variable. Therefore, the following declarations handle phase one of the implementation:

```
type POINTER = ^NODES;
     STUDENT_RANGE = 1..50000;
     NODES= record
              STUDENT: STUDENT_RANGE  ; (* Student number *)
              LINK: POINTER         (* Link to next student *)
            end;
var  COURSE,NEW_NODE : POINTER;
     CS101 , M101 , E101 : POINTER;
```

The second convention is that the logical ordering of the nodes will be an ascending sequence of student numbers. A sample of three course rosters is presented in Figure 4.14.

Now we can develop some algorithms for processing a course list. The first procedure illustrates the important technique of traversing a list and processing each node. For this purpose, the procedure is designed to print a class roster of all students presently enrolled in a course. We will assume that a procedure exists that accepts a student number as an input argument and prints the relevant information about that student on the class roster. Since it is very important for you to understand clearly how the movement from one node to the next is implemented, I suggest that you work through the procedure by using any one of the three courses depicted in the previous figure. Our first procedure using the linked list information structure is found below.

```
procedure ROSTER (COURSE : POINTER);
var PTR : POINTER:                   (* External pointer to step
                                        from node to node *)
```

Figure 4.14

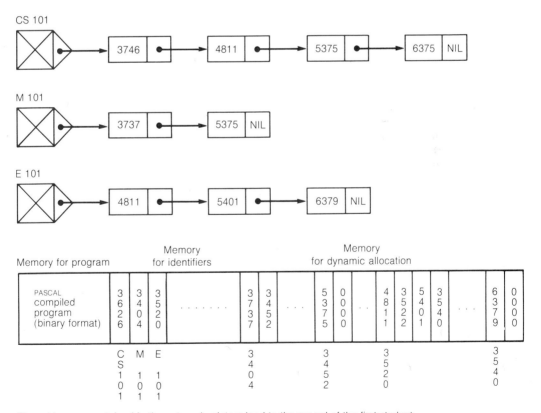

The addresses contained in the external pointers lead to the record of the first student.

```
      ST_NUMBER : STUDENT_RANGE;
begin
if COURSE <> nil then          (* Check for non-empty class list *)
        begin
        PTR := COURSE;   (* Initialize pointer to first node
                                              in course list *)
        while PTR <> nil do
            begin
              ST_NUMBER := PTR ^ .STUDENT; (*Retrieve field
                                         from node *)
              PRINTINFO (ST_NUMBER);
                            (* IMPORTANT *)
              PTR := PTR ^ .LINK          (* Step to next node *)
            end  (* while *)
        end
  end ; (* PROCEDURE *)
```

The algorithm is very easy to state. After checking for the empty list, the procedure processes each node in its logical sequence. The key step to this procedure and to many of the list processing procedures is the statement:

```
PTR := PTR ^ .LINK
```

The address in a pointer variable, PTR, is used to access a field that contains an address. The latter address replaces the first address in the original pointer variable. This is equivalent to graphically changing the arrow of a pointer to point to the next node in the linked list.

This statement demonstrates the essence of singly linked lists. The logical ordering is explicitly contained in the node, and the contiguous nature of the storage area is transcended. To reach the next storage location you do not use

```
P : = P + 1
```

as you have in the past. Please take some time to reflect on the importance and uniqueness of this concept and how it works.

To reinforce the method of traversing a linked list, let's develop a boolean function to determine whether a particular student is enrolled in a given course. The algorithm traverses the list until the student's number is found or the end of the list is encountered. Notice how the special case of an empty list is handled quite easily and subtly. The student number and the course pointer variable are the input arguments.

```
function CHECK (ASTUDENT: STUDENT_RANGE; COURSE : POINTER): boolean;
var PTR : POINTER;
begin
PTR := COURSE;          (* Initialize pointer to first node,*)
                        (*        if list is empty .        *)
CHECK := false;         (* pointer will have nil value *)
while (PTR <> nil) and not (CHECK) do
      if ASTUDENT <> PTR ^ .STUDENT then
                                (* No match - step to next node *)
                                      PTR : = PTR ^ .LINK
                                  else
                                (* Matching student number *)
                                      CHECK := true;
end; (*Function CHECK*)
```

Once again, access to the information within a node is through the pointer variable and movement through the list is by way of the link field. Maybe you can begin to ask yourself what could be simpler.

Now let us look at two procedures that perform a change to the order of the singly linked list. One will add a new node after a specified node; the other will locate a node to be deleted, then delete that node from the list.

To insert a node into a singly linked linear list, we must determine where to insert it and indicate where the change is to occur. The method of determining the location will be postponed; it is similar to the function CHECK. We will concentrate instead on specifying the place for an insertion to occur and implementing the change.

There are two possible ways to specify where a change is to occur:

1. Inserting the node after the node designated by a pointer variable;
2. Inserting the node before the node designated by a pointer variable.

For singly linked lists, of course, inserting the new node before the designated node is inappropriate. Therefore, for the insertion operation on a singly linked list, it is best to request that a new node be inserted *after* a designated node. This will make the insertion procedure straightforward, though it will cause a minor difficulty for the procedure to determine the proper location for the insertion in the ordered list. This difficulty and its solution will be the main topic of another procedure.

The following diagram, which correlates the PASCAL statements to a changing graphic representation of a typical singly linked linear list, will clarify the procedure. Three distinct cases must be accommodated:

1. The empty list.
2. The insertion of a new node at the front of a nonempty list.
3. The insertion of a new node at a location somewhere after the beginning of the list.

The procedure has three arguments: the external list pointer for the course, a pointer variable that points to the node after which a new node is to be inserted, and the student's identification number. The code is as follows:

```
procedure INSERT (var COURSE:POINTER;
                      HERE:POINTER;
                      DATA : STUDENT_RANGE );
var NEW_NODE : POINTER;              (* Pointer for a new node *)
begin
                          (* Procure a new node from available pool *)
new (NEW_NODE);
with NEW_NODE ^ do begin
   STUDENT := DATA;   (* Fill data field of new node *)
   (* FIRST CASE - EMPTY LIST)
   if COURSE = nil then
               begin                 (* New node is list *)
               LINK := nil;
                       (* External points to new node*)
               COURSE := NEW_NODE
               end
```

```
(* SECOND CASE - INSERT AT FRONT *)
(* Special convention used here *)
else if HERE = nil then
        begin                    (* New points to first *)
        LINK := COURSE;
                                 (* New becomes first *)
        COURSE := NEW_NODE
        end
else
(* THIRD CASE - INSERT IN MIDDLE *)
   begin                         (* Shift pointer of prior node *)
   LINK := HERE ^ .LINK;
                    (* Prior node points to new node *)
   HERE ^ .LINK := NEW_NODE
   end
end (* with NEW_NODE ^ *)
end; (* PROCEDURE *)
```

NEW_NODE

POOF!

NEW_NODE
37415

Case 1

COURSE   NIL

NEW_NODE
37415

COURSE   ⊠ •------→ NEW_NODE
                     37415   NIL

Case 2

NEW_NODE
37415

COURSE   ⊠ •------→ 42653 •----→ etc.

COURSE   ⊠ •------→ NEW_NODE
                     37415 •
                            ↓
                     42653 •----→ etc.

Continued

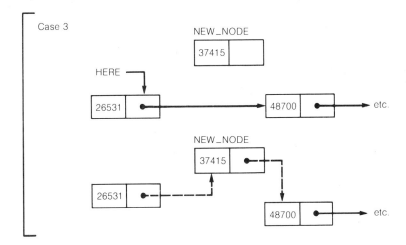

This procedure illustrates the way in which the links can be altered and the external list pointer updated if necessary. Be sure that you understand how each PASCAL statement accomplishes its ministep in the overall process.

One convention in the procedure was not previously stated. In the second case, it is necessary to specify a node that does not exist—since to insert "before the first node" and "after the designated node" are contradictory expressions. So I adopted the convention that a *nil* value for the designator HERE implies that the insertion should occur after the external list pointer (i.e., before the first node).

For the operation of deletion, I will point out a limitation of singly linked lists. If we search through a linked list with the intention of finding and deleting a node with a specific value, we will pass the node that must experience a change to its link field before encountering the desired node. Figure 4.15 illustrates the situation.

When traversing the linked list and checking for a match on the data field, the pointer variable PTR will end up pointing to the node to be deleted. But we need access to the node before this node. How can this be accomplished while we are using a linked list that possesses foresight but not hindsight?

Figure 4.15

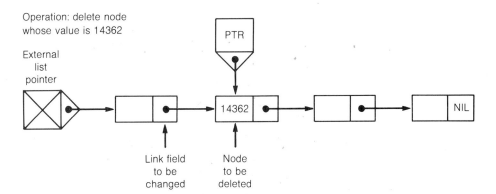

The solution is demonstrated in the next procedure. The idea is to use a second pointer variable that follows directly behind the first pointer. When the first pointer is pointing at the node to be deleted, the other pointer, which I shall call a **shadow pointer,** will point to the node that must be altered. Simple imagination in action! Care will need to be taken for special cases, but this will only add to the challenge.

The procedure will contain two sections. The first looks for a node with a particular student number. A shadow pointer will indicate the node to be changed and a boolean flag will indicate when a match has been made. The second section of the procedure performs the alterations to the necessary link field or external list pointer and returns the deleted node to the available pool.

```
procedure DELETE (var COURSE : POINTER; ASTUDENT :STUDENT_RANGE);
(  *PROCEDURE to locate a node in a linked list with a given value in its data
field and to delete the node. If the list is empty or the given value does not
match any in the list then no action is taken*)
var PTR, SHADOW : POINTER;
    MATCH : boolean ;
begin
(* Initialize pointers prior to searching the list *)
PTR := COURSE ;
SHADOW := nil ;
(* Initialize boolean variable *)
MATCH := false ;
(* While a match is not made and the pointer is not at the end *)
while not (MATCH) and (PTR <> nil ) do
if ASTUDENT = PTR ^ .STUDENT then
                          (* Match found *)
                                MATCH := true
                     else
                                (* Step to next node as
                                   shadow pointer follows *)
                                begin
                                  SHADOW := PTR ;
                                  PTR := PTR ^ .LINK
                                end;
(* delete node pointed to by pointer variable *)
(* CASE 1 - Empty list or No match - no action taken *)
if (COURSE <> nil) and MATCH then
    (* CASE 2- Delete first node *)
        if SHADOW = nil   then
                              begin (* Delete first node *)
                                COURSE := PTR ^ .LINK ;
                                dispose (PTR)
                              end
                          else
    (* CASE 3 Delete other node *)
                              begin (* Delete node by shifting
                                          pointer to prior node *)
                                SHADOW ^ .LINK := PTR ^ .LINK ;
                                dispose  (PTR)
                              end
end; (* PROCEDURE *)
```

Figure 4.16

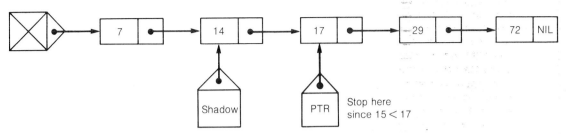

The node indicated by the shadow pointer is the node to be changed.

The shadow pointer, which enables us to remember the last node visited before the node being investigated, is useful during the insertion operation as well. Here too it is necessary to pass the node whose link field must be changed before determining the location within the linked list for a new node to be inserted.

Figure 4.16 shows a linked list of ascending numbers. To add the value 15 to the list, you would start at the first node and ask: is 15 less than the value in the data field of this node? If the answer is no, you move to the next node and repeat the question. When you reach the node whose data field equals 17, the answer to the question is yes and you have found the spot. You must insert the new node before this node. But since this is not directly possible with a singly linked list, what do you do? Right you are—a shadow pointer does the trick.

When you encounter the node whose data field has a value greater than the value to be inserted, you can insert the new node *after the node pointed to by the shadow pointer.* (This operation is already provided in a previous procedure.) As an exercise write a procedure that adds a new student to a course list, given only the external pointer to the course and the student's identification number. Convince yourself that a shadow pointer is necessary for an ascending or descending ordering.

The next part of the implementation concerns a feature that is not strictly necessary, but whose inclusion simplifies all of the procedures given by removing the special cases from consideration. All of the special cases involve either the empty list or the first node in the list, and the special responses all involve changing the external list pointer. Any approach that eliminates the need for special processing and checking without incurring a larger expense elsewhere is worth trying. The imaginative idea is the introduction of the **head node.** The following conventions will eliminate many headaches.

1. The list will have one node that is always pointed to by the external list pointer.
2. This node will never be deleted.
3. No node will be inserted before this node.

Figure 4.17 shows various course lists with this new feature.

What benefits do these conventions provide? The first and second conventions ensure that the external list pointer will never have a *nil* value. The last convention

Figure 4.17

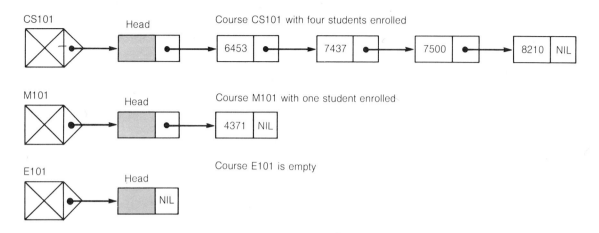

means that the external list pointer will not be affected when a node is inserted into the list. Collectively, the conventions say that it is not necessary to check for an empty list and that the external list pointer will never be changed during an insertion or deletion operation. This eliminates much of the special checking and processing. For example, the procedure for inserting a new node after a designated node HERE in a singly linked list COURSE is noticeably simplified with a head node:

```
procedure INSERT ( HERE : POINTER;
                             DATA : STUDENT_RANGE ) ;
var NEW_NODE : POINTER;
begin
new ( NEW_NODE ) ;
NEW_NODE ^.STUDENT := DATA ;
(* Insert after head node or other node *)
NEW_NODE ^ .LINK := HERE ^ .LINK ;
HERE ^ .LINK := NEW_NODE
end ; (* PROCEDURE *)
```

Thus, with a head node as a part of the implementation, the special cases of inserting a node into an empty list or at the front of the list become a matter of inserting a new node after the head node. This, of course, is equivalent to inserting a new node after any node in the list, hence the four-step procedure above is all that is required.

By reviewing the procedure LIST _ BUILD of the previous section, you will see that it sets up an external pointer and a single node. This can be interpreted as establishing an empty list with a head node. An added bonus occurs when the data fields of the head node can hold information about the list itself. For example, the number of students enrolled in the course can be stored in the student number field of the head node.

However, some of the other procedures will have to be altered to take the presence of the head node into account. For example, the printing of the roster would skip over the head node before beginning the printing.

Another situation aided by the presence of the head node occurs when the same list is pointed to by more than one external list pointer. This might happen, for example, if the math department and the computer science department offered a joint course in numerical analysis, but each department had its own course number. Two external pointers, say M142 and CS150, would point to the same list of students.

Let's assume that a rumor circulated among the students that a certain Dr. Digital was going to teach the course and that the students, filled with fear of failing, decided to remove their names from the course list. Eventually, the list would become empty, and the external list pointers would have to be updated. How would the procedure know that there were two (or more) external list pointers to be changed? Ouch! A headache. Once again, the head node comes to the rescue. With the head node present, both external list pointers continue to point to the head node, and the link field of the head node is set to NIL to indicate that no students are enrolled in the course.

This points out an important distinction that must be made when a head node is used: the difference between implementation and abstraction. An implemented singly linked linear list with a head node is never without nodes (i.e., empty). To derive certain benefits, the implementation is set up so that there is always at least one node contained within a list.

Thus we must distinguish between the logical list, which can be empty, and the physical list, which always contains at least the head node. Whenever an application checks to see if the logical list is empty, the physical list is actually checked to see if it contains only the head node.

Another feature that can be added to a linked list is the circular attribute. The implementation of circularly linked list is a simple extension of what we have just seen. The INSERT procedure can be used directly for adding a node to a circularly linked list. You will find the main difference in any algorithm that traverses the linked list. Previously, the *nil* pointer value indicated the last node in the list. In this case, a new test must be developed for determining when the traversal has accessed all the nodes.

The procedure below traverses the list, starting at the external list pointer, CIR _ LIST, until a complete circuit is made. It uses a generic procedure PROCESS that can be designed to process the node in any desired manner. It assumes a simple node structure of one data field and one link field. The circularly linked list does not contain a head node.

```
procedure CIRCULAR_TRIP ( CIR_LIST: POINTER );
var    PTR: POINTER ;
begin
  if CIR_LIST = nil then
                   writeln ( 'no nodes to PROCESS' )
                 else
                   begin
                    PTR := CIR_LIST ;
                    repeat
                       PROCESS (    PTR ^ .DATA );
                       PTR := PTR ^ . LINK
                    until PTR = CIR_LIST;
                   end
end;
```

As you see, not only the test condition—PTR = CIR _ LIST—but also the control structure for the traversal—*repeat–until*—is different. By testing for the empty list first, the code in the *else* block is ensured of at least one node in the list. Therefore, the node can be processed and the next node stepped to before the end-of-traversal test is performed.

If you tackled the traversal procedure and used a *while* control structure then you might have written:

```
while   PTR <> CIR_LIST do
              begin
                PROCESS ( PTR ^ . DATA);
                PTR := PTR ^ . LINK
              end
```

When does this logic fail? As soon as the pointer variable is initialized.

```
PTR :=  CIR_LIST;
```

A solution is to process the first node outside the *while* loop and to initialize the pointer variable to point to the node after the first node. This gives us another version of the CIRCULAR _ TRIP procedure block:

```
begin
if CIR_LIST = nil then
              writeln ( ''no nodes to PROCESS'' )
            else
            begin
                PROCESS ( CIR_LIST ^ .DATA );
                PTR :=  CIR_LIST ^ . LINK;
                while  PTR <> CIR_LIST do
                          begin
                           PROCESS ( PTR ^ .DATA );
                           PTR := PTR ^ .LINK;
                          end
            end
end;
```

Both versions handle the empty list and the case of a circular list with only one node—that is, a node that points to itself. Verify for yourself that this latter case is correctly processed in both versions.

The first version is simpler and more elegant than the other version. These are important programming qualities to cultivate. Strive for the important balance between simplicity and elegance, clearness and cleverness. At times overzealous cleverness can confuse the picture and add a complexity to the solution that is unneeded and is rarely appreciated by the programmer who takes over the project weeks later.

The procedure CIRCULAR _ TRIP illustrates the alteration needed for processing a linked list with the circular attribute. An expanded example of a circular singly linked list is included in Section 4.4, which presents a computer-assisted instruction application concerning the blood flow through the body. It will provide a more complete picture of the operations on a singly linked list with the circular attribute.

The implementation of the singly linked list using PASCAL features—pointer variables and the dynamic allocation system—is complete. It has provided for all the characteristics and behavior of the abstract model of a singly linked linear list. The operations of INSERT and DELETE have been presented, with special attention given to the special cases. During the implementation we saw how the changes to spots after a designated node are natural to the singly linked linear list, while changes before a node are not directly possible. We also saw how the explicit structural information contained in a node provided a means to traverse through the list. Sometimes, the traversal technique took us past the node to be changed and we had to rely on our friendly shadow to rescue us. We added a head node to the implementation and found simplicity entered the INSERT procedure. And all the time, the PASCAL memory management system was patiently and effectively tending the pool of available nodes. Through the web of interrelations, the whole—linked list processing—became larger than its parts—pointers, procedures, pools, and PASCAL.

4.3.3   USING A SELF-MANAGED AVAILABLE POOL

The implementation of the singly linked list provided an excellent example of the importance of the implementation language. PASCAL provides the building blocks for list processing—pointer variables. It supports the use of these building blocks through the dynamic allocation system. Hence, list processing in PASCAL is a natural extension of the language.

However, such widely used languages as FORTRAN and BASIC, which do not provide this capability, force the programmer to use fewer resources to accomplish the same feat of linked list implementation. These resources include simple identifiers and arrays. This section offers a preview of the techniques that will be used in the next section to implement the doubly linked list without relying on PASCAL'S pointer variables and dynamic allocation system. Using only a physically ordered array of records, an important convention, and a touch of magic, we will emulate the missing resources.

How can we preserve the logical relationship and the capacity for change of a linked list without relying on a physically ordered array of records?

The solution lies in adapting a new perspective toward the array. Yes, once again an array of records will be used as the storage space for the linked list of nodes. The important new perspective lies in the contents of the records in the array and in how we "see" the records being used. The declared records will mimic the structure of the nodes. Thus they will have one or more data fields of appropriate type and the extra-special link field(s).

The crucial convention that we will use is that **the integer value that is stored in the link field of the record will signify the subscript of a record that is the location of the next node in the logical ordering.** With this convention for the link field, the records in the array can be seen as individual, connectable, numbered boats floating in a large pool. When a boat is needed, any boat will do. All that needs to be remembered is the number of the boat selected. In this way, we can have physically noncontiguous records logically next to each other. With this new perspective, the implementation of linked lists begins to take shape as our storage entity, the array of records, adapts to the needs of linked list processing.

Abracadabra—the magic arrives! Again we introduce Bruce, the magician. Bruce's magical and managerial skills will be at our disposal. He will aid us in three ways.

First, he will designate all records as available for use by the linked list procedures that we will design and call. We must remember to ask him to perform this task before using any list operations. Second, he will provide us with an integer subscript value whenever we need a record. We will use this feature during the INSERT operation by just saying POOF! The integer we receive is the subscript of a record that is available for use. And finally, he will accept a subscript from us and add the indicated record to his list of available records. During the deletion operation, we will complete the operation by calling out to Bruce with a ZAP command. We will merrily use his magical services without investigating his method. Subsection 4.3.5 will be used to investigate his magical managerial method, for ultimately we are responsible for even the magic.

Figure 4.18 depicts the transition from the abstract model of a singly linked list with a simple node structure to an array of records with a single data field and a link field.

Exchanging the individual nodes of Figure 4.18a for the arbitrarily selected records of Figure 4.18b does not change the logical ordering. The transition is completed by exchanging the arrows linking the nodes (and records) of Figure 4.18b for the subscript values in the link fields of Figure 4.18c. The abstract model's logical ordering is preserved in the implementation model of Figure 4.18c. Now, the operations on the linked list can be performed on the implementation model by PASCAL procedures.

The records of Figure 4.18c can be grouped into two categories. The first group contains the four records used by the linked list. The remaining records are available for use when new nodes are added to the list. This group is called the **available pool** of records and is deftly managed through the wizardry of Bruce. In subsection 4.3.5 he reveals his skills through a set of PASCAL procedures. Figure 4.18d suggests how Bruce keeps a list of available records.

The use of an array as an available pool of records enables the records to be used by any information structure that shares the same node structure. Therefore, more than one linked list can access the records of the available pool without interfering with each other. Also, as we shall see in Section 4.4.1, the stack and queue, as linked structures, can share the space of the array via the available pool concept, assuming they share the same node structure.

During the implementation, certain PASCAL identifiers will take on a special character. I will give these special identifiers a specific label, because of their importance and usage: they will be called **pointer-identifiers.** The label was selected purposely to be similar to the PASCAL term, *pointer variables*. Although they are similar, they are not the same. They will be used in the same way but the underlying organization of memory to which they refer is different.

Pointer-identifiers will point to or identify records of an array that are or will be used as nodes in a linked list. Therefore, pointer-identifiers have integer values within the subscript range of the array of records.

In addition, pointer-identifiers can have a value of NIL. To implement this special value, a value of -1 will be valid for a pointer-identifier. Hence, the array can have a subscript range from 0 to MAX, while a pointer-identifier will have a value of -1 to MAX. Make a note of the newly adopted convention for the integer -1.

One such pointer-identifier will represent the external list pointer of the abstract model. Another pointer-identifier will be used when Bruce tells us the subscript of

Figure 4.18

a. Abstract model of the singly linked list.

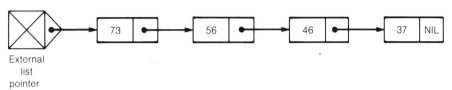

External
list
pointer

b. Linked list as an
array of records.

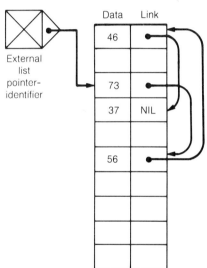

c. Subscripts into the
array as arrows

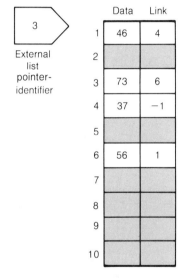

Darkened records constitute
the available pool.

d. List of
available records

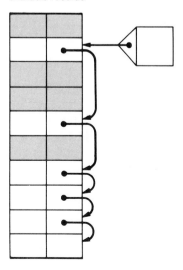

an unused record, when we are inserting a new node. In performing various operations, various pointer-identifiers will be used, such as a pointer-identifier to indicate which node is to be deleted. Pointer-identifiers of this type, ones that we will be working with during a procedure, are called working pointers.

It is important to emphasize the logical operations on pointer-identifiers. It is logical to assign an integer value to a pointer-identifier (this is like drawing an arrow to a node). Using the value of the pointer-identifier as the subscript into the array of records is also logical (this is like accessing the information within the node). But take care! Adding to or subtracting values from a pointer-identifier is not illegal (PASCAL-wise) but it is illogical (linked list-wise). Therefore, PASCAL statements such as PTR := PTR + 1 should not appear when you are using a pointer-identifier, since the physical ordering of the records is no longer relevant to the concept of the array as a pool of records.

With this preview as a backdrop and Bruce looking over our shoulders, let us embark upon our journey into the land of doubly linked list implementation.

4.3.4 IMPLEMENTING THE DOUBLY LINKED LINEAR LIST

Using the new perspective presented in the last section, we can begin the implementation of the doubly linked list model. As usual, the first step is the setting of conventions.

The storage consideration is our starting point. We will need some type declarations to declare PASCAL equivalents of the linked list components. The following do the trick:

```
const MAX = 300 ;
type PTR_IDENTIFIER : -1..MAX;
     NODES = record
                DATA  : (* matches the specifications of the
                                node structure *)
               PRIOR : PTR_IDENTIFIER;
               NEXT  : PTR_IDENTIFIER
             end ;
```

IMAGINATION CHALLENGE

Gather up some marking pens of various colors. For each of the following actions, imagine yourself in the midst of the action. With a sense of the motion and with your emotions, quickly select a colored marker and expressively draw the feelings of the action.

1. Diving
2. Skating
3. Reading
4. Falling
5. Slipping
6. Weeping

These statements implement two previously stated conventions: (1) the NIL value is represented by a −1, and (2) the link fields are represented by integers within the subscript range of the array. This leads us to our next step—allocating memory for the array of records that will house the list of available records and the linked list being implemented. The following statement does this and also allocates space to a few pointer-identifiers:

```
var LIST : array [0..MAX] of NODES ;
    FRONTDOOR, BACKDOOR : PTR_IDENTIFIER ;
    PTR, HERE, NEW_NODE : PTR_IDENTIFIER ;
```

The pointer-identifiers—FRONTDOOR and BACKDOOR—will be used as external pointers to the doubly linked list. Remember that the linear ordering may be processed in either direction. These pointer-identifiers indicate the first nodes in the forward and backward direction, respectively.

Once the direction has been selected, the method of traversing the doubly linked list is similar to traversing a singly linked list. For a forward traversal, the PASCAL instruction

```
PTR  := LIST[PTR].NEXT
```

would implement the movement from one node to the next. The pointer-identifier PTR would initially be assigned the value of FRONTDOOR.

Let's stop at this point and compare the two statements

```
PTR := PTR^.LINK
```

and

```
PTR := LIST[PTR].NEXT
```

The first statement causes a record in main memory, indicated by the address in PTR, to be accessed; a value is then stored in PTR. This value, found in the LINK field, is another address—the address of the next node in the logical sequence.

The second statement causes a record in an array, indicated by the subscript in PTR, to be accessed; a value is stored in PTR. This value, found in the NEXT field, is another subscript—the subscript of the next node in the logical sequence.

So you see that the process is identical, with the array playing the role of main memory and the subscript replacing the physical memory address. Once we supply Bruce's managerial procedures—POOF and ZAP—to simulate PASCAL's *new* and *dispose* procedures, we will have created a miniature dynamic allocation system.

The reverse traversal starts at its respective external pointer, via

```
PTR := BACKDOOR
```

and progresses through the linked list by way of

```
PTR :=  LIST [PTR].PRIOR
```

In both cases the traversal would be terminated whenever the pointer-identifier PTR equals −1, the NIL indicator. As you can see, the use of two link fields has not complicated this traversal operation using the doubly linked structure. You need only be very careful in specifying which link field to use.

The algorithms for inserting or deleting a node also parallel those given before. However, the doubly linked feature provides more freedom than singly linked lists, in this instance. The designations for inserting a new node either before or after a given node are of the same level of difficulty; apart from the setting up of pointers, the same algorithm can be used.

To illustrate the steps in the algorithms for processing a doubly linked list, a new application—prices on the New York Stock Exchange—will be presented. As part of the application we have a new structure. The type declarations that describe the node are:

```
const MAX = 300 ;
type PTR_IDENTIFIER : -1..MAX;
     NODES = record
                  STOCKNAME : string[20] ;
                  CATEGORY : 0..9 ;
                  CURRENTQUOTE : real;
                  STARTQUOTE : real ;
                  PRIOR : PTR_IDENTIFIER ;
                  NEXT : PTR_IDENTIFIER ;
             end ;
var LIST : array [0..MAX] of NODES;
    FRONTDOOR, BACKDOOR : PTR_IDENTIFIER ;
```

The records contain four data fields, representing a stock's name, its category (such as industrials, petrochemicals, utilities, electronics, etc.), and its current and starting price quote from the New York Stock Exchange.

In inserting a new node, I will assume that there will be two arguments, both pointer-identifiers. One pointer-identifier, HERE, points to the record in the array after which the insertion is to take place. The other pointer, NEW _ NODE, will indicate a previously unused record that was procured through Bruce's magic from the available pool of records. I will also assume that the data fields of the new record have already been filled with the pertinent data and that the only fields that need to be assigned values are the PRIOR and NEXT link fields. The special case of inserting a new node at the beginning of the list is indicated by HERE having a value of −1. No head node is assumed to exist.

The three possible positions at which a new node can be inserted are illustrated in Figure 4.19. The figure shows the linked list before and after the insertion has taken place. The algorithm for the insertion operation follows.

```
procedure INSERT_AFTER (NEW_NODE, HERE : PTR_IDENTIFIER;
                             var FRONTDOOR, BACKDOOR :
                             PTR_IDENTIFIER) ;
(* LIST array is globally available *)
var HEREAFTER : PTR_IDENTIFIER;
begin
(* CASE 1 * At front of LIST *)
if HERE = -1 then begin
                  LIST [FRONTDOOR] . PRIOR := NEW_NODE ;
                  LIST [NEW_NODE] . PRIOR := -1  ;
                  LIST [NEW_NODE] . NEXT := FRONTDOOR ;
                  FRONTDOOR := NEW_NODE
             end
```

```
         else
(* CASE 2 * AT end of LIST *)
if LIST[HERE] . NEXT = -1 then begin
                    LIST [HERE] . NEXT := NEW_NODE ;
                    LIST [NEW_NODE] . PRIOR := HERE ;
                    LIST [NEW_NODE] . NEXT := -1  ;
                    BACKDOOR := NEW_NODE
              end
         else
(* CASE 3 * Between two nodes *)
              begin
                 HEREAFTER := LIST [HERE] . NEXT ;
                 LIST [HERE] . NEXT := NEW_NODE ;
                 LIST [NEW_NODE] . PRIOR := HERE ;
                 LIST [NEW_NODE] . NEXT := HEREAFTER ;
                 LIST [HEREAFTER] . PRIOR := NEW_NODE ;
              end
end ; (* PROCEDURE *)
```

This procedure handles the special case of inserting a new node before the first one by assuming that the argument HERE will be set to −1 before the procedure is called. In either the first or second case, the two external pointers must also be available to be altered.

The doubly linked nature of the nodes can be used to insert a new node before any given node in the following way. Assume GIVEN is a pointer to the node in question and NEW _ NODE is a pointer to a new node to be inserted before the node GIVEN. The following instructions accomplish the insertion.

```
if GIVEN = FRONTDOOR then HERE := -1
                   else HERE := LIST [GIVEN] . PRIOR ;
INSERT_AFTER (NEW_NODE, HERE, FRONTDOOR, BACKDOOR) ;
```

In this way, we can move from the given node to its prior neighbor and insert the new node after its neighbor, accomplishing our task. We set up the special conditions in case the request puts the new node before the front of the list. Thus, insertions before or after a given node will require basically the same amount of processing time, a definite advantage compared to singly linked lists.

This same advantage applies to deletion. Since we can get to the node before or after a given node, we can easily delete the node before or after this node. Remember this increased flexibility in using doubly linked lists in algorithms when looking through your bag of programming tricks for list processing applications. As an exercise, write three procedures: (1) one to delete a given node from a list; (2) one to delete a node before a given node; and (3) one to delete a node after a given node.

To illustrate this flexibility and point out the advantages of being able to begin either a forward or a backward traversal from any node, let's set up the following problem. Imagine yourself as part of the programming staff for a stock brokerage firm that is setting up a real-time information retrieval system for all the stocks on the New York Stock Exchange. With the recent volatile nature of the stock market and the keen competition from other firms, the management wants a system that provides current information about any stock and about its performance relative to other stocks in the day's trading at any time during the day. These requirements demand a

Figure 4.19

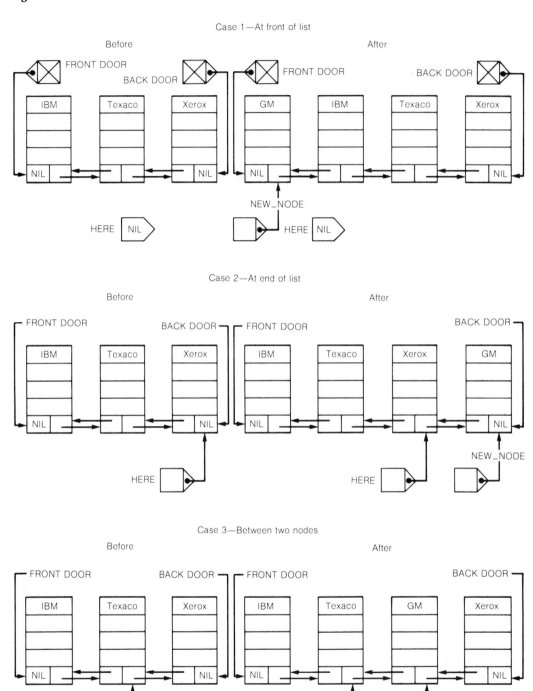

real-time system where changes are reflected immediately in the underlying information structures. The number of stocks involved, the amount of information per stock, and the frequent changes to the logical relationship among stocks has contributed to the project director's decision to use a doubly linked linear list that is ordered by the amount of change in price noted so far in the day's trading. The record to be used as a basis for the list and the designation of the list itself is given below:

```
type PTR_IDENTIFIER : -1..5000;
     STK_POINTER : 1..300;
     STOCKS = record
                 STOCK : STK_POINTER ;  (* Pointer to data *)
                 CURRENT : real ; (* Most recent price quoted *)
                 STARTQUOTE : real ;
                 PRIOR : PTR_IDENTIFIER ;  (* Link fields *)
                 NEXT : PTR_IDENTIFIER ;
             end ;
     var STOCKLIST : array [1..5000] of STOCKS ;
```

The STOCKLIST array keeps the ordering of the stock's current performance relative to all others. Therefore, the data fields of the record are limited to those necessary to keep the ordering.

The pointer field designated by STOCK deserves some additional comments. Since considerable data will be stored concerning each stock, it is necessary to access this block of data directly. The STOCK pointer, a new type of pointer field, is designed for this purpose. Data about all stocks will be kept in a large data base. This data base can be accessed from various procedures of the information retrieval system through the STOCK pointer. It is through the STOCK pointer that procedures processing the active STOCKLIST gain access to data about a particular stock from the data base. In this way, data that seldom change or are infrequently accessed, such as the category of the stock, are excluded from the active, changing list of ordered stocks.

The project director gives you the specifications for a maintenance procedure. The firm's computer will be tied into the New York Stock Exchange's central computer facility. Each time that a stock experiences a change as reported by the central computer system, your firm's computer recognizes the new change and a maintenance procedure is called to update the STOCKLIST.

Your task is to develop the procedure for locating the stock's new position in the ordered list and performing the necessary changes in the list to reflect the new situation. You know the structure of the STOCKLIST, the format of the record STOCKS, and the conventions set up by the project director. You also know that the arguments to the procedure will be the stock's new price quote and a pointer-identifier to the stock's record in the STOCKLIST.

As you sit at your desk with pencil in hand, a fresh pad of paper on the desk, and your favorite information structures textbook by your side, you ponder how lucky you are to be given the pointer to the stock's record in the list rather than the stock's name or identification number. Otherwise, you would have to perform a linear search for the stock's current position in the list. With 5000 possible stocks in the list, your procedure to respond in real time would have been in considerable jeopardy. Since the project director is an advocate of structured programming, you know that the conversion from stock name to record subscript number is contained in another procedure. You wonder briefly how this other procedure does its thing and recall overhearing her discuss hash tables with a colleague. Your attention then returns to the task at hand.

You decide to follow the project director's example and follow a structured programming strategy. So you consider the major subtasks necessary to accomplish your task. On the pad you write:

TASK: REPOSITION stock in STOCKLIST based on new price quote.

1. REMOVE record from STOCKLIST.
2. LOCATE new position of record in STOCKLIST.
3. INSERT record in new position in STOCKLIST.
4. UPDATE current price field of record.

Four subtasks must be developed as part of the procedure. Focusing your attention on the first subtask, you write:

Subtask: REMOVE record from STOCKLIST

1. Have record BEFORE point to record AFTER.
2. Have record AFTER point to record BEFORE.

Note: Do not ZAP record being removed, as it will be inserted later; check for special cases at the front and end of the list.

Without adding the details to the first subtask, you now consider the strategy for the second subtask. This is the most unique of the four. You recall that the ordering of the stock is based on the amount of change in the stock's price so far today (CURRENT minus STARTQUOTE) and that there is a descending ordering (the first record has the largest positive amount of change, the second record has the next largest change, etc.). Therefore, the new position is located toward the front of the list if the new difference in the stock's price is greater than the old difference. Otherwise the new position is located closer to the end of the list. With this important insight, you outline the steps for the second subtask on another sheet of paper.

Subtask: LOCATE new position of record in STOCKLIST

1. Start from where the record was removed.
2. If new price difference is greater than old difference
   then traverse the list backward until new location is found
   else traverse the list forward until new location is found.

Notes: Upon completion a pointer will indicate the record after which the insertion subtask should occur; criteria for deciding when the new location is found will be supplied during the detail level.

The doubly linked attribute is quite handy in this algorithm, since the search for the new location begins at one point in the list and progresses only in the direction necessary.

The third and fourth subtask are very straightforward. One is a standard doubly linked list operation and the other involves accessing a field of a record. As an exercise, write the pseudocode for each subtask.

With the general strategy outlined and the strategy for each subtask clearly specified, you arrive at the detail level by producing the code for the procedure. After a bit of head scratching, pencil sharpening, erasing, and textbook reviewing, the following appears on your pad:

```
procedure REPOSITION (NEWQUOTE : real; STOCKPTR:PTR_IDENTIFIER) ;
(* STOCKLIST is globally available *)
var BEFORE, AFTER, PTR : PTR_IDENTIFIER;
   NEW, OLD : real ;
 begin
(* SUBTASK 1 - Remove record from stocklist *)
BEFORE := STOCKLIST[STOCKPTR] . PRIOR ;
AFTER := STOCKLIST[STOCKPTR] . NEXT ;
if BEFORE = -1 then begin (* Remove from front *)
                    FRONTDOOR := AFTER ;
                    STOCKLIST [AFTER] . PRIOR :=  -1
                end
            else
if AFTER = -1 then begin (* Remove from end *)
                   BACKDOOR := BEFORE ;
                   STOCKLIST[BEFORE] . NEXT :=   -1  ;
                end
            else begin (* Remove from between two *)
                   STOCKLIST [ BEFORE] . NEXT := AFTER ;
                   STOCKLIST [ AFTER] . PRIOR := BEFORE
                end
(* SUBTASK 2 - Locate new position in stocklist *)
with STOCKLIST[STOCKPTR] do begin
OLD := CURRENT - STARTQUOTE ;
NEW := NEWQUOTE - STARTQUOTE ;
if NEW > OLD then begin (* Traverse toward front *)
                PTR := BEFORE ;
                while (PTR <>  -1) and
(STOCKLIST[PTR].CURRENT - STOCKLIST[PTR].STARTQUOTE < NEW )
                        do  PTR := STOCKLIST[PTR].PRIOR ;
                (* Upon completion PTR will either be nil, *)
                (* i.e. insert before front of list *)
                (* or will point to record before the location *)
                (* to insert the update record *)
                  end ;

           else begin (* Traverse toward end *)
                PTR := AFTER ;
```

```
                    while (PTR <>  -1)  and
       (STOCKLIST[PTR].CURRENT - STOCKLIST[PTR].STARTQUOTE > NEW)
                     do PTR := STOCKLIST[PTR].NEXT ;
                 (* Special case or back up one record *)
                 if PTR = -1  then PTR := BACKDOOR
                              else PTR := STOCKLIST[PTR].PRIOR ;
                 (* Upon completion PTR will point to the record
                     before the location to insert the update record *)
              end
end; (* with *)
(* SUBTASK 3 Insert record in new position *)
   (* Insert new record, STOCKPTR, after record, PTR *)
INSERT_AFTER(STOCKPTR, PTR, FRONTDOOR, BACKDOOR ) ;
(* SUBTASK 4 Update current price field *)
STOCKLIST[STOCKPTR].CURRENT := NEWQUOTE ;
end ; (* PROCEDURE *)
```

You are now convinced that this procedure does the job. You have effectively clipped the links to a node, taking care of the special links at the front and end of the list. From that point in the list you have traversed the list toward either the beginning or the end until no more records remain to check or the correct position in the ordering is located. In traversing toward the end, you backed up the pointer one record so that the pointer meets the requirements of the standard INSERT _ AFTER procedure. Finally, you polished off the job by updating the current quote field of the stock being repositioned. With some additional in-line documentation you will be ready to present your procedure to the project director for review and then advance to the testing phase of the process.

You should feel quite good about this procedure, since you have shown your skills at three important tasks of doubly linked list processing: deleting, traversing, and inserting. You have taken advantage of the main flexibility of the doubly linked attribute—the ability to move in either direction from a given node.

Since this maintenance procedure went so well, you might try your hand at a different kind of list processing procedure—information retrieval. The management wants to receive the information that satisfies the following requests:

List the best ten stocks based on today's performance.

List the worst ten stocks based on today's performance.

List the best N stocks based on today's performance.

List the best N stocks in the petro-chemical category.

For each category, provide a list of today's ten best-performing stocks.

These requests require the basic traversal method for linked lists, though some require selective processing of the records. As an exercise, design procedures for each request and list the additional procedures or information needed to satisfy each request.

The doubly linked list can be enhanced by adding the circular attribute in one or both traversal directions. Implementation of this new feature parallels that presented for a singly linked list with the circular attribute given at the end of subsection 4.3.2.

Once again, the important difference in the algorithms is the test for a complete traversal. For a doubly linked list, the test is the same: repeat until the working pointer-identifier equals the external list pointer. If two external list pointers are used, the direction of the traversal determines which one is involved. If only one external list pointer is used, as was suggested in Section 4.2, the initialization of the working pointer-identifier and the control logic depend on the traversal direction. As an exercise, write the pseudocode for each of the four possible situations: forward or backward traversal for an implementation with either one or two external list pointers.

Section 4.4 contains an application using the doubly linked list with the circular attribute. This application concerns the reversible energy cycle known as the Krebs energy cycle. It is in the context of a computer-assisted instruction program that helps students learn about this cycle. Feel free to skip ahead to this section to find out more about the combined benefits of the doubly linked list and the circular attribute.

The present section has given you a way to implement the doubly linked linear list information structure, the most flexible and dynamic information structure presented so far. Its potential is proportional to the insight and imagination that you apply when tackling varied programming tasks. With this structure you have greatly increased the power that you can wield against the future challenges that you will face.

4.3.5 REVEALING THE MAGIC

You may have wondered why I am so confident of Bruce's magical poofing and zapping skills. Before his secret was revealed, I was as amazed and skeptical as you. Afterwards, its simplicity only added to my amazement. Let me pass this magical secret on to you.

As our resident sorcerer for linked list management, Bruce is responsible for ensuring that all available nodes are organized so that they are available upon request for use by an application program. In the spirit of efficiency, he also ensures that any node returned after use is not lost but is properly recycled and made available again.

He accomplishes this feat with some creative foresight and insight. The nature of a node for a linked list is that it has at least one link field. So Bruce figures that before all processing begins (since all records in the array are then unused and available) he will link together all these nodes. He establishes an external pointer to indicate the beginning node in this linked list of available nodes. In this way, he knows where the first available node is.

When a node is given away through a POOF, he finds the next node through the link field of the first one. By continuing to remove the first node of the available list, he can honor all requests until the available list of nodes is exhausted.

Normally this situation is a two-way street: some nodes are returned after being used. When the ZAP operation is called, Bruce adds the newly available node to the

TRADE-OFFS

The doubly linked list provides a very flexible information structure for an ordered list of data elements. Important factors to consider include the ratio of link fields to data fields and the linear access to the list.

Assume that you plan to process the data from an experiment. Five hundred samples were taken and the project leader wants you to write a program to sort the 500 values.

If you select an array, then 500 memory locations will be used. You plan to read in the 500 values and then call a sort procedure that you have written to finish off the task.

Another approach comes to you after a morning swim. You will input the values one at a time. You will then insert the value into its proper location in an ordered doubly linked list. Since little movement of the data is required, you think this is a good idea. At the conclusion of the input, the values will already be sorted in the doubly linked list—another advantage of this approach.

What are the cost factors? In terms of memory, one data field and two link fields. This means 1500 memory locations will be allocated to store the 500 values and their logical connections—three times the amount needed for the array approach.

In terms of time, how many comparisons will be needed to locate the proper position? Here lies the main disadvantage of the linked list structure. The structure and its implementation force a sequential search. The very efficient binary search mentioned in an earlier chapter depends on the contiguous arrangement of the records, and therefore can not be used.

Thus if 300 elements are in the list then the worst case requires 300 comparisons, the best case requires one comparison, and on the average there will be 150 comparisons. As it turns out, the execution time of the linked list approach to sorting numbers is proportional to the square of the number of data elements. In Chapter 8, you will see that this time can be greatly improved on.

So your morning swim was refreshing but it was not inspiring. The linked approach would use three times the memory as well as more execution time than other available sort algorithms. It seems that you have forgotten when the linked list is most useful—for a list that will experience frequent changes to the ordering. And now you have another concern to monitor—the ratio of data fields to link fields.

front of the available list, where it is then available for another POOF request. To maintain this strategy Bruce must simply perform standard deletion and insertion operations to the front of the linked list of available nodes. What could be simpler?

Let's watch Bruce perform his magic. Assume that the node structure is described with the PASCAL record structure below. The storage space for the nodes is reserved with the accompanying array declaration.

```
const MAX = 200 ;
type PTR_IDENTIFIER = -1..MAX;
NODES=    record
              DATA  : real ;
              PRIOR : PTR_IDENTIFIER ;
              NEXT  : PTR_IDENTIFIER
          end ;
var LIST : array [0..MAX] of NODES;
    AVAIL_PTR : PTR_IDENTIFIER ;
```

Bruce's first step is to link together all of the records in the array. The order in which they are linked is not important. The most straightforward way would be with the PASCAL code:

```
for K : = 0 to MAX - 1 do
    LIST[K] .NEXT := K + 1 ;
LIST[MAX].NEXT := -1 ;
```

Next, Bruce must set aside a special pointer-identifier to point to the next available record in the newly linked list. This is accomplished by the PASCAL statement:

```
AVAIL_PTR := 0 ;
```

Collecting this into one package, he creates the following procedure:

```
procedure CREATE_POOL (var AVAIL_PTR : PTR_IDENTIFIER);
(* The array LIST is assumed to be a global identifier
    for this procedure. *)
var K : integer;
begin
(* Link available nodes thru a link field of node *)
for K := 0 to MAX - 1 do
    LIST[K].NEXT := K + 1 ;
LIST[MAX].NEXT := -1 ;
(* Set up pointer to next available node *)
AVAIL_PTR := 0 ;
end ;
```

This procedure must be called by the application program before any requests for a node can be correctly serviced. It is only called once during the process.

Now that Bruce's foresight has been implemented, he is ready to sit back and maintain the organization through any sequence of calls to POOF and ZAP.

Figure 4.20 shows how Bruce will handle one situation, the return of a node. His secret strategy, in this case, is to add the returned node to the front of the available list by having it point to the node presently on the front of the list. Likewise, the pointer-identifier that shows the first available node now points to the newly returned node. ZAP, the chore is done. And the operation is coded as simply as it is said:

```
procedure ZAP (RETURNEE : PTR_IDENTIFIER);
(* AVAIL_PTR and LIST are assumed to be global identifiers *)
begin
(* Returned node points to present first available node *)
LIST[RETURNEE].NEXT := AVAIL_PTR;
(* Update available node pointer *)
AVAIL_PTR   := RETURNEE ;
end ; (* of MAGIC *)
```

Figure 4.20

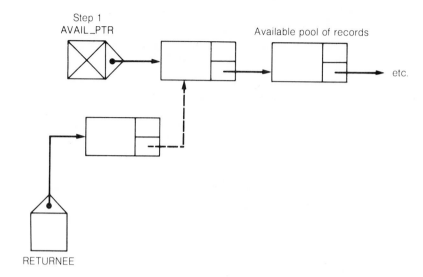

Copy AVAIL_PTR value to NEXT link field of record pointed to by RETURNEE.

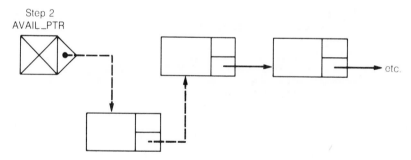

Copy value of RETURNEE pointer-identifier to AVAIL_PTR pointer-identifier. Dashed lines indicate changes.

Bruce must also be able to pull an available node out of his hat. All his planning was designed to make this trick happen with ease. Let's look at the procedure that he has provided:

```
procedure POOF ( var NEW_NODE : PTR_IDENTIFIER);
(* AVAIL_PTR and LIST are assumed to be global identifiers *)
begin
(* Assign pointer the next available node *)
NEW_NODE := AVAIL_PTR ;
(* Remove node from available list *)
AVAIL_PTR := LIST[AVAIL_PTR] . NEXT
end ; (* of POOF *)
```

This appears to be a fine finale for Bruce's magic performance. But a ghost from the past has been overlooked. What happens if Bruce tries to POOF a new node and none are available? The underflow of available records is a potion that is stronger even than Bruce's magic. To protect against this harmful magic, two additional statements must be added to the procedure—one to check for this condition and another to provide adequate notification and apply some sort of remedy if possible. As an exercise, be a ghost buster and patch up POOF so that the underflow of available nodes is detected and handled gracefully.

With these three symbiotic procedures—CREATE _ POOL, POOF and ZAP—the secrets of Bruce's magic are yours. You are now equipped with all the tools of the trade for maintaining and implementing any of the varied versions of the linked list information structure.

The following program skeleton alludes to the way that the application program, the available pool management procedures, and the linked list processing procedures are collectively arranged. They are logically tied together by the assorted conventions that have been stated over the last two sections.

```
program LIST_PROCESS ;
type PTR_IDENTIFIER : ... (* as specifications demand *)
     NODES = record
                 .
                 .
                 .
              end ;
var  LIST : array [ ... ] of NODES ;
     AVAIL_PTR, START, PTR, SPTR, HERE, AFTER :PTR_IDENTIFIER;
(* available pool management procedures *)
procedure CREATE_POOL( ... );
   .
   .
   .
end;
procedure POOF( ... );
   .
   .
   .
end;
procedure ZAP( ... );
   .
   .
   .
end;
(* linked list processing procedures *)
procedure INSERT_AFTER( ... ) ;
   .
   .
   .
end;
procedure DELETE( ... );
   .
   .
   .
```

```
        ZAP( ... ) ;
         .
end;
procedure LOCATE( ... ) ;

         .
         .
         .
end;
(* main program begin here *)
begin
         .
         .
CREATE_POOL ;
         .
         .
         .
         .
if  ... then begin
                 .
             POOF( ... );
                 .
             INSERT_AFTER( ... );
                 .
                 .
             end
         else
             DELETE ( ... ) ;
         .
         .
         .
end.
```

One important feature of this magic is that Bruce is completely unprejudiced. He does not care if many distinct linked lists access his available pool of nodes, as long as each uses the same node structure. He is equally glad to recycle nodes from various structures to make them available to all who share the pool. Such a generous soul is a treat to find in the field of hard-wired logic, but then he is a figment of imaginative software.

In cases where more than one node structure exists then the available pool for each node structure must be managed. Some major changes are necessary.

First, the use of global variables in the three procedures is unworkable. Each procedure must be designed so that the array of records and the available node pointer are included in the argument list. This generalizes the three operations so that (1) CREATE _ POOL can be called for each pool needed and (2) the ZAP and POOF operations are applied to the available pool that is supplied at the time they are called.

The second change occurs to the linked list program itself. When the procedures are called, the number of arguments must be adjusted. For instance, the following code would generate two available pools and set up an empty list with a head node for each type of node structure present:

```
CREATE_POOL(AVAIL1,LIST1);   (* Create pool for doubly linked *)
CREATE_POOL(AVAIL2,LIST2);   (* Create pool for singly linked *)
POOF( HEAD1 , AVAIL1 , LIST1 ) ;
    EXT_PTR1 := HEAD1 ;
    LIST1[HEAD1].PRIOR := -1;
```

```
   LIST1[HEAD1].NEXT := -1;
POOF( HEAD2 , AVAIL2 , LIST2 );
   EXT_PTR2 := HEAD2 ;
   LIST2[HEAD2].NEXT := -1;
```

For this program, the following node structures have been declared: NODE1 is the record description given above, with two link fields; and

```
NODE2 = record
          DATA_FIELD : real ;
          NEXT : PTR_IDENTIFIER ;
        end ;
The following identifiers are also set up :
  var  LIST1 : array [0..MAX1] of NODE1 ;
       LIST2 : array [0..MAX2]of NODE2 ;
```

With this sample as a guide you can expand Bruce's magic to manage as many different available pools as your application may demand.

■ "JUST FOR REFERENCE"

Singly Linked List Using Pascal's Dynamic Allocation

Basic steps for implementation include—

- describing node with a record structure
- describing link fields with pointer variables
- obtaining a record through *new* procedure and returning a record through *dispose* procedure
- using link field to explicitly order records
- using identifiers of POINTER type for pointers

Main considerations with the operations are as follows—

- traversal (moving through the list): PTR := PTR ^ .LINK is the key statement
- inserting (adding a node to the list) is stated as insertion after a given node
- deleting (removing a node from the list) is stated as delete node after a given node.
- Locating (finding a node with a given value or condition): shadow pointer is used to access predecessor node

Head node is a nondeletable node at front of the list that—

- may contain information about the list as a whole
- must be skipped in the traversal operation
- eliminates the two special cases of empty list and front of list
- is useful when multiple external list pointers point to the same list

TRADE-OFFS

If you are using PASCAL to develop an application program involving linked lists then you could still use the self-managed available pool. But would you want to? What are the trade-offs between the self-managed version and the dynamic allocation version of linked list implementation?

The self-managed system requires a stated maximum number of available records. This introduces a constraint to the size of the linked list being implemented. The dynamic allocation system also has an available memory constraint; however, it is much larger, since the rest of allocated memory is available for dynamic record assignments.

What happens when the application program uses linked lists with different node structures? For this case the dynamic allocation implementation receives five stars. By declaring a pointer type and a record structure for each distinct node structure, the *new* procedure can supply the correct amount of memory for each type of node. This is a very flexible feature.

The self-managed implementation, on the other hand, receives five lemons. As presented, the available pool is a collection of homogeneous records. Attempting to accommodate, say, three different node structures would cause several difficulties: (1) space for three arrays of records would need to be allocated—one for each node structure; (2) CREATE _ POOL would have to be generalized and called three times; and (3) the procedures POOF and ZAP would have to be adapted to use the appropriate pool to satisfy a request involving each of the node structures.

In summary, the dynamic allocation system of PASCAL has many positive points in its favor. So if the implementation language is PASCAL, then use its resources to the fullest. When these resources are not available, then use your resources to the fullest by implementing the self-managed system.

Circular attribute characterizes a list in which last node points to first node—

- traversal can begin at any node
- *repeat–until* control structure is used in the traversal, with the test for completion being PTR = START _ PTR

Doubly Linked List Using a Self-Managed Pool

Basic steps for implementation include—

- declaring a pointer-identifier type and a record for the node structure
- declaring an array of records for the available pool
- managing the available pool through procedures CREATE _ POOL (arranges records into a pool), POOF (locates unused record), and ZAP (returns a record)

- using two external list pointers for the two directions of traversal (forward and backward)

Main considerations for the operations are as follows—

- traversal—select the direction and use the correct external list pointer and the appropriate link field for the direction selected
- insertion—may be specified either before or after a given node
- deletion—may be specified either before, after, or at a given node
- locating—no shadow pointer is needed

Added features (head node and circular attribute) are the same as singly linked list.

Bruce's Management Procedures for the Available Pool

CREATE _ POOL sets up the pool of records for use by the application program (it must be called before the other procedures are called); to implement—

- link all records of the array together except the last one, which receives a NIL value
- initialize pointer-identifier AVAIL _ PTR to point to first record in the array

ZAP returns a record to the linked list of available records; to implement—

- link returned record to current first available record
- update pointer-identifier AVAIL _ PTR to point to returned record

POOF delete the first record from the linked list of the available pool and supplies it to the application; user is notified if no records are available. To implement—

- assign pointer-identifier NEW _ NODE the value of AVAIL _ PTR (i.e., the first in the list)
- update pointer-identifier AVAIL _ PTR to the current second node in the list (i.e., first node's link field)

EXERCISES

1. Explain how the individual, unattached nature of abstract nodes is simulated by an array, a collection of contiguous storage locations.

2. In what ways does using a head node simplify the implementation of a linked list?

3. When you are implementing a linked list, three auxiliary routines help manage the available pool of records. Name each routine and briefly describe its function.

4. Write procedures to implement the functions in parts a–j below. Assume the following record definition for the node of the ordered singly linked list. Assume that no head node is used. The external list pointer is designated as EXT _ PTR.

```
type    POINTER :  -1..50;
        NODES   =  record
                   DATA : integer;
                   LINK : POINTER ;
                   end ;
var LIST : array[0..50] of NODES ;
```

a) Calculate the sum of the data fields of the list.

b) Create a list with ten nodes whose data fields are the multiples of two—2, 4, 6, .., 20.

c) Return a pointer to the last node in the list.

d) Delete the nth node if it exists.

e) Return all nodes whose data fields are negative to the available pool.

f) Produce a reversed copy of the list pointed to by EXT_PTR. The new list is pointed to by PTR_EXT.

g) Search the list for a node whose value is GIVEN and print the value of the node before and after the GIVEN node if the search is successful.

h) Search the list for a node whose value is GIVEN and split the list into two lists. The list pointed to by EXT_PTR should contain the nodes before the GIVEN node and include the GIVEN node. The remaining nodes should form the second list and be pointed to by the external pointer REST.

i) Perform the same function as (h) above except that the GIVEN node is the first node in the list pointed to by REST.

j) Assume that you have another ordered list pointed to by MORE. Merge the two ordered lists into one pointed to by EXT_PTR. Duplicate nodes are to be returned to the available pool.

5. Which procedures in problem 4 would be aided by the presence of a head node?

6. Which procedures in problem 4 would be aided by the lists being doubly linked?

7. Assume that you have a doubly linked list with two data fields, an account number and a balance due. The list is ordered by account number. Write a procedure that reorders the list by the balance due, with the highest amount first in the list.

8. You want to represent polynomials such as $5x^4 + 2x^3 - 7x^2 - x + 4$ as a linked list. Each node will contain the coefficient and exponent of a term in the polynomial. Consider whether to use a singly or a doubly linked list and define the record structure for the nodes. Write procedures to add, subtract, and evaluate polynomials represented as linked list.

9. Write a procedure that transforms a singly linked list into a doubly linked list with a head node.

10. This problem can be assigned as a major programming project:

During the operation of a multiprogramming operating system, the computer's memory is shared by a number of different programs, called JOBs. The operating system must keep two lists: a list of allocated blocks and a list of free blocks of memory. The diagram below shows a typical allocation.

JOB 1 5K	FREE 5K	JOB 3 8K	JOB 2 4K	FREE 10K	JOB 4 16K	FREE 24K

0 address ————————————————————————————→ MAX address

Consider how each list would be ordered and whether it would be singly or doubly linked and whether or not it should be circular. Define the record structure for each list and write a procedure that returns the starting address of the memory allocated to a request for job X of size n K. Consider the three strategies—BEST FIT (locate the free block that fits the best), WORST FIT (locate the free block that fits the worst), and FIRST FIT (locate the first free block that fits)—in terms of how you would arrange the two lists.

11. Write a procedure that deletes a given node by copying the contents of the successor node into the fields of the node to be deleted and returns the successor to the available pool.

12. The POOF procedure in subsection 3.5 lacked a check for underflow, the situation of no available records. What condition would be used to detect this situation?

13. Revise the POOF procedure so that it checks for the underflow condition and prints a warning message.

14. Revise the POOF procedure so that it is a boolean function that returns a true value if a node is available and a false value if overflow occurs. There is no change to the rest of the assumptions given in this section.

15. Instead of using POOF and ZAP, you can use PASCAL's built-in procedures *new* and *dispose*. What is different about the declaration of the node structure? What operations are no longer necessary?

4.4 Applications

4.4.1 LINKED STACKS AND QUEUES

Section 4.3 introduced an idea that can be combined with an earlier idea to provide an imaginative solution to a common problem in system programming. In Chapters 2 and 3, the concept of multiple stacks or queues sharing the same storage space was presented. Both cases presented the possibility of having to shift entire stacks or queues whenever one had used all the available space. Bruce's unbiased nature and the nature of the available pool of nodes that he manages inspire a suggestion for implementing stacks and queues as linked lists. Let's see how the idea unfolds.

If we look carefully at how Bruce manages the available pool, we see a familiar behavior pattern. Where does he obtain a new node from? Where does he place a returned node? At the front of the linked list of available nodes.

Bruce has organized the available pool of nodes as a linked stack. The operations of POOF and ZAP are actually the stack operations of POP and PUSH.

We can set up a linked stack for an application program by using Bruce's available pool management procedures as a model. Let's use the dynamic allocation facility of PASCAL to manage the storage requirements. Let's also assume that we have defined the following types for a stack to be used in an application with return addresses and a register set:

```
type  POINTER = ^STACK_NODE ;
      STACK_NODE = record
                       RET_ADDRESS: integer;
                       REGISTERS:array[0..7] of integer;
                       LINK : POINTER
                   end ;
var   TOP,NEW_NODE:POINTER;
```

When a subroutine is called, its return address and current register set is placed on the top of the stack. First, storage must be allocated and then the appropriate fields must be filled with the necessary values. Assuming the presence of a procedure FILL _ IN to supply the values and using PASCAL'S built-in procedure *new*, the following two instructions prepare the way for the PUSH procedure:

```
new(NEW_NODE);          (* allocate a node,set up pointer*)
FILL_IN(NEW_NODE);      (* set RET_ADDRESS and REGISTERS*)
```

Since it is equivalent to an insertion at the front of the list, the PUSH procedure need only connect the links. In addition, no overflow check is required since storage has already been allocated by procedure *new*. The PUSH procedure is coded as follows :

```
procedure PUSH (NEW_NODE:POINTER; var TOP:POINTER);
begin
(* Connect new node to node currently on top of stack*)
NEW_NODE^.LINK := TOP ;
(* Update stack pointer to point to new node *)
TOP := NEW_NODE ;
end ;
```

The two steps in this procedure are similar to those found in Bruce's ZAP procedure.

The POP procedure mimics Bruce's POOF procedure. Writing this procedure in the context of linked stacks is left as an exercise.

Multiple stacks can easily be included in an application program without additional overhead as long as they share similar node structures. By having different stack pointers—TOP1, TOP2, TOP3, for instance—the various linked stacks can use the procedures *new, dispose,* POP, and PUSH without any strings attached, so to speak.

Implementing a queue parallels this last technique. A second external list pointer would point to the last node. This allows the REAR element to be identified and the relationship pattern of a queue to be implemented. Figure 4.21a illustrates this setup for a queue.

This straightforward technique is not the only alternative. The circular attribute can be used quite elegantly for the linked queue implementation. As Figure 4.21b shows, an external pointer can be used to point to the last element in a circular list (the rear element of the queue) and the circular nature of the list can be used to access the front of the queue through the link field of the rear element of the queue. The instruction would look like this:

```
FRONT := REAR^.LINK  (* set up pointer to front of queue *)
```

The circular attribute and some imagination creates the ability to change the front and rear elements of a list. Therefore, by writing a procedure to insert a new node after the node pointed to by REAR, a linked list operation, the operation ENTER a new node into the queue is accomplished. By stepping from the rear element to the front element and performing a delete operation on the linked list, the queue operation of REMOVE is also accomplished. Meanwhile, taking the linked approach to the queue implementation has opened a new opportunity for the queue. Now changes can easily be made anywhere in the queue and the implementation of a priority queue can be developed. Details on this flexible species of the queue family appear in the next section.

Figure 4.21

a. Two external list points—FRONT and REAR

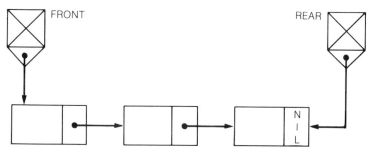

b. Circular attribute provides access to FRONT through REAR external list pointer.

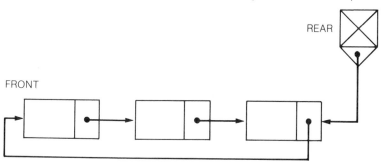

Assuming that a singly linked list with the circular attribute is used to implement the queue and that REAR is a pointer variable, the procedure for removing the front element of a nonempty queue is as follows:

```
procedure REMOVE (var REAR: POINTER );
var FRONT : POINTER ;
begin
(* Set up pointer to front data element *)
FRONT := REAR^.LINK ;
(* Check if only one data element is in queue *)
if FRONT = REAR then
                begin
                dispose (FRONT) ;
                REAR := nil
                end
            else
                begin
                REAR^.LINK := FRONT^.LINK ;
                dispose (FRONT)
                end
end;
```

The special case of changing the external list pointer is handled by setting it equal to nil. The ENTER procedure is left as an exercise for the reader.

With these linked implementations we have gained a flexible growth potential for stacks and queues. We can also have both queues and stacks share the storage space without a large overhead devoted to bookkeeping and without a need for costly data movement. But these gains have a cost. Because of the link field, this new implementation for stacks and queues requires more storage space. In addition, each stack or queue operation (insertion/deletion) will require another operation (POOF/ZAP) upon the linked list of available nodes, which incurs an added expense in time. Each side of the scale has the potential for outweighing the other, depending on the application in which the stack and queue are needed.

4.4.2   WHAT'S YOUR PRIORITY—DOLLARS OR SENSE?

The linked implementation for the queue information structure can also be used when insertions or deletions occur within the queue rather than only at the rear or front. We have all experienced a situation in which the natural ordering of a queue is disrupted when a person from the middle of the line is served before the person in the front because of some special condition.

Such phenomena can occur in other controlled environments with defined operating policies, producing beneficial results. This happens with the information structure called a priority queue. With this structure we have a field that designates the priority of the node (such as how much money the user is willing to offer). By using a linked implementation we can make changes at any position within the queue at a small overhead cost.

To illustrate some of the important aspects of the priority queue, let's invite our old friend QMAN back. Mr. QMAN is the fellow responsible for scheduling the use of the line printer in a multiuser environment. In Chapter 3 he was the pillar of equity and fairness, operating under the policy of first come–first served. But in these trying economic times he has developed an affinity for capital (as in dollars) and has instituted a clever new policy for the printer queue. He will still assign the printer to the user currently on the front of the queue. But when the user places the original request for the printer's services, she may also specify a priority number (in units of dollars). When QMAN (whom I shall now call $QMAN, for obvious reasons) places this request in the priority queue, he will use the priority number to determine the correct position and then link the request into the queue (and automatically debit your student account accordingly—aren't computer systems wonderfully efficient?). Since this new policy is not official, $QMAN does not advertise the change. If a user is unaware of this new feature and does not provide a priority number, QMAN naturally adds the request to the rear of the line.

To further illustrate $QMAN's devious ways, let's look at the procedure for adding a new request to the printer queue. The node structure is similar to the one given in Chapter 3. The link field will, however, be implemented by using PASCAL's pointer variables. The type declarations to match this approach are assumed to be in force. The important PRIORITY field has been added. Therefore, the node has five fields: account number, disk address of file to be printed, length of file, priority value, and link field. The procedure to perform the new policy of $QMAN will be as follows:

```
procedure  ENTER$ (REQUEST: NODE  ;var REAR: POINTER):
(* Assumptions for this procedure:
   REQUEST is a record containing the account number,
      disk address and length of file and the
      priority amount - zero if not supplied
   REAR is the external pointer to the rear of the queue *)
(* The algorithm will enter the request at the rear
      of the queue if the priority is zero. Otherwise it will
      traverse the circular list using a pointer and shadow pointer
      until either the correct priority position
      is found or one complete circuit is made *)
(* DECLARE LOCAL VARIABLES *)
var CIRCUIT : boolean;
    FRONT,PTR, SHADOW,NEWNODE: POINTER;
begin
FRONT := REAR ^ .LINK;
new (NEWNODE) ;
with NEWNODE ^ do begin
                    ACCOUNT := REQUEST.ACCT;
                    DISK := REQUEST.DISK;
                    LGTH := REQUEST.LEN;
                    PRIORITY := REQUEST.PRIORITY
                 end ;
(* Test for regular case of no priority *)
if REQUEST.PRIORITY = 0 then                 (* REGULAR ENTERING OF NEW NODE *)
                        begin
                          NEWNODE ^ .LINK  := REAR ^ .LINK;
                          REAR ^ .LINK  := NEWNODE;
                          REAR   := NEWNODE
                        end
                          else
                        (* Begin search at front of queue *)
                            begin
                            PTR : = FRONT;
                            SHADOW := REAR;
                            CIRCUIT := false;
                        (* Until proper position or full circuit *)
                        while (REQUEST.PRIORITY < PTR ^ .PRIORITY)
                                 and not (CIRCUIT)
                            do begin
                                SHADOW := PTR;
                                PTR := PTR ^ .LINK ;
                                if SHADOW = REAR then CIRCUIT:=true
                               end;
                        (* Link new node into queue *)
                        NEWNODE ^ .LINK := SHADOW ^ .LINK;
                        SHADOW ^ .LINK := NEWNODE;
                        (* Adjust external list pointer *)
                        if CIRCUIT = true then REAR := NEWNODE;
                        (* Don't forget the donation!! *)
                        COLLECT_DOLLARS (REQUEST.ACCT)
                        end
       end;
```

Upon looking at the procedure you see that it consists of a standard queue insertion operation and a regular circular linked list traversal with a conditional check for a special node and a safety check for a complete circuit. We have seen these operations before in separate sections. It is good to see how we can combine skills to solve problems in new and creative ways.

The priority queue is used in operating systems to better use the facilities of the computer system based on the requests that are present. A request that requires only a small amount of the computer's resources can be placed ahead of a request that will occupy the computer's attention for a considerable time period, thus giving the little person a break for a change.

4.4.3   CIRCULATION AND CIRCULAR LISTS

The instructor of a physiology course wants to develop a tutorial program for the blood flow cycle within the human body. She wants the program to be able to answer four types of questions that students pose. The instructor has selected the blood flow cycle that goes from the heart (left side) to the intestines, then the liver, then the heart (right side), then the lungs, and finally to the heart (left side), to begin its circuit again. Figure 4.22 depicts the circuit in both the physiological model and the information structure model.

The four questions that the instructor has selected are:

1. To which organ does blood first flow from organ A?
2. Blood entering organ A comes from which organ?
3. What is the blood flow cycle starting at organ A?
4. What organs are between organ A and B in the blood flow cycle?

Figure 4.22

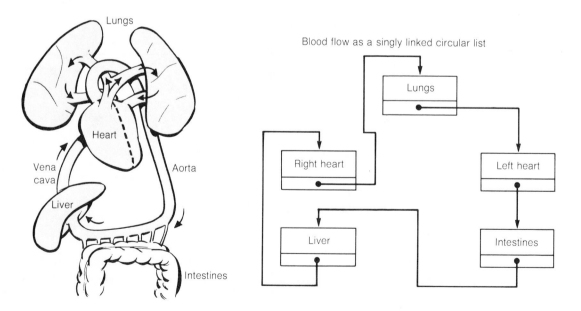

The program will respond to each type of question based on the organ or organs given by the student. The student may specify any of the five organs as organ A.

Let's begin the program development by looking at the conventions for the information structure. To represent the blood flow cycle between the organs, we establish a singly linked circular list. To implement the list, we use PASCAL'S dynamic allocation system. The first step is to declare a pointer type and a record structure:

```
type POINTER = ^ORGAN_NODE  ;
     ORGAN_NODE = record
                      ORGAN : string[11] ;
                      LINK : POINTER
                  end ;
```

Access to the circular list requires an external list pointer, LISTPTR. Since the blood flow cycle does not inherently have a first organ, I will arbitrarily select one organ, the lungs, for LISTPTR to point to initially. As each procedure uses the circular list, the external pointer will rotate around the circular list so that it always points to the last organ about which a question was asked.

Since I expect no changes to the circular list and the presence of a head node is helpful mainly in handling changes, there is no great need for a head node.

I will assume the presence of three procedures to aid in the problem solution. The first one I will call INITIALIZE. It will create the singly linked circular list by procuring nodes and by filling the data field and link field with the necessary values. It will also initialize the external list point, LISTPTR, to point to the lungs. The second procedure, ERROR, will be used to print messages to the student in case of errors. The last procedure, PRINT, will be used to print the names of the organs when necessary. The format of the output can be tailored to the specifications of the instructor at a later time.

From this point, I can begin by developing the procedure to answer the first question—to what organ does blood flow after leaving organ A? I will assume that the variable NODE is a pointer to the node that contains the name of the organ specified by the student. This is a very simple procedure since it requires only that I look forward in the circular list:

```
procedure QUEST1 ( NODE : POINTER ) ;
var NAME : string[11] ;
    NEXTNODE : POINTER;
begin                              (* Use link field of node to
                                      locate next node *)
NEXTNODE := NODE^. LINK;
NAME : = NEXTNODE^.ORGAN;         (* Retrieve name of organ from
                                      next node *)
PRINT (NAME)
                                  (* Print name of organ *)
end ; (* PROCEDURE *)
```

Two important steps precede action performed by this procedure. First, a menu of question options is displayed and a selection solicited. The selection is then checked for validity before one of the four option modules is called. This first step is a good exercise in designing a user-friendly interface. The second step takes place at the beginning of each of the four modules. The user is asked to supply the name of an organ around which the context of the selected question is framed. For the first time the information structure is accessed. The data supplied by the user must be transformed into a pointer to the node that contains that name. Therefore, the list operation LOCATE must be performed so that the pointer variable can be passed to the procedure QUEST1. Simple as the QUEST1 procedure is, the steps that prepare the way should not be overlooked. Figure 4.23 presents the overall design of the tutorial program. This design would have been the top-level process in developing the program.

The second question—from what organ does blood flow to organ A?—provides more of a challenge since it requests information not explicity contained in this information structure. It requires information about a node before a given node. As is the case with all singly linked lists, such information cannot be provided directly.

Two strategies can be pursued to answer this question. The first is to begin at the given node and take four steps through the linked list. Since there are five nodes in the list, it will always take four steps to arrive at the node before a given node. (If the list were of variable length, the presence of a head node would allow a counter to be kept in its data field so that this strategy could be applied.) Though this strategy would work for question 2, I will not use it because it depends on the list remaining unchanged, which makes the procedure data-dependent.

The second strategy is to make a full circuit through the list, using an auxiliary pointer (initially pointing to the given node) and a shadow pointer until the auxiliary pointer points to the node from which I started. The shadow pointer can thus, be used to provide the information to answer the question. Because this strategy produces procedure that does not depend on the length of the circular list, a change to the list does not require a change to the procedure. Its execution time does depend on the length of the list, since the procedure will always make one complete circuit.

A similar strategy, which does not always require a complete circuit, uses the external list pointer and a shadow pointer. Since, (by my previous conventions), the external list pointer is free to rotate around the circular list, I can take my chances that it is close to the desired node. In the worst case, it will be pointing to the given node, and I will make a full circuit. In the best case, it will be pointing to the node prior to the given node, and I will need to take only one step before the shadow pointer points to the correct node.

This last approach seems like the best strategy to follow for procedure QUEST2. Again, I am assuming that NODE is a pointer to the node that contains the name of the organ specified by the student. Here is the coded procedure.

```
procedure QUEST2 ( NODE, LISTPTR : POINTER ) ;
var SHADOW : POINTER ;
    NAME : string[11] ;
begin
SHADOW := LISTPTR ;                    (* Initialize shadow pointer *)
LISTPTR := LISTPTR^.LINK ; (* Take first step with external list
                                          pointer *)
while LISTPTR <>  NODE do              (* Until external list
                                           pointer
                                           reaches given node *)
              begin
                SHADOW := LISTPTR ;   (* Take another step forward *)
                LISTPTR := LISTPTR^.LINK ;
              end ;
```

Figure 4.23

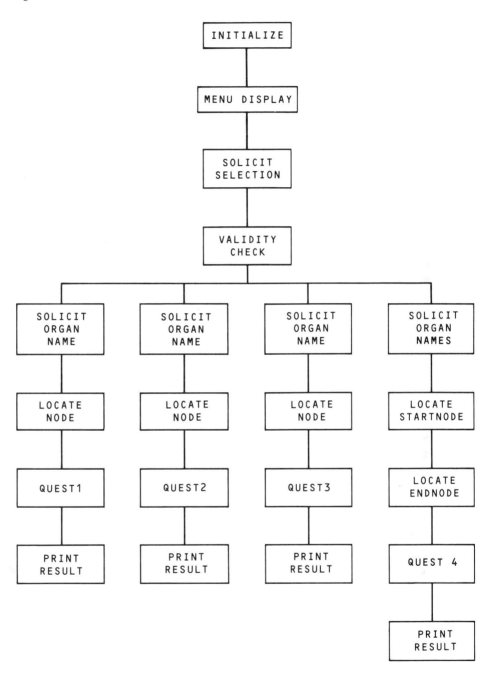

```
NAME   := SHADOW^.ORGAN ;          (* Retrieve name from previous node*)
PRINT (NAME)                       (* and print it *)
end; (* PROCEDURE *)
```

This procedure demonstrates the basic way to make a full or partial circuit of a circular list and to determine when to stop traversing the list. One pointer remains stationary as another is used to move from node to node until the two pointers are equal. We can apply this technique immediately by using it in the procedure to answer question 3—what is the sequence of organs through which the blood flows starting at the organ pointed to by the pointer variable NODE?

```
procedure QUEST3 (NODE : POINTER) ;
var PTR : POINTER ;
    NAME : string[11] ;
begin (* Print name of first organ and step to next node *)
NAME : = NODE^.ORGAN ;
PRINT (NAME) ;
PTR : = NODE^.LINK ;
            (* Until both pointers point to the same node *)
while PTR <> NODE do
            begin (* Print name of organ *)
               NAME : = PTR^.ORGAN ;
               PRINT (NAME) ;
                    (* And step to next node *)
               PTR : = PTR^.LINK
            end
end ; (* PROCEDURE *)
```

Once again we have a flexible procedure that does not require any changes if the number of nodes in the circular list is increased. This is an aim that you should incorporate into your programming strategy—the procedure should be independent of the data and depend solely on the nature of the information structures.

For the last question—what organs lie between organ A and organ B?—three separate cases must be considered. One is an error condition that occurs if the same organ is specified for organ A and organ B. The next case is a legitimate question with a special answer—if organ A is next to organ B in the sequence, no organs are between them in the blood flow cycle. The last case is the typical situation where the name of the organ(s) can be printed out. I will assume that there are two input arguments to this procedure, STARTNODE and ENDNODE, pointers to the nodes of the organs specified by the student. The procedure is given below:

```
procedure QUEST4 (STARTNODE, ENDNODE : POINTER) ;
var PTR : POINTER ;
    NAME : string[11] ;
begin
(* CASE 1 Start and end node are the same *)
if STARTNODE = ENDNODE then ERROR_MESSAGE
(* CASE 2 Start node points to end node *)
else if STARTNODE^.LINK = ENDNODE then
                        begin
                              NAME := 'NONE EXIST' ;
                              PRINT (NAME)
                        end
(* CASE 3 Typical situation - print names *)
```

```
else      begin
          PTR := STARTNODE^.LINK ;
          while PTR <> ENDNODE do
                begin
                  NAME := PTR^.ORGAN ;
                  PRINT (NAME) ;
                  PTR := PTR^.LINK
                end
          end
end ; (* PROCEDURE *)
```

The statements for processing the third case are similiar to procedure QUEST3 since the process is the same—a traveling pointer continues its journey along the path until it reaches a stationary pointer.

The four presented procedures and the two assumed ones can now be incorporated into a main procedure that interacts with the student. The main procedure would accept and interpret a student's request, accept the name of an organ and determine which node contains this name, and then call the necessary procedure, using the located node as an input argument.

The main procedure is concerned with the information structure in only two ways. It must initialize the singly linked circular list by calling the procedure INITIALIZE. And it must locate the node that contains the name of the organ input by the student. This could be done by another procedure, which uses the external list pointer, LISTPTR, as the starting node and steps through the list until a match is made or a full circuit of the list is made (which constitutes another error condition). Therefore, the external list pointer will be pointing to the node with the last inputted organ name.

If the instructor of the physiology course decides to expand the information in the blood flow cycle by including the names of the arteries and veins through which the blood flows between the organs, it will be necessary to change the lists, and some maintenance modules will be needed.

This application has provided a natural way to illustrate the processing of a singly linked list with the circular attribute. The way to detect a full circuit, the way to find a node before a given node, and the benefit of letting the external list pointer float around the list were important concepts developed in this section. Beginning at the beginning—the flow diagram of Figure 4.23—and following the conventions, you can develop the entire tutorial program by supplying the details of the modules that still lie in the sphere of abstract design. Thus another important concept that is illustrated in this section is the modular top-down design of application programs. May the subtlety of the illustration gain substance and reach the level of conscious application in all of your program designs!

4.4.4 THE KREBS ENERGY CYCLE

Dr. Digital's good friend, Dr. Maynard G. Krebs, has visited his office with a request. Dr. Krebs is preparing a lesson on the metabolism pathways of the human body for his class in human physiology. Dr. Krebs explains that the nutrients we ingest in the form of foods are used in various chemical pathways to provide either building materials or energy for each of our hard-working cells. Different nutrients (carbohydrates, proteins, and lipids) may take different pathways to produce energy for a "hungry" cell.

What Dr. Krebs is looking for is a hard-working student who is hungry for a little academic adventure. He wants a computer program that can assist his students in learning the sequence of chemicals involved in a particular metabolic pathway. Dr. Krebs has provided a diagram of the pathway, originally introduced in Figure 4.13 and now reproduced as Figure 4.24.

At first you may feel a bit overwhelmed by what you see. But listen to the words of Dr. Krebs concerning the diagram of this metabolic cycle: "The chemical pathway can be used either to store energy (the anabolic direction) or to release energy (the catabolic direction). Each chemical in the cycle is linked to two other chemicals; associated with each link is an enzyme that works as a catalyst.

"For example, isocitric acid is transformed with the aid of the enzyme aconitase to citric acid in an energy-storing (anabolic) reaction. Alternatively, the enzyme isocitric dehydrogenase converts isocitric acid to oxalosuccinic acid in an energy-releasing (catabolic) reaction.

"Notice also that at certain spots in the cycle other chemicals are produced (or consumed, depending on the direction). For instance, carbon dioxide is produced when oxalosuccinic acid is converted to ketoglutaric acid and consumed when the chemical reaction is reversed.

"A chemical that is produced in a catabolic (energy-releasing) reaction is consumed in the associated anabolic (energy-storing) reaction and vice versa. There are

Figure 4.24

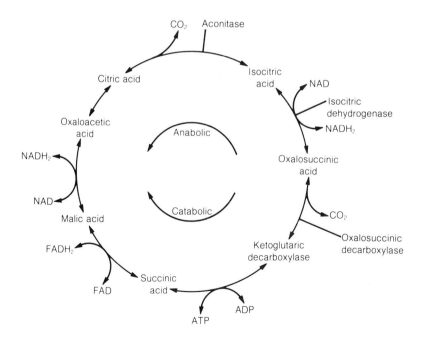

other aspects of the cycle, but these will be covered in later lessons. The areas that I am concerned with now are:

1. The sequence of chemicals in the metabolic cycle.
2. The enzymes associated with each individual chemical reaction.
3. The other chemicals produced during each reaction."

Let's consider a record structure that can be used to implement the metabolic cycle as a doubly linked circular list that includes the additional information about the enzymes and by-products. All the data will be chemical names or pointers. One approach is to set up a separate array of all the chemicals involved in the diagram. The record will contain pointers to the following chemicals: (1) the next and prior chemical in the sequence, (2) the enzymes used in the catabolic and anabolic directions, and (3) the chemical by-products of the reaction. Thus for each direction there will be three pointers in each record. The pointer to the chemical produced as a by-product could possibly be the NIL pointer, if there is no by-product. Figure 4.25 illustrates the node structure and presents the PASCAL code describing the record.

The application program will be based on two information structures: a doubly linked circular list of nodes consisting of seven pointers and a list of chemical names. This design allows for more than one node to point to the same chemical name, thus realizing a savings in memory.

A procedure that we will call INITIALIZE is needed to store the chemical names in the CHEMS array and to set up the doubly linked circular list with all the pointer fields correctly initialized. Writing this procedure would be a good appetizer for a hungry student of information structures.

Before you can develop any other procedures, you must know more about the way in which the student will access the information within the information structure. You need to ask Dr. Krebs about the format of the dialog between the student and the program. Your conversation with him results in a sample dialog between a student and the program. It is illustrated below with editorial comments in parentheses and student responses underlined.

```
HELLO, I AM HERE TO ASSIST YOU IN LEARNING THE KREBS METABOLIC
        ENERGY CYCLE. WE WILL BE WORKING TOGETHER TO LEARN THE
        SEQUENCE OF CHEMICALS IN THE CYCLE, THE ENZYMES THAT
        AID THE INDIVIDUAL REACTIONS, AND THE CHEMICALS THAT ARE
        PRODUCED OR CONSUMED BY THESE REACTIONS.
1. FIRST OFF, WHAT IS YOUR NAME, YOU COMPLEX BAG OF CHEMICAL
   PATHWAYS?
   ? WILMA
   MY NAME IS GILLIGAN,
   I AM A PRETTY COMPLEX BUNCH OF ELECTRONIC PATHWAYS MYSELF.
   OK, LET US GET STARTED,
2. AT WHICH SPOT IN THE PATHWAY DO YOU WANT TO START?
   ?OXALOACETIC ACID      (A response of ''ANY'' means the program
                           should randomly select a starting point.)
3. DO YOU WANT TO MOVE IN
   A CATABOLIC (ENERGY-RELEASING)
   OR ANABOLIC (ENERGY-STORING) DIRECTION?
   ? ANABOLIC
```

Figure 4.25

Sample node

Chemical name pointer	
Next anabolic chemical pointer	Next catabolic chemical pointer
Anabolic enzyme pointer	Catabolic enzyme pointer
Anabolic by-product pointer	Catabolic by-product pointer

Pointer to Oxalosuccinic acid	
Pointer to isocitric acid	Pointer to ketoglutaric acid
Pointer to isocitric dehydrogenase	Pointer to oxalosuccinic decarboxylase
Pointer to NIL	Pointer to carbon dioxide

Pascal type and variable declarations for node structure.

```
type  CHEM_NAME  = string [19];
      CHEM_POINTER = -1..24;
      POINTER = ^ CHEM_NODE
      CHEM_NODE = record
                    CHEM:CHEM_POINTER ;
                    NEXT_CHEM_ANABOLIC:POINTER;
                    ENZYME_ANABOLIC:CHEM_POINTER;
                    BY_PRODUCT_ANABOLIC:CHEM_POINTER;
                    NEXT_CHEM_CATABOLIC:POINTER;
                    ENZYME_CATABOLIC:CHEM_POINTER;
                    BY_PRODUCT_CATABOLIC:CHEM_POINTER;
                  end;
   var CHEMS: array[1..24] of CHEM_NAME ;
       KREBS_CYCLE : POINTER; HERE, NEXTNODE,
       HERE, NEXTNODE, KREBS_CYCLE : POINTER;
```

```
            4. HOW MANY STEPS IN THE SEQUENCE
               DO YOU WISH TO MOVE IN THE ANABOLIC DIRECTION?
               ? ALL              (An integer less than nine will allow a
                                      partial circuit of the circular list)
               OKAY, WILMA, HERE WE GO.
            5. WHICH CHEMICAL FOLLOWS OXALOACETIC ACID
               WHEN THE CYCLE IS STORING ENERGY?
               ? MALIC ACID        (For all questions in this section,
               CORRECT YOU ARE.        after two incorrect answers, the
                                          correct answer is to be given)
            6. WHICH ENZYME ASSISTS THIS REACTION :
               ? MALIC HYDROGENASE
               NO, GIVE ANOTHER ANSWER
               ? MALIC DEHYDROGENASE
               OKAY, WILMA
            7. WHICH CHEMICAL IS A BY-PRODUCT OF
               THE OXALOACETIC TO MALIC ACID REACTION?
               ? NONE
               CORRECT
```

```
8. WHICH CHEMICAL IS CONSUMED DURING THIS REACTION?
   ? NONE
   THAT IS ALSO CORRECT
   NOW TO THE NEXT STEP IN THE SEQUENCE, WILMA.
   WHICH CHEMICAL FOLLOWS MALIC ACID
   WHEN THE CYCLE IS STORING ENERGY?
   ?FUMARIC ACID
```
(Continue in the same pattern)

In addition to the procedure that produces the question sequence, accepts and analyzes the answers, and prints a response, certain questions will require a procedure that can access the information in the doubly linked circular list pointed to by KREBS _ CYCLE. For instance, question 2, which selects the starting point, will need a procedure that traverses the linked list in either direction until a specific node (selected randomly or by way of the answer) is located by a temporary pointer. The method for the traversal is the same as for previous algorithms. Either the NEXT _ CHEM _ ANABOLIC or the NEXT _ CHEM _ CATABOLIC pointer variable can be used.

Responses to questions 3 and 4—direction of movement and number of steps—do not require the information structure to be accessed; instead they initialize parameters that influence the remaining repetitive process. With question 5, the first substantive question, the doubly linked attribute is helpful since the next chemical may be the result of either an anabolic reaction (reached by the NEXT _ CHEM _ ANABOLIC pointer) or a catabolic one (reached by the NEXT _ CHEM _ CATABOLIC pointer). This access is also something we have implemented in a different context, the stock market example.

Questions 6 and 7—enzyme involved and chemical by-product—are very similar in that they require information other than structural information to be accessed from the record. The new twist is that the information is not contained directly within the record. Instead, a pointer to the information is available in the record. This pointer can be used to access the name in the CHEMS array. The student's answer can then be verified for correctness.

The last question—which chemical is consumed—definitely poses the major challenge of this problem. We must determine the correct answer to the question in order to check it against the student's answer. But which chemical, if any, is consumed is not contained either directly or indirectly in the record we currently have access to. The solution comes from a statement of Dr. Krebs' when he was explaining the diagram: "A chemical that is produced in a catabolic reaction is consumed in an anabolic reaction and vice versa." Therefore, since the catabolic reaction of oxalosuccinic acid to ketoglutaric acid produces carbon dioxide, then the anabolic reaction of ketoglutaric acid to oxalosuccinic acid consumes carbon dioxide. So we must look at the next record in the direction selected by question 3 (anabolic or catabolic?) and see if any chemical is produced when the reaction is reversed. The PASCAL code would look like the following, assuming the direction chosen was anabolic and HERE is a pointer to the record being investigated:

```
NEXTNODE := HERE ^ . NEXT_CHEM_ANABOLIC ;
CONSUMED := NEXTNODE ^ . BY_PRODUCT_CATABOLIC;
```

Now the identifier CONSUMED is either the NIL pointer or a pointer to the chemical that is consumed during the anabolic reaction between the chemical of the HERE record and the NEXTNODE record. The same method would be used if the original reaction was catabolic, except that the ANABOLIC and CATABOLIC modifiers would be interchanged.

We have now considered how the processing of each question relates to the doubly linked circular list. We can see how the circular nature of the list allows us to begin our tutorial session at any node in the list and make a partial or full circuit of the list. The doubly linked attribute provides a convenient way to mimic the reversible nature of our problem. We may also notice that the linked list is never changed after it is initialized. Though the ease with which linked lists can be changed is an attractive characteristic, it was not one which we needed in this application.

Now that the information structures for the problem have been designed, the format for the dialog has been specified, and varied considerations in processing the questions and accessing the information structures have been discussed, I'll leave it to you to fill in the details.

As you go through the mental processes of completing the project, remember that each of your body's cells is exercising the Krebs metabolic cycle to support your efforts. So treat them right and watch how you eat!

4.4.5   LISTS WITH SUBLISTS

In previous sections we have used linked lists with a homogeneous nature—that is, lists where all the nodes have identical structures. In this section this constraint will be lightened to provide for a general form of the linked list information structure.

Consider the following example. While preparing a pamphlet on the feeding of fruit trees, an agronomist finds that certain subgroups require the same nutrients. The structure of the list appears as follows:

Fruit Tree Feeding Plans

Tree	Feeding Plan
Apple	2
Pear	5
(Peach, Nectarine, Plum)	6
Fig	1
Cherry	3
(Lemon, Lime, Grapefruit)	8
(Orange, Tangerine)	4
Mango	9
Passionfruit	7

While the list consists of nine data elements, three of the elements are actually lists in themselves. How can we model this new relationship in an information structure?

If we consider a list to be a collection of objects that are either data elements or lists, we widen our scope of possible arrangements. With this new twist we can accommodate the agronomist's table.

Let us use our imagination to come up with a notation for this new generalized list. We can write the list as an ordered list of elements, indicating elements

IMAGINATION CHALLENGE

Draw six STRAIGHT and CONNECTED lines that will cross through all sixteen dots.

Rule 1: Do not lift the pen from the paper.
Rule 2: Do not retrace any drawn line.
Rule 3: These are the only rules.

```
·  ·  ·  ·
·  ·  ·  ·
·  ·  ·  ·
·  ·  ·  ·
```

that are themselves lists by enclosing them in parentheses. For example, the fruit tree list could be written as:

Trees = (apple, pear, (peach, nectarine, plum), fig, cherry,
         (lemon, lime, grapefruit), (orange, tangerine), mango,
         passion fruit)

This notation indicates that the list consists of nine data elements, six of which are individual trees and three of which are groups of trees.

The next step is to represent this list in a graphic way. Each fruit tree will have a node and will be linked to the next node in the list. The table is graphically represented as a linked list in Figure 4.26. As you can see, the nodes have the same structure even though certain fields have a different interpretation. One field of the node either indicates the name of the fruit tree associated with the node or contains a pointer indicating the first node in a sublist. Thus three of the nodes in the diagram contain pointers in their first field, since three sublists exist. In each of the three special nodes that indicate the beginning of a sublist, the field that normally contains the feeding plan number can be either unused or used for some other purpose. Since I wish to harvest a little extra educational benefit from the example, I will use this field to indicate the number of elements in the sublist. In algorithms that process the list, this may become a useful added ingredient.

Figure 4.26

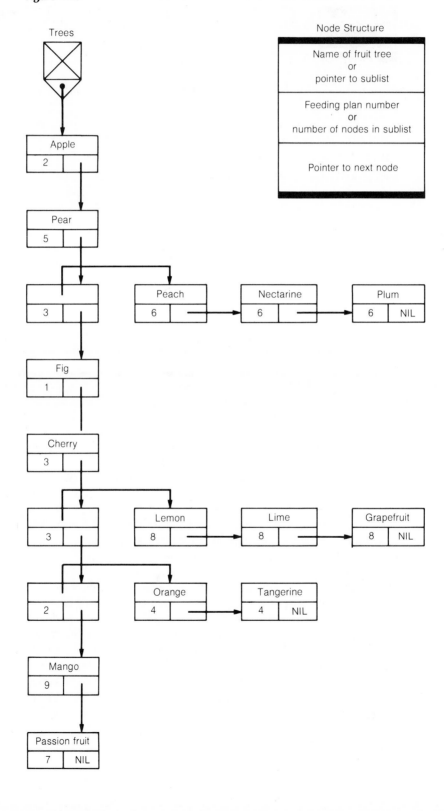

From an abstract perspective, this is how a generalized list is set up. Now let us move into a more practical setting and consider the implementation process.

The node structure can be implemented with arrays of records, with each record designed to facilitate the particular field requirements. The new problem that we encounter when implementing the generalized list is how to determine the significance of a field that can have two different interpretations, such as the field that stores either a feeding plan or the number of elements in a sublist. Once the difference is distinguished, different actions can be taken. But what convention can we establish to make the original distinction? If we add another field to the node, a boolean field, we can let the value of this field indicate which of the interpretations is to be taken for this node. For our agronomist friend, we would set up the following structure:

```
type NODES = record
                TAG : boolean  ;  (* to signify different kinds of nodes *)
                PTR : -1..17 ; (* pointer to tree name or beginning of
                                      sublist *)
                VALUE : 1..9 ;    (* feeding plan value or number in
                                      sublist *)
                NEXTNODE: -1..17; (* pointer to next node in list or
                                      sublist *)
             end;
        NAMES = string[12] ;
var LIST: array [1..17] of NODES;
    TREENAMES : array [1..14] of NAMES;
```

In this implementation, we have deviated from the graphic model by establishing a linear list of tree names and assuming the nodes will point to the names rather than containing the name directly. We did this so that the two values a field may have are of the same data type—a very important consideration during the implementation process.

The integer field PTR, therefore, will be either a subscript into the TREENAMES array or a subscript into the LIST array. The interpretation will be determined by the TAG field, where we will establish a convention such as TAG = *false* means PTR indicates the location of the tree name and TAG = *true* means PTR indicates the beginning of a sublist. Thus all algorithms that process the list will have to check the TAG field before proceeding with an activity on a node.

An alternate technique is suggested by the availability of variant records in PASCAL. Variant records allow a record to have a different structure based on a given tag field. Variant records for this example would be set up as follows:

```
type TREENAME = string[12] ;
     POINTER =  0..17 ;
     VARIANT_NODE  = record
                        LINK : POINTER   ;
                        case   TAG : boolean of
                 false   : (TREE: TREENAME;FEEDPLAN:1..9);
                 true    : (SUBLIST_PTR:POINTER;COUNT:1..10)
                 end ;
```

However, variant records are one of the most complicated features of PASCAL, and considerable study should precede their use.

We can see how sublists work by playing with another example. A leading toy manufacturer, Rosenblum Toys, Inc., has asked you to provide a program that will calculate the production costs of any toy in its inventory. The company already has the information structured in a certain way, and you will have to adhere to these conventions. After toying with the offer for a few seconds, you agree to the proposal.

Your first step is to determine what the information structures are. The data processing manager gives you the information found in Figure 4.27, including the node structure for each part that is used to assemble a toy, the PASCAL record that describes the node structure, and a sample parts list of two toys, the yellow submarine (a motorized boat that submerges when the level of rock music is above a certain decibel level) and Rita the heater maid (a motorized microcomputerized robot that can be programmed to turn on your electric blanket at night before you retire or to heat up water for tea when you awake and that has a radio hard-wired to the local rock music station).

Figure 4.27

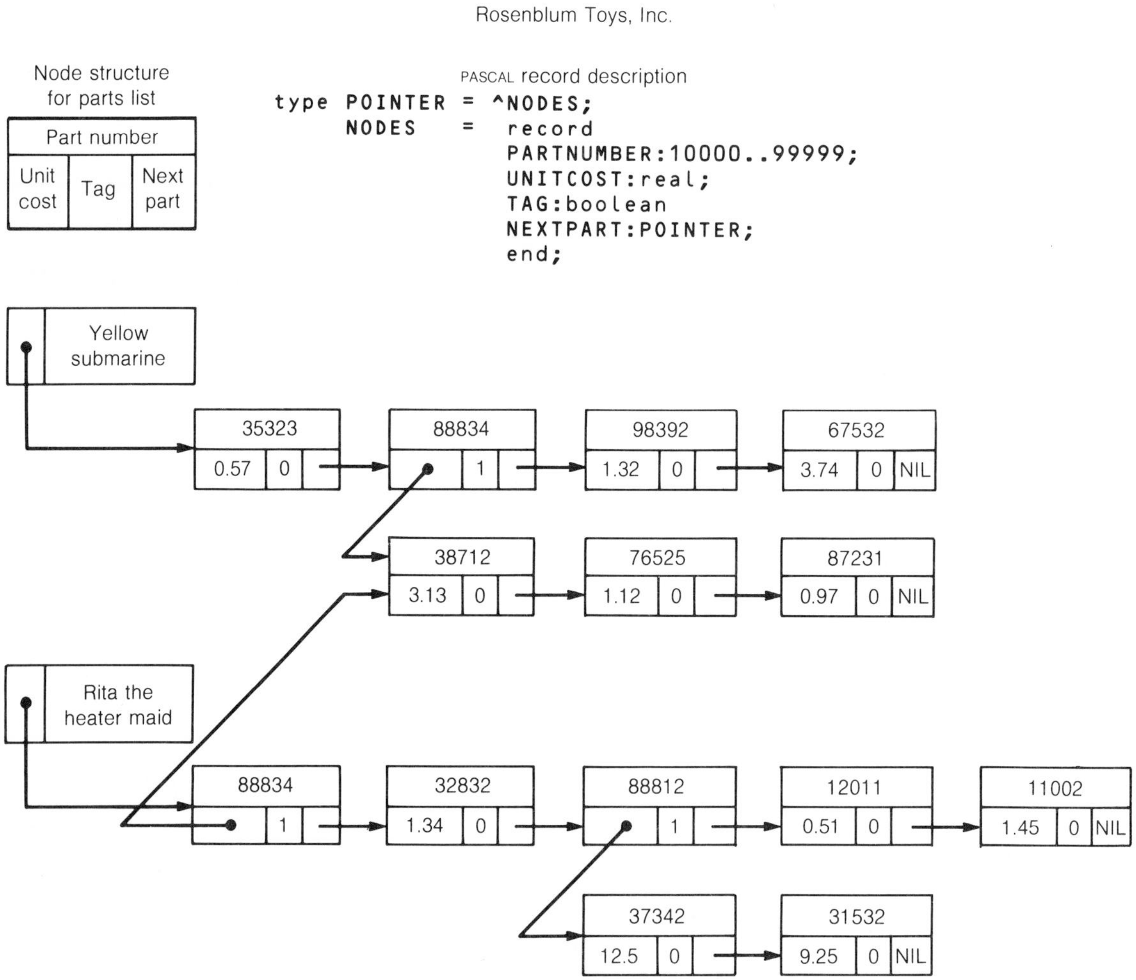

Rosenblum Toys, Inc.

From the information sheet you determine the significance of the TAG field and its associated field UNITCOST. When the tag is 0 then the field UNITCOST refers to the unit cost of the part in the list. Otherwise the field becomes a pointer to the first part in a subassembly (like the motor or the microprocessor). In this example, the list of parts for a toy can contain a sublist for a subassembly.

Each sublist is shared by more than one parts list. This is important because it shows that the person who designed the information structure was aware of the savings in memory space achieved with this imaginative idea. In the diagram, both toys share the same motor assembly.

You now can begin to design a strategy for the task at hand—calculating the unit cost of a yellow submarine. The strategy you select will have to sum the unit cost of all elementary parts as well as calculate the unit cost of any subassembly that may be encountered. What follows will basically be a casual walk-through along the linked list, following the NEXTPART link field to the next node, adding the unit cost to a running total, and occasionally, under the direction of the TAG field, taking a side stroll to calculate the cost of a subassembly, until the path comes to an end. The PAS-CAL procedure that you have designed is given below:

```
procedure COST ( PTR: POINTER; var: TOTAL:real);
(* Procedure to calculate the total cost to *)
(* assemble the toy pointed to by the pointer PTR *)
(* LIST is a global variable that contains the nodes for the *)
(* linked list and the node structure is as described *)
(* in Figure 4.27   *)
const SUBASSEMBLY = true;

var Q: POINTER;

begin
(* Initialize running total *)
TOTAL : = 0.0;

(* Begin casual walk thru until path ends *)
while PTR <> nil  do
      begin
      (* Check if node is for an elementary part or a subassembly *)
      if not (PTR ^ .TAG = SUBASSEMBLY) then (* Add unit cost to total *)
                      TOTAL : = TOTAL + PTR ^ .UNITCOST
            (* Else take a side stroll for subassembly *)
                      else begin
                            Q := PTR ^ .UNITCOST;
                            (* Q is a temporary pointer during stroll *)
                            while Q <> nil do
                            begin (* Add unit cost from subassembly *)
                              TOTAL := TOTAL + Q ^ .UNITCOST;
                              Q := Q ^ .NEXTPART;
                          end (* while block *)
                              end; (* else block *)
```

```
(* Step to the next node in the parts list *)
PTR := PTR ^ .NEXTPART;

    end (* while block *)
end; (* procedure *)
```

The procedure takes care of the toys that are assembled with either elementary parts or subassemblies, since we have been able to indicate with the TAG field when a sublist is a part of the list. We can provide more flexibility if sublists themselves are allowed to have sublists—if, in other words, the microprocessor subassembly has a part which is itself a subassembly. This would increase the depth of our information structure to another level. If we did this, we would also have to increase the depth of our side stroll in the procedure by another level.

Continuing increases of depth by allowing all sublists to contain sublists would quickly make the strategy used in this procedure not only highly inefficient but unworkable. If you are to provide the absolute flexibility mentioned above—that is, if you want all sublists to be able to contain sublists—you must look at the problem in an entirely new way, designing recursive algorithms to process completely generalized lists, since they are recursively defined.

This ends the chapter on linked lists. I hope that it has given you some new skills and tools to create software toys to entertain yourself and those who use your programs.

■ "JUST FOR REFERENCE"

Linked stacks—

- mimic the management of the available pool of records
- use PUSH to parallel ZAP, adding a node to the front of list
- use POP to parallel POOF, removing a node from the front

Linked queues can be implemented in two ways—

- by using a singly linked list with two external list pointers that show the front and rear of the queue
- by using a singly linked list with the circular attribute and one external list pointer that points to the rear element of the queue, whose link field is used in turn to locate the front element

Priority queue can be implemented by using a linked list, thus allowing insertion/deletions anywhere in the queue; the linked list is ordered by the priority field.

Circular list examples include—

- blood flow in the body—external list pointer was allowed to float around the list, giving the LOCATE operation a better average efficiency
- Krebs energy cycle—node structure consisted entirely of pointer fields; a special procedure was needed to initialize the circular doubly linked list

Generalized lists are lists that contain both data elements and sublists. Features are—

- node must include a tag field to determine interpretation of fields with multiple meanings
- PASCAL'S variant record feature can also be used
- recursive list definition opens up the opportunity for recursive algorithms

EXERCISES

1. Write the POP operation for a linked implementation of a stack.

2. Write a procedure FLIP that interchanges the first two data elements on a stack that is implemented as a linked list.

3. Can you think of any reason why a linked list with the circular attribute would be used to implement a stack?

4. Write the ENTER queue operation for a queue that is implemented as:

   a) a singly linked list;

   b) a singly linked list with the circular attribute.

5. Another approach to implementing a queue with a linked list is to use a circular singly linked list with a head node. Let two of the fields of the head node point to the FRONT and REAR elements of the queue. Write the INSERT and DELETE queue operations for this alternate approach to the linked implementation of the queue.

6. The procedure ENTER$ of subsection 4.4.2 adds a job of priority N before all other jobs of priority N currently in the queue. Alter the procedure so that the job is entered after the jobs of equal priority.

7. Occasionally, after submitting a job to $QMAN, the user may realize that the printout is not needed. For this occasion, write a procedure that deletes a given job from the priority queue. Remember to check for special cases and error conditions.

8. For the application presented in subsection 4.4.3, write the procedure LOCATE. Use the assumptions stated in the section and state any additional conventions that you adopt.

9. The professor of subsection 4.4.3 decides to add the arteries and veins to the blood flow problem; you decide to add a head node to the circular list. Discuss the ways that the inclusion of a head node affects the implementation and how it would aid or hinder the additions that will be made.

10. If you include a head node in a singly linked list with the circular attribute, what condition defines the empty list?

11. For the tutorial program on the Krebs cycle, a procedure was needed to initialize the circular doubly linked list and the array of chemical names. Write this procedure.

12. The following is an alternate description of the node used in the example of subsection 4.4.3.

```
type    TRIO  =  record
                    NEXT :  POINTER ;
                    ENZYME : CHEM_POINTER ;
                    BY_PRODUCT : CHEM_POINTER
                 end ;
        CHEM_NODE =  record
                       CHEM : CHEM_POINTER  ;
                       ANABOLIC : TRIO ;
                       CATABOLIC : TRIO
                    end ;
```

Using this new declaration, write procedures to answer questions 5, 6, 7, and 8 of the sample dialog. Assume the answers to questions 2 and 3 are the same as in the example.

13. Design a flow diagram for the complete tutorial program for the Krebs energy cycle and implement it in PASCAL.

14. Describe how you might design the Krebs energy cycle program without using linked lists.

15. Using the node structure described in subsection 4.4.5 for the fruit tree feeding plans, write a procedure that searches through the list of nodes pointed to by LIST _ BEGIN and locates the node whose tree name equals the identifier FRUIT _ TREE. Once the name is found your program should print its name and the feeding plan. If it is not found a message should be printed. State any assumptions that you make.

16. Write the same procedure using the variant record version of the node structure.

17. The data processing manager of Rosenblum Toys, Inc., has another assignment for you. A maintenance program is needed to update the unit cost field of all toys with a given part. Assume that you are given a pointer to a toy, PTR; a part number, PART _ NUM; and the new unit cost, UCOST. Assume that you do not have to check sublists for the part number. If the part number is present then update the unit cost field; otherwise do nothing.

18. For the toy inventory example, assume that subassemblies can recursively contain further subassemblies. Write a recursive procedure that calculates the unit cost of a toy pointed to by PTR.

19. Redo the above procedure by using a stack instead of recursion.

THE WORKOUT ROOM

PROJECT 1: *Getting the Blood Flowing*

Starting with the flow diagram of the blood flow example of subsection 4.3, develop the entire tutorial program. Provide the user-friendly interface for the student to select questions and another user-friendly interface for the instructor to add arteries and veins to the initial set of organs.

PROJECT 2: *Playthings*

Expand the toy inventory example of subsection 4.5 to include the following routines, which can be selected from a menu of options:

1. A routine to print the parts included in a given item.

2. A routine to add a part or subassembly to a given item.

3. A routine to order the parts in a given item by increasing part number.

4. A routine to print a summary of the number of parts in each subassembly of a given item.

5. A routine to print the part number of all parts that are in common to two given items.

PROJECT 3: *Standing by Your Word*

Since you take life *very* literally, you have decided to develop the world's first true WORD processing program. You are going to represent textual information as a linked list of WORDs. You begin with the following declarations:

```
type   POINTER = ^NODE ;
       WORD = packed array[1..15] of char;
       NODES =   record
                       DATA : WORD ;
                       PRIOR : POINTER ;
                       NEXT :POINTER ;
                 end ;
```

You plan to implement the following operations:

1. Inserting a word after the current cursor position (this is the default operation).

2. Deleting the word at the current cursor position.

3. Replacing a word at the current cursor position.

4. Moving the cursor forward *n* words.

5. Moving the cursor backward *n* words.

6. Exchanging the word at the current cursor position with the word before it.

Make whatever assumptions are necessary to make the WORD processor relatively functional, adding additional operations as you desire.

PROJECT 4: *Directory Access System*

Operating systems must manage the files on your diskette and in your account. One responsibility they have is to keep track of the files you have saved. Some systems allow the user to have multiple accounts in which files can be catalogued. The following example describes a hypothetical system.

The user may select one of five accounts, labelled USER0 through USER4. Each account is assigned a security level from 0 to 7 to control access. The user may save, delete, and move files within the five accounts. Each file is also assigned a security level from 0 to 5. The operating system provides the following operations, whose guiding policies are explained in the parenthetical comments.

1. Adding a file to directory N. (No policy is necessary.)

2. Deleting a file from directory N. (File security level is less than directory security level.)

3. Moving a file from directory M to directory N. (Directory M security level is less than or equal to directory N.)

4. Listing files in directory N—standard. (Only files with security level less than or equal to directory N.)

5. Listing files in directory N—enhanced. (Only files with security level less than or equal to the security level of directory N plus 2.)

6. Reporting directory N's status. (List the number of files in each security level not greater than directory N and list the total number of files with security level greater than directory N.)

7. Change security level of directory N. (No policy is necessary.)

You are the senior software engineer for the OPSYS group and must implement this directory access system. The information structure to be used is illustrated below. An array of external list pointers will be used to find the list of files held in each directory. The directory's security level is also included in the array. Each file will have a file control block, FCB, that is prepared by another part of the system. You will have access to it through the FCB_PTR, which is part of the node structure described below. Declarations are also included. Design the user interface and each of the modules to perform the seven operations described above. Thoroughly test your system and then get rich by marketing it to the mega-microcomputer market.

NODE DECLARATIONS FOR THE DIRECTORY ACCESS SYSTEM

```
type FILE_PTR = ^NODE ;
     FCB_PTR  = ^FCB  ;
     NODE = record
                FILE : packed array[1..8] of char;
                INFO : FCB_PTR ;
                NEXT : FILE_PTR
            end ;
     FCB  = record
                TRACK : 0..39 ;
                SECTOR : 0..15 ;
                SECURITY : 0..5
            end ;
     DIR_NODE = record
                    ACCOUNT_SECURITY : 0..7 ;
                    FIRST_FILE : FILE_PTR
                end ;
var  ACCOUNTS:  array[0..4] of DIR_NODE ;
```

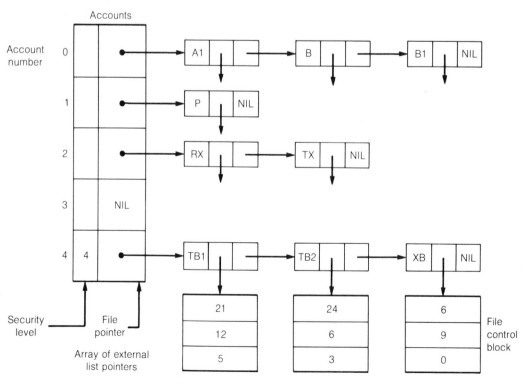

INSIGHTS WITH DR. DIGITAL

Scene: *Dr. Digital is in his office, using his word processor to compose a set of right brain exercises, when Wilma comes in with a copy of the following diagram. The diagram was given to Dr. D's morning class to illustrate a strategem for approaching problem solving. It seems that Dr. D has quite a few questions to answer.*

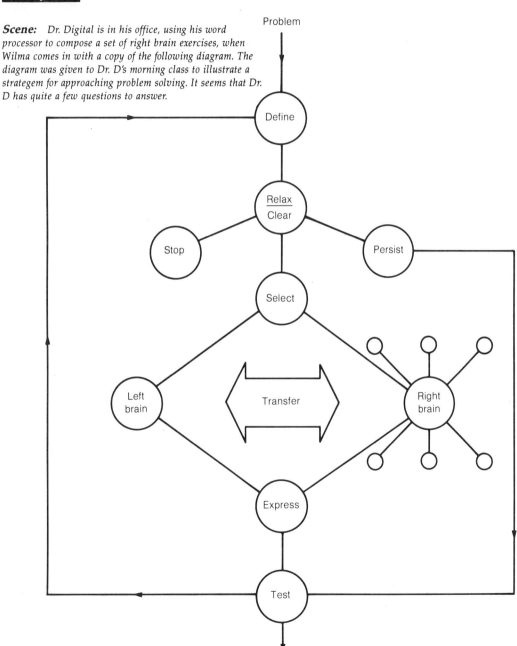

Problem

Define

Relax
Clear

Stop   Persist

Select

Left
brain   Transfer   Right
brain

Express

Test

Solution

Wilma: Hello, Dr. D! I see that you are plugged into microspace. Can I press your reset button and set up a little human interface for awhile?

Dr. D: Interrupt acknowledged, Wilma! Just let me control-KD this file and I'll be on-line in real time with you in no time. [Pause with the whirring sound of the disk drive.] Okay, what's on your mind?

Wilma: Well, this diagram that you gave us this morning. I've got a number of questions about it.

Dr. D: Okay, but before you focus our attention on the details, let me ask you a question. What do you see or imagine to be the general purpose of the diagram?

Wilma: Oh, how does it fit into the Big Picture? Well, the flow diagram provides alternate strategies for problem solving. Once the problem is defined, I can select a strategy of either the left or the right brain type. After expressing a possible solution, I can then test to see if it solves the defined problem. If it doesn't, then my choices are to try again, to choose another strategy, or to throw in the towel. How's that for a verbally painted big picture?

Dr. D: Well done—your left brain correctly translated the right brain image of the diagram. A very important point to emphasize is that this problem-solving approach enables you to consciously select the strategy that best suits the problem—instead of falling into a habitual pattern of problem solving.

Wilma: You know I appreciate that option, seeing how I've had problems with problem solving in the past. But some part of my brain is still not clear on this left-brain, right-brain stuff. [With a smile.] Can you perform one of those conceptual surgeries again?

Dr. D: Sure. Neurologists and psychologists have discovered that the two hemispheres of the brain have specialized and different functions. The left brain is the "thinker" in that the functions of verbalization, mathematical reasoning, classification, and judgement are centered there. So the left

brain exhibits the attributes of objectivity, abstractness, analytical reasoning, and control. The other hemisphere, the right brain, is the "dreamer." The functions of imagination, artistic expression, feelings, and drawing are found there. The right brain is characterized by the flavors of intuitiveness, playfulness, fantasy, creativity, and subjectivity.

Between the two is a continual interplay, depending on what is consuming your conscious energy at the time. However, education as we practice it is largely a left-brain activity, so it is possible to develop a preference for left-brain problem-solving strategies.

Recently, Wilma, experts have begun to suggest the need for a balance, a time to draw out and blend the artist and the scientist within each of us. Therefore, right-brain problem-solving strategies are becoming important skills to learn and—more important—to exercise. Imagination and visual thinking deserve a larger slice of the educational pie. Does this clear up the distinction for you, Wilma?

Wilma: Seems to have been a successful implant, Dr. D. My left brain thanks you and my right brain hugs you. Now, we can get down to some of those questions that are floating around upstairs.

Dr. D: Sure thing, Wilma. My biocomputer is on-line and ready for inputs.

Wilma: Okay, Dr. D, the first question is—how to define the problem?

Dr. D: Let's see. The goal is to recognize the nature of the problem, using both hemispheres. By raising questions, gathering information, and identifying hurdles and feelings, you begin to delimit the problem. At some point you will have to state the problem. Try expressing it both verbally and graphically, drawing on both hemispheres. Finally, list the objectives and criteria by which a solution can be evaluated. After you have moved to this clearer head space, you can relax and move on to the next step.

Wilma: Now, Dr. D, this next

step—relaxing—is most confusing. Whenever I'm working on an assignment, I feel guilty if I'm goofing off.

Dr. D: Maybe when you realize why relaxing is important then you won't feel guilty. By taking a swim in the ocean or a walk in the park, you are recognizing the fact that much thinking and insight occurs outside the conscious arena. Besides, because the next step is a three-way fork in the road, a clear mind will be a definite benefit at this crucial intersection. Do you think, Wilma, that you can take a break now without feeling those pangs of guilt?

Wilma: For sure, Dr. D—I clearly see that I make the choice to feel relief or to feel guilt. From now on, I'll choose the healthier option. I wish the decision of which type of problem-solving strategy to select—left-brain style or right-brain flavor—was as easy. Any insights on this, Dr. Digital?

Dr. D: Whether you are selecting your first strategy or selecting a new strategic direction, the problem is the same. On what factor do you base your decision? To paraphrase Robert McKim, the designer of the diagrams: "The master carpenter masters many tools and masters the matching of the tool to the task." Likewise with the master problem solver. But to reach the level of mastery one must practice, experiment, fail, and try again—thereby gaining experience. An especially important skill is flexibility, removing the locks, letting the judge go on vacation. Survey the field of strategies, looking for clues, and select the one that feels right. That's my advice.

Wilma: Dr. D, let's say I chose to look into the tool kit that I carry in my right hand. What kind of left-brain strategies will I find?

Dr. D: First, you'll notice the verbal strategies—the listing of facts and details, which depends on your ability to create categories. Next, you'll see some mathematical tools to use. The strategies that depend on logic, both inductive and deductive, will also be available. Overall, they will be the tools that you are most familiar

with. Try to be impartial in your selection of a left-brain tool, so that habitual patterns do not develop.

Wilma: What if I chose the other path, Dr. D? Can you give some examples of right-brain strategies?

Dr. D: Okay, Wilma. In the book *Experiences in Visual Thinking*,* author R. McKim divides visual thinking (another term for right-brain problem-solving strategies) into three aspects: seeing in a new way, imagining new things, and drawing what you see or imagine. When solving problems, you can use one, two, or all three aspects.

For example, when you have a bug in your program you could draw diagrams to trace the logic flow and the data flow through the parts. Or you could imagine that you are the computer and "execute" the program one line at a time so that you "see" it from a new perspective. You could even manipulate the program's image to see the effect.

There is a story about a virtual genius of visual thinking, Nicolas Tesla. He was able to create an image of a machine with details as precise as a blueprint. He said that he could actually test his mental inventions by having them run for weeks—after which time he would examine them thoroughly for signs of wear.

Wilma: Imagine that! Amazing! What did he invent?

Dr. D: The fluorescent lights on the ceiling and the AC current that powers our society. And much more.

So by opening your eyes to a new view, by opening your mind's eye and by graphically representing objects, concepts, and relationships you will be applying your right hemisphere to problem solving.

Wilma: Well, I've exhausted my question queue about the diagram, Dr. D. It all seems pretty clear to me now, but I'll have to go over it a few times before all the pieces fall into place. By developing the right-brain strategies, I will be adding some powerful tools to that programmer's tool kit that you keep mentioning. With practice on problems and challenges, I should master their use and their selection.

Dr. D: Yes, and I would strongly suggest that you get a copy of *Experiences in Visual Thinking* and enjoy the numerous exercises

and challenges to the dual-processor biocomputer that you carry in your head.

Wilma: I'm on a path to the library right now. Thanks for your help, Dr. D, and enjoy your return to microspace.

*Second edition, 1980. Brooks/Cole Publishing Company, Monterey, CA; a division of Wadsworth, Inc.

5

Trees

5.1 Setting the Stage

The famous poem that heads this chapter was penned by Joyce Kilmer to commemorate the beauty of the common tree, whether an acacia, a sycamore, an oak, a poplar, or a palm. The tree kingdom supplies us with wood for shelter, pulp for paper, syrup for pancakes, and oxygen for our atmosphere. On this physical plane we are much indebted to our lanky wood neighbors. In addition, trees nourish our feelings and emotions in many ways. Can you remember the joy of playing in their branches, diving into the cushion of autumn colors, or sharing a picnic in the cool shade of a favorite senior citizen of the tree family?

But it is the more lofty plane of concepts and ideas that now draws our attention to trees. Aside from Newton's enlightening experience under the apple tree, scientists of the computer arboretum have been able to look at the structure of the tree (with help from genealogy) and apply its structural concepts to data in a hierarchical relationship. The conceptual tree has its roots embedded in various fields of computer science: compiler design, operating system programs, data base systems, and a variety of applications programs. In all these cases, the programmer needs to preserve the order of a graduated series of classified data. Because the branched structure of actual trees mimics the abstract relationship pattern that is needed, the tree information structure has been formalized into a useful tool for dealing with hierarchically ordered data.

In the rest of this section we will look at ways the tree structure has been applied to different areas of thought. We will then see how the general characteristics of the examples can be abstracted, adding a new programming tool, the tree information structure, to our collection.

Genealogy, with its family trees, provides the background for the tree structure. In recording an individual's ancestors, the order of the generations is important. Genealogists have developed charts that clearly depict the relationships among the various ancestors. The chart shows direct relationships between two ancestors on the same line of ascent. To develop a feel for this system, fill in the names of your ancestors on the pedigree tree below.

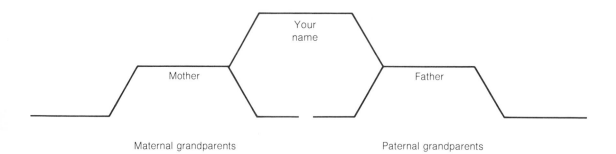

In this pedigree tree, two branches rise upward from each individual. The tree can be extended to whatever level of ancestors is desirable (or known). In the chart, your position at the root of both lines of ancestors makes clear your direct relationship with your maternal and paternal ancestors, as well as the indirect relationship between, say, your father's grandmother and your mother.

You were pivotal to the pedigree tree because other names ascended from yours. But it is important to notice that sections of your mother's and father's pedigree trees are also included within yours. We shall see that selecting a different pivot point or root will always create another tree structure to consider.

If you reverse your perspective by picking an ancient ancestor of yours and listing his descendants, you will create a genealogical tree called the lineal tree. How does this new tree differ from the first? The number of branches from your ancestor is no longer restricted to two, because the number of offspring can vary from zero to many. In addition, the pedigree tree can go back indefinitely, but the lineal tree has a fixed level until a new offspring arrives.

By redirecting your focus, you can find lineal subtrees for any descendant of an ancient ancestor. Within the lineal tree you can easily identify the common family relationships of not only your siblings but your first and second cousins. Figure 5.1 gives a sample of a lineal tree for a brief section of Noah's biblical descendants.

In the fields of botany and zoology, scientists have taken a similar approach to the classification of groups of plants and animals. Since individual pedigree trees don't apply here, the hierarchy and classification are based on similarity of form, function, and development of anatomical parts. Figure 5.2 shows a typical simplified family tree for one group of animals. It also illustrates a hierarchical classification and ordering. For instance, in Figure 5.2a the order Marsupialia is divided into four suborders: Diprotodonta, Peramelida, Polyprotodonta, and Caenolestoidea, with two of these groupings being further split into the families represented by the wombats, kangaroos, the native cats, and Tasmanian wolves. This hierarchical ordering can be expressed as a set of ordered pairs:

Figure 5.1

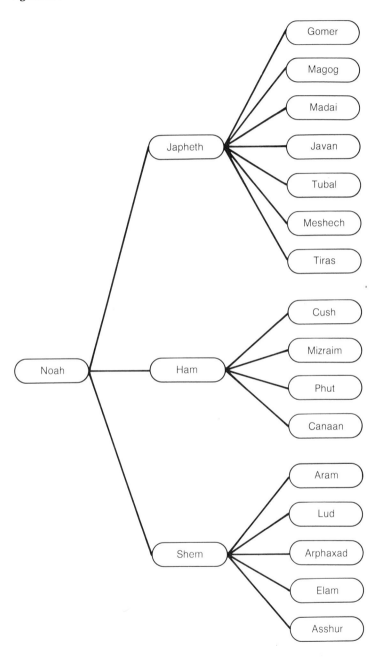

Figure 5.2a

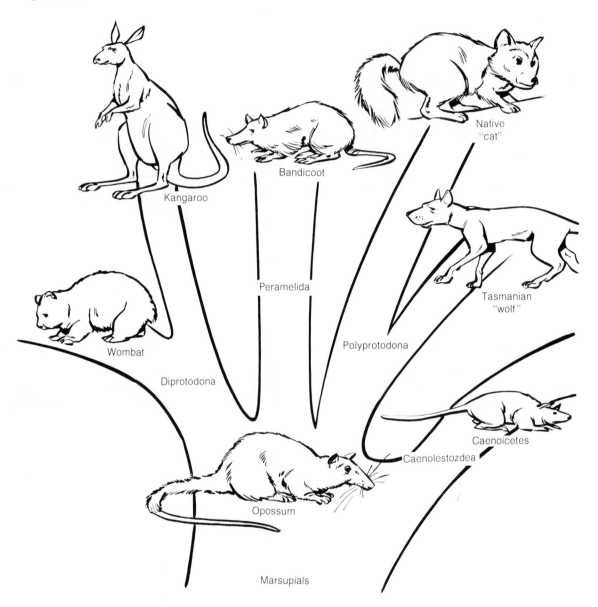

Tree of marsupials =
{(Mar.,Dipr.) , (Mar.,Pera.) , (Mar.,Poly.) , (Mar.,Caen.) ,
(Dipr.,wombat) , (Dipr.,kangaroo) , (Poly.,cat) , (Poly, Tas. wolf)}

A similar set notation will be used to describe trees in the later sections of this chapter.

With this notation, it is easy to see that the grouping Marsupiala is the most general and that kangaroos are related to the grouping Marsupiala by a transitive property.

Figure 5.2b

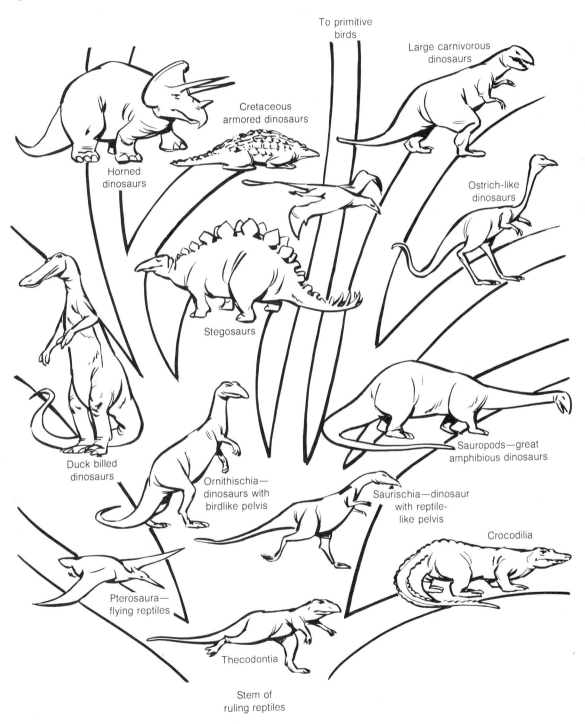

To primitive birds

Large carnivorous dinosaurs

Cretaceous armored dinosaurs

Horned dinosaurs

Ostrich-like dinosaurs

Stegosaurs

Duck billed dinosaurs

Sauropods—great amphibious dinosaurs

Ornithischia—dinosaurs with birdlike pelvis

Saurischia—dinosaur with reptile-like pelvis

Crocodilia

Pterosaura—flying reptiles

Thecodontia

Stem of ruling reptiles

The set of ordered pairs makes it clear that no ordering exists between the kangaroo and the Tasmanian wolf, although they share a common classification in Marsupiala. Therefore, the tree diagram is a pictorial expression of a hierarchical relationship among a set of elements. It clearly shows how an element is related to another element of the set.

The lineal and family trees of genealogy provide two concrete examples of the tree information structure. The relationship pattern that they possess is different from those presented in earlier chapters. Let us move on to the next section where the hierarchical relationship is formalized into our first nonlinear information structure.

■ "JUST FOR REFERENCE"

Hierarchical structures in genealogy and science include—

- pedigree tree—depicts the relationship among the ancestors of a selected individual; exhibits the transitive nature of the relationship; stretches backward in time to any desired depth
- lineal tree—depicts the relationships of a selected individual and his descendents; allows for variable number of relations for each individual; stretches forward in time to a fixed depth
- anatomical family tree—based on groupings of animals (or plants), not a selected individual; groupings based on form, function, and anatomical parts; relationships express evolution of subgroups; exhibits transitive nature; stretches forward in time

IMAGINATION CHALLENGE

You and five friends find yourselves faced with a farfetched problem that revolves around a ping pong ball. The ball has mysteriously bounced into a vertical pipe whose diameter is just bigger than the ball itself. The pipe is four inches tall and firmly embedded in the concrete floor. Looking around the room, the following "tools" are available:

1. a hammer
2. a light bulb
3. 100' of clothesline
4. a box of Wheaties
5. a monkey wrench
6. a wire coat hanger
7. a file
8. a chisel

Describe several ways to get the ball out of the pipe without damaging the ball, the pipe or the floor, so that you can get on with the Pied Pipe Ping Pong Program.

Each type of tree has certain common features—

- all contain subtrees of the same type (i.e., your pedigree tree contains your mother's and father's pedigree trees)
- each tree can be expressed as a pictorial expression of the underlying mathematical construct, a relation set of ordered pairs

EXERCISES

1. Is it possible to determine your great-grandmother's brother from your pedigree tree?
2. Is it possible to determine your father's maternal grandfather-in-law from your pedigree tree?
3. Write a phrase that characterizes the relationship between two related individuals in your pedigree tree.
4. List other animal species for which pedigree trees are kept.
5. Name two features that distinguish the lineal tree from the pedigree tree.
6. Some sales promotion organizations are based on a hierarchial relationship: you sponsor a number of new salespeople, they in turn sponsor additional salespeople. You receive benefits from the sales of people you sponsored and the sales of the people whom they sponsored. To which type of tree structure is this organization most closely related?
7. Draw the lineal tree of your maternal grandmother and write it out in the notation of a relation set—that is, a set of ordered pairs of names.
8. Describe how the lineal tree of exercise 7 is composed of specific subtrees.
9. Write an expression that defines the relation set of the lineal tree of exercise 7.

5.2 Formalizing the Structure: Binary Trees

5.2.1 ABSTRACT DESCRIPTION OF THE BINARY TREE

With this small family of samples, we can now look at the tree information structure in a more abstract way. The pedigree tree is in a class by itself. Each element has at most two branches leading from it. In our example, there were exactly two branches or none. But this will not be a general constraint of the binary tree.

The binary tree is very important to computer science. A formal description captures its nature: **A binary tree T is either an empty set or a finite set of elements that is divided into three disjoint subsets R, S1, and S2, such that the set R is a singleton set containing one element and the sets S1 and S2 are binary trees in their own right.** The sets S1 and S2 are called subtrees of the binary tree T while the set R is called the root of the tree T.

Relating this to your pedigree tree of Section 5.1, the set of elements is the set of you and all your ancestors to a certain level. You are the set R, the root of the tree; set S1 is the ancestors on your mother's side (which is your mother's pedigree tree); and S2 is your paternal ancestors.

In this formalization it is important that a binary tree be allowed to have no elements, so that the recursiveness of the definition will have a sufficient terminal condition. This special case shall be called the **empty binary tree.** It plays an important role in the development of most algorithms, and is a tribute to the human mind that a figment of the imagination can acquire such substance.

Consider the important features of this description:

1. The designation of one element as the root.
2. The division into two subsets besides the root set (either or both of which may be empty), which constitutes the binary nature of the structure.
3. Disjoint subsets, a necessity for separating trees from the graph information structure of the next chapter.
4. Two subsets that are themselves binary trees, which constitutes the recursive nature of the structure.
5. The empty binary tree as the terminal condition for the recursion.

In the next section various terms used to discuss binary trees will be introduced. I will also select a standard orientation for drawing a binary tree structure.

5.2.2 TERMINOLOGY AND STRUCTURAL DIAGRAMS

The illustrations of three trees of Section 5.1 demonstrate two different graphic orientations: vertical for the pedigree family tree and horizontal for Noah's lineal family tree. A third orientation—the one used most frequently in computer science texts and articles related to trees—places the root of the binary tree at the top with the subtrees extending downwards. This orientation, shown in Figure 5.3, will be used for easier reference in the text and algorithms.

In drawing a binary tree, I shall always consider the tree to be an ordered binary tree. This means that the order of the subtrees is important. Exchanging elements E

Figure 5.3

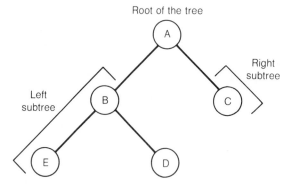

and D in Figure 5.3, for example, would produce a different binary tree, although its structure would be similar to that of the original binary tree. To further emphasize this attribute, I shall refer to the two subtrees of any element as the **left** and **right** subtrees.

All elements within the binary tree are called **nodes** and are further classified as root nodes, branch nodes, or leaf nodes. Using Figure 5.3 as a basis, the following elements can be classified into the three categories:

Node Category	Tree Elements
root	A
branch	B
leaf	C,D,E

Nodes A and B and nodes A and C are related in similar ways. The terms **parent** and **child** are used to refer to this relationship. The root node A is the parent of the branch node B, and the leaf node C is the child of the root node A. Since we are dealing with ordered binary trees, we also refer to the left and the right child of a node. Thus B is the left child of A, and D is the right child of B. The root node of a binary tree has no parent, a branch node has a parent and one or two children, and a leaf node has no children.

Nodes D and E illustrate another relationship that may exist between nodes. This relationship is expressed by saying that nodes D and E are **siblings.** Siblings are the left and right child of a common parent node. In Figure 5.3 another pair of nodes also exhibits the sibling relationship; which nodes are they?

Let's define a quantity to indicate the "distance" to the root. This quantity is useful in constructing trees that are evenly balanced. This attribute of distance from the root is formalized by the concepts of **level number** and **depth.** A level number is assigned to each node in the binary tree. The concept of depth is applied to the binary tree itself. The level number indicates the number of ancestor nodes in a direct line back to the root. By assigning a level number of zero to the root of the tree and using the rule that the level number of a child node is one more than that of the parent node, all nodes will be assigned a unique level number. Depth is defined as the highest level number of any node in the tree. Given the depth of a binary tree, you can compute the maximum number of nodes within the tree. If the depth of a binary tree is d then the maximum number of nodes equals

$$2^{(d+1)} - 1$$

For example:

Depth	Maximum Number of Nodes
0	1
1	3
2	7
3	15
4	31
5	63

Figure 5.4 **Ordered binary tree of depth 2**

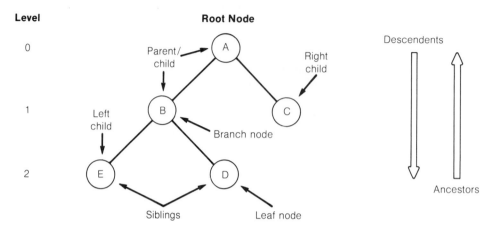

The terms **ancestors** and **descendants** are also used to refer to a collection of nodes in the binary tree. They refer to the same ideas as their common and genealogical usage. Descendants of a particular node have higher level numbers and are on a continuous line down the tree. Ancestors of the leaf node D are the nodes B (level 1) and A (level 0).

The various terms that have been described are illustrated in Figure 5.4, using the binary tree of Figure 5.3.

The following example shows how the formal set description can be applied to the binary tree of Figure 5.4. We will also use this notation in a later section. We must be able to list all the sets for all the subtrees and all the roots of all the subtrees until only empty subtrees are left.

T	= set of elements	= {A,B,C,D,E,}	
	relation Set	= {(A,B), (A,C), (B,E), (B,D)}	
R of T	= root of binary tree T	= {A}	
S1 of T	= left subtree of T	= {B,D,E}	level 0
S2 of T	= right subtree of T	= {C}	
R' of S1	= root of subtree S1	= {B}	
S1' of S1	= left subtree of S1	= {E}	level 1
S2' of S1	= right subtree of S1	= {D}	
R' of S2	= root of subtree S2	= {C}	
S1' of S2	= left subtree of S2	= empty binary tree	level 1
S2' of S2	= right subtree of S2	= empty binary tree	
R" of S1'	= root of subtree S1'	= {E}	
S1" of		= empty binary tree	level 2

S1'	= left subtree of S1'	
S2" of		= empty binary tree
S1'	= right subtree of S1'	
R" of S2'	= root of subtree S2'	= {D}
S1" of		= empty binary tree level 2
S2'	= left subtree of S2'	
S2" of		= empty binary tree
S2'	= right subtree of S2'	

This method of listing the roots and subtrees of any ordered binary tree can be used to verify that any claimed relation set of elements is indeed a binary tree. With the abstract binary tree described and a set of terms defined, we can now talk about the parts and relationships within a binary tree. It is now time to start at ground level and discover how to plant this information structure in the program environment.

■ "JUST FOR REFERENCE"

A binary tree is a set that can be divided into three disjoint subsets, R, S1, and S2, in which R is a singleton set and S1 and S2 are themselves binary trees.

Important features of the definition are that—

- the binary tree can be an empty set
- the subsets S1 and S2 are called subtrees of the root R and are considered ordered
- the ordering enables S1 to be labeled the left subtree and S2 to be the right subtree
- the binary tree also forms a relation set of ordered pairs of nodes
- this relation set is transitive

Terminology of relationships among nodes—

- **parent-child**—an ordered pair in the relation set
- **root**—node with no parent
- **branch**—node with a parent and one or two children
- **leaf**—node with a parent and no children
- **sibling**—node that shares a common parent with another node
- **level number**—the level number of the parent node plus one
- **descendants**—all children of a given node, recursively
- **ancestors**—all parents of a given node, recursively

EXERCISES

1. The definition of a tree information structure is a recursive definition. What is the terminal condition for the definition?

2. Define the terms root node, branch node, and leaf node.

3. The terms left and right subtree are a result of the binary tree having a special attribute. What is this attribute?

4. Draw a binary tree of depth 3 that has four pairs of siblings, five leaf nodes, one node that has an only left child, and another that has an only right child.

5. Write a formula that defines the level number of a node.

6. A tree of depth 4 can have a maximum of how many leaf nodes?

7. Counting subtrees of subtrees, a tree of depth 3 that contains the maximum number of nodes, 15, has how many subtrees?

8. Given the binary tree below,

   a) Write the relation set that is depicted.

   b) Show how the graphic representation satisfies the recursive definition of the binary tree using the notation at the end of subsection 5.2.2.

9. In binary tree of exercise 8, what policy appears to determine whether a node is a left or right child of a parent node?

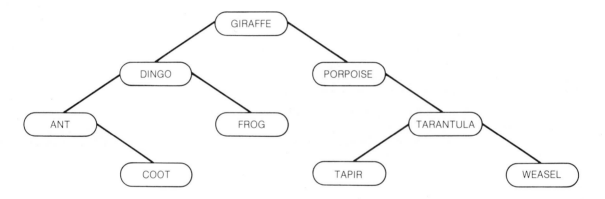

10. Based on the policy that you stated in exercise 9, add the following animal names to the binary tree of exercise 8:

    First egret, then human, then pelican, then wombat. What is the level number of each of these new nodes? (Hint: the new tree will have a depth of 4).

5.3 Implementing the Structure: Binary Trees

5.3.1 TREE NODE STRUCTURE AND A POOL OF TREE NODES

As we slip back into our role as computer programmers, we must begin to conjure up the spirit of imaginative implementation to transform the tree idea into a practical programming tool. The abstract binary tree must grow from the raw materials found in the program environment into an active and alive addition to the environment.

Once its supporting systems have taken root and the binary tree has found a successful niche to inhabit, it is up to you to find places for it to flourish.

The hierarchical, nonlinear structure of the tree does not fit the linear structure of the array. By taking a cue from the similar dilemma encountered with linked lists, we can apply the two methods presented in Chapter 4. In this way, we can mimic the nonlinear, branching structure of the binary tree by using the raw materials found in an available pool of array elements or provided through PASCAL'S dynamic allocation system.

To mimic the branching nature of the tree node structure, each record structure must have two pointer fields. This enables us to locate the left or right child of the tree node. Since each tree element has some data associated with it, the record contains either the data fields themselves or a pointer to the data. In Figure 5.5, two node structures using both implementation versions—self-managed and PASCAL'S managed pool of records—are presented. The choice of which to use depends on the size of the data fields and the need to move the data fields around, as well as whether the data will be referenced by other information structures (as in a data base system).

Now that the node structure is described, the support for the available pool is necessary. If you select the self-managed approach then you have responsibility for the managerial magic that Bruce revealed to you.

Figure 5.5 **Two node structures for binary trees**

Left child pointer		Data field(s)		Right child pointer

Left child pointer	Data pointer	Right child pointer

Dynamic allocation versions

```
type POINTER = ^NODE ;

     NODE =
       record
         LCHILD:POINTER;
         DATA1: (data
         DATA2:  types
         .        as
         .
         .        appropriate)
         RCHILD:POINTER;
       end;
```

```
type POINTER = ^ NODE;
     D_POINTER = ^DATA_RECORD;
     NODE =
         record
           LCHILD:POINTER;
           DATA_PTR:D_POINTER;
           RCHILD:POINTER;
         end;
```

Self-managed versions

```
type PTR_IDENTIFIER = -1..MAX;
     NODE = record
             LCHILD:PTR_IDENTIFIER;
             DATA1:
             DATA2:
               .
               .
               .
             RCHILD:PTR_IDENTIFIER
           end;
```

```
type PTR_IDENTIFIER= -1..MAX;
     DATA_PTR = 1..NUM_DATA;
     NODE = record
             LCHILD:PTR_IDENTIFIER;
             DATA:DATA_PTR;
             RCHILD:PTR_IDENTIFIER
           end;
```

You would begin by designing the CREATE _ POOL procedure to link the records in an array together. Notice that either pointer-identifier—LCHILD or RCHILD—may be used for this purpose.

The procedures for maintaining the pool are next—POOF and ZAP. As you recall, Bruce treated the pool of available records as a linked stack, so you must incorporate this behavior into the workings of the procedures.

Throughout these procedures, you are dealing with an array of records. This array is allocated space through a statement such as :

```
var TREE : array [1..MAX] of NODES ;
```

So with memory space set up and procedures posed to serve the caller, you are ready to move on to procedures that operate upon the tree structure.

The alternate potion can also be applied in the form of PASCAL's built-in magic—pointer variables and dynamic allocation. The record structure would be set up as in Figure 5.5, using pointer variables. PASCAL's procedures *new* and *dispose* would replace Bruce's POOF and ZAP, and the dynamic allocation system would replace the declared array TREE of the self-managed version. As usual, the choice is yours, based on the language available and the application being developed. You should be comfortable with either option in the remainder of this chapter.

5.3.2 BUILDING AND CLIMBING IN THE BINARY TREE

In nature, the first stage for trees is growth. In using binary trees in a program environment, we must also have some way to implement the tree's growth. In some applications, all the data for all the nodes are known in advance, and the entire tree can be built at one time. For example, a computer-assisted instruction program on the botanic classification of edible plants uses information that is well known and unchanging; the information tree can be structured before the program is developed. With other applications, the growth is slower, and the need for a new node arises after some of the tree has already been built and accessed. Such is the case with artificial intelligence, where decision trees will be built based on the changing conditions of the task at hand.

When the tree structure is fixed and known in advance, the programmer must use some method to 'build' the tree structure. One method is to assign each tree node to a specific record and to set up the pointer fields to preserve the relationships. A procedure can be written to initialize the records to match the arrangement planned by the programmer. After the initialization procedure is called, the application program can access the newly built tree structure. With this method, no available pool is required.

A method that is applicable to nonfixed, unknown tree structures as well is to write a procedure that adds a node to an existing tree based on the ordering relation defining the tree structure. The fixed tree is built by adding each node one at a time to the partially built tree. After a sequence of calls to the above-mentioned procedure, the resultant tree would be the same as that obtained using the first method.

The second method is more general, since you can add a node at any time during the execution of the application program. Thus the structure of the tree can change as nodes are added. The tree does not have to remain fixed, nor do all the nodes have to be known before the application program is off and running.

The basic algorithm for adding a leaf node to a nonempty binary tree is given below:

1. Get a tree node from available pool.
2. Locate position of new leaf node in tree.
3. If new leaf node is a right child
   then connect new leaf node to RCHILD field of parent else connect new leaf node to LCHILD field of parent.
4. Fill data field(s) and place NIL in LCHILD and RCHILD pointer fields of new leaf node.

An example can illustrate this method of building a tree, demonstrating the usefulness of the binary tree in the computer science field. We have all used an assembler or compiler to translate our higher-level language to a machine-usable one. Assume that we want to build and access a symbol table used by assembler. In this application, not all the symbol names are known in advance. Furthermore, between the addition of the next symbol name and the last one added, some processing by the assembler is likely to occur. Each symbolic name has a set of attributes (relocatable, nonrelocatable, etc.) associated with it; this information is kept in a separate structure. The tree node structure thus consists of three pointer fields. The arrangement is shown graphically in Figure 5.6.

To use this arrangement in a PASCAL procedure, we need the following declarations:

```
type POINTER = ^NODES;
     DATA_POINTER = 1..MAX ;
   NAME = record
           SYM: (*Data
           ATTR1: types
           ATTR2: to be
           ATTR3: declared here*)
           end;
   NODE = record
           LCHILD:POINTER;
           DATAPTR:DATA_POINTER;
           RCHILD:POINTER;
           end;
var NAMES: array [1..MAX] of NAME;
    NAME_COUNT:0..MAX;
```

I have left the data types of the symbolic name and its attributes unspecified, as they are not crucial to the discussion of trees and are assembler-dependent.

In building the symbol table, I will assume the existence of a couple of procedures that are supplemental to the main job of building the tree. When a new symbolic name is encountered during the assembly process a procedure that adds the symbolic name and its attributes to the NAMES array, using the next available unused location, is needed. The list of names in the array need not be sorted because the logical ordering, in this case alphabetically sorted, will be contained in the tree structure. Thus the names may be stored sequentially as they arrive from the calling procedure. Another important feature of the list of symbolic names is that deletions will not occur. This reinforces the decision to store the names sequentially instead of implementing a linked list. Based on these two factors, we can determine the next unused

Figure 5.6

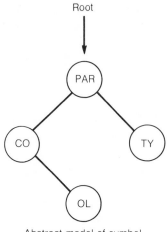

Abstract model of symbol
table as binary tree

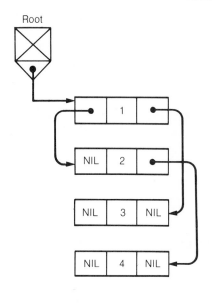

Dynamically allocated
nodes representing
the binary tree

1	PAR	432	R	0
2	CO	474	R	0
3	TY	462	N	1
4	OL	430	N	0

Array of symbol names
and attributes

location of NAMES by keeping a counter of the number of names currently in the
list, NAME _ COUNT. With this implemented, the procedure can pass as a return
argument the subscript value of the location where the newly encountered symbolic
name was placed in the NAMES array. This will become the value of DATAPTR.

If you are to write the procedure as an exercise, we must agree on the argument
list.

The calling statement shall be:

```
ADDTOTABLE (SYMNAME,AT1,AT2,AT3,PTRTODATA);
```

where the input arguments are SYMNAME, the symbolic name as a string of four characters, and AT1, AT2, AT3, the associated attributes; and where the return argument is PTRTODATA, the subscript value of the location where the symbolic name and its attribute have been stored in the array NAMES. Notice that two entities are assumed to be global: the array NAMES and the counter for the number of names in the list.

Now, I am ready to become an aide in the arboretum and design a procedure to add a new leaf node to the tree of symbolic names. My algorithm will be based on the earlier one, with the inclusion of the special case of adding a leaf node to the empty tree. To do this, I will need an external pointer to direct me to the root of the binary tree, which I shall call SYMBOLTREE. The empty tree will be indicated by this external pointer having the *nil* value.

One step in the aforementioned algorithm was to locate the position of the new node in the tree. This step will depend on the following ordering principle of the nodes: the left child of a node is lexicographically (alphabetically) less than its parent, and the right child is greater than its parent. Therefore the symbolic name CO is the left child of the symbolic name PAR and the symbolic name OL is the right child of the symbolic name CO. This enables me to determine the proper position of a new leaf node in the binary tree that represents the symbol table. Finding the correct position is the main task of the procedure. It also uses a technique reminiscent of the shadow pointer technique of linked lists.

```
procedure    ADDTOTREE(PTRTODATA:   DATA_POINTER;
                   var SYMBOLTREE: POINTER);
const LEFT = 0; RIGHT = 1; (*Any distinct values will do*)
var SYMNAME , TREENAME: string[4];
    NEW_NODE, PARENT, CHILD:POINTER;(*Pointers to tree nodes*)
    DIRECTION:LEFT..RIGHT; (*Indicator for left or right branch*)
begin (*Retrieve symbolic name from record in names array*)
SYMNAME := NAMES [PTRTODATA].SYM;
new (NEW_NODE); (* Get a new tree node from available pool *)
(*Test for empty binary tree, make new node the root*)
if SYMBOLTREE= nil then SYMBOLTREE:=NEW_NODE
    else
    (* Locate position of new node in tree*)
    (*Initialize pointer to root of tree*)
    begin
    CHILD := SYMBOLTREE;
    while CHILD <> nil do
        (*Update parent shadow pointer and continue looking*)
        begin
    PARENT := CHILD;
    TREENAME := NAMES[PARENT^.DATAPTR].SYM;
    (*Determine if new symbol is less than tree symbol*)
    (*This statement determines the ordering within the tree*)
    if SYMNAME < TREENAME then
        begin (* Move left  *)
            CHILD := PARENT^. LCHILD;
```

```
                DIRECTION := LEFT
            end
      else (*Move right*)
            begin
                CHILD := PARENT^.RCHILD;
                DIRECTION := RIGHT
            end
        end;  (*When child is nil*)
    (*Determine if new node is left or right child of parent*)
    if DIRECTION = LEFT then
                PARENT^. LCHILD := NEW_NODE
                else
                PARENT^. RCHILD := NEW_NODE
      end; (*of section to locate position of new node*)
  (*Fill data field and pointer fields of new node*)
  with NEW_NODE ^ do begin
                DATAPTR := PTRTODATA;
                LCHILD := nil ;
                RCHILD := nil
              end
    end;  (*of procedure to add a new leaf to the tree*)
```

If the tree is empty then SYMBOLTREE will point to NEW _ NODE and its data field and pointers will be filled. The tree experiences its first growth. Otherwise, the procedure steps from the root to either its left or right child until it can step no further. At this point it has located the node to which to attach the new leaf node. Thus it experiences another touch of springtime growth. Using this procedure and calling ADDTOTABLE whenever a new symbol is encountered, the symbol table and its associated alphabetically ordered binary tree are gradually built until the assembler has encountered all symbolic names. At this point the information structure is completely built and ready to be used.

I did, however, intentionally leave out one important feature. I didn't take into account the possibility of duplicate symbolic names. This error condition is not detected by this procedure and it should be. Enthused readers can modify the procedure so that an error message is produced and the procedure terminates without affecting the symbol table or symbol tree. Is the procedure ADDTOTREE or ADDTOTABLE the more appropriate place for the error detection to occur?

You have watched the construction of a binary tree by slow addition of leaf nodes in their proper positions. We could also have used the root of another tree and attached an entire subtree to the binary tree in much the same way.

Shifting back to the assembler application, after the symbol table is constructed the assembly process begins another pass through the assembly language code. During this pass, it must use the attribute information in the table to assemble the machine code into the object file. A typical action during the second pass is encountering a symbolic name and looking up its attributes in the symbol table. This can be done in either of two ways:

1. You could undertake a linear search of the NAMES array until the symbolic name is found and then fetch the attributes. The execution time for this task is proportional to half the length of the symbol table: on the average, 16 comparisons are needed if 32 names are in the table.

2. The second option uses the binary tree to perform the search. The search algorithm is similar to the algorithm for locating the correct position for a new node.

Since the binary tree has been ordered during its construction, this feature can be used for searching out a particular symbolic name. Basically the strategy is:

Look at the left child if the searched-for symbolic name is less than the symbolic name in the tree,

or

look at the right child if the searched-for symbolic name is greater than the symbolic name in the tree

until there is a match (the two names are equal) or a leaf node is encountered (meaning the searched-for symbolic name is not in the tree).

Does this search strategy improve the search time needed to find the desired attributes? In the optimum case, a tree with 31 names will take a maximum of five comparisons. However, this depends on the shape of the binary tree, which is determined by the sequence in which the symbolic names are encountered and placed in the binary tree. Figure 5.7 depicts two examples that represent the worst and best cases. The worst case is one that requires the most work (i.e., execution time), and the

Figure 5.7

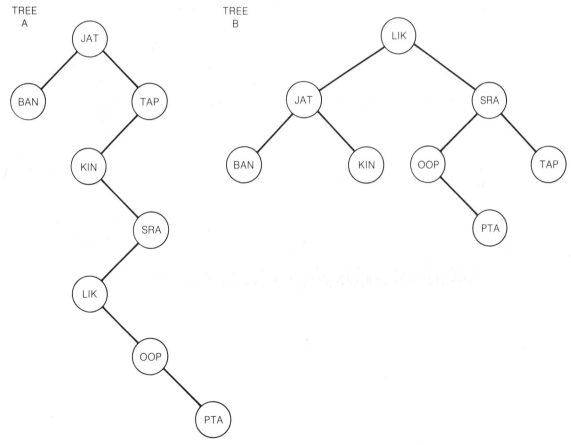

Sequence of symbolic names added to each binary tree:
a. JAT, TAP, KIN, SRA, BAN, LIK, OOP, PTA
b. LIK, SRA, JAT, KIN, BAN, OOP, TAP, PTA

Figure 5.8

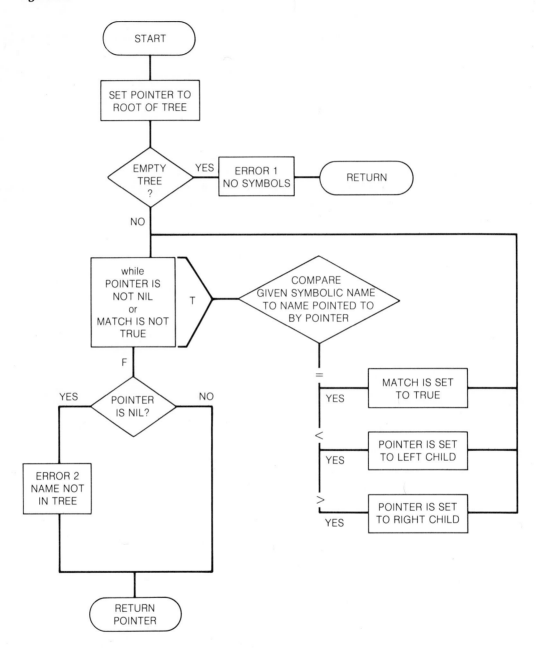

best case takes the least. Both trees contain the same set of symbolic names, but the order in which they are encountered is different.

Finding the attributes of the symbolic name OOP for tree A of Figure 5.7 will require six comparisons before a match is found. It will require only three comparisons with tree B. Tree A is close to the worst case of a linked linear list, which gives us the same execution time as the first option using a linear search. Tree B is close to the best case of a tree that is evenly balanced and requires the minimum number of comparisons (equivalent to the binary search, which is proportional to log base 2 of the number of elements in the tree).

The shape of the tree is described by the largest level number, the depth, and the number of nodes in the tree. Assume L is the largest level number of any node in the binary tree and N is the number of nodes in the binary tree. By considering the ratio

$$\frac{L}{\log_2(N + 1) - 1}$$

the nearness to a completely full, evenly balanced binary tree can be determined. As the ratio nears unity, the tree's shape approaches the evenly balanced binary tree; as the ratio grows farther from unity, the binary tree becomes more unbalanced.

It still is not possible to say exactly how efficient the tree search will be. In all but the worst case, it will be better than the linear search. So for the needs of the assembler's second pass, the tree search is the better option.

The flowchart found in Figure 5.8 gives the complete algorithm for locating an arbitrary symbolic name in the binary tree. This flowchart includes the detection of two error conditions.

5.3.3 ACCESSING ALL AND ALTERING PART OF THE TREE STRUCTURE

In binary tree processing, the need often arises to process all nodes in the tree exactly once. To ensure that the condition "exactly once" is met, a systematic method must be devised. Processing (or visiting) every node exactly once is called **traversing** the binary tree. Computer scientists traditionally use three similar methods to do this.

INORDER Traversal

Continuing with the assembler symbol table example, when the assembly process is completed, an assembly listing is normally produced. This listing includes the symbol table (symbolic names and attributes). The simplest way to produce the list is to print the array NAMES, which contains this information as a simple linear list. But simplest is not always best. By traversing the binary tree in a special way, we can produce an alphabetical list of symbolic names. This should not be surprising, since the crucial decision of whether to take the left branch or right branch during node insertion was based on a lexicographic criterion.

The idea behind this traversal is to visit (process) all the nodes in the left subtree of the root *before* visiting the root and to visit all the nodes in the right subtree *after* visiting the root. It is important to note that this method is applied to the subtrees in similar fashion. Thus, for our symbol table tree, all the symbolic names in the left subtree, which are alphabetically less, will be printed before the symbolic name of the root node; all the symbolic names in the right subtree, which are alphabetically greater, will be printed after. In this way an alphabetical list is printed.

The idea has the flavor of recursion, of the divide-and-conquer variety. The strategy is to traverse a tree by traversing its subtrees until the empty binary tree is encountered. I will present both the nonrecursive and recursive implementations of this idea.

For example, with the simple tree below the nodes are visited in the following sequence:

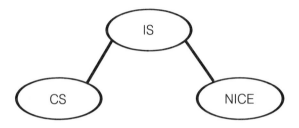

1. Left subtree (CS)
2. Root node (IS)
3. Right subtree (NICE)

In this simple example, it is easy to see how the traversal technique, called INORDER traversal, produces an alphabetical list of three symbolic names. However, on a binary tree that reaches to a greater depth, a large knot in the INORDER traversal technique must be untied. By looking at the binary tree B in Figure 5.7, we can appreciate the difficulty; then we can untie the knot with some imaginative fingers.

Before the symbolic name LIK can be printed, the subtree with root JAT must be traversed. But before JAT can be printed, the subtree with root BAN must be traversed. This is easy, so the symbolic name BAN is printed. But what do we do next? From your vantage point as a human, it is easy to say, "back up to the root node JAT and print it." But from the vantage point of a procedure, it's not so simple. How does the procedure remember to back up to the correct one of the two symbolic names waiting to be returned to, JAT or LIK? The procedure must remember which root nodes have been passed and, more important, the sequence in which they have been passed. The relationship is that the last root node passed over is the first root node to be returned to, a LIFO relationship.

At the beginning of our adventurous path, we met the stack information structure. We now have the good fortune to meet it again in a new context. The stack can be used in an INORDER traversal procedure to keep track of the root nodes that must be visited after their left subtrees are traversed. By pushing the root node on the stack before taking its nonempty left branch and popping the stack after the left subtree has been traversed, we can be sure the INORDER will return each time to the correct root node.

The INORDER traversal method and the important function of the stack in this method can be demonstrated by a detailed walk-through of the algorithm. The binary tree of Figure 5.9 will be our traversal lab specimen.

Figure 5.9

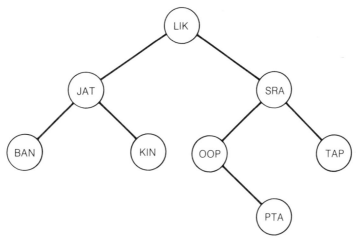

Sequence of nodes visited during INORDER traversal:
BAN   JAT   KIN   LIK   OOP   PTA   SRA   TAP

To illustrate the INORDER traversal method using a stack, let's use the set notation for the tree and all of its subtrees. For this example, we have TREE = root R, left subtree S1, and right subtree S2 where

R = (LIK)
S1 = (BAN, JAT, KIN)
S2 = (OOP, SRA, PTA, TAP)

The basic strategy for the traversal algorithm is listed below:

Steps for INORDER Traversal of a Nonempty Tree

1. PUSH root onto stack.
2. Traverse left subtree (S1).
3. POP stack—root.
4. Visit root.
5. Traverse right subtree (S2).

When applying these steps to our sample tree, we must remember three things. First, to traverse a left or right subtree that is empty means to do nothing and to continue with the next step. Next, for our assembler application, to visit the root means to print the symbolic name pointed to by the root. Third, in this illustration the stack will contain the symbolic name, though in the succeeding PASCAL procedure and in actual practice, it is more efficient to PUSH and POP pointers to the symbolic name. Having laid this groundwork, let's put on our climbing shoes and begin our walk through the binary tree.

Bottom

        STACK   empty
        Initially

R = {LIK}
S1 = {BAN, JAT, KIN}
S2 = {OOP, SRA, PTA, TAP}

Step 1   PUSH root = (LIK)

Top
```
| LIK |    |
```

Step 2   Traverse left subtree = {BAN, JAT, KIN}
           where R = {JAT}, S1 = {BAN}, S2 = {KIN}

  Step 1   PUSH Root = JAT

Top
```
| LIK | JAT |
```

  Step 2   Traverse left subtree = {BAN}
          where R = {BAN}, S1 = S2 = empty

    Step 1   PUSH root = BAN

Top
```
| LIK | JAT | BAN |
```

    Step 2   Traverse left subtree = empty

    Step 3   POP stack—root = BAN

Top
```
| LIK | JAT |
```

    Step 4   Visit root   *BAN* (printed)

    Step 5   Traverse right subtree = empty

  Step 3   POP stack—root = JAT

Top
```
| LIK |    |
```

  Step 4   Visit root   *JAT* (printed)

  Step 5   Traverse right subtree = {KIN}
          where R = {KIN}, S1 = S2 = empty

    Step 1   PUSH root = KIN

Top
```
| LIK | KIN |
```

    Step 2   Traverse left subtree = empty

    Step 3   POP stack—root = KIN

Top
```
| LIK |    |
```

    Step 4   Visit root   *KIN* (printed)

    Step 5   Traverse right subtree = empty

Step 3   POP stack—root = LIK

```
| empty |    |
```

Step 4   Visit root   *LIK* (printed)

Step 5   Traverse right subtree = {OOP, SRA, PTA, TAP}
where R = {SRA}, S1 = {OOP, PTA}, S2 = {TAP}

Step 1   PUSH root = SRA

Top

| SRA | |

Step 2   Traverse left subtree = {OOP, PTA}
where R = {OOP}, S1 = empty, S2 = {PTA}
Step 1   PUSH root = OOP

Top

| SRA | OOP | |

Step 2   Traverse left subtree = empty

Step 3   POP stack—root = OOP

Top

| SRA | |

Step 4   Visit root   *OOP* (printed)

Step 5   Traverse right subtree = {PTA}
where R = {PTA}, S1 = S2 = empty
Step 1   PUSH root = PTA

Top

| SRA | PTA | |

Step 2   Traverse left subtree = empty

Step 3   POP stack—root = PTA

Top

| SRA | |

Step 4   Visit root   *PTA* (printed)

Step 5   Traverse right subtree = empty

Step 3   POP stack—root = SRA

| empty | |

Step 4   Visit root   *SRA* (printed)

Step 5   Traverse right subtree = {TAP}

where R = {TAP}, S1 = S2 = empty

Step 1   Push root = TAP

Top

| TAP | |

Step 2   Traverse left subtree = empty

Step 3   POP stack—root = tap

| empty | |

Step 4   Visit root   *TAP* (printed)

Step 5   Traverse right subtree = empty

The INORDER traversal therefore produces the following sequence of printed symbolic names:

BAN JAT KIN LIK OOP PTA SRA TAP

Our alphabetical listing is produced **by this traversal method and, quite importantly, by the method used to build the tree in the first place.** It is the complementary nature of both algorithms that provides us with the capability of producing a sorted list from the hierarchial tree structure.

To move from the illustration to the PASCAL procedure for implementing the IN-ORDER traversal technique, we must dig into our programming bag and pull out one stack that can hold pointers to the symbolic names and the procedures EMPTY, PUSH, and POP. We shall use the structure that was described in Section 5.3.2, NAMES. The identifier PTR will be used to point to the nodes as we traverse the tree. The operation of visiting the node will be handled by another procedure, PRINTNODE, which can be tailored to the desired specifications. For safety's sake, the possibility of trying to traverse an empty tree will be checked before the main traversal steps begin. The procedure will at first appear to be different than the illustration. But by carefully following its flow, you will see that it does indeed faithfully implement the strategy outlined. Let's now look at our first traversal procedure for a binary tree.

```
procedure INORDER (SYMBOLTREE:POINTER);
(* Nonrecursive traversal procedure using pointer variables
   and dynamic allocation  *)
(* Assume a stack is a global structure supported by the
   procedures EMPTY, POP, PUSH*)
var PTR:POINTER;
begin (*Test for nonempty tree*)
if SYMBOLTREE <> nil then
    begin
    PTR:=SYMBOLTREE;
    (* While stack has a node in it or PTR points to a node *)
    while (not EMPTY) or (PTR <> nil) do
        begin
        (* Move down left branch until leaf node *)
        while PTR <> nil do
                begin
                    (* STEP 1 PUSH root pointer *)
                    PUSH (PTR) ;
                    (*STEP 2 Traverse left subtree begins*)
                    PTR := PTR ^ .LCHILD
                end;
(* Return to nodes that were passed by*)
        if not (EMPTY) then
                begin
                    (* STEP 3 POP STACK - to pointer*)
                    POP(PTR);
                    (*STEP 4 Visit root*)
                    PRINTNODE (PTR);
                    (*STEP 5 Traverse right subtree begins*)
                    PTR := PTR ^ . RCHILD
                end   (*STEPS 3, 4*)
        end (* Main while loop*)
    end
end;    (* Procedure for INORDER traversal*)
```

The coded strategy of this procedure first checks for a nonempty tree as an argument. If the argument SYMBOLTREE indicates an empty tree has been passed, no action is taken. The main *while* control loop is based on two conditions: the stack of root nodes to be visited is not empty or the pointer is indicating that a right subtree is still to be traversed. If both conditions are false, the procedure will terminate. The next *while* control structure is designed to traverse the left subtree recursively by pushing the root of the left subtree, then traversing the root's left subtree until it is empty. After this condition is reached, three steps are taken: the root of the most recent subtree is removed from the stack; the root is visited via PRINTNODE, and finally the working pointer is set to the right subtree of the root in preparation for its traversal. The method used to traverse the right subtree is to consider it as another tree and to start the process from the top at the main *while* control loop. Therefore, the procedure "calls itself" with part of the original data and recursion is emulated.

This procedure allows us to process all nodes in a binary tree exactly once. When we combine this ability with the ability to locate any given node and to build a sorted binary tree, we have a firm base on which to stand regarding binary tree processing. These three capabilities are used frequently in computer science in situations that require the hierarchical relationship for which trees are best suited. The binary tree building technique is commonly called a tree sort (when you want to sort N numbers or keys into ascending order) and the phrase **tree search** refers to finding a particular number or key after the group has been sorted. The tree search is the same as the algorithm for searching for the attributes of a given symbolic name presented earlier. In effect, we have just developed some multipurpose programming tools.

POSTORDER Traversal

Though the INORDER traversal is very powerful, it does not suit all needs. The following example is found in the area of compiler design and is related to a topic presented in conjunction with stacks—the postfix algebraic expression. Since algebraic expressions are made up of operators that use either one or two arguments, the root of the tree can be the operator and the subtrees can be the operands (where one subtree is empty for unary operators). In this way, the operand itself can be another algebraic expression and hence a subtree. Figure 5.10 shows two binary trees that represent two distinct algebraic expressions. By reordering the sequence of steps of the INORDER traversal methods, the POSTORDER traversal method is created. The sequence for a POSTORDER traversal is:

1. Traverse left subtree.
2. Traverse right subtree.
3. Visit root.

This recursive algorithm produces the sequence of visited nodes indicated in Figure 5.10. Check for yourself that the POSTORDER traversal does indeed produce the sequences given.

As you can see, INORDER doesn't distinguish between the two distinct expressions, while POSTORDER produces two different sequences. The two distinct sequences happen (not by chance or magic, either) to be the postfix notation of the original infix expressions.

Figure 5.10 **Binary trees as algebraic expressions**

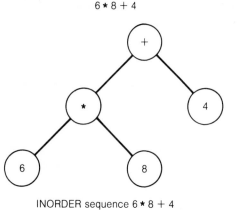

6 ✶ 8 + 4

INORDER sequence 6 ✶ 8 + 4
POSTORDER sequence 6 8 ✶ 4 +

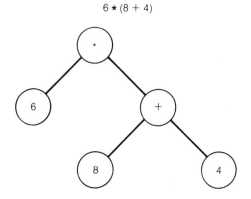

6 ✶ (8 + 4)

INORDER sequence 6 ✶ 8 + 4
POSTORDER sequence 6 8 4 + ✶

How can this approach be used by the compiler designer? If (and this is a very big "if") the assignment statements in a program can be transformed into binary tree expressions, the expression can be evaluated very efficiently by using postfix notation (derived from the POSTORDER traversal of the tree) and the stack algorithm presented in Chapter 2. Because it offers the added advantage of unambiguous postfix notations, this option is very attractive to the compiler designer. So it is helpful to consider more than one method for walking through a binary tree. We have found an area close to our home ground where it bears fruit.

The POSTORDER procedure will be presented in a different way. It is not surprising that recursion can be applied to binary tree processing, since the definition of a tree is recursive. For traversals, recursion is quite apt. If we write a procedure for traversing a tree, we must traverse subtrees at two points. Why not call the original procedure at these two points, since each subtree is a tree in its own right?

The concept of recursion applied to the new traversal method, POSTORDER, yields a surprisingly elegant PASCAL procedure. Assume that the procedure VISIT processes the node in whatever way is specified by the application.

```
procedure    POSTORDER (TREEPTR:POINTER);
begin    (* RECURSIVE POSTORDER TRAVERSAL PROCEDURE*)
      if TREEPTR <> nil then
                  begin
                  (*STEP 1 traverse left subtree*)
                  POSTORDER ( TREEPTR ^ .LCHILD);

                  (*STEP 2 traverse right subtree*)
                  POSTORDER ( TREEPTR ^ .RCHILD);

                  (*STEP 3 visit root*)
                  VISIT (TREEPTR)
                  end
      end;
```

This procedure looks more magical and mystical than even Bruce could have conjured up. It took refined minds to see the beauty of this concept and even more wizardry to implement the concept. J. McCarthy, a virtual giant in the field of computer science, is credited with introducing the idea of recursion in his 1960 article, "Recursive Functions of Symbolic Expressions and Their Computation by Machine."[*] McCarthy quickly brought his brain child to bloom by including recursion in the LISP programming language that he and others presented in 1962. The idea is attractive enough to have been included in most major programming languages since then.

The procedure does indeed work, though at first it seems unbelievable, as is often the case with magical things. You can use the POSTORDER traversal procedure to traverse any example that we have seen. As you step through the procedure, be sure to notice the characteristic of suspended action while another smaller but similar task is tackled, and finally the return to the point where the action was suspended. Also notice that the only time the procedure does not call itself is when an empty subtree is being traversed. Recall that this is similar to behavior found in the INORDER traversal. With the POSTORDER recursive procedure as a model, write the INORDER traversal recursively.

Don't let the simple appearance of the procedure fool you. The recursive power is expensive in increased execution time. The power's magic lies in having a built-in stack and the maintenance routines for the stack embedded in the programming language. This added execution time—overhead that is reduced when the programmer manages the stack as in the INORDER traversal procedure—is a major factor to consider. Using PASCAL involves a trade-off: you can have elegance if you can bear the expense, or you can economize and "grow your own."

PREORDER Traversal

The third traversal method is analogous to the other two. It is called PREORDER because the root of the tree is visited before its subtrees are traversed. The three steps for this traversal are:

1. Visit root.
2. Traverse left subtree.
3. Traverse right subtree.

This traversal runs a course like the others, but a different sequence of nodes is visited. With the binary trees of Figure 5.10, which represent algebraic expressions, we obtain the sequences:

```
+ * 6 8 4    and    * 6 + 8 4
```

These are the prefix notations for the expressions. Note that the three types of traversal are closely connected to the three notations for expressing algebraic formulas.

A PREORDER traversal of an individual's pedigree tree would result in a sequence where the individual whose tree it is, is followed by his maternal ancestors and then by his paternal ancestors. (This is assuming a tree ordered as in Section 5.1). The sub-

---

[*]CACM Vol. 3, No. 4, April 1960, 184-185.

groupings are the same: the mother is followed by her maternal ancestors and then by her paternal ancestors.

Another interesting application of PREORDER traversal is in situations similar to the table of contents of a book. In these situations, there are multiple sections, each of which can have one or more subsections, each of which can in turn have one or more subsections, etc. Such structures are also found in botany and zoology, where life is divided into kingdoms, kingdoms into phyla, phyla into one or more classes, classes into one or more orders, orders into one or more families, families into genera, and finally genera into one or more species. The following binary tree (Figure 5.11) representing the subdivisions of a hypothetical book, *The History of Trees*, shows how PREORDER traversal is applied.

Why the binary tree is organized in this particular way is a later topic for subsection 5.5.2. Notice that the right child ancestors of each root node are in the same grouping—that is, at the same level organizationally.

The PREORDER traversal of the table-of-contents binary tree produces a sequence

Figure 5.11

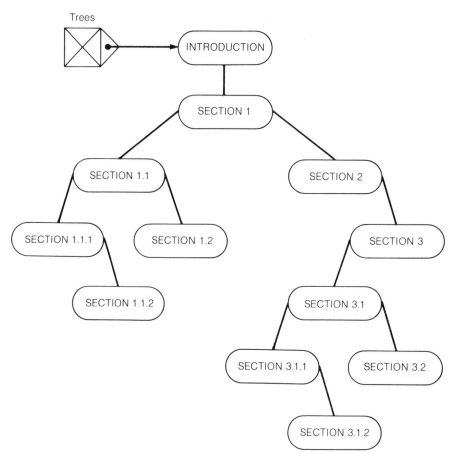

of nodes that is compatible with the order in which you would read the sections. The sequence is:

```
Introduction Section 1 Section 1.1
Section 1.1.1 Section 1.1.2 Section 1.2
Section 2 Section 3 Section 3.1
Section 3.1.1 Section 3.1.2 Section 3.2
```

A PREORDER procedure could be useful for a university library information retrieval system in which students could view sections of textbooks on a video display system. Notice how the original structure of the tree in conjunction with the traversal method produces the desired ordering of the table of contents.

The procedure for the PREORDER traversal may be written either recursively or nonrecursively. It parallels the POSTORDER and INORDER procedures.

We now have three different ways to walk through a binary tree. Because each has its own distinct flavor, each is attractive to particular applications. Your next challenge is to develop the skill to sense quickly the flavor hiding in various applications of binary trees and select the complementary traversal.

Deleting a Node from a Binary Tree

Altering part of the structure of a binary tree is not a simple task, because of the structure that may reside below the point where the change is being made (for instance, the subtrees of a node to be deleted). There are no simple algorithms that can delete an arbitrary node from a tree and preserve the order of the structure. You must approach the problem as a collection of cases, with each case defined by certain conditions and handled by special processing. In presenting the following operation for deleting a node from a tree, I will assume that the binary tree is built and ordered so that an INORDER traversal will produce an ordered list. This is the same setup as existed with the symbol table for the assembler or that would exist for a collection of keys stored in a tree in ascending order.

To specify the deletion operation, we must have two parameters: a pointer to the node to be deleted and a pointer to the parent of the node to be deleted. The pointer variable N will refer to the node to be deleted; the pointer variable P will refer to its parent. Node N may be either the left or right child of P, and this possibility must be accounted for in all cases. I will assume in all cases that the tree is being implemented by using dynamically allocated records, with three fields in each record—LCHILD, DATA, and RCHILD. The PASCAL code for performing the deletion process for each case will be presented as program segments, not as complete procedures.

The easiest deletion operation, deletion of node N and its subtrees, is a basic pruning operation. The only processing necessary is to change the link field of the parent P so that it no longer points to N and then to return N and all the nodes in its subtrees to the available pool. The deletion is performed by:

```
if P ^ .LCHILD = N then P ^ .LCHILD := nil
                    else P ^ .RCHILD := nil
```

IMAGINATION CHALLENGE

The following diagram shows an assortment of handscapes. Using only your skills of visual imagery, determine whether the left or right hand is being depicted. No "hands-on" testing is allowed. (With perseverance you can overcome this challenge hands down.)

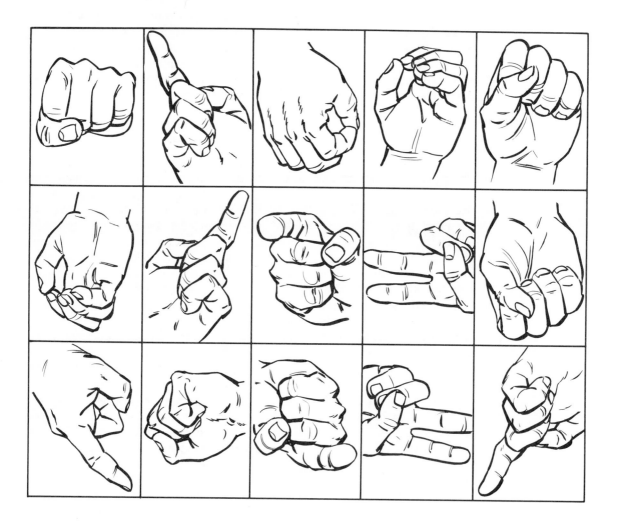

*Adapted from Thurstone's Visual Intelligence Test

A special procedure must be designed to return a subtree to the available pool (see exercises).

The operation for deleting node N but retaining the nodes of its subtrees within the tree structure without destroying the ordering is more difficult and challenging. Node N's position in the tree and hence in the ordering, and the location and depth of its subtrees determine how the deletion is to be handled. There are four distinct cases to consider, the last of which requires the most complicated processing:

1. Node N has no children.
2. Node N has an only right child.
3. Node N has an only left child.
4. Node N has two children—which have two subcases—
   a) Left child of node N has no right child.
   b) Left child of node N has a right child.

While each case will be presented separately, they would be collected and placed in one procedure.

Case 1—No Children

Defining Conditions

```
N ^ .LCHILD = nil
N ^ .RCHILD = nil
```

Processing Statements

```
if P ^ .LCHILD = N then
                    P ^ .LCHILD := nil
                    else
                    P ^ .RCHILD := nil ;
dispose(N);
```

Comments

This is the simplest case, a simple process of cutting the link of parent P and returning node N to pool.

CASE 1

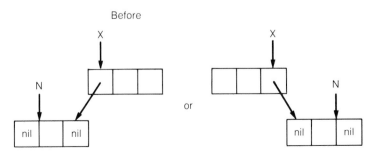
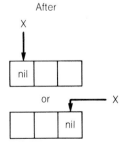

Case 2—An Only Right Child

Defining Conditions

```
N ^ .LCHILD = nil
N ^ .RCHILD <> nil
```

Processing Statements

```
A:=N ^ .RCHILD;
if P ^ .LCHILD = N then
                        P ^ .LCHILD:=A
                        else
                        P ^ .RCHILD:=A;
dispose(N);
```

Comments

Let the only child of node N become the left or right child of the parent P. Return the node to the pool. Any subtrees of node A are retained and the order is preserved.

CASE 2

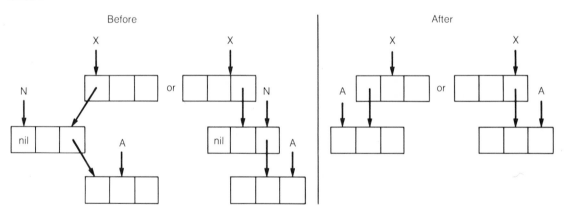

Case 3—An Only Left Child

Defining Conditions

```
N ^ .LCHILD <> nil
N ^ .RCHILD = nil
```

Processing Statements

```
A := N ^ .LCHILD
if P ^ .LCHILD = N then
                        P ^ .LCHILD:=A
                        else
                        P ^ .RCHILD:=A;
dispose(N);
```

Comments

This case is similar to case 2 and the same approach is used.

CASE 3

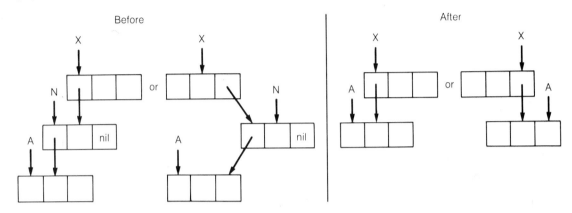

Case 4—Two Children

Defining Conditions

```
N ^ .LCHILD <> nil
N ^ .RCHILD <> nil
```

Processing Statements

```
A:=N ^ .LCHILD;
```

Subcase 1—Node A Has No Right Child

Defining Condition

```
A ^ .RCHILD = nil
```

Processing Statements

```
A ^ .RCHILD := N ^ .RCHILD;
if P ^ .LCHILD = N then
                 P ^ .LCHILD:=A
                 else
                 P ^ .RCHILD:=A;
dispose(N);
```

Comments

Node A, the left child of N, takes the place of N in the structure, since the left child of N is less than all the descendants in the right subtree of N and greater than all of its own descendants (it has no right child). The order of A, B (A's sibling), and of the descendants of A and B is preserved.

CASE 4

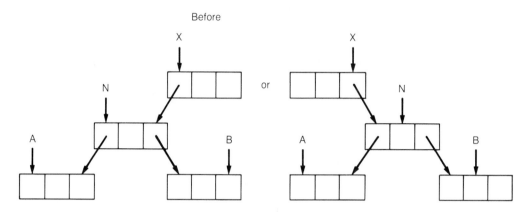

Before

or

Subcase 2—Node A Has a Right Child

Defining Condition

```
A ^ .RCHILD <> nil
```

Processing Statements

```
FINDMAXINSUBTREE (A,MAX,PARENT);
N ^ .DATA  := MAX ^ .DATA;
REMOVEMAX (MAX,PARENT),
```

Comments

This case and its solution require certain explanations. The procedure FINDMAXIN-SUBTREE is assumed to use the following strategy: Using a simple "go right" technique, locate the node that has the MAXIMUM data field in the tree pointed to by A. This node will be the last node visited in an INORDER traversal of the left subtree of N and will be the "rightmost" node in the subtree. The position of this node in the tree will be indicated by the output argument MAX, a pointer. For a related purpose, the parent of the node pointed to by MAX is returned as PARENT. Once the procedure has performed its purpose, the data field of node N is changed to contain the data field of node MAX. Since the data value is greater than or equal to all the nodes in the left subtree of N and is less than all the nodes in the right subtree of N, the hierarchial structure of the tree is preserved. All that is left is to remove the node pointed to by MAX from the subtree that it is contained in. This is the purpose of the procedure REMOVEMAX. There are two possibilities for this removal task, both illustrated after the diagram for subcase 2.

SUBCASE 1

Before

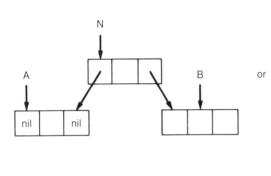

or

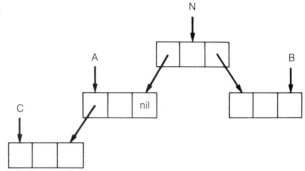

N was a left child of X

After

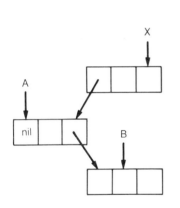

or

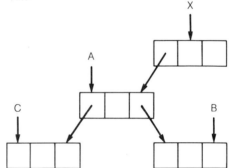

N was a right child of X

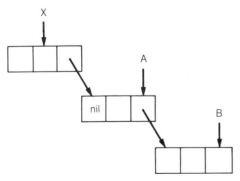

or

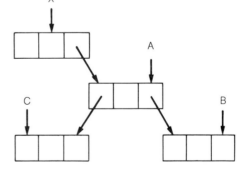

SUBCASE 2

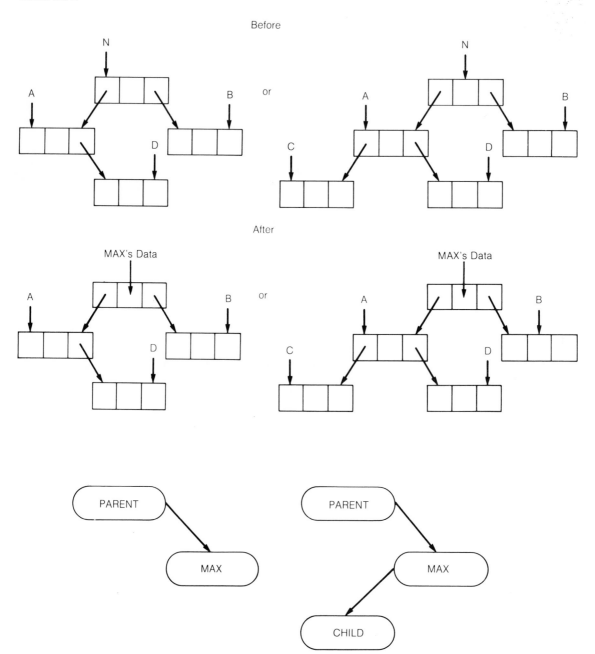

These two situations are analogous to deleting node MAX in cases 1 and 3 above and therefore can be handled analogously, or recursively.

To develop the procedure DELETE it is necessary only to set up the needed logical structures to detect which of the four cases prevails. The determination is made by using the defining conditions and *"if-then-else"* statements. For each case, the processing statements are included. The last phase is the coding of the two procedures, FINDMAXINSUBTREE and REMOVEMAX. This step can be performed as a separate procedure or placed directly in-line. Look carefully at cases 1, 2, and 3 to see how they can be combined into one section of code.

The deletion operation for binary trees is the most complicated of all the deletion operations on information structures (so far!). Tree structures are thus not recommended for applications requiring numerous deletions. The usual life cycle of a binary tree is to grow only at its leaf nodes until a stable structure is achieved and then to be accessed and walked through to a ripe old age before being recycled into the available pool of tree nodes. But should the tree need pruning, the previous algorithm will solve the problem without having to call out a tree surgeon.

5.3.4 A FRIENDLY SPIDER LEAVES A TRAIL OF THREADS

Nature is a consistent friend of scientists. It inspires them to apply its principles to areas of scientific study. If you have enjoyed a day in the forest and spent some time looking at the trees, you may have noticed another of nature's friendships—the tree and the spider. Between the branches, the spider spreads its welcome mat of silk threads and waits nearby, wondering who is coming for dinner. Though rarely observed, a special spider called INJOY has found a way to repay the trees for their friendship. Soon we shall see how the INJOY spider (kingdom Animalia, phylum Arthropoda, class Arachnida, order Pretoposta, family Fantasia) has found its niche among the branches of the binary tree.

The INJOY spider has learned to live undetected for many years among the branches of the binary tree. While living on these structures it has learned to walk through the trees in ways that you have not yet seen. It has developed the ability to traverse the binary tree, visiting each node only once, without the knowledge and therefore the use of stacks or recursion. This phenominal behavior was discovered by two clever computer scientists named A. J. Perlis and C. Thornton. They called such trees **threaded** trees. Let's look at INJOY's intriguing method for getting around the hierarchical neighborhood of tree nodes.

Assume that we are observing a tree spider from the suborder INORDER. An individual of this order can walk through a binary tree in an INORDER sequence. The spider begins at the root of a binary tree and follows the left branches until it can go no farther. This is seen by the series of hops from node F to C to B to A in Figure 5.12. It then visits node A (by checking to see if any food goodies are left). Next it attempts to walk along the right branch. Since node A has no right branch, the INJOY spider has left a silk thread that it can follow to the successor of node A. In this case, it follows the thread (threads are too weak for hopping, so it gently walks) to node B and checks again for food.

TRADE-OFFS

In this chapter we saw how the tree structure can be used to store a sorted list of data elements. In Chapter 4, linked lists were useful for the same task. What trade-offs exist between the two structures as tools for storing and processing sorted lists?

Let's compare memory usage. If we use a doubly linked structure for the linear list, then the node structures are identical and the amount of memory needed to store a list of 1023 data elements is the same. Some say that the tree structure underutilizes its space, since all the leaf nodes have two NIL values, while the entire linked list has only two NIL values. Whether these locations are inefficiently used is really a subjective interpretation because they do convey structural information (and can be used to "thread" the tree—see subsection 5.3.4). As regards memory, therefore, the scales are evenly balanced.

The speed at which operations can be performed is another factor. Let's compare them in four operations—searching for a data element, inserting a data element, deleting a data element, and traversing the entire list.

The tree structure has a big advantage in the search operation. Let us assume an assembler symbol table with 1023 identifier names. The time it takes to search a linearly linked list is proportional to the length of the list. On the average, 512 investigations will be made before a data element is found. The branched nature of the tree, on the other hand, supports a binary search. The execution time for a search of a fully balanced tree is proportional to log base 2 of the number of data elements. The maximum number of data elements investigated will be ten (with an average of five or six). When the averages are compared, the tree betters the linked list by a factor of 100.

Once the position for the new data element is located, the insertion operation can occur. The linking of a new node into either structure requires essentially the same execution time—a constant amount. Deletion, however, is a different matter.

The linked list's deletion operation takes a constant amount of time, independent of the number of data elements. For the binary tree, the existence of an entire subtree below the node to be deleted complicates the matter. Multiple cases can occur. At the worst case, the execution time depends upon the depth of the subtree. Hence the deletion of data elements from a binary tree poses a significant disadvantage.

What about traversing the entire list? It seems obvious that for both structures, execution time is proportional to the number of data elements in the list. However, the use of recursion or a stack to perform a tree traversal adds an overhead cost that favors the linked list because the constant of proportionality is smaller for the linked list traversal operation.

In summary, the two structures are relatively equal in the areas of storage, insertion, and traversing the sorted list. In the areas of searching for a data element and deleting a data element, there is an even split—the tree is better for an application involving frequent searches, the linked list for one with frequent deletions. By focusing on the frequency of occurrence of these two operations, a sound decision can be made.

Figure 5.12

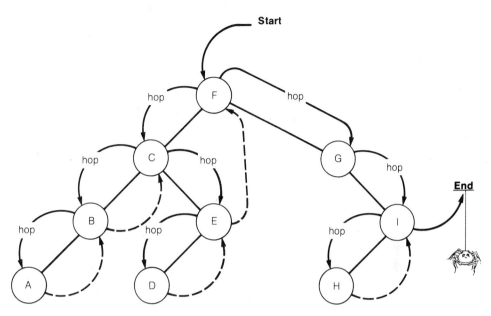

The nodes can be traversed without the use of a stack or recursion. Hops occur by following the links (solid lines), while threads are used to find the next node (dashed lines).

From node B it tries to walk right again, but again finds its silk thread and follows it to node C, which it visits. From node C it tries once again to walk right. This time it does find a branch and takes a hefty hop to node E. To the INJOY spider, hopping to the right is like being in a new tree, so it begins its intriguing traversal sequence from the beginning. That is, from node E it begins a stroll down the left branches until it can go no farther. This stroll is a short hop to node D. It visits node D for a tidbit of food and begins again on its walk to the right. At node D it finds a thread leading off to the right, which it follows to node E. After a short visit, INJOY follows another thread back to the root F for a visit before it begins to traverse the right subtree in the same way. By following this clever pattern, INJOY will have visited every node in the binary tree exactly once. Oddly enough (though those who study nature may find this oddity to be a disguised elegance), the nodes are visited in an INORDER sequence.

It is the forethought of the INJOY spider that allows it to exercise this unusual behavior. The placement of the threads is the key to its existence. Another important feature is its ability to detect when the end of the walk has occurred. This is illustrated by its resting posture at node I. You will notice that node I has no right branch and no thread leading from it, another example of the forethought exhibited by this amazing arachnid.

Can we learn a lesson from INJOY and design an algorithm for traversing a binary tree with threads to the INORDER successors, without stacks or recursion? Let's give it a try, since we hail from kingdom Animalia, phylum Chordata, class Mammalia, order Primates, family Hominidae, genus *Homo*, species *Homo sapiens* (sometimes).

In this situation the self-managed implementation is quite useful. It provides a convenient way to distinguish threads from links. Hence we shall use it here. To distinguish branches from threads let us establish a convention: threads will be negative integers whose absolute values refer to the subscript of the next array element in the INORDER traversal. The last node in the traversal that has no branch or thread will have a zero (NILL) in its link field. The array TREE will be used as the pool of available tree nodes and the pointer-identifier ROOT will point to the root of the tree. An important change is the *type* declaration

```
type PTR_IDENTIFIER : NEGMAX..MAX ;
```

to accommodate the negative subscript values.

```
procedure HOP_AND_WALK(ROOT:PTR_IDENTIFER);
const NILL=0;
var SHADOW,PTR,SUCC:PTR_IDENTIFER;
begin
PTR := ROOT;
SUCC := ROOT;
(*While a successor exists - keep hopping and walking *)
while SUCC <> NILL do
                  begin (*Hop left until leaf node encountered*)
                  SHADOW := NILL;
                  while PTR <> NILL do
                              begin
                                SHADOW := PTR;
                                PTR := TREE[PTR].LCHILD
                              end;
                  (*Skip this if no left subtree*)
                  if SHADOW <> NILL then
                              begin
                              VISIT (TREE[SHADOW].DATA);
                              (*Move to the right*)
                              PTR := TREE[SHADOW].RCHILD;
                              (*While a thread, walk to
                                  the successor node*)
                              while PTR < 0 do
                                    begin
                                      SUCC := - PTR ;
                                      VISIT(TREE[SUCC].DATA);
                              (* Move to the right again *)
                                      PTR := TREE[SUCC].RCHILD
                                    end ; (*while*)
                              SUCC := PTR
                  (*   Either another thread was present*)
                  (*   and the next successor was visited *)
                  (*   or it is a right branch in *)
                  (*   which case the traversal of the *)
                  (*   right subtree begins from the top *)
                              end  (* if-then*)
    end  (* While successors exist *)
end;  (* PROCEDURE HOP_AND_WALK *)
```

Yes, I think we have done it. If you work through this procedure using Figure 5.12's binary tree, you should experience the same hops and walks that INJOY does. What an interesting pair they are—the parallel powers of imagination and intellect.

We have some options in the implementation of the threads within the binary tree. We have signified a thread by using negative integers, branches by positive integers, and neither by zero. Alternatively, we could make the distinction by defining the node structure with the following record description:

```
NODES =  record
            LCHILD:POINTER;
            DATA:(* Whatever is needed *)
            RCHILD:POINTER;
            TAG:boolean
         end;
```

The boolean identifier TAG can be used to indicate whether the identifier RCHILD is a branch or a thread. Which Boolean value signifies a branch or thread is an arbitrary choice and is another implementation convention set by the programmer. In this way either the self-managed or the PASCAL-managed pool of records and pointers can be used.

The way that the threads in the binary tree of Figure 5.12 are set up defines the tree as a **right in-threaded** binary tree. This is not our only option, as Figure 5.13 shows. The threads can be connected to the successor encountered during the PREORDER or to the predecessors during the POSTORDER traversals. In these cases the trees are called **right pre-threaded** and **left post-threaded.** These trees are inhabited by IN-JOY's close cousins, PREJOY, who is rather clumsy when it comes to hopping, and POSTJOY, who seldom leaves her home among the branches, in case dessert comes a-visiting.

Tree traversal algorithms for these threaded trees are similarly to HOP _ AND _ WALK for in-threaded trees. The strategies will obviously be different, but the detection and use of threads is the same.

We can also take advantage of the NIL LCHILD fields as we did with the NIL RCHILD fields. If it becomes necessary to find the predecessor of a node in a particular ordering, the shadow pointer technique would have to be used. If the LCHILD fields that are NIL are used to point to the predecessor of a node, it becomes easier to answer the question "who's in front of me?" As an activity for yourself, take the trees in Figures 5.12 and 5.13 and replace the LCHILD fields that are NIL with threads to the predecessors.

If the construction of the threads is an expensive programming factor, the benefits of easier traversals may be outweighed. The easiest time to put the threads in place is when the tree is being built and new nodes are being inserted into the tree. When the proper position for the insertion is found, the thread of the new parent is inherited by the new child as it is passed down to the RCHILD field of this new leaf node (assuming a right in-threaded binary tree). If the decision to use threads is made after the tree has been built, a procedure can be designed to traverse the tree in the old way of Section 5.3.3. During this traversal the threads can be left so that an easier traversal method is then available.

By using threads we reduce execution time by eliminating stack operations. This is shown by D. Knuth in his book *Fundamental Algorithms.** By removing the stack a certain amount of memory space is gained. The threads do not use extra space or reduce the space necessary to store the tree because the LCHILD and RCHILD fields

*The Art of Computer Programming, Vol. 1. Fundamental Algorithms, 2nd ed. Addison-Wesley, 1973.

Figure 5.13

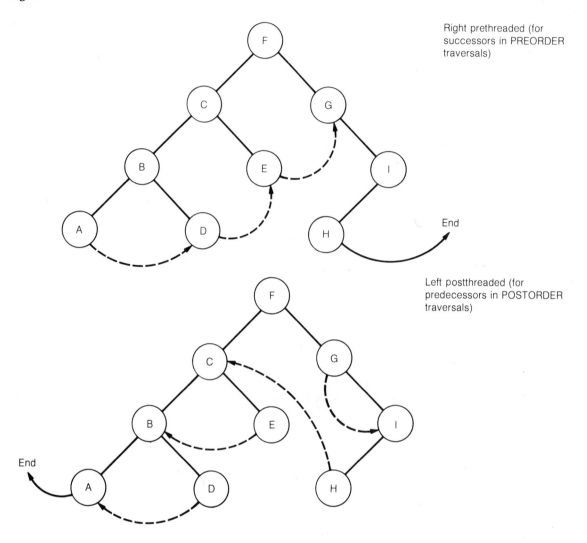

Right prethreaded (for successors in PREORDER traversals)

Left postthreaded (for predecessors in POSTORDER traversals)

are needed anyway. Even though many of these fields may have NIL values, they are important because they contribute to the structural information of the tree (they indicate when a node has no subtree). But with threads, Perlis and Thornton did find a way to increase the information content of the fields without detracting from their structural function. For this they deserve a hopping ovation.

▪ "JUST FOR REFERENCE"

Node structure of binary trees includes either—

- PASCAL record with two pointer-identifier fields and available pool of records with maintenance routines, or

- PASCAL record with two dynamic pointer fields supported by PASCAL

To build the binary tree structure either—

- fixed, known tree can be assigned storage locations by an INITIALIZE procedure, or
- a procedure for locating position and adding a new leaf node can be called repeatedly until initial tree is built; this procedure can also be used as tree grows

Accessing tree structure—By utilizing the ordering used in building the binary tree, a search algorithm takes the right branch if "greater than" condition is true or the left branch if "less than" condition is true until the "equals to" condition is true or until no additional nodes are available for testing.

Traversing the tree means visiting each node exactly once in a specified order. The three types of traversal are—

- PREORDER—visiting root first
- INORDER—visiting root in between
- POSTORDER—visiting root last

Recursive definition of traversal involves three steps—

- visit the root of the tree
- traverse the left subtree of the root
- traverse the right subtree of the root

Deleting a Node from the tree—

- involves varied degrees of difficulty, depending on whether node is a leaf or a branch
- may require restructuring if node is a branch, depending on the position and number of children

Threaded binary tree uses the NIL link fields to point to the successor nodes for a given traversal type. Features include—

- link field must be designated either a branch or a thread, through sign, boolean field, or variant record
- advantage is that the traversal algorithm does not use recursion or a stack and therefore is more efficient

EXERCISES

1. Given a pointer to a binary tree, write a procedure that lists the leaf nodes in the tree.
2. Given a pointer to a binary tree, write a procedure that lists the leftmost node at each level.

3. Given a pointer to a binary tree, write a procedure that prints the node or nodes with the highest level number.

4. Given a pointer to a binary tree and an integer less than or equal to the depth of the tree, write a procedure to list all the nodes at that level.

5. Given a pointer to a binary tree and a pointer to a node in the tree, write a procedure to determine the level number of the node.

6. Given a pointer to a binary tree and a pointer to a node in the tree, write a procedure to determine the sibling of the node if one exists.

7. Given a pointer to a node in a binary tree, write a procedure to determine the number of descendants of the node.

8. Given the following ordered sequence of words, draw a binary tree such that an alphabetical list of the words is produced by an INORDER traversal of the tree:

    HAT   FAT   RAT   SAT   MAT   CAT   BAT   OAT

9. Write a procedure to search a binary tree for a given value. Base the procedure on the algorithm given in Figure 5.8.

10. The form of a binary tree determines the number of comparisons needed to locate a given value. Draw a completely full binary tree of depth 3 with 15 nodes, each containing a word, with the words ordered alphabetically. Draw a linked list of 15 nodes, ordered alphabetically. For each word determine the number of comparisons needed to locate the word in the tree and in the list. Make a table of these values.

11. Given a pointer to a node, write a procedure to return the node and all of its descendants to the available pool.

12. Given the following tree of computer science courses, give the sequence of nodes visited by each of the three traversals: PREORDER, INORDER, and POSTORDER.

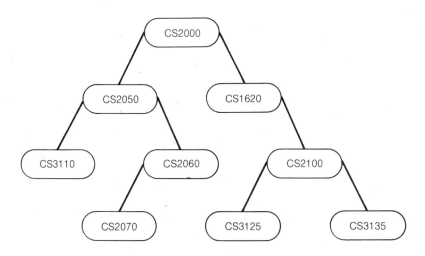

13. For the binary tree below, show the contents of the stack while the tree is being processed by procedure INORDER.

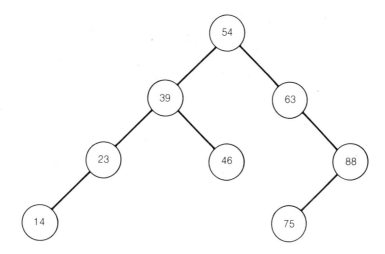

14. Write the PREORDER traversal procedure in both a recursive and a nonrecursive way.

15. Transform the POSTORDER procedure to a nonrecursive procedure, using the technique presented in Chapter 2, subsection 2.5.3.

16. Using the tree in exercise 13 as data, draw the environments of the recursive procedure POSTORDER in the style presented in Chapter 2, subsection 2.5.2.

17. Using the tree in exercise 13 as data, show the contents of the stack as the tree is traversed in a nonrecursive POSTORDER procedure.

18. Given the following algebraic expression, draw a binary tree that yields the postfix expression when traversed in a POSTORDER way:

    X / Y - B * (U * Z - X / (N - 1))

19. Write a procedure that traverses the tree of exercise 18 and produces the infix expression with only the necessary parentheses in place, based on the hierarchy of operators.

20. Using the outline in this section, write a procedure to delete a given node from a binary tree, incorporating the four possible cases that can occur.

21. Write the procedures FINDMAXINTREE and REMOVEMAX that accompany the procedure of exercise 20.

22. The most complicated case in deleting a node is solved by finding the maximum value in the left subtree of a given node. Another approach is to locate the minimum value in the right subtree of the same node. Write the procedure to perform this task.

23. Write a procedure for an INORDER traversal of a binary tree that leaves the tree a right in-threaded binary tree.

24. Write the procedure HOP _ AND _ WALK using dynamic allocation with
    a) Tag fields.
    b) Variant records.

25. Given the binary tree of exercise 13, draw the threads that facilitate a PREORDER traversal. This yields a right pre-threaded binary tree.

26. Write the procedure to traverse a right pre-threaded binary tree.

27. Write a procedure for a PREORDER traversal of a right in-threaded binary tree. Is a stack necessary for this procedure?

28. Using the binary tree in exercise 13, draw threads so that the NIL left link fields point to the predecessors and the NIL right link fields point to the successors during an IN-ORDER traversal. This yields an in-threaded binary tree that has only two link fields that are still NIL. Write a procedure that traverses a binary tree and produces an in-threaded binary tree.

5.4 Formalizing the Structure: General Trees

5.4.1 THE ABSTRACT DESCRIPTION OF THE GENERAL TREE

In the Section 5.1 we examined several examples of the tree information structure. The pedigree family tree had only two branches. The other two examples did not fit this pattern—the lineal tree allowed for multiple branches from one individual, and the family tree for animal classifications showed multiple evolutionary lines from the same common ancestor. Therefore, the binary tree must have a relative in the information structure family to match this new pattern of relationships. Let me describe this new species of information structure in a formal way.

An **ordered general tree** GT is a nonempty set of elements, that can be divided into $(m + 1)$ disjoint subsets, R, S1, S2, . . . , Sm. The sets S1, S2, . . . , Sm are considered ordered and are ordered general trees in their own right. The set R has a single element and is called the root. The sets S1, S2, . . . , Sm are called subtrees of the general tree GT.

For Noah's lineal tree, Noah is the root R and the subsets are all descendants of Noah's first son (S1), his second son (S2), and his third son (S3). Each of these three sets can be further subdivided to create the lineal trees of Noah's sons.

If the ordering of the sets S1, S2, . . . , Sm is not important to the use of the tree, the general tree is classified as an **oriented** general tree. This distinction will be important when we are drawing general trees. An ordered general tree is drawn only one way, while an oriented general tree can be drawn several different ways. This implies that two general tree diagrams with two subtrees interchanged will be considered different trees if they are ordered general trees, different orientations of the same tree if they are oriented general trees.

Think of the general tree as an acquaintance of the binary tree (and vice versa) rather than a descendant or ancestor. This outlook is helpful for several reasons. The general tree always has at least one element, while the binary tree can be empty—a basic structural difference. An oriented general tree with two branches from each node looks very much like a binary tree. But since it is oriented, the concept of left child and right child is meaningless, and the close resemblance quickly fades away. In the same way, if we have a node with only one child in a general tree there is no need to classify it as a left or right child as in the binary tree. Therefore, the binary attribute of binary trees produces characteristics that are not found or needed in general trees.

5.4.2 TERMINOLOGY AND STRUCTURAL DIAGRAMS

The terminology used for binary trees carries over to general trees, with no changes in the definitions. The familiar terms of parent, child, sibling, ancestors, and descendants apply equally well to the general tree structure. The nodes within the general tree may be either root, branch, or leaf nodes. A new term, **degree,** indicates the number of children a node has. With this new term, it is easy to see that a node is a leaf node if it has degree 0. The level number and depth of a node in a general tree are defined the same as for a binary tree.

Since a node in the general tree can have any number of children, the terms left and right child are no longer applicable. To refer to specific children of a node, I shall use the terms **leftmost, rightmost, next,** and **only** child.

The diagrams used to illustrate general trees are pretty straightforward, but they can be clarified by giving an ordered general tree in set notation and drawing the diagram that would represent it. The set is given below and consists of nine elements. The diagram of this tree is found in Figure 5.14.

$$\textbf{GT = (A, B, C, D, E, F, G, H, I,)}$$

R = (A)	Level 0
S1 = (B, D, E, F)	
R = (B)	Level 1
S1 = (D)	
S2 = (E)	Level 2
S3 = (F)	
S2 = (C,G,H,I)	
R = (C)	Level 1
S1 = (G,H,I)	
R = (G)	Level 2
S1 = (H)	Level 3
S2 = (I)	

Figure 5.14

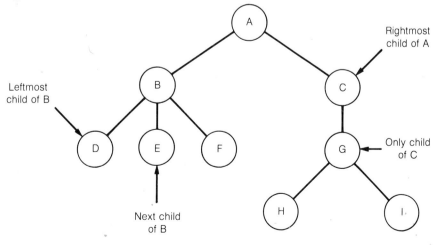

Rightmost child of A

Leftmost child of B

Only child of C

Next child of B

The diagram can be used to demonstrate the use of the new terms related to children of a node. The leftmost child of node B is node D; the next child of node B is node E; and node F is the rightmost child of node B. In the rightmost subtree of the root A exists a node C, which has an only child, G. In the drawing, the branch to the only child, a vertical line, will always be drawn so as to avoid any left or right orientation. Also in this same rightmost subtree is a node G that has a degree of 2, with rightmost child I and leftmost child H.

In dealing with oriented general trees it is important to focus on the relationship of the nodes, not on the topography of the diagram. Figure 5.15 shows a lineal tree oriented in two useful ways.

Both of these orientations can be helpful for different applications. But the tree remains a tree of descendants of the root individual Joan with three children and three grandchildren. The relationships are preserved and the significance of leftmost and rightmost children will be determined by the programmer's conventions.

■ **"JUST FOR REFERENCE"**

A general tree is defined as—

- a nonempty set of elements
- divided into $(m + 1)$ disjoint subsets, R, S1, . . . , Sm
- R has one element
- S1, . . . , Sm are general trees in their own right

A general tree may be—

- ordered—the subtrees have a prescribed order
- oriented—the subtrees have no prescribed order

Figure 5.15

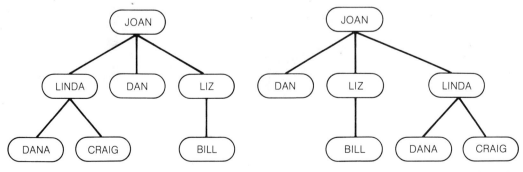

Oriented by birth—youngest is leftmost   Oriented by number of descendants (i.e., by degree)

Differences between the binary tree and the general tree—

- binary trees can be empty, general trees cannot
- nodes of degree 1 in a general tree have no need for a left/right classification of the subtree
- oriented general trees whose nodes all have degree less than or equal to 2 resemble binary trees but do not have a unique representation

EXERCISES

1. Given the general tree below, develop the set notation that verifies it is a general tree.

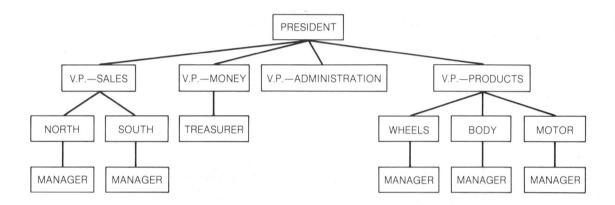

2. Draw the above general tree as an oriented general tree based on the criterion of degree. Let the leftmost sibling have the largest degree.
3. Given the following general tree, give the level number of each node, the degree of each node, the ancestors of each node, and the depth of the tree.

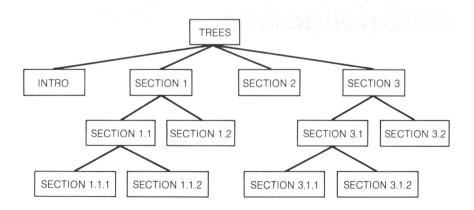

5.5 Implementing the Structure: General Trees

5.5.1 TREE NODE STRUCTURE: A DILEMMA

The implementation of the general tree presents an interesting challenge to the programmer. The natural approach to solving the implementation problem is not well suited to the physical environment of the computer or the capabilities of most computer languages. This natural approach to representing the node structure for a general tree would be to have a field for each data value of the node and a link field for each child. The records to handle nodes with 0, 1, 2, ..., N children must have the capability of being variable in size. If children may be added after the tree is built then the node structure must be dynamically expanded (at execution time) to include the new child's link field. The management of any pool of available nodes either by you or by Bruce the magician would become an initial overhead cost that would be difficult to offset by any possible savings of a general tree. So, what to do? It seems like a problem that could require us to resort to magic. But we have another power to aid us—the power of imagination.

The main problem with the natural approach is the variably sized node structure. If a new approach can be devised that uses a fixed node structure, it may offer a better solution. Let us return to the definition and use it as a basis for constructing a plan for representing general trees. We will set up two node structures, one for roots and one for subtrees. The node structure for roots contains the data fields for the root and a link field to the leftmost subtree of the root. The use of the tag field will be explained later.

Root data fields	T A G	Leftmost subtree pointer

The node structure for the subtrees identifies two entities. The first is a pointer to the next rightmost subtree of the parent node of this subtree. This enables the ordering of the subtrees of a root to preserved. All the subtrees of a given root node are connected into a linked list through this pointer field. Figure 5.16 gives a right-brain image of this approach.

The second entity that the subtree node indicates is the set of elements that constitutes the subtree itself. Two cases can occur: either the subtree consists of only one element, or else it consists of a root and its subtrees. In the first case, the data for the lone element can be recorded in the subtree node itself. In this instance, the node contains the data fields of the root of the subtree and a pointer to its next rightmost sibling subtree.

In the latter case, the recursiveness of the definition can be applied and the subtree node can contain a pointer to a root node, which can then lead recursively to its subtree nodes. Thus the two mutually exclusive cases can be included in the same node

Figure 5.16

General tree

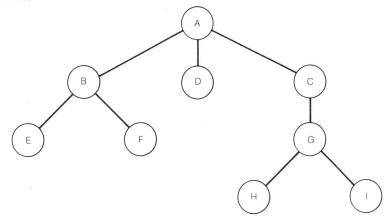

Set notion: GT = (A,B,C,D,E,F,G,H,I) where R = {A}, S1 = {B,E,F}, S2 = {D}, S3 = {C,G,H,I}

Representation
of general tree

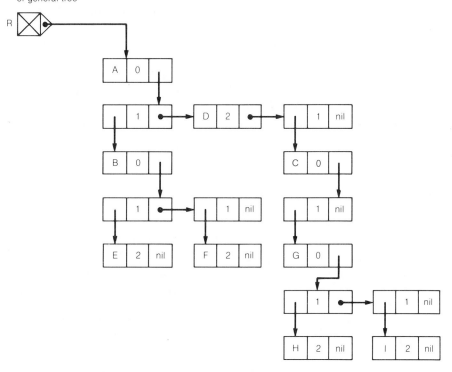

```
Tag significance

 0    Root node
 1    Subtree
 2    Subtree with only one element
```

structure and a boolean tag field can be used to determine the appropriate interpretation.

Root data fields or pointer to root node	T A G	Next subtree pointer

The important fact to keep in mind with this last node structure is that since a general tree cannot be empty, the terminal case for the recursive definition for the general tree is a tree that has only one element, the root, and no subtrees. The subtree node structure takes advantage of this fact by letting two mutually exclusive cases share a field of the node.

The tag field in the root node can be used to distinguish this structure from the subtree node. Because the two nodes now have identical structures, one available pool of nodes can be set up, and we can begin with a management cost that is workable.

One underlying assumption must be emphasized. The data types of the two quantities sharing a field in the subtree node must be compatible. It would not be possible, for example, for an integer pointer and a character data field to share this field. In such a situation some convention must be chosen to ensure compatibility. Of course, when we use PASCAL for the implementation, the variant record feature is well suited to having a pointer and character as different interpretations of a single field.

Let us see how a general tree looks under this implementation and examine a procedure that uses it. Figure 5.16 presents a diagram of a general tree, the set notation of the general tree, and the general tree under the conventions of this implementation.

Using this arrangement, we can develop a procedure that prints the children of any given root node. The nodes will be in an array of records called GT which have the following record description:

```
type  PTR_IDENTIFIER=0..MAX;
      NODES = record
                 SHARED_FIELD:PTR_IDENTIFIER; (*Pointer to root data
                                 or to root node of a subtree*)
                 TAG: 0..2;            (* Root and subtree cases
                                 tag field*)
                 SUBTREE:PTR_IDENTIFIER (* Pointer to leftmost subtree
                                 or next rightmost
                                 sibling subtree *)
              end;
var   GT:array[1..MAX] of NODES;
      DATA:array[1..MAX] of char;
```

An understanding of the intended use of the fields is necessary before looking at the procedure. The first field, SHARED _ FIELD, is used to point to the data field of a root (contained in the array DATA) or to the root node of a subtree (contained in the array GT). The second field, TAG, indicates which interpretation is appropriate. The distinction is between a root node and a subtree node, as described earlier. The last field of the record, SUBTREE, also has two interpretations, based on the type of node represented. If the node is of the root type, it is a pointer to the leftmost subtree of the root; if the node is of the subtree variety, it is a pointer to the next rightmost sibling subtree. Once again the tag field indicates the distinction.

The tag field will have three values since one case has two versions—a subtree with one element or with more than one element. The following conventions are adopted for the tag field.

Tag	Significance
TAG = 0	Root node—contents: pointer to ROOT data fields; pointer to leftmost subtree of ROOT.
TAG = 1	Subtree node—for subtree with more than one element. Contents: pointer to a ROOT node for subtree; pointer to the NEXT rightmost sibling subtree.
TAG = 2	Subtree node—for subtree with only one element. Contents: pointer to ROOT data fields; pointer to next rightmost sibling subtree.

Having planned the information structures, we now determine the strategy for the procedure. After checking for a valid input argument and the simple case of a root with no children, the procedure will start at the leftmost subtree of the root and use the next rightmost sibling subtree field to locate all the children.

Based on this stratagem and the tag conventions, the procedure ALL _ MY _ CHILDREN for printing the children of a given root of a general tree follows:

```
procedure ALL_MY_CHILDREN(RT:PTR_IDENTIFIER);
(*RT is a pointer to a root node in general tree*)
const NILL = 0;
var PTR,CHILDPTR:PTR_IDENTIFIER;
begin
(*Check for error on input argument*)
if GT[RT].TAG = 1 then writeln ('not a Root NODE - invalid input argument')
    else (*Check for root with no children*)
    if GT[RT].TAG = 2 then writeln ('Root has no children')
    else (*Starting at root node look at subtrees*)
    begin
    PTR := GT[RT].SUBTREE (*Leftmost subtree*)
    (*While subtrees remain*)
    while PTR <> NILL do
        begin
          (*CASE 1 Subtree has one element*)
          if GT[PTR].TAG = 2 then CHILDPTR := PTR
          (*CASE 2 Subtree has more than one element*)
                  else CHILDPTR := GT[PTR].SHARED_FIELD;
          (*Write data for this child of root*)
          WRITECHILD(CHILDPTR);
          (*Step to next rightmost sibling subtree of root*)
          PTR := GT[PTR].SUBTREE (*Next subtree*)
        end (*while*)
    end;
end;
```

This approach to implementing the general tree is quite similar to the method for implementing generalized lists in Chapter 4. This should not be surprising as the set notation for general trees is also similar to a generalized list. The tree of Figure 5.16 could be written as a generalized list as follows:

GT = (A , (B , (E) , (F)) , (D) , (C , (G , (H) , (I)))

where the root of a subtree is followed by a parenthetical list of its subtrees.

The above method has the advantage of using the storage space efficiently because it shares one field. If this sharing is not possible and separate node structures (and hence separate available pools) are needed, the extra cost must be considered.

The previous approach can be refined to provide a different perspective on the implementation problem. The main idea of this alternate method is to link each node in the general tree, not directly to its children but to its leftmost child and its own next rightmost sibling. The new node structure is:

LEFTMOST CHILD	DATA FIELD	NEXT SIBLING

This produces only one node structure, no shared fields, and no tag fields. In effect, each parent is linked through its LEFTMOST CHILD field (similar to a HEAD node) to a linked list of its children (through the NEXT SIBLING field). The general tree of Figure 5.16 is shown again in Figure 5.17 from this new perspective.

Since each node has two unique link fields, we have transformed the relationship of the general tree into what seems to be a binary tree. This new view of the general tree is the topic of the next section.

5.5.2 THE RETURN TO THE PRIMITIVE

For ordered general trees, two relationships are well defined: parent–leftmost child and sibling–next rightmost sibling. If the relationship exists, it is unique—that is, the parent–leftmost child relationship is not shared by two distinct pairs of nodes. Therefore, all of these relationship pairs can be used to characterize (describe logically) any ordered general tree. This feature can be used to describe a transformation of an ordered general tree into a binary tree. The transformation process can be described by the following rules. For each node N in the ordered general tree G,

1. The left child of the corresponding node N' in the binary tree B is the leftmost child of the node N in the general tree G.

2. The right child of the corresponding node N' in the binary tree B is the next rightmost sibling of the node N in the general tree G.

3. The data fields of node N' are the same as the data fields of N.

For ease of reference, I'll call the binary tree B the **binary correlative tree** of the ordered general tree G. This gives a very natural correlation between the two trees. Since the correlation is unique for ordered trees, it also gives us the ability to generate

Figure 5.17

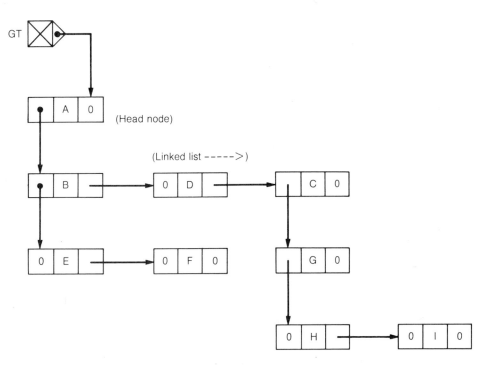

algorithms for the binary correlative tree (henceforth called BCT) in place of the general tree. Figure 5.18 illustrates the two trees side by side.

This transformation has consequences. Starting at the top of the BCT, the root node will never have a right subtree, since the root node of the general tree will never have a sibling. At the next level, the binary tree B becomes a bit lanky, stretching downward with longer branches. Because of the transformation, we lose the direct information about the level number of a node. Thus node DANA is at level 2 in both trees, but node BILL is at level 2 in tree G and level 4 in tree B. However, the level number of a node in the general tree is indirectly contained in the structure of the binary tree. How many left branches must be taken from the root of tree B to get to node BILL?

Although the degree of any node in the general tree cannot be directly transformed into the binary tree, this structural information can be determined with an algorithm on the BCT. The following procedure calculates the degree of a node from the general tree G using the binary tree B. Assume that PASCAL pointer variables are being used in the implementation and that the following declarations are in force:

```
type POINTER = ^NODE;
     NODE    = record
                 LCHILD : POINTER;
                 DATA : as appropriate
                 RSIBLING : POINTER;
               end;
```

Figure 5.18

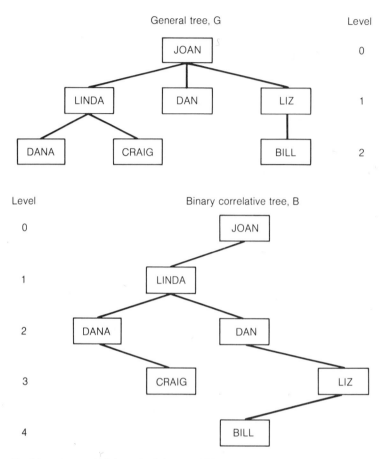

General tree, G

Level

0

1

2

Level

Binary correlative tree, B

0

1

2

3

4

The binary tree node links to the leftmost child of general tree through the LCHILD field. The RCHILD field is connected to the next sibling from the general tree.

The input argument is a pointer to the node whose degree is sought. The computed degree is an output argument.

```
procedure DEGREECOUNT (NODEPTR:POINTER;var DEGREE:integer);
var PTR:POINTER;
begin (*NODEPTR points to parent whose degree is sought*)
DEGREE:=0;
PTR := NODEPTR^.LCHILD;(*Go to leftmost child*)
   (*In BCT, go along right branch until it ends*)
   while PTR <> NIL do
             begin
                DEGREE := DEGREE +1;
                PTR    := PTR^.RSIBLING
             end
end;(*PROCEDURE DEGREECOUNT*)
```

This procedure can be used to develop various algorithms that must process all the children of a given node, since all children in the general tree implies all right branches (next rightmost siblings) in the binary correlative tree.

Since the BCT is a binary tree, we can use our binary tree skills with our present topic, the BCT of a general tree. One useful feature was developed in subsection 5.3.4 with our friendly spider INJOY and its silk threads. By threading the BCT of a general tree, we can answer certain questions more easily. For instance, if the BCT is developed as a right in-threaded binary tree, each node with a thread (which turns out to be a rightmost child in the general tree) points to its parent from the general tree. If you return to Figure 5.18 and draw in the threads to make tree B a right in-threaded tree, you will see that this is the case. Therefore, the threaded binary correlative tree can be used to answer the question, "Who is the parent of this child?" The following procedure, which is similar to DEGREECOUNT, answers this question by returning a pointer to the parent of a node pointed to by the input argument. Once again, threads will be denoted by use of a boolean tag field, where a value of true implies a link exists and false implies a thread exists.

```
procedure WHOISDADDY (CHILD:POINTER: var PARENT:POINTER);
var PTR:POINTER;
begin
(*Beginning at the designated child*)
(*Go along the right branch thru siblings*)
(*Until a thread is found*)
PTR := CHILD;
        while PTR^.TAG = true do
                        PTR := PTR^.RSIBLING;
PARENT := PTR^.RSIBLING
end;
```

If we were to use other ways of implementing general trees, such an operation would require much more programming effort. The transformation from general tree to binary tree and the addition of the threaded attribute enable us to harvest a tasty programming plum.

Another natural operation to perform on general trees is traversing the general tree. In subsection 5.5.3 we shall see how the binary correlative tree provides us with the medium to perform this operation without a "tree"-mendous effort.

5.5.3   WALKING THROUGH THE GENERAL TREE

Our walk through the land of binary trees was fairly simple and was expressed in terms of visiting the root before, between, or after its left and right subtrees. With general trees the walk-through concept can be extended in two out of three of the previous traversals. It is possible to visit the root of a general tree before or after its various subtrees. However, an INORDER traversal of a general tree would require an arbitrary decision concerning the placement of the root visit between its subtrees.

The two traversals for a general tree are summarized below in a form similar to the binary tree traversals.

Preorder

1. Visit root of general tree.
2. Traverse in PREORDER fashion the leftmost subtree of the root, if any.
3. Traverse in PREORDER fashion the remaining subtrees of the root, if any.

Postorder

1. Traverse in POSTORDER fashion the leftmost subtree of the root, if any.
2. Traverse in POSTORDER fashion the remaining subtrees of the root, if any.
3. Visit root of general tree.

Both traversals are natural choices for visiting all the nodes of a general tree. They are specified for ordered rather than oriented general trees. Using the general tree from Figure 5.18, the PREORDER and POSTORDER traversal sequences are given below:

PREORDER: JOAN LINDA DANA CRAIG DAN LIZ BILL
POSTORDER: DANA CRAIG LINDA DAN BILL LIZ JOAN

Using the binary correlative tree from Figure 5.18, the PREORDER and INORDER traversal sequences are given below:

PREORDER: JOAN LINDA DANA CRAIG DAN LIZ BILL
INORDER: DANA CRAIG LINDA DAN BILL LIZ JOAN

This situation is not a coincidence. It applies for all general trees and their binary correlative trees. Therefore, to perform a PREORDER traversal of a general tree, it is sufficient to perform a PREORDER traversal of its BCT, a procedure that we have already written.

The POSTORDER traversal of a general tree is equivalent to an INORDER traversal of its BCT. This may not surprise you if you have considered the effect the correlative transformation has on the relationships of siblings and descendants of siblings. You might also have noticed that designing the binary correlative tree as a right inthreaded tree streamlines the POSTORDER traversal of the general tree because the INORDER traversal of the binary correlative tree is greatly simplified.

Therefore, the natural traversal paths for general trees require no additional programming once the general tree has been transformed to its binary correlative tree. What began as a dilemma caused by the variability of general trees (the need for variable node structures) and the inflexibility of the computer and computer language has evolved back to the primitive concept of a binary tree and the operations upon it. Behind each transmutation stands the power of imagination.

5.5.4 THE EXOTIC TROPICAL GENERAL TREE

If you have ever been in the tropics or have even dreamed of being in the tropics, somewhere in your memory is an image of long palm trees swaying in the breeze. The typical tropical palm seems to have only a trunk and no branches and therefore is a bit exotic because of this straight and linear appearance. I'm not saying that palm

IMAGINATION CHALLENGE

Here is a challenge to your imagination's partnership with the brain's other hemisphere. The goal is to determine the number of blocks present in each block structure. This will require the combined efforts of your right brain's visual imaging system and your left brain's ciphering and analytic abilities. By looking at the diagrams below, state how many blocks are contained in each of the half dozen block structures.

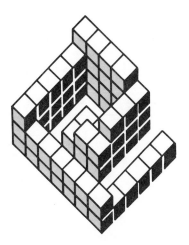

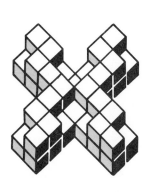

Adapted from the Army General Classification Test

trees inspired the next implementation approaches, but I want to set a mood consistent with their main feature.

The approaches we have seen so far involved linking nodes together logically and keeping them in an available pool. This next family of approaches does not rely on an available pool but uses as its basis a preselected ordering of the nodes in a linear sequence of contiguous memory locations. The nodes of the tree will be ordered and then stored sequentially in a block of memory locations. Hence the analogy to the palm tree—no explicit branches will exist, and the logical structure must be deduced from other information. Keep in mind that the hierarchical relationships of the tree will be inherent in the carefully selected ordering that is used.

The general tree of Figure 5.16 will be used in all examples that follow.

Preorder with Right Subtree Pointer

The first sequential implementation requires that the information of the tree be stored in its preorder sequence. Thus the ordering for the general tree of Figure 5.16 would be:

$$A \quad B \quad E \quad F \quad D \quad C \quad G \quad H \quad I$$

(from either the general tree or from the binary correlative tree). To provide sufficient information to adequately describe the relationships of the general tree, the following quantity is stored with each node: the address of the node in the preorder sequence following the left subtree (in the binary correlative tree) of the node. For instance, node B would indicate node D, since the left subtree of node B ends immediately before node D. The storage scheme for the general tree would be:

Index	Node	Pointer
0	A	9
1	B	4
2	E	3
3	F	4
4	D	5
5	C	9
6	G	9
7	H	8
8	I	9
9	*	

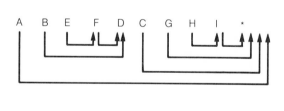

This strategy works because a preorder sequence guarantees that the left subtree follows the root, and this additional field indicates where the right subtree begins. Because both subtrees of the binary correlative tree can be accessed from any root, algorithms can be written using this sequential representation.

Consider three typical operations for a general tree. A PREORDER traversal of the general tree is extremely simple as it now entails only a sequential listing of the nodes. To list the descendants in the left subtree of a given node the following steps would be required. Assume N is the subscript of the node and the node is declared as follows:

```
type PTR_ID : 0..MAX ;
     NODE = record
                 DATA:char;
                 RIGHT_SUBTREE: PTR_ID
            end;
var TREE:array[0..MAX] of NODE;
```

The procedure for listing the elements in the left subtree is:

```
procedure LIST_LEFT(N:PTR_ID );
var UPPER, LOWER:PTR_ID;
begin
UPPER := TREE[N].RIGHT_SUBTREE;
LOWER := N+1;
while LOWER < UPPER do
          begin
            PRINT_OUT(TREE[LOWER].DATA);
            LOWER := LOWER + 1
          end
end;
```

Since all the left descendants of a node follow the root sequentially, you need know only where the root is and where the left subtree ends (which is before the right subtree begins).

The last operation is to find all the children of a given node. Locating the first child is simple in the BCT. By taking the left branch from the given node, the first (i.e., leftmost in the general tree) child is found. The second rule in the BCT transformation provides the remaining children. From the first child a right branch leads to the next sibling, that is, the second child. Repeating the right branch movement yields the rest of the children. Therefore, by moving to the right subtree of each child, the next child is found as the root of the next right subtree. By using node A as the given node, walk through the following procedure segment to verify that the children B, D and C of Figure 5.16 are visited. Once again, assume that N is a pointer to the node whose children are to be visited.

```
UPPER :=TREE[N].RIGHT_SUBTREE;(*Upper boundary or scope*)
CHILD := N+1;        (*First child is next*)
                     (*sequential location*)
while CHILD < UPPER do
          begin
            VISIT(TREE[CHILD].DATA);
            CHILD := TREE[CHILD].RIGHT_SUBTREE;
            (*Move to right subtree within
                  scope of given node*)
          end;
```

If there are no children, the *while* condition fails immediately.

This approach has some a priori conditions that limit its use. The tree must be known in advance and experience no changes to its structure. The dominant ordering required must be preorder, and the array storage scheme must be planned in advance.

Postorder with Degree

Another sequential tree representation that has the same prerequisites is called postorder with degree. In this approach, the nodes of the general tree are listed in postorder. This provides the arrangement: leftmost, next, to rightmost subtrees followed by the root in sequential memory locations. Within each node is stored the degree of the node. This enables us to know how many descendant subtrees precede this node in the postorder sequence and therefore in memory. Hence, if we know the postorder sequence and the degree of each node, we can describe the structure of the general tree. Figure 5.19 shows how the subtree arrangement is implied by these two facts. The general tree illustrated is from Figure 5.16.

This arrangement has a backward flavor because it is based on the postorder sequence and the degree. Thus each node tells us how many children, and therefore subtrees, precede it in the array. The algorithms using this implementation also exhibit this backward flavor.

As an exercise, write the two procedures for the previous linear implementation for the postorder-with-degree arrangement. To find the descendants in the leftmost tree, you will have to step over, without processing, the rightmost subtree and any other in-between subtrees before beginning the main task of the procedure. Backtracking is also necessary for finding all the children of a given node.

For a different challenge, create a list of operations that can easily be performed with the postorder-with-degree arrangement. In this way, you can determine the advantageous areas of application for this particular arrangement.

If you're thinking that linked implementation of these complex relationships is your only option, these two examples should shake your complacency. Keep your imagination open to using old tools in new ways.

Figure 5.19

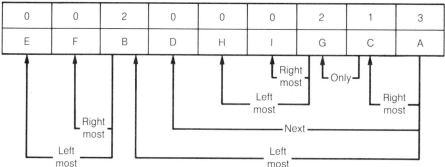

■ **"JUST FOR REFERENCE"**

The challenge of the general tree is its nonhomogeneous node structure, a result of the variable number of children.

Definition method—

- declare two node structures—one for the root of a general tree and one for the subtrees of a general tree
- each subtree node points to the root node of the subtree and to the next rightmost subtree
- each root node contains the data associated with the root and a pointer to the leftmost subtree of the root

Binary correlative tree method simplifies implementation of the general tree—

- declare one node structure containing the data associated with each tree node and two link fields
- one link field points to the leftmost child of the general tree node and the other link field points to the next rightmost sibling of the general tree node
- this provides a unique transformation of an ordered general tree to a binary tree
- algorithms and traversals on the general tree can be implemented upon the BCT (binary correlative tree)
- hence, a general tree PREORDER traversal is produced by a PREORDER traversal on the BCT and an INORDER traversal on the BCT yields a POSTORDER traversal on the general tree

Linear arrangement method—

- for a fixed tree structure with a preselected traversal ordering, the nodes can be arranged in a linear array
- the nodes are stored consecutively based on the selected ordering
- with each node is stored an attribute which helps characterize the general tree's structure
- for a preorder arrangement, the location of the first node in the right subtree is stored
- for the postorder arrangement, the degree of the node is stored

EXERCISES

1. What characteristic of the general tree provides the greatest hurdle in the implementation process?
2. The first approach presented in the book was based on the definition of the general tree. A single node structure was used. This approach was possible because a field was shared by two compatible quantities. Assume that your application does not allow for such sharing and define the record structure for two distinct nodes—a root node and a subtree node—based on the general tree definition.

3. Using the two distinct nodes of exercise 2, draw the general tree of Figure 5.16 with these new entities and compare the efficiency of each approach.

4. Rewrite the procedure ALL _ MY _ CHILDREN using the new approach with two distinct nodes.

5. Assume that you know that each node in a general tree will have a maximum of five children. A straightforward way to declare the record structure is:

```
NODE = record
       DATA: {as appropriate}
       CHILDREN: array[1..MAX_CHILDREN] of POINTER;
       end;
```

Using this new node structure, write the procedure ALL _ MY _ CHILDREN and compare the advantages and disadvantages of this new approach.

6. Write a procedure that accepts a general tree information structure in the form presented in exercise 5 and produces the BCT.

7. Write a procedure that accepts a general tree information structure in the form presented in exercise 2 and produces the BCT.

8. Write a procedure that accepts a general tree information structure in the form of a BCT and lists all the leaf nodes of the general tree.

9. Write a procedure that accepts a general tree information structure in the form of a BCT and lists all the descendants in the rightmost subtree of the general tree.

10. Assume that a BCT of a general tree has been in-threaded. List the operations upon the general tree that can easily be performed on the in-threaded BCT.

11. Using the linear array approach presented in subsection 5.5.2—in which the nodes are arranged in preorder with pointers to right subtrees—write a procedure that lists the elements in the right subtree of a given node.

12. Adapt the procedure DEGREECOUNT to the linear array approach in which the nodes are arranged in preorder with pointers to the right subtree.

13. Adapt the procedure DEGREECOUNT to the postorder-with-degree linear array approach.

14. Write a procedure LIST _ LEFT for the postorder-with-degree approach. The procedure lists the descendants in the left subtree of a given node.

15. Write a procedure ALL _ MY _ CHILDREN to list all the children of a given node for an implementation that uses the postorder-with-degree linear array approach.

16. Write a procedure that accepts a binary tree in a linked format and converts it to one of the two linear array approaches. Which one requires the most programming effort?

17. Write a procedure that accepts a binary tree in one of the linear array formats and converts it to a linked format.

5.6 Applications

This section presents three situations that can be resolved by applying the tree structure. Its intent is to show how the tree structure fits without indicating any particular algorithms. You are invited to develop your own problem specifications based on the initial and somewhat sketchy descriptions and to design the algorithms and information structures to solve the problem you define. We have come down this path together for quite awhile, and I have the confidence to let you step forward on your own as we begin to leave this forest of trees. So we will branch and amble on our separate paths, sure to meet again in the next chapter.

5.6.1   A TREE OF PAGE POINTERS

In writing this book, I have selected examples relevant to my own state of affairs. Presently, I am pondering how to create the index for this book. This index must have several attributes. It will be a large list of alphabetically ordered word phrases, each associated with a page range or number. The need to frequently access the entries in the table and to rearrange the ordering when word phrases are added dictates a flexible information structure. So I have decided on an alphabetically ordered binary tree structure. When the tree undergoes an INORDER traversal, the book's index should be produced.

As was mentioned earlier, when you are using a tree sort system such as a book index, the efficiency of the search is determined by how well balanced the tree is. So to optimize the search time for any word phrase in the index tree, I will build the tree as an AVL tree (named after the two scientists who came up with the idea in 1962, Adelson-Velskii and Landis). This structure is more commonly called a **height-balanced** tree. The idea is that the height (the largest number of nodes from the root to any leaf node) of each nodes's subtrees differs by at most one. This property guarantees that the tree remains balanced. The constraint is easily satisfied if the tree is rebalanced if necessary when a new node is added. The rebalancing algorithms are not difficult once all the possible cases are determined.

Some preliminary ideas are important before the algorithm can be presented. For each node in the AVL tree the **balance value** is defined and stored as part of the node. This is defined as the difference between the height of its left and right subtree and referred to as BAL _ VAL. Before a new node is inserted, the BAL _ VAL of all nodes is either 0 or 1. (You may want to allow +1 or −1 to indicate the orientation of the imbalance.) After the new node is inserted, various subtrees will be affected, and the ancestors of the node will have a BAL _ VAL of 0, 1, or 2.

For the purpose of the algorithm, the location of the youngest (smallest level number) ancestor whose BAL _ VAL becomes 2 will be important if it exists. So within the algorithm this node (and its parent) must be located and pointers must be made available. Call this special node the PIVOT _ NODE.

Also important to the algorithm are two operations that will be applied to the PIVOT _ NODE, and possibly to its children. The goals of these operations are to balance the tree rooted at the PIVOT _ NODE and to preserve the in-order ordering of the nodes. They perform a left or right rotation of the unbalanced tree around the PIVOT _ NODE. The operations LEFT _ ROTATE and RIGHT _ ROTATE are illustrated in Figure 5.20 using the two simplest cases. Sample PASCAL code to perform the operation is also provided.

Two important features about these operations should be emphasized: First, the INORDER traversal of both trees produces the same sequence of nodes, as desired.

Figure 5.20

a

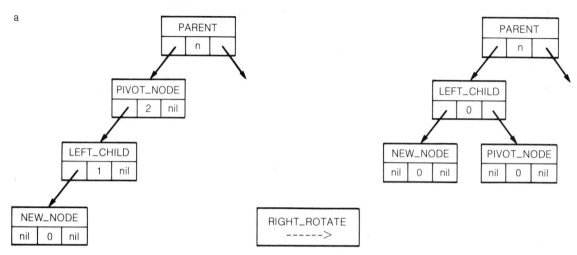

Note: The integer refers to the BAL_VAL of the node. The labels PARENT, LEFT_CHILD refer to the nodes and are not the data fields.

PASCAL code (* ASSUMING DYNAMIC POINTERS ARE IN USE *) arguments : PARENT,PIVOT_NODE ;

```
LEFT_CHILD := PIVOT_NODE^.LEFT ;
PTR := LEFT_CHILD^.RIGHT ;
LEFT_CHILD^.RIGHT := PIVOT_NODE ;
PIVOT_NODE^.LEFT := PTR;
PARENT^.LEFT := LEFT_CHILD;
```

b

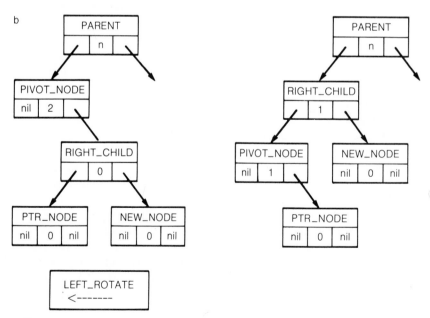

The PASCAL code left as an exercise.

Second, the BAL_VAL of the PARENT node is unaffected; therefore all of its ancestors are unaffected.

Based on these preliminary ideas, the algorithm, to insert a new node into an INORDER AVL tree follows:

Locate correct position for NEW_NODE, indicated by HERE, and, in the process, indicate the PIVOT_NODE and its PARENT and the direction from PIVOT_NODE. (Check for possible duplicate node error!)
if no error found then begin
    Insert NEW_NODE in AVL tree, given pointer HERE.
    Update all BAL_VAL of ancestor nodes from NEW_NODE to PIVOT_NODE inclusive.
   (* Balance AVL if necessary *)
   if PIVOT_NODE = nil then AVL is still balanced.
  else
    case
      NEW_NODE added to the left subtree of the left subtree of the PIVOT_NODE:
        perform RIGHT_ROTATE on PIVOT_NODE;
        (* as in Figure 5.20a *)
      NEW_NODE added to the right subtree of the right subtree of the PIVOT_NODE:
        perform LEFT_ROTATE on PIVOT-NODE;
        (* as in Figure 5.20b *)
      NEW_NODE added to the right subtree of the left subtree of the PIVOT_NODE:
        perform LEFT_ROTATE on the left child of PIVOT_NODE and then perform RIGHT_ROTATE on the PIVOT_NODE;
      NEW_NODE added to the left subtree of the right subtree of the PIVOT_NODE:
        perform RIGHT_ROTATE on the right child of PIVOT_NODE and then perform LEFT_ROTATE on the PIVOT_NODE;
  end (* cases for rebalancing *)
    (* note BAL_VAL of all affected nodes must be updated after the rotate operations *)

One way to distinguish the four cases is to use a direction flag to indicate whether the left or right subtree was followed from PIVOT_NODE and, by assuming BAL_VAL has a value of +1 or −1, to indicate the orientation of the imbalance. Your imagination, however, can be used to develop an alternate approach.

By drawing some diagrams you can verify that the responses to the last two cases return the balanced attribute to the AVL tree. With some concentrated effort you should be able to design the set of conventions necessary to express the AVL insert-and-balance procedure in PASCAL. If you don't have time now to complete the project, you will find it among the exercises at the end of this section.

Another attribute of the index list is that some entries will have subentries that should be listed under them. Take this section of the index as an example:

node,
  deletion of
  insertion of
  structure of
    in linked lists
    in trees

Each node in the index tree can point to the root of another tree that contains its associated subentries. Figure 5.21 shows this idea graphically. The major question is whether the subentry attribute will occur frequently enough to justify the extra tree structure or whether a linked list of subentries is sufficient. Consider these two options and select the one that feels more appropriate.

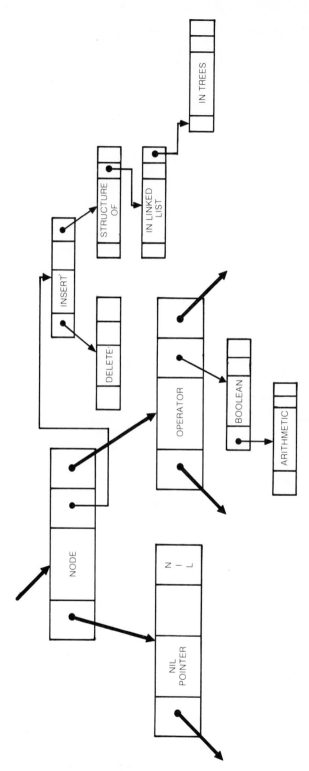

The key phrases are alphabetized and may point to subphrase trees such as

```
NODE
    DELETE
    INSERT
    STRUCTURE OF
        IN LINKED LISTS
        IN TREES
```

Figure 5.21

With this brief description and assorted scattered ideas, you can begin on your own path with a backpack full of unsorted phrases and page numbers. Upon completing your algorithmic journey you should be accompanied by a collection of information structures, PASCAL procedures, and one fine index specimen recovered while climbing through the index tree.

5.6.2 FINDING ONLY WHAT BELONGS TO YOU

In developing the algorithms for the previous example and coding the procedures to implement them, you started by creating a few files on some computer system. But you not only created them—you plan to locate them again to make corrections and improvements. In performing these operations you undoubtedly interacted with the file management section of the operating system. This section is responsible for keeping track of the files that you create and allowing only you to access them. It provides this service for all who share the computer system.

In a university environment it is not uncommon to have 1000 or more users, each with 10 to 20 files in their accounts. Therefore, the file management section must keep the records on the whereabouts and access privileges of more than 15,000 files and provide near-immediate responses to all user requests concerning file operations. A hierarchically structured file system provides quick access and protection from illegal access. In Figure 5.22, you can see a typical tree structure that illustrates the main features of such a file system.

The root node of the tree contains a directory that indicates where the information about a group or single user account can be found. The file management section uses this directory to direct itself to the correct subtree. If the request comes from a group user, the group user account node is located and the directory at the next level is consulted to verify that the request comes from a valid user within the group. When this verification is complete, the next level is reached and the user's account directory is consulted to find the location of a particular file on an auxiliary storage device. So three directories are consulted before the file is located and the request serviced.

For single users, the path to a leaf node in the tree—a file—may be one step shorter. Using the root directory, the single user's directory is located. Within this second directory the whereabouts of a file can be easily discovered. Some single users may use a library of files, used by all other files. The file management section must provide this additional level by creating another directory for the designated files.

The file management section must be capable of executing a number of operations. At the top level, it must add new accounts to the root directory. Adding and deleting files affects only the leaf nodes and their parents at the bottom level of the tree.

The file directory tree of Figure 5.22 poses some interesting challenges for implementation. Because the directory is a general tree, each node can possess a variable number of subtrees. In addition, four different nodes appear in the tree: SINGLE account node, GROUP account node, LIBRARY file node, and FILE node. This will entail extra tag fields and, possibly, additional programming for the available pool management procedures.

Figure 5.22

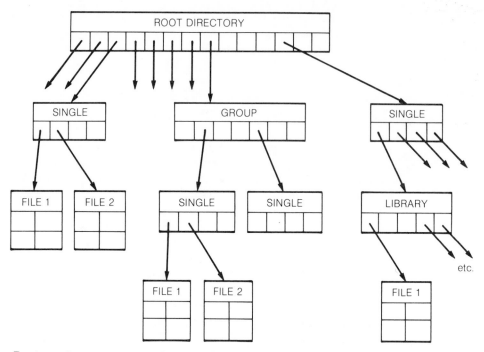

Two types of accounts can exist: SINGLE USER and GROUP USER. The information about a file is found in the leaf nodes.

Once again, the choice between a linked list of file nodes or a binary tree of file nodes is presented. The search time for a linked list is proportional to the length of the list, while the search time for a binary tree depends on the height of the tree. Inserting and deleting new file nodes in the linked list is simple, while the deletion operation on a binary tree is more complicated. Either arrangement will suffice; the decision rests on the number of changes expected and the level of efficiency desired.

This arrangement can provide the protection the user expects and the quick responses he demands. The tree information structure has easily found its niche in an important corner of the operating system. You may either use it or design it, depending on which hat you are wearing.

5.6.3 AN INTELLIGENCE TREE

Ode to an Intelligent Tree

*I hope that I shall never see
A decision tree more smart than
me.*

*— by an anonymous
programmer*

TRADE-OFFS

The development of the algorithm to preserve the balanced nature of an AVL—height-balanced—tree during the insertion and deletion operation is a nontrivial activity. It requires a full understanding of the multiple cases that can occur and the appropriate rotational operations for each case. How does the program's performance benefit from the increased execution time of the dual-processor biocomputer of the programmer?

The goal of height-balanced trees is to ensure an efficient search time, even in the worst case. It achieves this goal at the expense of the insertion and deletion operations.

The AVL search operation is proportional to the log base 2 of the number of elements in the tree. A binary tree that is built without regard to balance can become a linked list and therefore have a worst case search time equal to the number of elements in the tree. With 1023 elements in the tree, we are talking about a factor of 100—1023 versus $\log^2 (1023)$.

During the insertion and deletion operations, after the proper location has been found, the AVL approach may require that a portion of the tree be rebalanced. This balancing task means that the insertion and deletion execution times are also proportional to the log base 2 of the number of elements in the AVL tree, in the worst case. In the best case, they are equivalent to the standard insertion/deletion operation—a constant execution time for adjusting link fields.

Thus AVL tree operations are equal in their worst case execution times—log base 2 of the number of elements. So the balance of AVL trees is both in the height of the tree and the execution of its operations.

From these statements you can see that, with some extra program development energy, an application that can use a binary tree that requires no deletions and then performs frequent searches of the tree is a golden opportunity for using your AVL binary tree tool.

The area of artificial intelligence and robotics is continuing to make advances in problem solving by machine. A machine with a general problem solving strategy is presented with a new situation requiring a sequence of decisions. By evaluating the present situation and internally pursuing the various options, the artificially intelligent machine selects the option most likely to bring the solution closer. By repeating this look-ahead technique, the machine eventually discovers a solution to the problem. Determining whether the solution is the best is a more difficult skill for both the machine and the scientists studying artificial intelligence.

The tree information structure is basically indispensable in the areas of artificial intelligence, problem solving, decision theory, and game playing. It provides the form by which the various hierarchical strategies can be expressed and pursued. Fig-

Figure 5.23

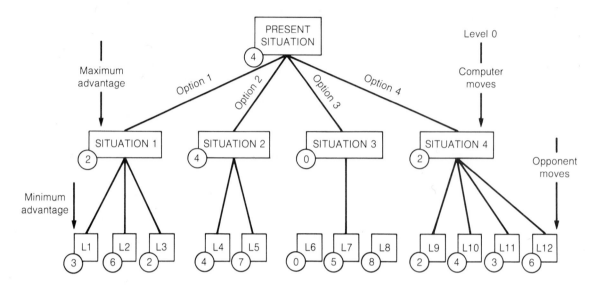

ure 5.23, a decision tree for a hypothetical game, shows how the tree provides this important medium of expression.

By starting from the present situation, the possible option subtrees can be generated. This provides the important feature of look-ahead intelligence found in chess-playing computers. The depth of the look-ahead foresight is determined by the depth to which the option subtrees are generated and investigated. If the solution is not among the future situations that can be seen at a given depth, some evaluation method must be used to select an option with a high probability of bringing the solution into sight.

To this end, a recursive function that assigns a value to each situation based on the value assigned to its children is developed. Assignment of a value to a leaf node is the terminal condition for the recursive function.

In the area of game playing, a technique known as minimax evaluation can be followed. Assume, for example, that the computer is playing a human opponent and has the next move. The decision tree above states that the level 0 to level 1 branches represent the computer's moves and level 1 to level 2 branches represent the opponent's responses to the possible moves. The computer can evaluate the new situation produced by each option based on how advantageous it is to the computer's goal of winning. The path selected would be based on the assumption that the opponent's options should minimize the advantage to the computer, and the computer's options should maximize the advantage. For example, in the decision tree of Figure 5.23 the numbers next to each leaf node represent the value of the evaluation function referred to earlier. Assume that 0 represents a game lost, and 9 represents a game won, from the computer's perspective. At this level, level 2, the opponent will have selected the move that gives him the maximum advantage (computer's game lost). Therefore, from each node at level 1, the computer can expect the opponent to select the move of minimum advantage to the computer. Hence, situation 1 is assigned a value of 2, the minimum value of its children, as are the remaining three situations. Notice that situation 3 provides the opportunity for a game lost and should be avoided.

Moving up one level to level 0, the computer's move, the option that provides the maximum advantage is situation 2, with a value of 4. With this technique the decision tree must be generated to a desired depth and the terminal situations evaluated. For each node at a particular level, the values of its children are surveyed and the minimum value (for odd levels) or maximum value (for even levels) is used. This recursive backtrack continues until the root situation is encountered and the choice is determined.

A refinement of this technique is called alpha-beta pruning. In simple terms, and definitely understating its complexity, the technique does not generate the remaining subtrees of a node when the parent's sibling subtree already produces a larger advantage than the node being considered. For instance, when the subtrees of situation 4 are being generated and evaluated, the siblings of situation 4 provide a maximum value of 4 so far, via situation 2. When node L9 is generated and evaluated as a 2, then situation 4's value can be no greater than 2, since we are taking the minimum value at this level. Therefore, it is not necessary to generate the nodes L10, L11, or L12 since they can not improve the advantage at level 1. Could a similar alpha-beta pruning have occurred with situation 3?

For more detailed information about these techniques and the use of trees in game playing, refer to some of the books listed in the bibliography. The incorporation of strategy into game-playing programs is a very challenging and individual endeavor. It also brings programmers into areas of thought-about-thought that may cause them to question some precepts that place us humans as a group into the classification of the most intelligent beings on earth. Some reading in this exciting field may produce changes in your perspective that you would never imagine.

▪ "JUST FOR REFERENCE"

Index tree—implementation of a book's index—is a tree of alphabetically ordered phrases and page numbers—

- Search time is optimized through AVL property—tree is height-balanced.
- Height balancing algorithm:

Locate correct position, insert new node, and determine PIVOT _ NODE if one exists.
If tree becomes unbalanced then perform appropriate LEFT _ ROTATE or RIGHT _ ROTATE on PIVOT _ NODE and possibly its children.

Account directory tree—tree of accounts available on a computer system—

- consists of heterogeneous node structures
- decides whether the list of files is implemented as a linked list or a binary tree

Decision tree is used in artificial intelligence, robotics, decision theory, and game playing—

- starts with a current situation and builds the optional response subtrees to a desired level

- uses the minimax technique to evaluate the potential success of each option
- uses the alpha-beta pruning technique to decide whether additional subtrees need to be generated

EXERCISES

1. For the application involving the index tree, design the information structures where each phrase can have some subphrases.

2. For the application involving the index tree, design the information structures where each subphrase can also have subphrases.

3. Design a PASCAL record structure to be used in the AVL index tree mentioned in subsection 5.6.1.

4. Develop an algorithm that locates the correct position for a new node in the AVL index tree and determines the PIVOT _ NODE if one exists.

5. Write the entire procedure for LEFT _ ROTATE and RIGHT _ ROTATE.

6. Justify the assertion that the two rotations on the AVL, LEFT _ ROTATE and RIGHT _ ROTATE, tree preserve the ordering.

7. Justify the assertion that the two rotations do not change the balance value of the parent of the PIVOT _ NODE once the insertion and rotation are performed.

8. Write a procedure to insert a new node into an AVL tree that preserves the height-balanced property.

9. Design the information structure for the account directory tree of subsection 5.6.2. What methods of implementing a general tree will you use? Will the files be stored as a linked list or a binary tree?

10. For the account directory application, develop algorithms to:

    a) Add a new account to the root directory.

    b) Add a new account to a group account.

    c) Add a file to an account.

    d) Add a file to a library.

    e) Delete a file from an account.

11. Discuss ways of approaching the heterogeneous node structure problem involved in the account directory application.

12. Draw a decision tree for a game of tic-tac-toe.

13. For the decision tree of exercise 12, define an evaluation function for the terminal nodes and use the minimax method to assign values to each node.

14. Using the decision tree exercise 13, play yourself a few games of tic-tac-toe.

15. Design a PASCAL record structure for tic-tac-toe and write a procedure that generates the possible moves, given a starting situation and whose move it is.

16. Write the recursive minimax procedure for a simple game of your choice.

17. Why do you think the alpha-beta pruning technique is important in the game theory of chess?

18. Draw a decision tree for a game or problem and define an evaluation function that illustrates the use of the alpha-beta pruning technique.

19. The example illustrating the alpha-beta pruning technique had the siblings at an odd level and thus the maximum sibling value was important. Construct a decision tree that illustrates the technique when the siblings are at an even level and the minimum sibling level is used.

20. Draw a decision tree that represents the options available for arranging four numbers into an ascending sequence.

THE WORKOUT ROOM

PROJECT 1   *Expression Tree*

1. Given an infix algebraic expression, write a program that builds an expression tree. Assume a strict left-to-right ordering of the operators—that is, no hierarchy of operators and no parentheses.

   Algorithm: Get first operand and make it the root of tree.
   Get the next entity.
   Repeat
   case entity of:
   operator: make operator node the root of the tree and the root node the left child
   of the operator node;
   operand: make the operand node the right child of the root node;
   end-case.
   Get the next entity.
   until expression delimiter is reached.

2. Given a postfix algebraic expression, write a program that builds an expression tree. Recall that with postfix expressions the hierarchy of operators is implicit in the expression and that no parentheses are needed.

   Algorithm: Get first operand.
   Repeat
   case entity of:
   operand: push operand node onto the stack;
   operator: if tree is empty then
   pop stack and make the operand node the left child of the operator node and set root pointer to operator node
   else
   make the root of the tree the left child of the operator node and set root pointer to operator node;
   pop the stack and make the operand node the right child of the root node;
   end-case.
   Get next entity
   until expression delimiter is reached.

3. Given an infix algebraic expression, write a program to build an expression tree. Assume that the hierarchy of operators is used and that no parentheses will be present. The algorithm is left to the reader. (Hint—assign priority levels to the operators and use a stack for the operators and one for the operands.)

PROJECT 2   *Learning Tree*

Write a program that learns! The program is an adaptation of the travel game Twenty Questions. (Remember? On long holiday trips someone would think of an object and you would have 20 yes/no questions with which to narrow down the options.)

In this interactive game, the player thinks of an animal and the computer asks a sequence of questions that are stored in a binary tree. The player's yes or no answer directs the program to the left or right child of the asked question. Either another branch node is found and the next question is asked or a leaf node is found. At the leaf node is found an animal name that matches the sequence of questions asked and answers given. The program asks the player whether this animal is the one he was imagining. The player may be a little surprised by the program's "intelligence" if the answer is yes. If the answer is no then the program has an opportunity to "learn" from the interchange. By asking three questions, the program can add another question node and an animal node to the tree. The three questions are:

1. What animal did you have in mind?

2. What question can be used to distinguish my guessed animal from your chosen animal?

3. For your chosen animal, is the answer to this question yes or no?

The more the program is used the larger the learning tree becomes. The depth of the tree and the "depth of understanding" of the program are both increased by continued use. An added challenge is to get the program to remember what it has learned.

PROJECT 3:   *Symbol Table Tree*

Write a program that processes the identifiers in a new language called NEWTON in the following way:

1. Reads the statements in the declaration section and—

   a) Assigns a memory address to each declared identifier. The amount of storage is determined by the data type being declared. Storage requirements are 1 byte for a boolean value, 2 bytes for an integer, and 4 bytes for a real number. Assume the first available address is 1000.

   b) Adds each identifier, its address, and its type to a symbol table tree information structure so that the identifiers are in alphabetical order. Check for doubly declared identifiers.

2. Reads the statements in the program section and—

   a) Checks each statement for two possible errors. One error is finding an identifier that has not been declared. The other error involves a mixed-mode arithmetic operation between a boolean identifier and either an integer or a real identifier.

   b) Prints a symbol table in alphabetical order containing each identifier, its address, and its type when the last statement is encountered.

   c) Prints a cross-reference table containing the identifier and all statement numbers that it is used in.

Sample Program

```
BEGINDEC
     INTEGER ab,tr,pert,knt$
     REAL x, aval,num$
     BOOLEAN flag, ans, resp, tval$
ENDDEC
BEGINPROG
     READ tr,aval, tval, pert$
     READ ans, x, ab$
     ADD ab TO tr$
     ADD pert TO knt$
     ADD tr TO knt$
     SUB ans FROM x$
     PRINT tr, x, cnt$
ENDPROG
```

Statement Formats

READ/PRINT   identifier,identifier, . . . ,identifier$

ADD/SUB   identifier TO/FROM identifier$

where $ is the end-of-statement delimiter and identifier is a character string of four or fewer letters.

PROJECT 4   *Decision Tree*

Write a program that uses a minimax strategy with a look-ahead decision tree to play the game 3/4-Square with a human opponent.

   The game is played on a square board divided into boxes. A sample four-square board is shown below with a sample game position. Each of two players alternate in placing a distinguishing character in a box until the game is won directly or the last box is filled. The game is won directly when a player has four characters forming a two-by-two square. If the game is not won directly, then every two-by-two square on the board is scored and the player with the larger score wins. Notice that the four-square board below has nine two-by-two squares contained within it. In general, an N-square board has $(N - 1)^2$ two-by-two squares. The scoring of the two-by-two squares is as follows:

   player has three out of four squares covered—1 point
   player has two out of four squares covered—draw

The diagram shows a sample four-square board with Y for you and M for me.

Y	M	Y	Y
M	M	Y	M
Y		M	
		Y	M

PROJECT 5 *General Book Tree*

Write a program for the Paul Bunyan National Forest Library. The library has an extensive collection of books on trees and lumberjacks. The librarians are developing a computerized reference system so that less paper is used for printing (and therefore fewer trees lose their lives). The table of contents of each book in the collection will be stored on the computer system. The librarians have selected the general tree information structure as the information storage medium. They want the system to provide the following services to library users. Given a book name, the system should:

1. Tell how many chapters are in it.
2. Given a chapter, tell how many sections it has.
3. Given a section, tell how many subsections it has.
4. Given a chapter, tell how many levels of subsections it has.
5. Given a chapter, tell how many pages are included.
6. Given a section, tell how many pages are included.
7. Determine which chapter is longest.
8. Given a word phrase, determine if a chapter or subsection begins with the phrase.
9. Provide a list of chapters.
10. Provide a list of all the chapters and their subsections and page numbers.

INSIGHTS WITH DR. DIGITAL

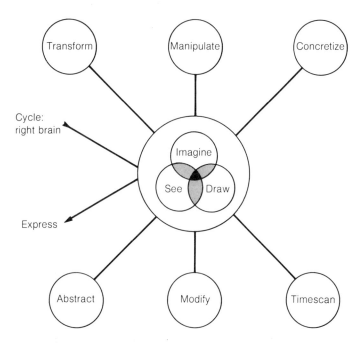

Scene: *Waldo is walking with Dr. Digital back from their information structures class and they stop at a shaded picnic table.*

Waldo: You're right, Dr. Digital. The implementation of general trees is a challenging problem. I think that a concept that you introduced to us—visual thinking—would be helpful here.

Dr. D: That's true, Waldo. The use of images to represent the thoughts that I have presented can be quite productive, and general trees are an excellent candidate.

Waldo: Dr. D., can you tutor me on how to think with visual images?

Dr. D: Sure. Where do we start?

Waldo: Well, I remember the diagrams on visual thinking strategies that you gave us before. Is that a good starting point?

Dr. D: I can't imagine a more appropriate frame of reference. Let's start with the components of visual thinking.

Waldo: Yeah, I recall how a relaxed attitude or activity can give the subconscious level a chance to simmer a potential solution. But I could use some help with the conscious level.

Dr. D: That's coming, Waldo. Another part of visual thinking is the form and way our thoughts are envisioned. The diagram illustrated the three types of images we use to express visual thoughts.

Waldo: Were they shown as three overlapping circles labeled seeing, imagining, and drawing?

Dr. D: Yes, that's correct. You can exercise conscious control over which context you use. For instance, you may draw a possible implementation scheme for the general tree or you may imagine a general tree being transformed into a simpler structure.

Waldo: I get the idea. An idea is formed at some level in my consciousness, and I can select the vehicle or image with which to represent the idea. Great!

Dr. D: You can then select the third component of visual thinking—operations upon the vehicle or image. These were represented in the diagram by satellite circles attached to the central core—the seeing-imagining-drawing triad. A thought percolates to a conscious level, a form is selected to represent the idea, and operations are performed on the visual image to adapt it to the current situation if needed.

Waldo: That all sounds good, Dr. D, but I can't even draw a respectable box, and my imagination quotient barely rivals my heart rate.

Dr. D: You've just expressed two of the most important self-limiting attitudes regarding visual thinking. You need to see these two activities in a different light.

Waldo: But Dr. D, I'd feel embarrassed to show anyone my drawings.

Dr. D: Try this, Waldo. Draw a general tree of depth 2 with eight nodes, the root having three children, one of which has no children and the other two having two children. [Waldo sketches the described tree on the back of his lunch bag.] Fine, you have taken a thought and given it form. So drawing for visual thinking purposes is a reflection of something in the visual mind. The sketch captures the essence of the idea and focuses the thought. It does not need to be a detailed communication to anyone else. Maybe using the word *sketch* instead of *draw* will reduce the performance anxiety that you associate with drawing.

Waldo: You know, that really helps. 'Sketching my ideas' sounds like an activity that I can do with confidence—given practice, of course.

Dr. D: Great! Speaking of confidence, that's all your imagination quotient needs—along

with continuous practice, of course. Waldo, do you daydream?

Waldo: Ahh—sure, Dr. D, . . . but not in your class. Why?

Dr. D: Then you imagine. Using scenes that you have seen, you create images for your mind's eye. With conscious practice, you can activate your imagination with any topic that you chose. Let's do an experiment. Close your eyes and take three slow, deep breaths. [Pause . . .] Imagine an implementation of the general tree in which the root of each subtree has a linked list of its children. [Pause a few moments.] Imagine the node structure for such an implementation. [Pause.] How's your imagination working, Waldo?

Waldo: Wow! I can actually see the image—each link an arrow, each level of the general tree a set of linked lists with the root node like a head node for a linked list. This is great, Dr. D, I even think that I could draw the image without much trouble. Seeing is believing, Dr. D. I believe my ImQ does have a chance for a bit of inflation.

Dr. D: I would venture to guess that you also believe that "seeing is seeing."

Waldo: Why sure, we all see the same things. Don't you see that oak tree over there?

Dr. D: Actually, we don't see the same! That's because we see images, not objects. What I see is a middle-aged deciduous tree showing the beginning shades of autumn. You see, Waldo, the act of seeing depends on your viewpoint. By taking a consciously active role in selecting the viewpoint, you can create a fresh image of the same object or event. You can see an event as it appears or you can see it as more than it appears and actively investigate it from different vantage points. In this way you exercise visual thinking by developing images from the seeing context.

Waldo: Not to punny, but I do see what you mean. By breaking my habitual seeing pattern, I can give my mind new images on which to feed. By using my imagination I can design images that the mind has never tasted, and by sketching the images, the mind crystallizes the visual thought in a form that I can analyze, compare, and develop. This is why the circles overlap; each type of visual imagery can interface with the others during the visual thinking process. What's more, each area is under my conscious direction if I so chose. Quite incredible, Dr. D, and right nice.

Dr. D: Quite incredible is how I'd describe your summary of our discussion! All that is left in your mastery of visual thinking is, of course, practice. How about practicing some visual thinking tonight on the problem of implementing the general tree whose nodes are nonhomogeneous? Now, let's see if you can practice it by throwing this imaginary frisbee.

(Waldo and Dr. D begin playing catch with a phantom Frisbee.)

6

Graphs

By logic and reason
We die hourly;
By imagination
We live.

— W. B. Yeats

6.1 Setting the Stage

6.1.1 MA BELL COVERS THE SOUTH

Each day that we function within this modern world we interact with various large systems possessing numerous interconnections, both among their own components and with other systems. When we take the time to look at these systems from a broad perspective, we encounter various organizational structures. In this section we take a perspective that allows us to see some common everyday systems as the graph structure. As I briefly present the situations, I will use the text and diagrams to slowly give you the flavor of the graph structure and to introduce the terminology currently in use.

The telephone system is used almost daily by virtually all of us for both local and long distance calls. Since it is not feasible to have each home phone in the United States directly connected to all other home phones, another arrangement has been designed. The telephone system designers selected certain cities to be nodes in the telephone communications network. Thus a call from Dime Box, Texas to Cozy, Georgia may first go to a communication center in Dallas, then be routed to Little Rock, Arkansas, next to Nashville, Tennessee, and finally to Atlanta, Georgia, where it is routed through a local (but similar) network to your cousin in Cozy. Each pair of communication centers is linked by a sequence of microwave transmitting stations.

Figure 6.1 shows a hypothetical communications network for the southern section of the United States. As you can see, each node city is connected to one or more other node cities by a direct path. It is safe to assume that it is a two-way path, since our conversations are two-way. It is also important to notice that there are alternate paths between cities. These paths may not seem as direct, but nonetheless they provide the needed communication link. For instance, if an autumn thunderstorm damages a microwave transmitter between Little Rock and Nashville, closing the path between

Figure 6.1

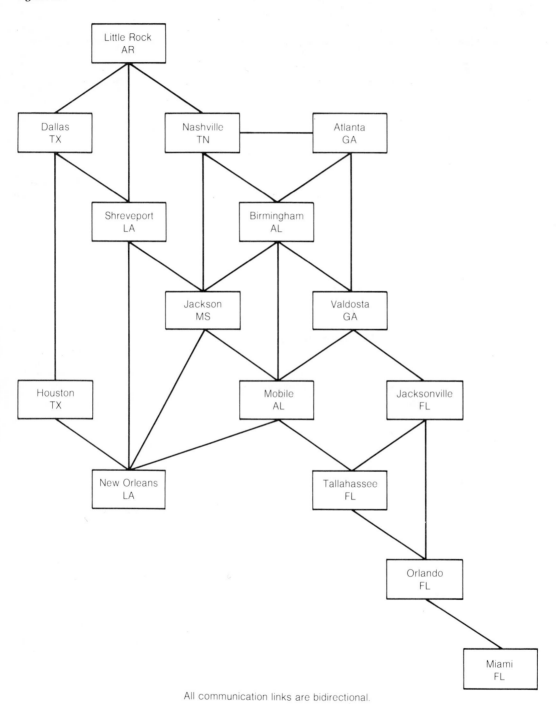

All communication links are bidirectional.

these two cities, your call to your Cozy cousin may be rerouted through Louisiana, Mississippi, and Alabama to Atlanta. Undoubtedly, you wouldn't notice the difference. You can take away any edge between nodes in this graph (except one) and construct another path (of a different length) that connects the two cities. The Orlando-Miami edge is critical to the southernmost section of the network and thus must be given special attention.

Other communication systems have a similar organization. The U.S. Postal Service uses a network to collect and distribute the mails. Airlines use regional airports with connecting flights from within a region to transport passengers across the breadth of the United States. In these three examples we see that the relationship pattern is not similar to any information structure that we have studied. There is no semblance of linearity or hierarchy—the appearance is more like the web of a slightly disoriented spider.

6.1.2 A NON-DOWN-TO-EARTH GRAPH EXAMPLE

Communication systems do not have to cover a large area, nor do they have to function exclusively between people. Among insects, bees use a set of dancing movements, and ants a chemical path to communicate the location of a food source. Another important type of communication system is a **computer network.** A collection of computers and a collection of communication links can be set up that permits one-way or two-way dialogs between selected computers. The scale of operation can range from the departments of a university, the branch office computers of a nationwide corporation, or the separate computer systems aboard the Space Shuttle. The important feature is not the scale but who can talk to whom—that is, how each computer is interconnected with the others.

The two networks illustrated in Figure 6.2 demonstrate the range that can be found in computer networks. Figure 6.2a represents a system where each department has a local computer system that can talk only with the central computer. Two departmental computers cannot talk together directly and thus only one data transfer within the system can happen at a time.

In a complicated endeavor like the Space Shuttle, illustrated in Figure 6.2b, various subsystems are monitored and controlled by a local dedicated computer. But fast intercomputer communication is essential: a changing situation noticed by one subsystem—for example, fuel pressure level—must be quickly passed on to the navigation and power subsystem computer. It is also important to allow for the possibility of simultaneous conversations between two pairs of computer subsystems, as the figure implies. Another important feature for the completely connected computer network on the Space Shuttle is its fault tolerance. Let's say that the communication link between subsystems 1 and 5 has a malfunction. Messages and data transfer can follow a slower but still reliable path through an intermediary subsystem such as subsystem 3. With this back-up process, simultaneous dialogs, and complete communication between subsystem computers, the Space Shuttle computers are capable of having their own huddle in space to evaluate the progress of the flight's game plan.

An important characteristic that helps distinguish these two extremes for computer networks is the number of communication links going into and coming from any

Figure 6.2

a. Centralized departmental computer network at Data U

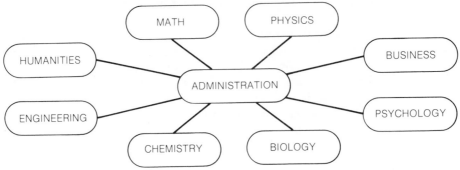

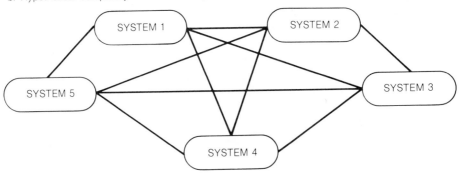

b. Hypothetical completely connected computer network for the space shuttle computer systems

All systems can communicate directly to all others.

one computer. This concept, called the degree of a node, will be important at different times during this chapter. Although we have not seen an example yet, graphs can exist in which the degree of incoming lines is different than the degree of outgoing lines. Can you think of any situations that require this relationship pattern?

The term network has been used in both a common and computer science sense; for the abstract model of the graph information structure, it will receive a slightly different, more precise definition. Even used somewhat informally, it conveys the essential nature of the graph information structure by describing the relationships among a set of elements, in this case computers.

6.1.3   THE MIGHTIER MOUSE RETURNS

The graph information structure can be found in several areas of artificial intelligence, robotics, and game theory. To give you an idea of how it contributes, let me bring back for a repeat performance the robot mouse that travels through a maze. To provide a little thrill to the example, it will be framed in the guise of a video game that I will call Pac Rat. The playing area is shown in Figure 6.3. Pac Rat starts in the goodies area, collects a hunk of cheese, and selects one of the three entrances. Pac Rat journeys along a path, encountering decision spots where alternative paths may be taken. The goal is to find a safe area where the goodies can be stored in case of a power outage or shortage of quarters. Of course, all video games must have a villain or two, so this one has three cozy cats that enjoy goodies of a different flavor than cheese. You can use your imagination to decide when each villainous cat leaves its den and what sound and sight effects to generate when one is lucky and becomes a fat cat à la Pac Rat. Other details and devious scenarios can be added by your enterprising mind.

To implant a bit of artificial intelligence into Pac Rat, the collections of all possible paths through the playing area can be included in the master program, which controls Pac Rat's movements. Each node will represent a starting spot, a decision spot, or an ending spot, and the edges connecting these nodes will indicate that Pac Rat can travel between the two.

The abstract graph that contains all the information for finding the paths in the playing area is found in Figure 6.4. You should take some time to verify to yourself that the relationships drawn into Figure 6.3 are indeed contained within the graph of Figure 6.4.

The key to proving the validity of the abstraction is to calculate the degree of each node, the number of edges connecting it to other nodes. In this way, you will find

Figure 6.3 **Playing area for PAC RAT video game**

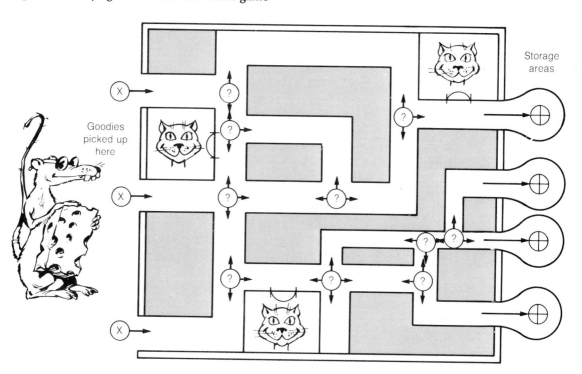

Figure 6.4 Abstract graph of paths in playing area of PAC RAT video game

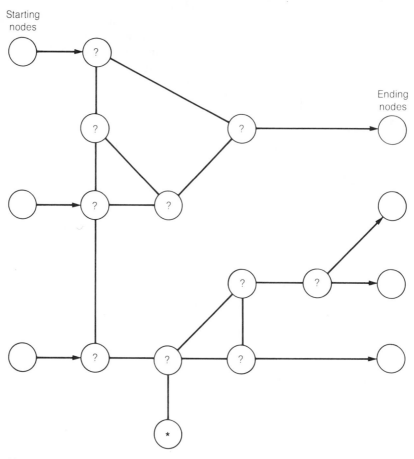

Starting
nodes

Ending
nodes

Note: All edges are bidirectional except those with arrowheads.

that each decision spot is represented and is connected to the correct other decision spots. The degree also gives you a way to distinguish the starting and ending nodes. So the degree attribute of nodes can be very important in characterizing the graph structure.

You might have noticed a node in the abstract model with an asterisk in it that does not appear directly as a decision spot in Figure 6.3. What does appear is a dead-end path, and this is why a dummy node is added to the graph. It will be easy to process this node, since there is only one path in and the same path out.

With the graph in the master program of the Pac Rat, we not only have a mightier but also a smarter mouse. In Chapter 2, our mouse had only hindsight; now it has foresight also and can plan a route to avoid meeting a cunning cat along the path. So the drama is set—for all intelligent plans, artificial or not, can quickly be laid asunder, substituting a bite of Pac Rat for a nibble of cheese.

■ **"JUST FOR REFERENCE"**

A telephone network has these characteristics—

- designated cities operate as national switching and dispatching centers
- nodes (cities) are linked by a microwave connection
- messages travel both directions along the link
- messages can be rerouted around damaged links
- relationships can be characterized as weblike

A computer network contains—

- a collection of computers that monitor and control specific areas
- a collection of links among the computers, whose arrangement influences the flexibility of the system

An artificial intelligence graph has these characteristics—

- collection of decision spots and the paths between them form a graph
- alternate paths allow strategy development
- the degree of flexibility is indicated by the degree of the node

EXERCISES

1. Describe a network situation that exists within:
   a) your home
   b) your work
   c) your head/brain
   d) your imagination
2. Develop a network arrangement that falls somewhere between the two extremes of Figure 6.2. Indicate some of the ramifications of the arrangement.
3. Develop a diagram of the paths in your living area, as in Figure 6.4.

6.2 Formalizing the Structure

The three examples in Section 6.1 can be used as a basis from which to generalize a description of the abstract model of the graph information structure.

Each example starts with a set of data elements (communication centers for the telephone network, computers in various departments, and certain locations on the playing area for Pac Rat). The elements are called the **nodes** or **vertices** of the graph. To describe the relationships among these data elements, a second set is needed. This is a set of pairs, with each member of the pair coming from the original set of data elements. The elements in this second set are called the *edges* of the graph. **The graph thus consists of two sets: a set of nodes and a set of pairs of nodes called edges.**

The set notation for a graph is given in Figure 6.5. The node set depicted has six elements, and the edge set has ten pairs of elements. This particular graph is called a **directed** graph or **digraph;** the defining criterion is that the pairs in the set of edges are ordered. This implies that the edges (TX, AR) and (AR, TX) are to be considered distinct. In such a case, the edges are called directed edges or **arcs.**

The first two examples from Section 6.1 allowed for two-way communications between any two nodes. This means that the pairs representing the edges do not have to be ordered because if (A, B) is in the edge set then (B, A) would also be a member. In general, graphs that possess this quality are termed **undirected.** Thus an undirected graph has an edge set that exhibits the symmetric property for relations.

It is possible that each edge of a graph may have a value associated with it (like the cost to ship something from New York to Georgia). A graph with this attribute is call a **weighted** graph. This is the technical definition of the term **network**—a weighted graph—though the term is frequently used without specific mention of the weights associated with each edge.

Three terms are used in the context of nodes. Two nodes are said to be **adjacent** if an edge exists in the edge set with these two nodes as members. Therefore, GA and AR are adjacent in the directed graph of Figure 6.5, since (GA, AR) is an element of the edge set of the graph. The next two terms refer to the number of nodes that are adjacent to a given node. Using Figure 6.5 as an example, the **indegree** of the node CA equals two, since CA is adjacent to two nodes where CA is the second member of the ordered pair defining the connecting edge. The **outdegree** of CA is one. This

Figure 6.5

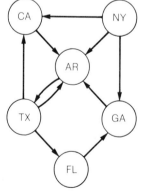

Set notation for the graph
$G =$ *(N,E)* where
$N =$ (CA, TX, AR, FL, NY, GA)—set of nodes
$E =$ {(NY,CA), (TX,CA), (CA,AR), (TX,AR),
        (TX,FL), (FL,GA), (GA,AR), (NY,GA),
        (NY,AR), (AR,TX)}—set of edges

means that only one edge leaves the node CA, since only one edge with CA first, (CA, AR), occurs in the edge set.

For undirected graphs, the terms indegree and outdegree are replaced by the term **degree,** which is defined simply as the number of edges that a node is a member of.

An important operation in dealing with graphs is determining whether two nodes are connected by one or more edges. Such a connection, if it exists, is called a **path.** A path between two nodes A and Z is an ordered sequence of nodes such that the first node in the sequence is A, the last node is Z, and each node (but the last) is adjacent to its successor in the ordered sequence. A **cyclic** path is a path from a node back to itself. When a path exists between two nodes, the two nodes are said to be **connected.** The **length** of a path is the number of edges it contains.

When a graph has the property that all nodes are connected to all other nodes by a path, the graph itself is said to be connected. If the length of all the paths is equal to one (that is, each node has degree equal to one less than the number of nodes) then the graph is called a **complete** graph. The computer network in Figure 6.2b is an example of a complete undirected graph.

In summary, the abstract information structure of this chapter is composed of two main ingredients, a set of nodes and a set of edges. The graph can come in different

IMAGINATION CHALLENGE

Consider the following sets of figures horizontally, vertically, and diagonally. Once you have figured out a pattern of change, draw the final figure in the lower righthand corner that completes the pattern.

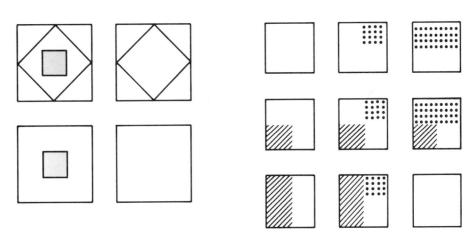

flavors: it can be directed or undirected, weighted, connected, or complete. Its nodes can be adjacent or connected and are part of its edges, which make up the paths through the graph. The number of paths originating from any node is indicated by the node's degree for an undirected graph or its outdegree for a directed graph.

At this point, we have seen examples of undirected graphs and, actually, quite a few directed graphs. The binary and general tree of Chapter 5 are directed graphs whose root node has an indegree of zero and whose other nodes have an indegree of one. You may recall that the term *degree* was defined for the nodes of a general tree. In the terminology of the graph, this meaning of degree is equivalent to the outdegree of a node. And the tree structure is no stranger to us now.

Let us begin to put on our programming clothes and see how we can take hold of this information structure and bring it into our software tool kit along with its hierarchical cousin, the tree.

■ **"JUST FOR REFERENCE"**

The graph model consists of two sets—

- nodes—a set of data elements
- edges—a set of pairs of data elements

The edge pairs—

- indicate the relationship between two nodes
- may be considered ordered or unordered, respectively yielding a directed or undirected graph

Terminology

Graphs—

- **directed/undirected**—edges are one-way or two-way, respectively
- **weighted**—each edge has a value associated with it
- **complete**—all nodes have a path of length 1 to all other nodes

Nodes—

- **adjacent**—an edge lies between two nodes
- **indegree/outdegree**—the number of incoming or outgoing edges, respectively, that a node is a part of
- **connected**—a path or ordered sequence of edges exists between nodes

Paths—

- **cyclic**—a path leads from a node back to itself
- **length**—measure of the number of edges that constitute a path

EXERCISES

1. For the graph illustrated in Figure 6.1, develop the set of nodes and the set of edges.

2. For the graph illustrated in Figure 6.1, list all paths of length 3 from Miami.

3. For the graph illustrated in Figure 6.2b, develop the set of nodes and the set of edges.

4. For the graph illustrated in Figure 6.4, give the degree of each node. For each node, list the nodes that are adjacent to it.

5. Draw a diagram of a connected digraph with six nodes that has the minimum number of edges to make it connected. Repeat the exercise for a connected undirected graph.

6. Draw a diagram of a complete graph with six nodes that has the minimum number of edges. How many edges will the graph have?

7. A simple model for a computer consists of five components: input device, output device, memory device, disk device, and central processing unit. Draw a directed graph of the model and attach weights to each arc. Let the transfer speed between devices be the weight's value.

8. Locate the block diagram of a well-known microcomputer system. View the diagram as a graph where each edge is defined by the existence of a signal path between two parts of the microcomputer. List the paths available and indicate all the cyclic paths.

9. Express a binary or general tree from Chapter 5 as a digraph. List the members of both the node and the arc set.

6.3 *Implementing the Structure*

6.3.1 A BIT ON EDGE

When either the structure of a graph will remain unchanged or only the edges may change, we can employ an implementation approach that uses an array whose elements are bits. The array indicates which nodes of the graph are adjacent. The conventions are as follows:

1. The array has the same number of rows and columns.

2. The number of rows and columns equals the number of nodes in the graph.

3. The nodes in the graph are numbered from one to the maximum number of nodes.

4. Each element of the array has a value of 0 or 1.

5. If the element in row J and column K is equal to 0 then there is no edge between node J and node K; if the value is 1 then an edge does exist between nodes J and K.

This collection of conventions provides a means to represent the structure of any graph. With respect to the existence of an edge it describes the relationships between all possible pairs of nodes. Further, the array occupies a minimal amount of storage space while preserving the structural integrity of the graph. (Although this approach looks good in theory, caution must accompany its practice. The dialect of PASCAL you use may implement boolean identifiers with bytes of memory. So investigate before you invest!) The adjacency bit array for the graph of Figure 6.5 is given below as Figure 6.6a.

Some immediate consequences of our conventions can be stated. For undirected graphs the array will have a symmetric attribute, since if row J, column K is 1, then row K, column J will also equal 1. In such a case, another savings in storage requirements can be realized by using a method of implementing symmetric matrices. Another obvious advantage is that the degree (or indegree and outdegree for directed graphs) of any node can be calculated by considering the number of ones in the proper row or column.

Since this method provides only structural information, additional conventions must be set up to accommodate information about the nodes or the edges. For example, a weighted graph requires that the weight associated with each edge also be stored. One way to approach this problem is to store the weight rather than a one in the array. The convention would now be stated thusly: if the value is nonzero then an edge exists from node J to node K and the nonzero value is the weight of the edge. Now, the structural and informational character of the graph is contained in the adjacency array. However, increased storage cost is the trade-off for increased informational content. The PASCAL declarations for this approach are presented in Figure 6.6b.

This implementation easily accommodates some graph operations. Determining whether an edge exists translates to a simple array reference and a test for a nonzero value. To delete an edge that currently exists in a graph, it is necessary only to store a zero in the correct row/column location. Adding an edge is performed similarly. These operations are so straightforward that they are given as exercises at the end of the chapter.

Another useful operation is determining the existence of all paths of a fixed length. As we shall see in Section 6.4, the adjacency bit array provides a particularly useful vehicle for this operation.

The use of an array to implement an information structure as flexible as the graph is a simple but not-so-obivous solution to the problem at hand. Its simplicity yields the advantages of minimal storage requirements and ease of performing various changes and operations on the graph. Because of its simplicity, however, certain constraints are produced that limit this method's application to a small subset of the potential graph population. Graphs that have a changing set of nodes or that have information associated with the nodes or edges will require an alternative approach. As you may have intuited, you are on the edge of discovering this new method, whether you "node" it or not.

6.3.2 THE LINKED STRUCTURE CONCEPT APPLIED TO GRAPHS

When you began to grasp the weblike nature of the graph information structure, your intuitive and intellectual senses probably visualized some sort of linked arrangement in the implementation process. The first approach, the adjacency array, was

Figure 6.6

a. Adjacency array for the directed graph of Figure 6.5.

```
type RANGE = 1..MAX_NODES;
     ADJ_VAL = boolean; {0 or 1 or weight range}
     ADJ_ARRAY = array [RANGE,RANGE] of ADJ_VAL;
```

		CA 1	TX 2	AR 3	FL 4	NY 5	GA 6
CA	1	0	0	1	0	0	0
TX	2	1	0	1	1	0	0
AR	3	0	1	0	0	0	0
FL	4	0	0	0	0	0	1
NY	5	1	0	1	0	0	1
GA	6	0	0	1	0	0	0

b. Adjacency array with weights

	1	2	3	4	5	6
1	0	0	4	0	0	0
2	2	0	3	5	0	0
3	0	4	0	0	0	0
4	0	0	0	0	0	3
5	3	0	4	0	0	2
6	0	0	6	0	0	0

where ADJ_VAL = 0..6; replaces the declaration above

probably unexpected. Though it has its place, admittedly covering a small area in the implementation of the graph, it has critical limitations—a small information content about the nodes and a fixed number of graph nodes. The need for a more flexible arrangement, capable of handling changes to the relationships within the graph, leads us back to your original intuitive approach—linked structures. As in previous situations, the linked structure provides us with the flexibility to add elements to the structure and redefine relationships without a large expense in programming and data movement. So in this section, we look at a progression of linked structures that can be used to preserve the relationships of the graph and provide the important characteristic of the capacity for change.

Let us begin with a diagram of a simple graph (Figure 6.7) and see a simple,

TRADE-OFFS

If you are implementing a weighted directed graph structure with 50 nodes and 100 edges, then consider the effects of using an adjacency array. First, the 50-by-50 array requires 2500 multibyte locations (since the graph is weighted). And 96% (2400) of these locations contain a zero value (since there are only 100 edges). This underutilization of space can be avoided.

The above situation is referred to as a sparse array—one where the majority of the elements are zero. Sparse arrays can be represented more effectively with a special linked structure that consists of two arrays of pointers—one for each row in the sparse array and one for each column. The pointers indicate the first nonzero element in the respective row or column. The sparse array's elements (in this case, the adjacency array's edge information) are stored in nodes that contain 5 fields: the row number (the FROM node); the column number (the TO node); the nonzero data value (the weight); a pointer to the next nonzero data value in the row and a pointer to the next nonzero data element in the column. (See accompanying figure to integrate this left-brain presentation with a right-brain picture.)

How storage-efficient is this new approach? The two pointer arrays require 100 locations. The 100 edges require five fields each, yielding a total of 500 locations for the edges. Thus, a minimum of 600 locations are used to represent the adjacency array (Assuming row/column numbers, pointers, and weight, each requires the same size location.) Compare this to a 50-by-50 array of locations, which uses a total of 2500 locations. The pointer arrays yield a 76% reduction in storage requirements, which is certainly worthwhile.

The next part of the trade-off analysis—which is left up to you—is to determine whether the development time or the execution time for procedures is increased by the linked nature of the sparse array implementation. Also, ask yourself if you have gained any added flexibility with this newly imagined approach.

	1	2	3	4	5
1	0	4	0	0	0
2	0	0	7	0	0
3	0	2	0	8	0
4	3	0	0	0	0
5	0	0	5	0	6

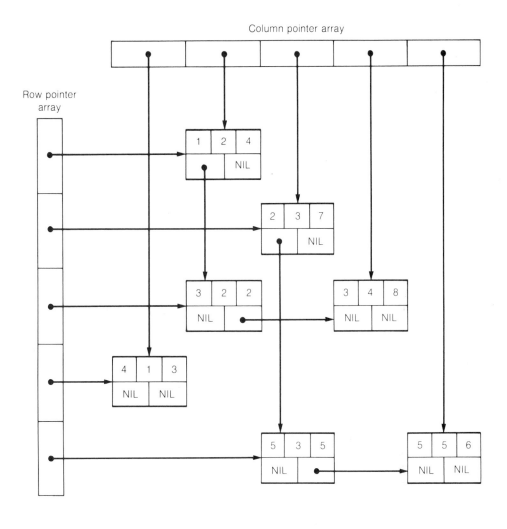

straightforward way to link the graph's nodes and edges. Since the graph consists of two sets of elements—nodes and edges—it seems logical that we will need two different pools of available nodes for our linked representation. (Notice here, the dual usage of the term *node*. In the first occurrence it refers to an element of the abstract information structure and in the second occurrence it is being used to refer to a storage element—an element used in the implementation. To distinguish between the usages, I will refer to the latter as the **storage node**.) This is quite reasonable, since nodes and edges are different in nature and thus their storage nodes will have different record structures. Each available pool of storage nodes will require its own set of procedures to manage its resources. This is true for the self-managed available pool.

Figure 6.7

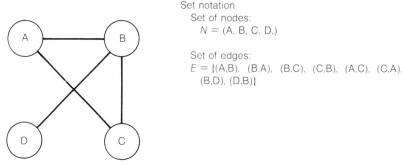

Set notation
Set of nodes:
$N = (A, B, C, D,)$

Set of edges:
$E = \{(A,B), (B,A), (B,C), (C,B), (A,C), (C,A), (B,D), (D,B)\}$

Each line is represented by two pairs in the set of edges

When we use PASCAL's dynamic allocation system in the later example, the *new* and *dispose* procedure in conjunction with two type declarations are all we need.

In order to represent the graph in Figure 6.7 with a simple linked structure, we must first agree on an arbitrary ordering of the nodes within the graph. This was done with the adjacency array so that the nodes could be associated with the rows and columns of the array. Let us take the obvious ordering—the node labeled A is first, B is second, C is third, and D is last. We can now set up an array of records where each record consists of two fields—the name of the node and a pointer field, to be described soon. The node names can be stored in consecutive records of the array. The PASCAL declaration below will suffice:

```
CONST MAX_EDGES=12;
      NUM_NODES=4;
type PTR_IDENTIFIER:0..MAX_EDGES;
     NODE = record
               NAME : char;
               EDGEPOINTER : PTR_IDENTIFIER
            end;
var NODE_LIST : array [1..NUM_NODES] of NODE;
```

With this declaration applied to the graph of Figure 6.7 we have the beginning of our structure.

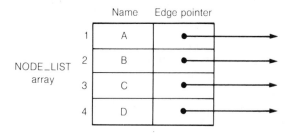

Next, the edges are incorporated into the structure. The storage node structure for the edge is simple since this is not a weighted graph. The PASCAL declaration that describes the storage node structure and allocates space for the available pool of storage nodes is given below:

```
type EDGE = record
               TONODE : char;
               NEXTEDGE : PTR_IDENTIFIER
            end;
var EDGE_POOL : array [1.MAX_EDGES] of EDGE;
```

With this said, let's look at a graphic representation of the linked implementation of the graph.

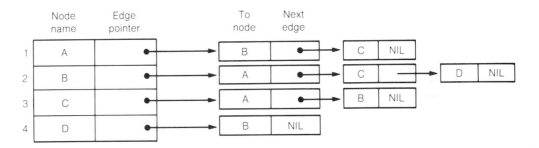

This representation provides a convenient way to implement the unweighted graph. All the edges leading from a given node can easily be found by following the EDGE _ POINTER pointer identifier. The operation of adding a new edge is a combination of (1) a linear search of the NODE _ LIST array for the FROMNODE name and (2) adding the node name of the TONODE to the linked lists of edges. This representation is referred to as a list of nodes and its adjacency lists. The adjacency lists themselves may be unordered or ordered. The operations of inserting and deleting edges are the basic linked list operations.

Assume that the identifiers NODEFROM and NODETO are the names of the nodes in a new edge to be added. The following PASCAL procedure will add an edge between the nodes:

```
procedure ADD_EDGE (NODEFROM, NODETO:char);
(* globals : NODE_LIST,EDGE_ POOL *)
var K:1..MAX_NODES;
    MATCH:boolean;
    NEW_EDGE:PTR_IDENTIFIER;
begin
MATCH := true;
K := 1;
while (NODEFROM <> NODE_LIST[K].NAME) and MATCH do
if K = MAX_NODES then MATCH := false
                  else K := K + 1;
if not (MATCH) then ERROR_RESPONSE (NODEFROM)
        else begin                    (*  get a new edge node *)
                                      (*  insert it at the front
                                          of adjacency list for
                                          node K *)
```

```
            POOF (NEW_EDGE);
            EDGE_POOL[NEW_EDGE].TONODE  := NODETO;
            EDGE_POOL[NEW_EDGE].NEXTNODE := NODE_LIST[K].EDGEPOINTER;
            NODE_LIST[K].EDGEPOINTER := NEW_EDGE
          end
  end;
```

Since the graph is undirected, the procedure must be called with the arguments NODETO and NODEFROM reversed. It does not check to see whether the edge already exists within the structure. If this is an important consideration, the logic for detecting it must also be included. As an exercise, you are invited to complete the procedure with the mentioned safeguard.

Actually, we have gained much with this linked representation, though it is simpler to add an edge to an adjacency array than to a list of nodes with adjacency lists. We can include more information in the storage nodes for both the nodes and edges, overcoming one limitation of the adjacency array. However, the main limitation—the difficulty of adding a node—is still present. By declaring the array LIST to have only four elements, we have restricted the number of nodes that can be represented.

In order to improve the capabilities of the implementation, we can either increase the upper bound of the array's declaration, thereby providing the extra space needed, or set up the list of nodes as a linked list. This latter approach is illustrated below with a directed graph.

With the extra link field for the nodes, another available pool and a second set of management routines will be needed. An alternative idea is to switch to dynamic

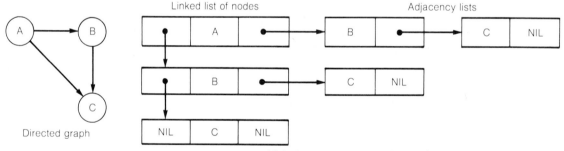

Linked structure representing graph

pointers and let the PASCAL system manage the storage. Taking this new avenue, the following PASCAL declarations are offered.

```
type NODE_PTR = ^NODE
     EDGE_PTR = ^EDGE
     NODE = record
              NEXT_NODE:NODE_PTR;
              NAME:char;
              FIRST_EDGE:EDGE_PTR
            end
```

7

```
EDGE = record
         TONODE:char;
         NEXT_EDGE:EDGE_PTR
       end
var NODES,NEW_NODE:NODE_PTR;NEW_EDGE:EDGE_PTR;
```

Let us exercise our new feature by adding a new node to the graph along with its adjacency list. First, let us assume that the identifier NODES points to the first node in the linked list of nodes. We can also assume that the list of nodes is ordered and that a procedure (similar to those in Chapter 4) for inserting a new node into a singly linked list already exists. For simplicity, let us add a node that has only one edge, where the identifiers NODEFROM and NODETO are of character type and NODEFROM is the new node being added. The PASCAL code below demonstrates the connections that must be made.

```
(* get the storage nodes for a node and an edge from the HEAP *)
new(NEW_NODE);
new(NEW_EDGE);
(* fill in the edge node's fields *)
NEW_EDGE^.TONODE := NODETO;
NEW_EDGE^.NEXT_EDGE := nil;
(*fill in the node storage node's fields except node link *)
NEW_NODE^.NAME := NODEFROM;
NEW_NODE^.FIRST_EDGE := NEW_EDGE;
(INSERT new node into the list of NODES *)
INSERT (NEW_NODE, NODES);
```

With this arrangement, we can add as many nodes and edges as there is available space. Additionally, we can use software tools and algorithms that we are familiar with. Our current approach has two distinct advantages over the adjacency array: (1) informational content within the structure and (2) the ability to add new nodes with their associated edges. But don't start to throw away the idea of the adjacency array.

Consider the following problem: For a directed graph, calculate the number of edges leaving a given node. Compare the algorithms given to solve the problem below.

	Linked List of Nodes
Adjacency Array	**with Adjacency Lists**
Add up the number of ones in the associated row of the array	Count the number of edges in the adjacency list of the given node.

Which algorithm is more efficient? The first one requires each column of a given row to be checked; hence if there are N nodes, there will be N iterations of a loop. The second algorithm requires an iteration for each edge represented in the adjacency list. This is very likely less than N and definitely never greater than N. So the algorithm for the adjacency array is proportional to the number of nodes, while the algorithm for the adjacency list method is bounded by the largest outdegree of any node. The second algorithm wins the prize—no big surprise!

Now consider this problem: For a directed graph, calculate the number of edges arriving at a given node. The algorithm are compared below.

Adjacency Array	Linked List of Nodes with Adjacency Lists
Add up the number of ones in the associated column of the array.	For each node in the linked list, search its adjacency list for the given node; increment counter if given node is found.

Now which algorithm takes the efficiency prize? The first algorithm is again proportional to the number of nodes. The second algorithm must now look through all the adjacency lists. As a worst case, it may have to sample every edge to discover that no edge arrives at the given node. Therefore, the execution time is proportinal to the numbers of nodes times the average indegree of the nodes. Because the implementation was not set up to look backward, so to speak, answering this "backward" question requires considerable expense. If this type of question must be answered frequently, then maybe we must dust off the adjacency array and bring it back into the limelight.

If you have become an avid fan of linked structures you may be saying, - "Wait, Mr. Author, I have an idea that may be able to solve the last problem without returning to "the Hulk"—the adjacency array. Let me draw a diagram and then I will explain the idea. I will start with a simple directed graph with four nodes and four edges. The set notation will be:

```
NODES = ( A, B, C, D )
EDGES = { (A,B), (B,C), (A,C), (D,B) }
```

Here's a sketch of my new improved linked graph structure:

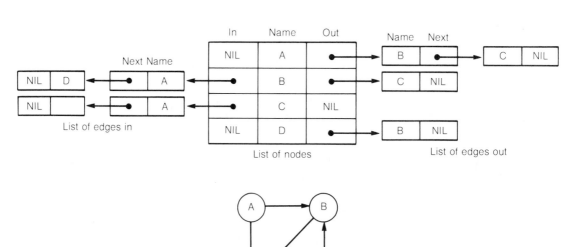

"What I am doing is adding an extra pointer field to the storage node for nodes and letting it point to another list of edges. This new list is the inverse of the adjacency list: it indicates the edges leading into a node rather than those leading from a node. With my linked structure, I can win both prizes, 'cause I can beat the Hulk to the answer in both problems!"

This extra set of lists does indeed provide the added information, which makes this a handy approach for accessing the information in either the FROM or TO direction. It also uses the same node structure for both the edges out and the edges in. It doubles the work of adding a new edge, since the list of both edges out and edges in must be updated. The same effect applies when an edge must be removed. If we measured efficiency in storage units, the presentation of the prizes may have to be reconsidered. All things considered, though, it's good to note that the outspoken reader has cultivated a touch of imagination regarding implementating information structures.

Another important feature of any implementation is the ability to delete a node from the graph. This operation requires information about both the FROM edges and the TO edges of the given node. Any structure that provides ready access to this information will produce simpler algorithms; therefore, the last approach provides a structure in which deleting a node and its associated edges is a breeze.

To present the deletion algorithm, let me state the PASCAL declarations to allow for dynamic pointers to both lists. I also want to label various elements so that the algorithm can be explained more easily. Notice that the list of nodes are linked together rather than being linearly stored in an array.

```
type NODE_PTR=^NODE;
     EDGE_PTR=^EDGE;
     NODE = record
              NEXT_NODE:NODE_PTR;
              EDGESINPTR:EDGE_PTR;
              NAME:char;
              EDGESOUTPTR:EDGE_PTR;
            end;
     EDGE = record
              NAME:char;
              NEXTEDGE:EDGE_PTR;
            end;
```

Let me refer to the list of edges leaving a given node as the *OUT–LIST* and the list of edges leading into the node as the *IN–LIST*. For any directed edge, let the node from which the edge leaves be referred to as the TAIL and the node to which it leads be called the HEAD.

The algorithm for deleting the edges associated with a given node which is to be deleted is:

> For all edges in the OUT-LIST of the node to be deleted,
>   delete this edge from the IN-LIST of the HEAD node.
> For all edges in the IN-LIST of the node to be deleted,
>   delete this edge from the OUT-LIST of the TAIL node.

In PASCAL this translates to the statements:

```
procedure LOCATE(NODE_VAL:char ; var LIST_PTR : NODE_PTR ) ;

( * procedure to locate a node with a given value, NODE_VAL,
  and return a pointer to the node * )

begin
| initialize to global external list pointer |
LIST_PTR := NODES ;

while LIST_PTR^.NAME <> NODE_VAL do
                    LIST_PTR := LIST_PTR^.NEXTNODE ;

end ;

procedure DELETE_EDGES(PTR:NODE_PTR);

var HEAD_PTR,TAIL_PTR:NODE_PTR;
    EPTR,SPTR,XPTR:EDGE_PTR;
    NAME_VAL,HEAD,TAIL:char;

|    procedure to delete a node pointed to by PTR
     and to delete all the edges that it is a part of |

begin
NAME_VAL := PTR^.NAME ;

| begin deleting edges in the OUT-LIST |

EPTR := PTR^.EDGESOUTPTR;

while EPTR <> nil do
          begin
          | locate tail node in list of nodes |
          TAIL := EPTR^.NAME ;
          LOCATE (TAIL, TAIL_PTR) ;

          | remove edge from IN-LIST of tail |
          SPTR := nil ;
          XPTR := TAIL_PTR^.EDGESINPTR ;
          | locate edge with matching head |
          while XPTR^.NAME <> NAME_VAL  do
                         begin
                            SPTR := XPTR ;
                            XPTR := XPTR^.NEXTEDGE;
                         end ;
          | check if edge is the first in the IN-LIST |
          | update appropriate pointer fields          |
          if SPTR = nil then
                         TAIL_PTR^.EDGESINPTR := XPTR^.NEXTEDGE
                  else
                         SPTR^.NEXTEDGE := XPTR^.NEXTEDGE ;
          dispose (XPTR) ;

          | remove edge from OUT-LIST of head |
          XPTR := EPTR ;
          EPTR := EPTR^.NEXTEDGE ;
```

```
              dispose (XPTR)

              end { while } ;

{ begin deleting edges in the IN-LIST }

EPTR := PTR^.EDGESINPTR  ;

while EPTR <> nil do
          begin
          { locate head node in list of nodes }
          HEAD := EPTR^.NAME ;
          LOCATE (HEAD,HEAD_PTR) ;

          { remove edge from OUT-LIST of head }
          SPTR := nil ;
          XPTR := HEAD_PTR^.EDGESOUTPTR ;
          { locate edge with matching tail }
          while XPTR^.NAME <> NAME_VAL  do
                              begin
                                SPTR := XPTR ;
                                XPTR := XPTR^.NEXTEDGE
                              end ;
{ check if edge is the first in the OUT-LIST }
{ update appropriate pointer fields          }
if SPTR = nil then
                    HEAD_PTR^.EDGESOUTPTR := XPTR^.NEXTEDGE
              else
                    SPTR^.NEXTEDGE := XPTR^.NEXTEDGE ;
dispose (XPTR) ;

{ remove edge from IN-LIST of tail }
XPTR := EPTR ;
EPTR := EPTR^.NEXTEDGE ;
dispose (XPTR)

end { while } ;

{ delete the node from the list of nodes }
{ use HEAD_PTR as a working pointer and TAIL_PTR as a shadow }

if PTR = NODES then  NODES := PTR^.NEXTNODE

              else begin
                    HEAD_PTR := NODES ;
                    TAIL_PTR := nil ;
                    while HEAD_PTR^.NAME <> NAME_VAL do
                                   begin
                                     TAIL_PTR := HEAD_PTR ;
                                     HEAD_PTR := HEAD_PTR^.NEXTNODE
                                   end ;
                    TAIL_PTR^.NEXTNODE := PTR^.NEXTNODE
                  end ;
dispose ( PTR )

end { procedure } ;
```

With this algorithm it is important to remember that the first part to be processed is each TAIL node for the edges in the OUT–LIST; in the second half of the procedure it becomes the HEAD nodes in the IN–LIST.

LOCATE is a procedure that looks through the list of nodes and finds the node that matches the name given as the first argument. When it locates this first argument, it returns its position in the list by way of the second argument.

The deluxe approach to implementing the graph is to include "the works" with the storage node structures, so that the algorithms that access the graph structure will have the important relationships easily at hand. This will entail a trade-off: for algorithm ease and against storage space utilization. The various path algorithms in the next section will give you an appreciation of this trade-off.

Using the graph from Figure 6.8 as a sample let us look at a storage node structure for both the nodes and edges of a graph.

The record structure of a storage node for graph nodes is presented below.

```
record
  NODEDATA1: (*DATA TYPES AS REQUIRED*)
  NODEDATA2:
    .
    .
    .
  NEXTNODE:NODE_PTR;            (*Pointer to next node*)

  INEDGES:0..MAX_EDGES;     (*Number of edges into node*)

  FIRSTINEDGE:EDGE_PTR;        (*Pointer  to first edge*)
                               (* in IN-LIST*)

  OUTEDGES:0..MAX_EDGES;       (*Number  of  edges  out of node *)
  FIRSTOUTEDGE:EDGE_PTR;       (*Pointer  to first edge*)
                               (*          in OUT-LIST*)
  MARK:boolean;                (*To  indicate if  node*)
                               (*      has been        *)
                               (*processed by algorithm*)
  end;
```

The record structure of a storage node for graph edges is as follows:

```
  record
    EDGEDATA:real;                    (*As required,
                                        such as weight *)

    TAIL:NODE_PTR;                    (*Pointer  to node
                                           that edge is from *)

    HEAD:NODE_PTR;                    (*Pointer to node
                                           that edge is to *)

    NEXTOUTEDGE:EDGE_PTR;             (*Pointer to next edge
                                          in the OUT-LIST of tail*)
    NEXTINEDGE:EDGE_PTR;              (*Pointer to next edge
                                          in the IN-LIST of head *)
    end;
```

Figure 6.8 **Directed graph with weights**

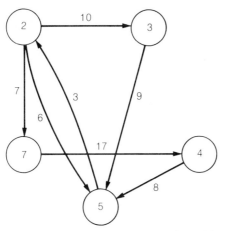

Node structures for representation of a weighted graph

Nodes

Node information	Next node
Number of edges in	Number of edges out
Pointer to IN_LIST / M A R K	Pointer to OUT_LIST

Edges

Weight	
Pointer to HEAD of edge	Pointer to TAIL of edge
Pointer to next edge in IN_LIST	Pointer to next edge in OUT_LIST

With these structures, each storage node for a graph node is potentially part of three linked lists: (1) it is always a part of the list of nodes; (2) it is possibly at the beginning of a linked list of edges that have this node as a tail (OUT–LIST); and (3) it may be at the beginning of a linked list of edges that have this node as a head (IN–LIST). In this way, the storage node for the graph node acts as a header for both the IN–LIST and OUT–LIST and contains the NIL value if either list of edges is empty.

Though it will have four pointers, the node for an edge is potentially a part of only two linked lists. Two of these pointers direct us back to the names and data of the nodes that comprise the edge. The two linked lists that an edge can be part of are the OUT–LIST of the tail of the edge and the IN–LIST of the head of the edge. Therefore, an edge node is part of an IN–LIST of one graph node and an OUT–LIST of another graph node.

The deluxe linked structure for the graph in Figure 6.8 is shown below as Figure 6.9. An external pointer is used to point to the first node in the linked list of nodes. This arrangement gives us the flexibility to process the graph's nodes or the edges associated with each node. To illustrate this point, let us look at the algorithm for printing the edges coming into a node, which does this for all the nodes within the graph. We can use the same record descriptions as given before, with the node number being the only field for NODEDATA and the edge's weight for the EDGEDATA. We will use two pointers, NPTR for the linked list of nodes and EPTR for the linked IN–LIST of edges. The external pointer for the beginning of the list of nodes is called START. The main section of the procedure follows:

```
begin
NPTR := START;

(*Until list of nodes is processed*)
  while NPTR <> nil do

(*Begin at the first edge in the IN-LIST*)
        begin
        EPTR := NPTR^.FIRSTINEDGE;

      (*Until all edges are processed  *)
        while EPTR <> nil do

              (*  Access edge information *)
              begin
                WEIGHT := EPTR^.EDGEDATA;
                HEAD_PTR := EPTR^.HEAD;
                TAIL_PTR := EPTR^.TAIL;
                (* Print information about edge *)
                PRINT_EDGE(TAIL_PTR,HEAD_PTR,WEIGHT);
                (* Step to the next edge in IN-LIST *)
                EPTR := EPTR^.NEXTINEDGE
              end;

        (*After finishing with the IN-LIST*)
        (*Move to next node in the list of nodes*)
        NPTR := NPTR^.NEXTNODE
        end;

(*After finishing with the list of nodes*)
end;(*PROCEDURE*)
```

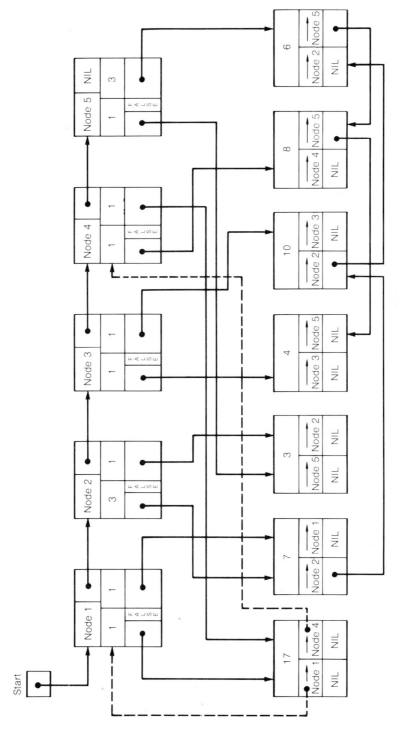

Figure 6.9

TRADE-OFFS

Tool Selection

We have two tools for the graph implementation task—the adjacency array and the list of nodes with adjacency lists. What are the pros and cons of each? This comparison will equip you with a tool of choice for the task at hand—selecting an implementation for a particular graph application.

The points in favor of the adjacency array are:

1. It is simple to conceptualize.
2. It is easy to program the operations of adding and deleting an edge, calculating the indegree and outdegree of a node, and determining if two nodes are adjacent.
3. It can use system programs to perform array multiplication to determine the number of paths of a fixed length.

The points against the adjacency array are:

1. The storage space is underused.
2. It is expensive in terms of time to find and list all paths of a fixed length, since the boolean matrix product requires a lot of execution time (of the order of N^2).
3. The addition or deletion of a node is difficult.
4. The array does not allow information about the nodes to be included in the structure.

These factors indicate that the adjacency array suits applications that have no changes to the number of nodes, require little information about the nodes, experience frequent changes to the number of edges, perform operations dealing with edge existence rather than path existence, and are not tight on available memory space.

Turning our focus to the adjacency list approach, the points in its favor are:

1. Information about the nodes and edges can easily be included in the structure.
2. It can use the standard linked list procedures.
3. The insertion of new nodes and edges is easy.
4. The IN–LIST and the OUT–LIST provide a lot of flexibility during the path algorithms.
5. The use of dynamic pointer variables permits the size of the graph to fluctuate over a large range.

On the other side of the coin:

1. It is not simple to conceptualize.
2. The deletion of a node involves searching all adjacency lists.
3. There are extra costs for maintaining the available pool (or pools) of records for the graph nodes and edges.

This approach is well suited for applications involving dynamic graphs where nodes and edges are added and deleted frequently. It would also be useful for applications that must determine the existence of paths between nodes or that must find paths with certain characteristics. Therefore, problems involving the shortest, longest, or most paths are best tackled with this tool.

This procedure turned into an exercise in traversing linked lists. You can also visualize the relative ease with which a new node and its associated edges can be added to the graph. The linked nature of the implementation facilitates this action.

This algorithm did not demonstrate the use of an important field—the **mark** field. Its usefulness arises when you need to know which nodes have already been processed or visited. This always occurs in algorithms that are involved in finding paths through the graph. The next section will cover three typical path problems and will use this simple field in the algorithms.

As a prelude, look at Figure 6.9 and follow the bouncing mark—#.

Start at node 1.
Mark, #, its mark field.
Find the first edge leading out of node 1.
Find the head of this edge. That is node 4.

Start at node 4.
Mark, #, its mark field.
Find the first edge leading out of node 4.
Find the head of this edge. That is node 5.

Start at node 5.
Mark, #, its mark field.
Mark the first edge leading out of node 5.
Find the head of this edge. That is node 2.

Start at node 2.
Mark, #, its mark field.
Find the first edge leading out of node 2.
Find the head of this edge. That is node 1.

Now—we have discovered a cycle within the graph—a path that begins and ends at the same node. How do we know this? The mark field of node 1 implies that this node has already been visited.

Admittedly, this example did not provide a systematic method for finding a cyclic path within the graph, as I purposefully selected the starting node. This example is intended to give you only a small taste of the usefulness of the mark field. Besides, I promise that the next section will fill your need for systematic methods of finding certain types of paths within a graph.

■ "JUST FOR REFERENCE"

Conventions for the adjacency array implementation of graphs include—

- numbering the nodes of the graph
- associating each node with a row and a column
- setting the array location (I, j) equal to 1 if node I is adjacent to node J; otherwise it is 0

Advantages and disadvantages of the adjacency array—

- indegree/outdegree are easily determined
- deleting/adding edges is done easily
- determining existence of paths is easy
- it is a storage-efficient method using bits
- capacity for storing information about nodes and edges is limited
- deleting/adding nodes is not easy

Conventions for the linked list implementation of graphs—

- each graph node is the header for one or two linked adjacency lists (IN–LIST or OUT–LIST)
- adjacency list consists of edge nodes that have the graph node as the tail (OUT–LIST) or the head (IN–LIST)
- graph nodes may be included in a linked list of nodes or in an array

Advantages and disadvantages of the linked list approach—

- it allows for added flexibility for changing number of nodes, edges, and relationships
- IN–LIST permits access to tails of edges leading in
- OUT–LIST permits access to heads of edges leading out
- deleting/adding edges is more complicated

- adding a new node and edge affects three linked lists: list of nodes, IN–LIST of edges, OUT–LIST of edges

The mark field is useful for path-finding algorithms.

EXERCISES

1. Design the adjacency array for the graph in Figure 6.1.

2. Using the graph in Figure 6.1, write a procedure that appropriately alters the adjacency array to reflect an addition or deletion of an edge. Assume the arguments are the names of the two cities and a boolean flag is set at true for an addition and false for a deletion.

3. Design an adjacency array implementation for a weighted graph like the one in Figure 6.8. State your convention for handling the weights.

4. Write a procedure to calculate the indegree of a given node for a graph that is implemented with an adjacency array.

5. Write a procedure that prints all the paths of length 2 from a given node. Assume that you are using an adjacency array to implement a graph of six nodes.

6. Write a procedure that prints all the paths of length 2 to a given node. Assume that you are using an adjacency array to implement a graph of six nodes.

7. Describe the main limitation encountered in using an adjacency array to implement a graph structure.

8. Assume that you are implementing a graph with a linked list of nodes and a linked list of edges, OUT–LIST. Revise the procedure ADD–EDGE to ensure that no duplicate edges are added to the OUT–LIST.

9. Assume that you are implementing a graph with a linked list of nodes and a linked list of edges, IN–LIST. Write a procedure that deletes an edge, given the two nodes that constitute the edge, HEAD and TAIL.

10. Write a procedure to calculate the indegree of a given node. Assume that the implementation is set up with a linked list of nodes and the OUT–LIST of adjacency lists.

11. For each of the implementation methods below, write a procedure to delete an edge specified by the arguments HEAD and TAIL.

    a) Linked list of nodes with OUT–LIST adjacency list.

    b) Linked list of nodes with IN–LIST and OUT–LIST adjacency list.

12. What advantages are gained by using a linked approach to implementing a graph structure?

13. What advantages and disadvantages arise when both IN–LIST and OUT–LIST adjacency lists are present in the implementation?

14. In a graph application that you are developing, during execution it may arise that a new node must be created and a set of edges to and from the node must be added. Write a procedure to handle this situation. Assume the node information is provided first (name, etc.), followed by an integer specifying the number of edges from the node. This is followed by the head nodes for the edges. Next comes the number of edges to the new node and the set of tail nodes for these edges.

15. Assume a graph application is implemented with a linked structure. Under certain conditions, a graph node must be split into two nodes and the edges connecting it to the other nodes shared between the two nodes. If the number of edges is even, each node

gets half the edges (the selection being unimportant). If the number is odd, the original node gets the first edge and the rest are shared evenly. Finally, two new edges are to be set up between the two nodes. Write a procedure that accomplishes the restructuring. Assume the argument passed is the name of the node to be split. State which version of the linked method is most appropriate for this procedure, and use it.

16. Using a linked list of nodes and an OUT–LIST adjacency list to implement a graph, write a procedure that prints all paths of length 2 from a given node. Suggest any improvements to the node structure for this problem.

17. Using a linked list of nodes and an IN–LIST adjacency list:

    a) Design an algorithm to print all paths of length 2 to a given node.

    b) Design an algorithm to print all paths of length 2 from a given node. Consider the need for a stack or special fields in the node structures.

18. Compare the storage requirements for implementing a weighted, directed graph with 25 nodes and 100 edges. Assume the nodal information is a name that uses a maximum of eight characters and that the edge weight is a real number. Calculate the amount of storage that would be needed for an adjacency array and also for a linked list of nodes with adjacency lists (OUT-LIST). Assume that all pointers require 2 bytes of storage.

INSIGHTS WITH DR. DIGITAL

Scene: *Wilma and Dr. Digital are looking for seating in the lounge of the Student Union building. Three students at a piano nearby are learning a musical piece.*

Wilma: Dr. D, let's find a seat near the window.

Dr. D: Okay, how about those to the left of the piano?

Wilma: Sounds fine to me. Such classic chairs for a student lounge. [Pause as they position themselves in the chairs.] Yesterday in class, you mentioned the idea of using different vehicles while thinking either visually or analytically. I've been trying to get a handle on this idea regarding information structures. So far nothing has chimed my bells.

Dr. D: Maybe you are starting with the wrong melody, so to speak. Let me pick another area to illustrate the concept and then replay the melody with an information structures theme.

Wilma: Okay, I'm game. You're the conceptual conductor—lead on!

Dr. D: See those three students at the piano? They are involved in a process using different vehicles to represent the musical thought being expressed. Let's listen to what is going on.

Learner: How can I remember this love sonata for Julie? She just loves the sound of music and I want to impress her with this song.

Novice piano player: It's simple—just memorize the notes, B-sharp, A, C, B, etc. When she comes by you just push your internal replay button and the sequence of notes will be displayed on your internal monitor. You translate the note to the corresponding finger movement on the appropriate key and repeat this for the next note. It's just like typing in that PASCAL program that you copied.

Learner: Wow ! That sounds too easy to be true. Is that how you play this sonata?

Master piano player: No, not at all—but it is how I learned to play it. By practicing the piece many times, the memory of a sequence of note symbols has been transformed into a sense of movement, both physical and emotional. For me, the music is a collection of allegros, bravuras, crescendos and dulces, blended into a wholistic momentum.

Learner: Oh, that would be much more impressive to Julie and draws . . .

Dr. D: This is a good time to draw the curtain on our eavesdropping. Did you notice the two perspectives on how music is represented in the mind?

Wilma: Yes. The first player suggested a simple vehicle, like a train of boxcars passing by the viewer one at a time. This method would produce one interpretation of the sonata.

Dr. D: And the nature of the vehicle would produce a rather flat musical image. The other vehicle, however, has a fuller, more multidimensional form tempered with feeling. It is important to notice that both vehicles are appropriate to different stages of the representational process.

Wilma: They also appear to correspond to a left hemisphere/right hemisphere distinction.

Dr. D: Very good point, Wilma! Say more.

Wilma: The novice's vehicle relies on the left hemisphere to memorize a sequence of letters as note symbols. That reminds me, Dr. D. I used to play songs on the piano using the do-re-mi-fa-so-la-ti notation. So I was basically using the same vehicle to represent music.

Dr. D: Yes, you were. My friend Dr. Abdo, a classical mathematician and pure pianist, memorizes the music by way of the graphic symbols appearing on sheet music. He is also

using a similar vehicle to represent the music while he learns a concerto.

Wilma: When the learner is practicing, the brain performs a mapping from the symbol—C or do or ♩—to the associated arm-hand-finger movement that produces the sound. Seems like a computerized robot could be programmed to do the same actions, Dr. D.

Dr. D: Long before computers, the player piano was doing exactly this to the delight of numerous listeners.

Wilma: The vehicle described by the second piano player seems to be a right-hemisphere activity. The memory of the notes no longer directly drives the arm, hands, and fingers mechanically. The feeling, momentum, and flow of the music are translated into the necessary physical movements. The piece is seen in its wholeness as each note blends with the ones before and after in forms called allegros and crescendos.

Dr. D: This is seen very clearly when my friend Dr. Abdo plays a classical concerto. Since they can contain upwards of six thousand notes, it is difficult to imagine him remembering each note in sequence. Instead, he probably performs the thinking operation referred to as "chunking" by Douglas Hofstadter in his analytical, artistic, and musical book, *Godel, Escher, and Bach: An Eternal Golden Braid.**A sequence of notes is replaced by a sense of movement, a "chunk" of the piece, a movement to a different level of perception. The sound is derived from the vehicle of sensory movement.

Wilma: How does hearing the piece affect the player?

Dr. D: Dr. Abdo says that the sound acts as a feedback system. It can verify that the movements are correct. But he can reproduce the movements without the piano sounding the music. The sound of the music is present in his mind while he is going through the movements. So in one sense the internal sound of the music is another vehicle by which the music is represented.

Wilma: Now I can apply these vehicle types to my understanding of the graph information structure.

Dr. D: Okay, let's hear the melody in the key of information structures.

Wilma: I can represent a graph as a left-brain vehicle, similar to our set notation or the adjacency array, and mentally perform operations on the graph by performing the associated operations on the set or the array.

Dr. D: This is adequate in the early stages of your programming endeavors. After developing programs using this vehicle, you may encounter a more sophisticated graph problem. Let's say you are trying to model the behavior of the subatomic particles during the chemical interaction of ions at the synapses of your neurons. The behavior of the subatomic particles has been represented by

Feynman diagrams, a graph information structure. The neuron itself is connected by dendrites and axons to numerous other neurons. This network of neurons can be represented as a three-dimensional graph information structure. To visualize the dance of life in the brain, a more wholistic vehicle must be used to represent the graph than the simple adjacency array or the set.

Wilma: The difference between the types of vehicles as they apply to graphs is clear to me, Dr. D. But to visualize the actual graph structure that you have described is mind-boggling. I'm afraid that I might just snap my synapses.

(As Wilma and Dr. D get up to leave the master piano player begins performing an anonymous fugue.)

*D. Hofstadter, Random House, 1980.

6.4 Applications

6.4.1 PATH FINDING

When graphs are used as information structures a frequent operation is finding certain paths between nodes. This becomes one of the basic foundations on which other processing can be built. Let's consider two important topics investigated during the path-finding operation.

The first deals with whether a path exists between two nodes. The question can be phrased in general, such as, Does a path exist between node A and node B?—or quantitatively—how many paths exist between node A and node B? The constraint of a certain path length or range of path lengths can also be added to the question of path existence. We will handle this in small increments, beginning with the general existence case, and progressing up the spectrum to more comprehensive and flexible cases.

The second topic will provide more information about the graph but naturally will pose a more challenging problem. Along with the existence of a path, the sequence of nodes comprising the path may be necessary information for making decisions about the path or the graph. We will see a couple of ways to collect this information as the existence question is being answered.

Path existence in adjacency arrays

The implementation of graphs using the adjacency array offers a convenient method for determining the existence of paths. This will be illustrated by looking at the solution to the question, does a path of length 2 exist between node I and node J where I and J can be any nodes in the graph? Figure 6.10 shows a simple directed graph and its adjacency array.

Our question, **does a path of length 2 exist between node 1 and node 3?,** can be expressed as:

Is there a path from node 1 to node 3 through node 1
or   is there a path from node 1 to node 3 through node 2
or   is there a path from node 1 to node 3 through node 3?

If any one of these three statements is true then the desired path exists. These three statements can be rephrased in the context of the adjacency array as:

if ADJ[1, 1] = 1 and ADJ[1, 3] = 1
or   if ADJ[1, 2] = 1 and ADJ[2, 3] = 1
or   if ADJ[1, 3] = 1 and ADJ[3, 3] = 1

then a path of length 2 from node 1 to node 3 exists.

The algorithm is to survey each node in the graph, designated node K, to check if there is an edge from the starting node, node I, to node K and an edge from node K to the ending node, node J. This algorithm is easily expressed as a PASCAL procedure that finds the first path of length 2 between two given nodes.

To prepare for the procedures that follow, let's set up the global variables and global constants upon which they depend. Our declarations include the number of nodes N and the adjacency array ADJ.

```
const N = *    (*number of nodes goes here*)
type RANGE = 1..N;
     ADJ_VAL = 0..1; (*boolean would also do*)
                    (*use a record for weighted graph*)
     PATH_ARRAY:array [RANGE, RANGE] of ADJ_VAL;
     var ADJ:PATH_ARRAY;
         ADJ2:PATH_ARRAY
```

Figure 6.10

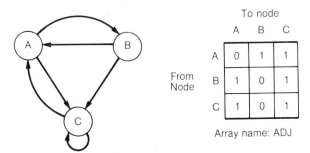

To node

	A	B	C
A	0	1	1
B	1	0	1
C	1	0	1

From Node

Array name: ADJ

With these preliminaries established, a procedure that determines whether a path of length 2 exists between nodes I and J follows. The existence is indicated by a boolean identifier PATH.

```
procedure PATH2 (I,J:RANGE;var PATH:boolean);
var K:RANGE;
begin
K := 1;
PATH :=false;
(*Keep looking for a path until all nodes are tested*)
while (K <= N) and (PATH = false) do
      (*Check if node K is middle node on path*)
      if (A[I,K] = 1) and (A[K,J] = 1)then PATH := true
                                  (*THIS IS AN IMPORTANT SPOT*)
                                          else K := K + 1
end;
```

The range of the question can be extended by rephrasing it as: **find all node pairs that are connected by a path of length 2.**

This problem can be solved by constructing another array, similar to ADJ, such that the value of the element at the intersection of the Ith row and Jth column is a 1 if a path of length 2 exists between node I and node J. The following procedure generates this new array from the adjacency array by using the procedure PATH2.

```
(* Existence of paths of length 2 *)
procedure ALLPATH2;
var NODE_I, NODE_J:RANGE;
    PATH:boolean;
begin
    for NODE_I := 1 to N do
        for NODE_J := 1 to N do
              begin
                PATH2(NODE_I,NODE_J,PATH);
                if PATH then ADJ2[NODE_I,NODE_J] := 1
                        else ADJ2[NODE_I,NODE_J] := 0
              end
end;
```

The procedure tests all combinations of nodes for a path of length 2 and constructs an array ADJ2 to indicate the pairs of nodes for which PATH is true. For our sample graph in Figure 6.10, Figure 6.11 shows the result of calling procedure ALLPATH2.

The three arrays in Figure 6.11 have much in common. The leftmost array is our adjacency array from which the other two are derived. The middle array shows that only nodes A and B are not connected by a path of length 2. This array is produced by the procedure ALLPATH2, which calls procedure PATH2. It indicates the existence of paths of length 2 between starting and ending nodes. The last array is produced by the standard algorithm for matrix multiplication, using the array ADJ times itself. It is neither luck nor magic that it resembles ADJ2 in structure. This last array indicates not only the existence but also the number of paths of length 2. This fact is easily seen by comparing the way that two corresponding array elements of ADJ2 and ADJ $\times$ ADJ are calculated.

Let us look at ADJ2[1,3] and the corresponding element of ADJ $\times$ ADJ. For ADJ2[1, 3] we have:

Node	A	B	C
A	0	1	1
B	1	0	1
C	1	0	1

ADJ

	1	2	3
1	1	0	1
2	1	1	1
3	1	1	1

ADJ2

	1	2	3
1	2	0	2
2	1	1	2
3	1	1	2

ADJ × ADJ

ADJ is an array of zeros and ones representing edges.

ADJ2 is an array of zeros and ones representing existence of paths of length 2.

ADJ × ADJ is the matrix product and represents the existence and number of paths of length 2.

Figure 6.11

$$ADJ[1, 1] = 1 \text{ and } ADJ[1, 3] = 1$$
$$\text{or}\quad ADJ[1, 2] = 1 \text{ and } ADJ[2, 3] = 1$$
$$\text{or}\quad ADJ[1, 3] = 1 \text{ and } ADJ[3, 3] = 1$$

For $ADJ^2[1, 3]$ we have:

$$ADJ[1, 1] \times ADJ[1, 3]$$
$$+\quad ADJ[1, 2] \times ADJ[2, 3]$$
$$+\quad ADJ[1, 3] \times ADJ[3, 3]$$

If we draw an analogy between the operators in each expression, we can say that ADJ × ADJ is arithmetic sum (+) of arithmetic products (×) and that ADJ2 is the logical sum (or) of logical products (and). Applying this to the entire array, ADJ2 can be called the boolean matrix product of the adjacency array ADJ. So now we have two options when we want to determine the paths of length 2 within a graph. We can either form the boolean matrix product of the adjacency matrix with itself or calculate the regular matrix product (and determine not only the existence but also the number of paths of length 2).

The next logical extension to our original question is to know which node is the middle node in the path of length 2. This information is easy to capture but requires some imagination in order to remember for all paths. If you refer back to procedure PATH2, you will see a comment within the procedure that says, "THIS IS AN IMPORTANT SPOT." For our present purpose, it is because at this spot we can capture the information that node K was between node I and node J on the path of length 2. Thus, at this spot another procedure can be called to record the connection between node K and nodes I and J. For procedure PATH2, this does not produce too much difficulty, but ALLPATH2 will require some fancy record keeping. Besides, we are capturing only the first path of length 2; to list the middle nodes of all paths between nodes I and J we definitely need to make some adjustments. These adjustments are left as exercises to the enterprising reader.

The next step is to increase the path length limit and determine the existence of a path of length 3. A clever change to the procedure PATH2 will provide a solution consistent with our needs. Consider that a path of length 3 from node I to node J is equivalent to a path of length 2 from node I to node K and an edge from node K to node J. This translates to:

if ADJ2[I, K] = 1 and ADJ[K, J] = 1 then a path exists.

If we change the procedure PATH2 to include an array argument that indicates paths of length $N - 1$, the new procedure can determine the existence of a path of length N. Here is our generalized version of the path existence procedure:

```
procedure PATH_LENGTH_N(I,J:RANGE;A:PATH_ARRAY;var PATH:boolean);
(* Globals - ADJ - adjacency array, N number of nodes *)
(*array A contains the information concerning paths of length N-1 *)
var K:RANGE;
begin
K := 1;
PATH := false;
(*Keep looking for a path until all nodes are tested or a path is found*)
while ( K <= N) and (PATH = false) do
        (*Check if node K is connected to node I*)
        (*by a path of length N - 1 and to node J directly*)
    if (A[I,K] = 1) and (ADJ[K,J] = 1) then PATH := true
                                      else K := K + 1
end;
```

Let's see how the general tool is used to accomplish some earlier tasks. This new procedure replaces PATH2 by calling the procedure with the following arguments:

```
PATH_LENGTH_N(I,J,ADJ,PATH);
```

since ADJ represents all paths of length 1.

To determine the paths of length 3 from node I to node J, the procedure ALLPATH2 must have been called to produce the array ADJ2. By issuing the following call:

```
PATH_LENGTH_N(I,J,ADJ2,PATH);
```

the existence of a path of length 3 from I to J can be determined. The boolean variable PATH is then used to set a location in the array ADJ3:

```
if PATH then ADJ3[I,J] := 1
        else ADJ3[I,J] := 0;
```

By embedding the procedure call and *if* statement within a pair of nested *for* statements, analogous to procedure ALLPATH2, the array ADJ3 is built, creating the essential code for producing the adjacency array for all nodes connected by a path of length 3. Once again, this algorithm is equivalent to calculating the boolean matrix product of ADJ2 and ADJ.

From this presentation, it should be obvious now that the determination of paths of length 4 depends on the arrays ADJ3 and ADJ; by inductive reasoning we can continue in this way for any desired path length. Therefore, the question of the existence of paths of an arbitrary length is answered by beginning with the adjacency array and determining the boolean products, where B×P denotes the operation.

$$ADJ \; B{\times}P \; ADJ \; = ADJ2$$
$$ADJ2 \; B{\times}P \; ADJ = ADJ3$$

and in general,

$$ADJN \text{ B} \times \text{P ADJ} = ADJN + 1$$

Once again let me remind you that the boolean product indicates only the existence of a path. If the number of paths is also desired, the arithmetic matrix product is used in the same way:

$$ADJ \times ADJ = ADJ^2$$
$$ADJ^2 \times ADJ = ADJ^3$$

and so on.

The question of the existence of paths can also be answered while using the linked implementation approach for graphs. The algorithm is more complicated, however, it is possible to easily keep track of the intermediate nodes along the path. The linked approach will be used to solve the next two questions about paths; I will leave its application to the present question as an exercise. By reading the next two sections you will easily see the nature of the algorithm for determining the paths of length N among a linked list of nodes and edges representing a graph. So let us forge on.

6.4.2 FINDING THE SHORTEST PATH BETWEEN NODES

The next operation on the graph information structure involves directed graphs in which each edge has an associated nonnegative weight. In this context, the idea of the shortest path can have two interpretations. One way of measuring shortness is to count the number of edges between the starting and ending node of the path. This

 IMAGINATION CHALLENGE

Look at the image below and describe it to a friend in a precise way. Now look at the image in another way and describe it to a second friend. Once again change your perspective and describe the shape to a third person. After each description, direct the listener to draw the shape that has been described. Compare the three drawings to the original image. How did your perception of the image aid in the formation of the most efficient description?

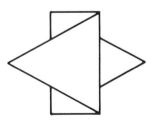

problem was handled in the previous section by taking successive boolean matrix products of the adjacency array with itself. We will deal with the alternative interpretation in this section. For each path from U to V, we compute a **path distance,** defined as the sum of the weights of the edges on the path between node U and node V. Thus when faced with a choice of different paths between the same nodes, we can select the one with the minimum distance. The path chosen by this criterion is considered the shortest path between the given nodes.

The algorithm I plan to present is attributed to an important person in the computer science field, E. W. Dijkstra. He presented this algorithm in the late 1950s, but it is not the only source of his fame. His name is frequently mentioned in connection with the origins of structured programming techniques. His idea for the problem at hand is to generate the shortest path to all nodes but to do so in increasing order. That is, given a starting node, determine the shortest path to any node that has not been reached yet. Initially, this will be the adjacent node with the smallest weight. This is followed by finding the next closest node, which will be either another adjacent node or will contain the previously selected closest node as an intermediate node on a path of length 2. Continuing in this fashion, either the shortest path to a particular node is found or the shortest path to all nodes is determined.

Figure 6.12 affords a brief glimpse of the technique. The directed graph with its weighted edges is given, with the starting node considered to be Dallas. A list of path distances generated in increasing order is also given.

In order to assist you in understanding the motivation behind the algorithm's method and to assist in framing the implementation, let me tell a short story in which the shortest-path problem arises. With the story's framework set, I can develop the algorithm for the solution and finally the PASCAL procedure.

Let me begin by assuming that you are the owner of a small, growing firm that provides equipment and supplies to the personal computer market. You are located in a medium-sized city and plan to expand your service to neighboring cities by way of the local freight delivery lines. You intend to expand to one new city at a time. The choice of when you expand will be determined by the financial status of the company, while the city you expand to will be whichever is the cheapest to service from the

Figure 6.12

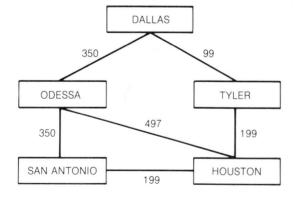

Shortest path from **DALLAS**	
Distance	To
99	**TYLER**
298	**HOUSTON**
350	**ODESSA**
497	**SAN ANTONIO**

cities that you already service. Figure 6.13 shows a graph of the cities in the surrounding area, the freight connections between the cities, and the cost factors for each connection. There are three primary freight companies operating out of cities A, B, and C; all have routes to and from city S (where you are located). There is some overlap between freight companies, so there can be more than one route to the same outlying city from city S. Since the area serviced by the freight line out of city B is quite hilly, the transportation costs in this area are noticeably higher. Let me assume that market conditions for your goods are approximately equal for all cities that are candidates for expanded service. In this way, once a decision to expand is made, you have only to find the city that lies the shortest distance away cost-wise, and is not presently being supplied.

Initially, the cities that are the most likely candidates for your first expansion are those directly connected to the source city S. So you have the following choices in front of you:

Candidate City	Cost Factor	Path
A	25	S.A
B	40	S.B
C	20	S.C

Figure 6.13

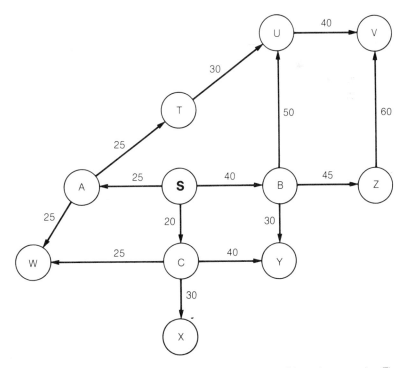

City S is the home base for the company. Surrounding cities are candidates for expansion. The weights represent cost of transportation.

where the notation S.A means a path exists from S to A.

You would obviously select city C, which has the minimum cost factor as the next (and in this case, first) city to service. Once this decision is made you now have two groups to consider:

Serviced Cities		
City	Cost Factor	Path
S	0	S
C	20	S.C

Candidates for Expansion		
City	Cost Factor	Path
A	25	S.A
B	40	S.B
W	45	S.C.W
X	50	S.C.X
Y	60	S.C.Y

You now service the source city, which has a negligible cost factor, and city C, which is the "closest" to the source with a cost factor of 20. The candidates for your second expansion step have been updated. This is a very important stage in the algorithm. **Once city C is included in the first group of serviced cities then all of the cities to which it is directly connected become candidates for service.** Hence cities W, X, and Y are added to the second group, with cost factors equal to the cost factor from city S to city C plus the cost factor from city C. This stage shows one of three possible cases that can occur, since none of the new candidates W, X, or Y is presently serviced or a candidate for expansion. In this case, the cities have only to be added to the list of candidates. The other two cases will be presented shortly. Notice also that the paths for the three new candidates are added, with the notation S.C.W. signifying that the path travels from city S to city C to city W.

Well, business is rolling right along and you are ready for expansion number 2 (are you also ready for case number 2?). A quick polling of the cost factors of the candidate cities shows that you plan to "go west, young woman," to city A in particular. With the choice made, you request that the two tables be updated to indicate the company's new status.

Serviced Cities		
City	Cost Factor	Path
S	0	S
C	20	S.C
A	25	S.A

Candidates for Expansion		
City	Cost Factor	Path
B	40	S.B
W	45	S.C.W
X	50	S.C.X
Y	60	S.C.Y
T	50	S.A.T
W	50	S.A.W

The update for the second expansion presents a new situation. A city directly connected to city A is already a candidate for expansion, city W. Therefore, there are at least two paths from the source city S to city W. When this occurs, the shorter of the two paths will be included in the candidate list. Thus the last entry in the above table, showing city W with a cost factor of 50, should not be included because the other path is shorter.

Case 2 can be generalized as follows: **if a new path to an existing candidate is found that is longer than the original path, then the new path is ignored and no update is necessary.**

Business and expansion continue as before and cities B, W, and X are added to the serviced cities of your now not-so-small firm. After these three expansions, your new data processing manager provides you with the following output of the expansion program:

Serviced Cities				Candidates for Expansion		
City	Cost Factor	Path		City	Cost Factor	Path
S	0	S		Y	60	S.C.Y
C	20	S.C		T	50	S.A.T
A	25	S.A		U	90	S.B.U
B	40	S.B		Z	85	S.B.Z
W	45	S.C.W				
X	50	S.C.X				

Verify for yourself that the output is correct. Note that when city B was added to the first group, a second path to city Y was ignored, as case 2 directs, and that the expansion to cities W and X caused no change to the list of candidates.

The next expansion phase provides an opportunity to illustrate the third and last case that may occur. When city T is added to the group of serviced cities and its adjacent cities are investigated as candidates, a new path from city S through city T to an existing candidate, city U, is discovered. But this time the new path is shorter than the existing path, so the new path and its cumulative cost factor should be entered in place of the present data in the candidate list.

Case 3 can be generalized as follows: **if a new, shorter path to an existing candidate is found, the new path supersedes the original path and is entered into the list as an update.**

With this final case presented, the algorithm for selecting the next city for expansion and updating the list of candidates for the next expansion can be summarized. So one afternoon while reflection on your successful expansion, you jot down this algorithm.

1. Select city with minimal cost factor from candidates.
2. Add selected city to list of serviced cities.
3. For each city directly connected to the selected city,
   either add the city as a new candidate,
   or ignore the city since a shorter path already exists,
   or update the cost factor and path if this is
      a shorter path.

You will extend your business slowly but surely to city Y, then to city U (via the path S.A.T.U), then to Z, and finally to the far-away city V (via the unexpected route of S.A.T.U.V). The final report from the data processing department summarizes the expansion.

Serviced Cities

City	Cost Factor	Path
S	0	S
C	20	S.C
A	25	S.A
B	40	S.B
W	45	S.C.W
X	50	S.C.X
T	50	S.A.T
Y	60	S.C.Y
U	80	S.A.T.U
Z	85	S.B.Z
V	120	S.A.T.U.Z

Satisfied with the performance of the SHORTEST PATH program, you call the software engineer who designed the program and ask for a presentation of the information structures she used to produce the solution.

You soon receive, through the data processing center's new electronic mail facilities, the following diagrams and explanations. One of the first points that you notice is that she has decided to use the self-managed system for the pool of records. You question this aspect briefly but accept the choice and go with it.

Node structure for:

NODES

Field	Contents
1	City name
2	Pointer to NEXT city node
3	Pointer to first edge out of this city
4	MARK field to indicate if this city is a candidate for expansion.
5	Pointer to first edge into this city
6	Cost factor of this city from the source city
7	A string that indicates a path from source to this city

EDGES

Field	Contents
1	Cost factor of edge
2	Pointer to HEAD node of edge
3	Pointer to TAIL node of edge
4	Pointer to next edge with same head node (IN–LIST)
5	Pointer to next edge with same tail node (OUT–LIST)

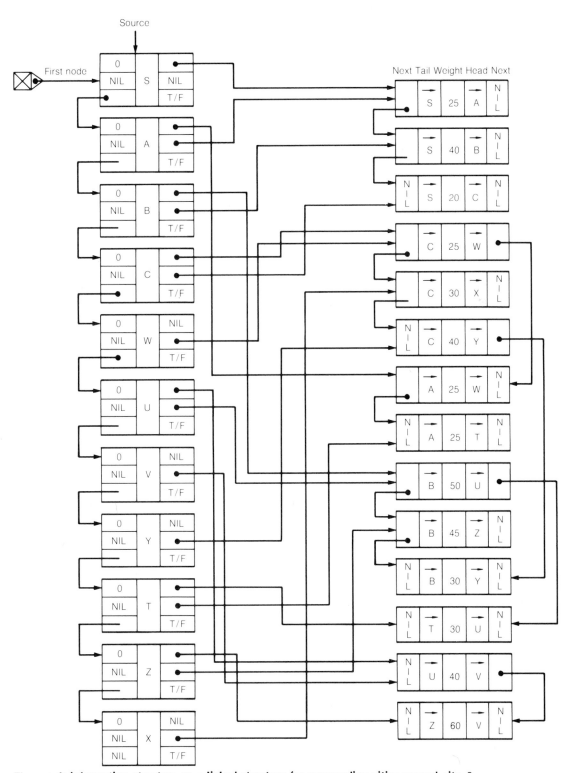

The graph information structure as a linked structure for surrounding cities around city S.

The PASCAL record declarations for nodes and edges are as follows:

```
type N_POINTER = 0..11;
     E_POINTER = 0..14;
     CITIES =
            record
              NAME:char;
              NEXTNODE:N_POINTER;
              FIRSTOUTEDGE:E_POINTER;
              MARK:boolean;
              FIRSTINEDGE:E_POINTER;
              PATHDIS:integer;
              PATH:string[8]
            end;
     EDGE =
            record
              COST:integer;
              HEAD:N_POINTER;
              TAIL:N_POINTER;
              NEXTOUTEDGE:E_POINTER;
              NEXTINEDGE:E_POINTER
            end;
(*Pool of storage nodes for NODES*)
(*Pool of storage nodes for EDGES*)
var NODES:array[1..11] of CITIES;
    EDGES:array[1..14] of EDGE;
```

After you look over the node structures and how they are used in the linked representation of the graph of cities that your company services, the PASCAL record structure arouses your curiosity about the program itself. You call the software engineer once again and ask her to bring a listing of the program to the presentation.

The software engineer, arriving early the next morning, aptly explains the algorithm and the information structure's conventions. A well-documented listing of the program is left with you, as reproduced below:

```
procedure SHORTEST_PATH(SOURCE: N_POINTER );
(* Declarations as presented above *)
const NILL = -1;
var FIRSTNODE : N_POINTER; (* Pointer to first city in linked list of cities *)
    CANDIDATE, MINDIS, PATHDIS: integer; OUTCITY, BESTCITY, CITY: N_POINTER;
    OUTEDGE : E_POINTER;
begin
(* Initialize linked structure of Nodes and Edges *)
(* and set all MARK fields to false *)
INITIALIZE ( FIRSTNODE );
(* Initialize source node's path and distance *)
NODES[SOURCE].PATHDIS := 0 ;
NODES[SOURCE].PATH := NODES[SOURCE].NAME ;
OUTEDGE := NODES[SOURCE].FIRSTOUTEDGE ;
CANDIDATES := 0 ;
(* Initially make all nodes adjacent to source
      candidates for expansion with distance
      equal to edge weight *)
while OUTEDGE <> NILL do
    begin
    OUTCITY := EDGES[OUTEDGE].HEAD ;
    CANDIDATES := CANDIDATES + 1 ;
```

```
            (* Mark node as a candidate *)
            NODES[OUTCITY].MARK := true ;
            NODES[OUTCITY].PATHDIS := EDGES[OUTEDGE].COST ;
            NODES[OUTCITY].PATH := NODES[SOURCE].NAME + '.' +
                                                NODES[OUTCITY].NAME ;
            (* Move to next edge leading out of source *)
            OUTEDGE := EDGES[OUTEDGE].NEXTOUTEDGE
         end ;  (* while *)
(*   while candidates exist, select best candidate and
          update candidate list *)
while CANDIDATES <> 0 do
      begin
      (* Select the candidate city (MARK field = true)
         with the lowest cost factor  *)
      BESTCITY := NILL ;
      MINDIS := 0 ;
      (* Initial city to investigate is initialized *)
      CITY := FIRSTNODE ;
      while CITY <> NILL do
            with NODES[CITY] do
                  begin
                  (* Determine if city is a candidate *)
                  if MARK then
                        if (BESTCITY = NILL) or (PATHDIS < MINDIS)
                        then begin
                        (* For first city or a better path
                            update best city data *)
                            BESTCITY := CITY ;
                            MINDIS := PATHDIS
                        end ;
                  (* Check next city for best city *)
                  CITY := NEXTNODE
                  end ; (* with and while *)
      (* Remove best city from the candidate list *)
      NODES[BESTCITY].MARK := false ;
      CANDIDATES := CANDIDATES - 1 ;
      (* For each adjacent city connected to the best city *)
      OUTEDGE := NODES[BESTCITY].FIRSTOUTEDGE ;
      while OUTEDGE <> NILL do
      (* Calculate path distance to the new potential candidate
          through the selected city *)
          begin
          PATHDIST := NODES[BESTCITY].PATHDIS + EDGES[OUTEDGE].COST ;
          TO_NODE := EDGES[OUTEDGE].HEAD ;
          (* If new distance is larger than previous distance
              then ignore the path because the city is already
              serviced by a shorter path or it is already a
              candidate by way of a shorter path *)
          with NODES[TO_NODE] do
                if PATHDIST < PATHDIS then
                (* Either add to list or update *)
                    begin
                    if not MARK then (* add to list *)
                        begin
                        CANDIDATES := CANDIDATES + 1 ;
                        MARK := true
                        end ;
```

```
                (* Set path distance to calculated distance *)
                        PATHDIS := PATHDIST ;
                        PATH := NODES[BESTCITY].PATH + '. + NAME
                    end ; (* if *)
            end ; (* while *)
        PRINT_STATUS(BESTCITY)
        end (* while for available candidates *)
end ; (* procedure *)
```

This algorithm can be adapted to any problem that requires you to find the shortest path in a graph. The important point to notice is the crucial role played by the boolean MARK field. It allowed us to keep track of which graph nodes still remained to be processed. It is also the criterion for ignoring a potential candidate, including a new candidate, or updating an existing one.

With the algorithm in mind and the program in hand, you are equipped to tackle the shortest-path problem as it applies to networks. If the shortest path to all nodes is desired, the program provides this solution. On the other hand, if the shortest path to a particular node is the goal, the same process is followed until the desired node becomes the head of one of the shortest paths from the source city. In either case, you will be able to solve the problem in a short time, hands down.

6.4.3   TASK SCHEDULING AND CRITICAL PATHS

Now let us change our objectives and set as our goal the discovery of the longest path through a graph. This activity has applications to project planning. Planning a large project demands that numerous considerations be taken into account. In order to se-

---

 # IMAGINATION CHALLENGE

New Year's Eve Dinner Party

What is the minimum number of guests that can be invited to your New Year's Eve party to ensure the condition that there are three strangers or that there are three acquaintances? (This condition will apply only before midnight since, you will then sing, "may old acquaintances be forgot!") Hint: Arrange the people in a circle and draw a solid line between acquaintances and a dotted line between strangers. You now have a complete graph. The party question becomes the graph question - does a cycle of length 3 exist that is entirely strange or entirely friendly? The solution can be reached by drawing the graphs by hand.

For a bigger challenge, solve the same problem for four friends or four strangers. Happy computing! This problem comes from a branch of mathematics called Ramsey theory. Frank Ramsey produced a theorem that is paraphrased as "Complete disorder is impossible."

quence the varied tasks and to project and meet a scheduled completion, time coordination is required.

The graph information structure offers project planners a vehicle through which to express the interdependent relationships that exist among the many tasks of a project. Once the relationship pattern is established with a graph, computerized algorithms are used to allocate resources to important tasks and to schedule the starting times of each task. Additional algorithms moniter the ongoing project and provide status statistics relative to the projections that are contained within the graph structure. In the event of a major delay during the project, the graph information is reevaluated. New critical areas or task bottlenecks are pinpointed so that alternate planning can begin.

The nature of the project can range from the construction of a dam, a skyscraper, or a home to the design and implementation of a data base system, an operating system, or a senior project for your college degree program. The methods involved are easily applied to all of these projects. The process described is known as **critical path analysis.**

The graphs that we will use in this analysis are less general than the ones available in previous sections. We will not allow a graph to have a cyclic path. Based on the nature of the problem being analyzed, task scheduling, this is not a surprising constraint. Otherwise, we would have a task's scheduled initiation dependent upon its completion.

Directed graphs used in project planning are referred to as **activity-on-edge** (AOE) or **activity-on-vertex** (AOV) networks. An AOE graph appears in Figure 6.14a. Its edges denote activities in progress. The nodes signify the state of the project when all activities leading into the node have reached completion. With this interpretation in mind and Figure 6.14 in hand, we can say that from the initial state, node 0, the activity T1 begins. Upon completion, we arrive at state or event 1, at which time activities T2 and T3 can commence and progress in parallel. Upon the completion of activity T2, T4 can begin, independent of T3. Once these are completed, T5 and T6 can begin independently. At some future time, activities T5 and T6 will conclude, yielding event 5—the completion event.

The AOV directed graph shifts the emphasis from the edges to the vertices (or nodes). The edges now describe a precedence relationship among the activities. In Figure 6.14b, the starting activity will be T1 since it has no predecessors. The finishing activity is TF since it has no successors. The precedence relationship expressed directly by the AOV graph (and indirectly by the AOE graph) is summarized in the table below (refer to Figure 6.14b).

Vertex Activity	Precedes Activities
T1	T2, T3
T2	T4
T3	T6
T4	T5
T5	TF
T6	TF
TF	none

Figure 6.14

a. AOE graph

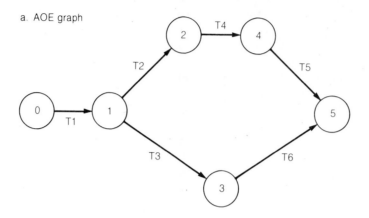

b. AOV graph

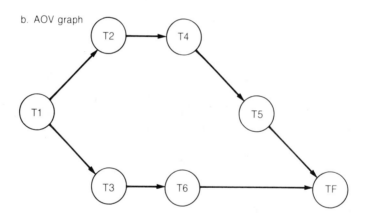

The precedence pairs are (T1, T2), (T1, T3), (T2, T4), (T3, T6), (T4, T5), (T5, TF), (T6, TF), which happens to be equivalent to the set notation for the graph information structure.

For each activity, there is an estimated amount of time for completing the activity. Depending on the type of network, AOE or AOV, this value is associated with either the edge or the vertex. By analyzing various paths from the starting to the finishing activity, based on the sum of the estimated completion times of all activities along the path, important scheduling considerations can be highlighted. The path that entails the largest time commitment is the most important, since the longest, time-wise, path determines the earliest possible completion time for the project. In the rest of this section, it will be the activities composing this longest path that you, the project programmer, and the project manager will be most concerned with.

Let's outline the plan for analyzing the project and scheduling the tasks. The project manager will list all the activities that must be performed during the project. You will input this list as the nodes for our AOV graph structure. The project manager will indicate which activities are prerequisite to the beginning of each activity. You will input this relationship information as the directed edges of our AOV graph. The project manager will give an estimated time for completion of each activity. You will include this information in each node of the AOV network structure. With all three of these ingredients arranged snugly in our information structure, you can now begin to develop algorithms to provide the scheduling information desired by the project manager.

The scheduling information falls into three categories. First, the project manager wants to know the earliest time each task can begin and the total amount of time needed to complete the project. Second, she also needs the latest time that a task finishes and the **slack time** for each activity. This is the amount of time an individual activity can be delayed without causing a delay in the scheduled completion time of the entire project. Finally, the critical paths through the network are important. In these paths, activities exist that have no slack time and therefore occupy a crucial role within the project. The algorithms that follow are concerned with these three areas.

Family Project

Let us begin this educational journey with the assumption that your father is a home builder by trade and you are a computer science professional. As you might suspect, a computer science career provides you with a good salary but little spare time away from the computer (who becomes the master of whom?). With your good salary, you plan to invest in a new home, but with so little time you must find someone else to build it. Naturally, you strike up a partnership with dear old dad. He has agreed to supervise the work if you will develop a task scheduling program for his use on your home and all future contracts. With an agreement reached, you begin the project.

Your first step is to create a list of tasks that must be done to reach the final state of Home Sweet Home. Your father has listed the necessary steps as they appear below:

Task	Description
0	start (ground-breaking ceremony)
1	excavate space for basement
2	build forms for foundation
3	pour concrete into the forms
4	install plumbing in basement
5	pour basement floor
6	build wooden walls on foundation
7	build roof on walls
8	install preliminary plumbing
9	install preliminary wiring
10	install heating and ventilation
11	lay brickwork on outside walls
12	install interior insulation
13	put up interior wall surfaces
14	lay down wooden floors
15	put in kitchen appliances and fixtures
16	finish all plumbing
17	do all finishing carpentry

18	put on final roof coating
19	install gutters on roof
20	paint all necessary surfaces
21	varnish wood floors
22	finish all electrical fixtures and outlets
23	prepare ground for landscaping
24	complete landscaping and walkways
25	finished house

You need to know which tasks may begin in parallel and which tasks must wait until others are completed. These data are provided by your dad in the list of ordered pairs shown below, where each integer refers to the task number from the list previously presented. The relationship between tasks expressed as (i,j) means task i must be completed before j begins.

Pairs	Comment
(0, 1)	Start
(1, 2)	Excavation leads to building forms for foundation then to
(2, 3)	pouring concrete into forms.
(3, 4)	Pour foundation before installing plumbing in basement
(3, 6)	and before building wooden walls.
(4, 5)	
(4, 8)	Basement plumbing precedes preliminary plumbing
(5, 10)	
(6, 7)	Notice that tasks 7, 9, and 10, depend on building
(6, 9)	the walls on the foundation.
(6, 10)	
(7, 11)	
(8, 12)	Notice that tasks 8, 9, and 10 must be completed before
(9, 12)	the interior insulation is installed.
(10, 12)	
(12, 13)	
(11, 18)	
(13, 14)	
(14, 15)	Task 14 marks a time when three other tasks can
(14, 16)	begin simultaneously.
(14, 17)	
(15, 20)	Task 20 provides a task which is the convergence of
(16, 20)	two other tasks, 15 and 16.
(17, 21)	
(18, 19)	
(19, 23)	
(20, 22)	
(21, 25)	The tasks on which the final task depends are
(22, 25)	indicated in three of the last four pairs.
(23, 24)	
(24, 25)	

You now have sufficient ingredients for the graph information structure: a set of nodes (the task numbers) and a set of edges (the ordered pairs of above).

By using your father's experience, the estimated time to perform each task is assigned to each node of the graph. Now you can begin to analyze the project's schedule. By drawing the graph you start the solution process with a right-brain aid. Using the notation i/h to represent nodes, you sketch out the task network. The i stands for the task number while the h indicates the number of work units needed to complete the task. The entire graph for your house construction project would look like the diagram on the following page.

With this graph we can begin to plan some algorithms to provide the information that the project manager needs. It is important at this point to notice a particular ordering among the node numbers and a particular attribute of the graph itself.

Each pair of nodes that is involved in a precedence relationship—that is, each adjacent pair—has the property that the node number of the tail node is less than the node number of the head node. You can easily verify this by looking at the preceding graph or by referring to the set notation given earlier. This particular ordering is called a **topological ordering** and is an important ingredient in the task scheduling process. In the house construction project, the topological ordering among the nodes was a by-product of how your father listed and numbered the tasks. In general, a topological ordering procedure would be a necessary preliminary processing step after the nodes and edges of the graph have been input.

The topological ordering procedure will have another important responsibility. In order to perform task scheduling analysis on a graph, it is necessary for the graph to be acyclic. This means that no cyclic paths can exist within the graph. This is quite reasonable, since a cyclic path would imply that a task must be completed before it can begin. The acyclic requirement ties in nicely with the topological ordering characteristic that is necessary. In a cyclic path, there will be a node P and an edge (P, P), but by the topological ordering relation this would be impossible. In other words, if during the topological ordering procedure the ordering cannot be completed, a cyclic path must exist, and the analysis of the graph by task scheduling methods cannot be continued. Thus a topological ordering procedure determines whether the node and edge input data are valid for task scheduling, and it orders the nodes such that the topological ordering relationship is in effect.

With the validity of the house construction graph assured, you now begin to develop algorithms to determine:

1. The earliest possible starting time for each task.
2. The latest possible finishing time for each task.
3. The amount of time each task may be delayed
   without delaying the entire project.

The algorithms for calculating these scheduling statistics will visit each node in the graph information structure by following each path either from the starting task to the finishing task or vice versa. We will calculate these values by hand for a small group of tasks to give us the flavor of the algorithm and later present the PASCAL code for all procedures needed in the task scheduling package.

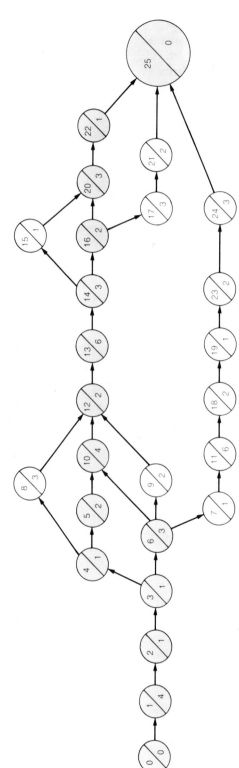

The task nodes indicate the task number (upper half of circle) and the activity time for the task. The starting task is labeled zero and the final task is labeled 25. Shaded tasks indicate critical tasks. Two critical paths exist in the graph.

Earliest Start Time

The **earliest starting time** of a task can be described as the time at which a task can begin if all goes well prior to the start. Thus, this value depends on the tasks that precede the task in question and the activity time of each predecessor task. Let's look at our house construction graph and calculate this statistic for a few tasks.

Task Number	Earliest Starting Time	Predecessor Task Number	Predecessor Earliest Starting Time	Activity Time
0	0	none	none	none
1	0	0	0	0
2	4	1	0	4
3	5	2	4	1
4	6	3	5	1
5	7	4	6	1
6	6	3	5	1
7	9	6	6	3
8	7	4	6	1
9	9	6	6	3
•	*at this point alternate paths exist*			•
10	9, 9	5, 6	7, 6	2, 3
11	10	7	9	1
12	10, 11, 13	8, 9, 10	7, 9, 9	3, 2, 4

As an exercise, complete the table.

For the starting task, you have no predecessor, so the earliest starting time depends entirely on events and conditions unrelated to the task scheduling. For task 1, since it has no predecessor tasks that consume time, its earliest starting time is also equal to 0. Task 2 depends on task 1, so the earliest starting time of task 1 plus its activity time (if all goes well) will be the earliest starting time of task 2, which is four time units after the project commences. You can see the same direct calculations for tasks 3 through 6.

From the statistics computed so far, task 7 can begin nine time units after the starting task if all goes well with tasks 1, 2, 3, and 6. Tasks 7 and 9 have the same earliest starting times, since they have the same predecessor, task 6.

A formula can be offered to computer the earliest starting time of a task with one predecessor.

If T is a task and P is the single predecessor task then:

`EST(T) = EST(P) + ACT(P)`

where EST denotes the earliest starting time of a task and ACT denotes the activity time.

As the diagram illustrates, with task 10 a new situation exists. This task has two predecessor tasks, so both need to be considered. The earliest starting times of tasks 5 and 6 are different (by 1), but their activity times are also different (by 1 again but in the opposite direction), so by either path the earliest starting time would equal 9 time units.

Task 12 illustrates the situation more distinctly. With three different paths to node 12, there will be three possible earliest starting times:

1. by way of task   8 = 7 + 3 = 10 units
2. by way of task   9 = 9 + 2 = 11 units
3. by way of task 10 = 9 + 4 = 13 units

Actually, there is only one possible choice. Thirteen time units will be the earliest starting time for task 12, since your father will have to wait for tasks 8, 9, and 10 to be completed before task 12 can be started. So when a task has multiple predecessors, the formula given earlier must be revised to:

```
EST(T) = maximum [EST(P) + ACT(P), for all predecessors P of T]
```

Thus a task must wait for the latest predecessor to finish before the task can begin: **the earliest starting time depends on the latest finish time.**

By following this method, you will eventually calculate the earliest starting times for all tasks. This includes task 25, the finish task. Since task 25 depends on three predecessor tasks, the latest finish time of these tasks determines the earliest starting time of task 25, which is also the earliest finishing time for the project:

1. by way of task 21 = 27 + 2 = 29
2. by way of task 22 = 29 + 1 = 30
3. by way of task 24 = 21 + 3 = 24

From this you can predict that the house will be completed, optimally, no earlier than 30 time units from the beginning of the project. An important statistic for both your father and you to know.

You also can provide your father a list of times when each task either may or must start. What determines the status of a starting time?

For a task that is the sole predecessor of another task, as task 7 is to task 11, the starting time is a must if task 11 is to start on time. Otherwise task 11 would miss its earliest possible starting time. In contrast, task 8, one of the three predecessors of task 12, has some leeway in its starting time. Since task 12 has an earliest starting time of 13 time units, and task 8 has an earliest starting time of 7 time units and requires only 3 time units to complete, task 8 may begin at time unit 7, 8, 9, or 10 and still meet task 12's deadline. The amount of flexibility between tasks can be computed from the following formula:

```
FLEX(P, T) = EST(T) - [EST(P) + ACT(P)]
```

This is the **flex-time** for starting task P before its successor task T. This is a measure of flexibility between tasks only and does not indicate an overall flexibility. However, those tasks that have a flex-time of zero do indicate an inflexibility of the task's starting time in relation to the project's overall completion time. Therefore, starting a task on time that has a nonzero flex-time will not speed up the project's completion time, but delaying a task with a zero flex-time will delay the project.

With one more planning step, you will be ready to develop an algorithm for calculating the statistics on the earliest starting times for each task. The next step is a plan for the structuring of the nodes and edges, which is important to the expression of the algorithm.

Since the EST (earliest starting time) of all tasks except the start task depends on the predecessor tasks, it will be necessary for each node to be linked to its predecessor nodes. This arrangement was previously implemented by using the IN–LIST linked list of all edges leading into a given node. You will also need to access the successors of nodes in order to progress through the network, calculating the EST for each node. So the OUT–LIST structure is also useful to the algorithm. One additional feature that is necessary, though the need is not obvious now, is a MARK field for each edge. This will be helpful in determining when the EST of all predecessors of a node has been calculated, for then the maximum value can be determined. Fields within the edge storage node will contain a pointer to the the head of the edge, a pointer to the next edge, and the mark field. The nodes representing tasks will have five (optionally six) fields: the task number, the EST for the task, the activity time for the task, a pointer to the IN–LIST, a pointer to the OUT–LIST, and an optional pointer to the list of all task nodes. The optional pointer field will be used if the list of task nodes is set up as a linked structure. If the task nodes are stored sequentially in an array, this field is not needed.

Figure 6.15 presents the storage node structures and a portion of the graph for the house project.

One additional information structure will be needed, a stack. When the EST of a node is calculated, its successor nodes become candidates for having their ESTs calculated. If one or more of the successor nodes have all their predecessors computed then the successor nodes can be processed. They are placed on the stack until all successor nodes are checked for this possibility. With these preliminary statements, you can sketch out the pseudocode for the algorithm to compute the EST for all nodes in the graph.

> Let P be the pointer to the START NODE.
> Set the EST of P, the start node, to zero.
> Push P on the stack.
> While the stack is nonempty,
> *Step 1*—(* calculate EST for last pushed task, by
>   surveying its predecessors *)
>   Let T equal the task on top of the stack, pop the stack.
>   Step through the IN–LIST of T and
>   Calculate EST plus activity time for each predecessor
>   Save the largest value calculated.
>   Store the maximum value calculated as the EST of T.
> *Step 2*—(* mark all edges that T is the tail of *)
>   For each edge E in the OUT–LIST of T,
>   Determine the head S, the successor of T.
>   Locate in the IN–LIST of S the edge with tail T.
>   Mark the edge.
>   If all edges in the IN–LIST of S are marked,
>   then all predecessor ESTs are calculated,
>   PUSH S on the stack.
> *Step 3*—(* output the newly calculated EST of task T *)
>   Print the EST of task T and the task number.
> *Step 4*—(* return to check status of stack and
>   calculate next EST if necessary *)

Figure 6.15 **A portion of the information structure**

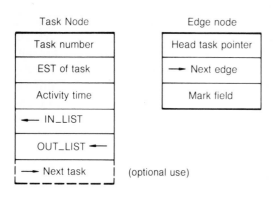

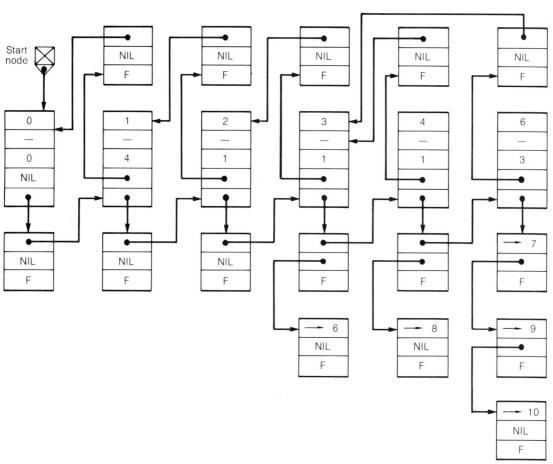

This algorithm will give your father the initial statistics about the starting times of all tasks. Readers may be a little unsure of the algorithm's ability to process all tasks, since a mark field was not used with the task nodes. This concern can easily be laid aside when you note that after each EST for a task is calculated, the algorithm checks all successors of this task to see whether their EST can be calculated and uses the stack to remember those tasks that can be processed but have yet to be handled.

Being a well-trained computer science professional, you are not satisfied with one approach to the solution, so you begin to consider alternate methods. You wonder whether another approach can be devised that does not use a stack but ensures all task nodes are processed. Earlier, an optional field was mentioned as part of the task storage node structure. It contained a pointer to the next task. Maybe this pointer and its associated linked list of nodes can be used to fashion an algorithm that steps from node to node, calculating the EST for each node.

To design an algorithm in this way, the ordering of the linked list of tasks is crucial. A strictly numerical ordering—node 0 linked to node 1, node 1 to node 2, and node N to node N + 1—will not necessarily work. Before the EST of a task can be calculated, the EST of all of its predecessors must have been already calculated. An increasing numerical ordering does not guarantee this property. An ordering that does provide this attribute, however, is the topological ordering that was used earlier to check for cyclic paths within the graph network.

An idea strikes you: if the next task pointer referred to the next task in the topological ordering of all tasks, when the next task in the linked list is moved to the predecessor EST values that its own EST depends on will already have been calculated. The calculation of this EST will then permit future tasks in the linked list to be calculated.

Thus if the tasks of the house construction graph were linked using the following topological ordering:

```
0, 1, 2, 3, 4, 5, 8, 6, 7, 9, 10, 12, 13, 14,
11, 18, 19, 23, 24, 15, 16, 17, 20, 21, 22, 25
```

then the algorithm could be rewritten using this new feature. It is important to notice that a topological ordering is not unique—that is, another ordering having the same desired attribute could be given because different paths can be taken from the same node. Thus, after node 6 of the house project graph, any of nodes 7, 9, or 10 could come next in the ordering. For the purpose at hand, no particular topological ordering will give us a noticeable advantage. It is also useful to remark that the previous algorithm using a stack generates a topological ordering in the sequence of task numbers that are printed, and hence a similar algorithm can be used to link the nodes together.

With this new field as part of the node structure, and this new strategy in mind, you sketch out another algorithm:

Let P be the pointer to the START NODE.
  Set the EST of P, the start node, to zero.
  Step to next task, T, in the topologically ordered linked list.
  While a next task, T, exists,
 Step 1—(*Initialize the EST of task T*)
   Set the EST of task T to zero.
 Step 2—(* finding largest EST from all predecessors of T *)
   For each predecessor task S in the IN-LIST OF T,

Calculate SEST as the EST of task plus the
activity time of task S ;
If SEST is greater than the present EST of task T
then set EST of task T to SEST.
Step 3—(* move through the list of tasks *)
Step to next task T in the topologically ordered
linked list.

Your wisdom in considering two solutions to the problem has demonstrated quite different approaches. From this vantage point you can weigh the advantages and costs of each approach and select the algorithm that best suits your needs and style. The opportunity to compare two solutions is one that you, as a computer science professional, should look forward to, and the skill to develop different approaches is one you should strive to cultivate.

The next step in the algorithm is illustrated in Figure 6.16. You have already designed the algorithm to calculate the earliest start time EST for any task T. The calculation of the **earliest finish time** is simply a matter of adding the activity time of the task to the EST of the task. Eventually this will lead to the earliest finish time of the final task, and you will have the earliest finish time for the project as a whole. This extra statistic can be calculated as part of the above algorithm, since both the EST and activity time are available.

Figure 6.16

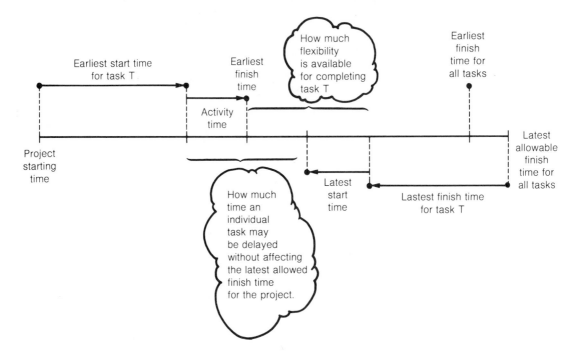

Latest Finish Time

Let's look at another area of concern. Because of various constraints, you may have a deadline for when you want the house completed. So you may set a latest allowable finish time for the project. From this time point, in a similar manner to calculating the EST, you can calculate the **latest finish time**, LFT, for all tasks in the network. The significance of this statistic is that if all goes well and each task is finished at its LFT, the project will complete at the latest allowable finish time.

You can just as easily determine the latest start time of a task by subtracting the activity time of the task from the LFT of the task. This yields the time the task must start to meet the project deadline. So if the task begins at its latest start time and all successive tasks go as scheduled, the project will reach completion as planned.

Two important differences exist in the calculation of the LFT. First, the latest finishing time of a task depends on the latest start time of the task's successors. A task must finish in time for all of its successors to begin on schedule. Therefore, the task's LFT depends directly upon the latest start time of its successors. **By looking at all of the latest start times of the successors and selecting the minimum value, the latest finish time is determined.**

This implies a second difference. The calculation of LFT moves from the final task to its predecessors and from the predecessors back to their predecessors until the starting task is found. Thus, a reverse direction is taken through the graph during the LFT calculations.

To perform this process, you plan to write a PASCAL procedure similar to the algorithm for calculating the EST, using the linked topological ordering convention previously stated. One important step is missing. It is necessary for the order of the linked list to be reversed. This will permit the desired reverse flow from finish to start task. This can easily be accomplished while traversing the linked list the first time. As an exercise, write a procedure that reverses the links in a singly linked list. Your PASCAL procedure assumes that this has been done and is written with the following record descriptions based on the node structure described in Figure 6.15, with two additional fields for our present and future purposes:

```
type TASK_NODES =
       record                          (* Task node structure *)
         TASK:integer;                 (* Task number *)
         EST:integer;                  (* Earliest start time *)
         ACTTIME:integer;             (* Activity time *)
         LFT:integer;                  (* Latest finish time *)
         CRTCAL:integer;              (* To be used later *)
         IN_LIST:E_POINTER;           (* Pointer to predecessor list *)
         OUT_LIST:E_POINTER;          (* Pointer to successor list *)
         NEXT_TASK:N_POINTER          (* Pointer to next task in *)
       end;                            (* reverse topological ordering *)
     EDGE_NODES =
       record                    (* Edge node structure *)
         TASK_PTR:N_POINTER;      (* Pointer to task at head or tail *)
         EDGE_PTR:E_POINTER;      (* Pointer to next task IN/OUT-LIST *)
         MARK_FIELD:boolean       (* To be used later *)
       end;
```

```
and with the identifier declarations of
     var    TASKS:array[1..25] of TASK_NODES;
            EDGES:array[1..30] of EDGE_NODES;
            FINISH_NODE:N_POINTER;  (* Pointer to finish task *)

procedure LATEST_FINISH_TIME
          (FINISH_TASK:N_POINTER;FINISH_TIME:integer);
const NILL = -1;
var PTR:N_POINTER;
    TASK_LFT:integer;
    SUC_PTR:E_POINTER;    (*Successor task-edge pointer *)
    SUC_TASK:N_POINTER;   (*              -node pointer *)
    SUC_LFT:integer;      (*              -latest finish time *)
    SUC_LST:integer;      (*              -latest start time *)
    SUC_ACTTIME:integer;  (*              -activity time *)
begin
(* Initialize finish task and working pointer through tasks *)
TASKS[FINISH_TASK].LFT:=FINISH_TIME;
PTR := FINISH_TASK ;
(*Calculate latest finish time for each task*)
while PTR <> NILL do
    begin
    (* Set LFT of task to maximum possible *)
    TASK_LFT := FINISH_TIME;
    (*Look at latest start time of all successor tasks *)
    (*           by using the OUT-LIST of edges *)
    SUC_PTR := TASKS[PTR].OUT_LIST;
    while SUC_PTR <> NILL do
              begin
              SUC_TASK := EDGES[SUC_PTR].TASK_PTR;
              SUC_LFT := TASKS[SUC_TASK].LFT;
              SUC_ACTTIME := TASKS[SUC_TASK].ACTTIME;
              SUC_LST := SUC_LFT - SUC_ACTTIME;
       (* Check for the minimum latest start time *)
              if SUC_LST < TASK_LFT then TASK_LFT := SUC_LST;
        (* Move to next successor by way of OUT-LIST *)
              SUC_PTR := EDGES[SUC_PTR].EDGE_PTR
              end;
(*Latest finish time of task has been calculated *)
        TASKS[PTR].LFT := TASK_LFT;
     (* This area will be updated later *)
     (*    involving latest finish time-LFT, *)
     (*           EARLIEST START TIME-EST, *)
     (*           ACTIVITY TIME-ACTTIME, *)
     (*    to calculate critical tasks   *)
     (* Move to next task in reverse topological ordering *)
        PTR := TASKS[PTR].NEXT_TASK
    end
end;
```

   This procedure, together with the earlier algorithm, gives your father two lists of statistics to aid him in his duties as project supervisor. He now knows the earliest time that any task can start, EST, and the latest time any task can finish, LFT, in order to meet an arbitrarily selected latest finish time for the project. Figure 6.17 summarizes the situation and also shows your next task as project programmer, the calculation of slack time for a task.

Figure 6.17

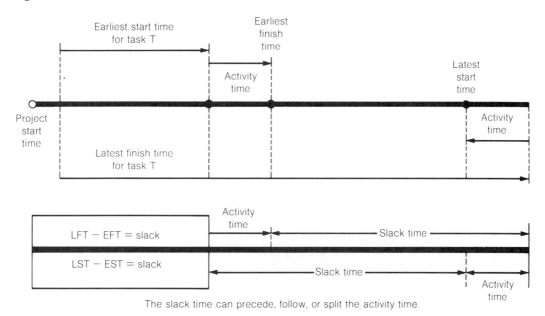

The slack time can precede, follow, or split the activity time.

Slack Time and Critical Tasks

The slack time can occur after, before, or during the activity of the task. Neither the project as a whole nor any of the task's successors will be delayed by the slack time. The value can be calculated in either of two ways:

```
latest finish time minus earliest finish time
or
latest start time minus earliest start time
```

A critical situation arises when the slack time of a task is equal to the slack time of the final task. This means that any delay longer than the task's slack time will delay the entire project. These are classified as **critical tasks.** For instance, if the earliest finish time for the project is 34 time units and the latest finish time is 36, then any task that has a slack time of 2 time units is a critical task.

You can easily include the calculations for a task's slack time into the previous procedure, LATEST_FINISH_TIME. The comments included in the procedure can be replaced by the following statements with the necessary additions to the identifier declaration section for TASK_EFT, TASK_SLACK and PROJECT_SLACK:

```
TASK_EFT := TASKS[PTR].EST + TASKS[PTR].ACTTIME;
TASK_SLACK := TASK_LFT - TASK_EFT;

TASKS[PTR].CRTCAL := TASK_SLACK;
```

or

```
PROJECT_SLACK := TASKS[FINISH_TASK].LFT-(TASKS[FINISH _TASK].EST +
                        TASKS[FINISH_TASK].ACTTIME);
TASKS[PTR].CRTCAL := TASK_SLACK - PROJECT_SLACK;
```

In the latter case, the amount of task slack time greater than project slack time is stored as the critical value. In this way all tasks with a critical value of zero are critical tasks.

With this procedure completed, the graph information structure has all the necessary data to provide the scheduling of all tasks—a table of statistics of earliest and latest start times, earliest and latest finish times, activity time and the overall slack time for all tasks, which indicates the critical tasks within the graph. A table of these values appears below. Assume two time units maximum allowable extension to project finish time.

TASK	ACT	EST	EFT	LFT	LST	CRTCAL
0	0	0	0	2	0	0
1	4	0	4	6	2	0
2	1	4	5	7	6	0
3	1	5	6	8	7	0
4	1	6	7	9	8	0
5	2	7	9	11	9	0
6	3	6	9	11	8	0
7	1	9	10	18	17	6
8	3	7	10	15	12	3
9	2	9	11	15	13	2
10	4	9	13	15	11	0
11	6	10	16	24	18	6
12	2	13	15	17	15	0
13	6	15	21	23	17	0
14	3	21	24	26	23	0
15	1	24	25	28	27	1
16	2	24	26	28	26	0
17	3	24	27	30	27	1
18	2	16	18	26	24	6
19	1	18	19	27	26	6
20	3	26	29	31	28	0
21	2	27	29	32	30	1
22	1	29	30	32	31	0
23	2	19	21	29	27	6
24	3	21	24	32	29	6
25	0	30	30	32	32	0
TASK	**ACT**	**EST**	**EFT**	**LFT**	**LST**	**CRTCAL**

A **critical path** is one containing critical tasks. It is a sequence of tasks that your father must pay particular attention to. Sufficient labor must be supplied to these tasks to ensure the house is completed by the projected finish time. The critical tasks have been shaded in the graph diagram given earlier.

Finding the Critical Paths

Your final task has now arrived—the critical path problem. You ponder what you already have. You consider what you want—the enumeration of all critical paths. You decide on two approaches.

Your first option is to alter procedure LATEST _ FINISH _ TIME again, so that all edges between critical tasks are marked as part of a critical path by using the MARK _ FIELD. This is easily done after the calculation of a task's slack time. If the slack time of a task indicates that a task is critical, the OUT–LIST of the task can be used to locate the critical successor tasks (since their slack time has just been calculated—remember the traversal is in reverse). The edges that lead out of a critical task to a critical successor task are then marked. After procedure LATEST _ FINISH _ TIME completes, you will have all the edges of all the critical paths marked; all that is left is to follow the marked edges from start task to finish task (not to imply that this is simply done).

Another choice is to leave the procedure LATEST _ FINISH _ TIME as it is and write a procedure that follows this strategy: (1) beginning at the start task, investigate its successors by using the OUT–LIST; (2) locate critical successor tasks by using the CRTCAL field of the task; (3) push the critical successor tasks onto a stack; (4) removing the top one, print the edge connecting the two critical tasks; and (5) using this critical successor task, recursively repeat the process for its successors. You will know when a critical path ends by the arrival of the finish task—the terminal condition. You then check the stack to see whether any more critical successor tasks exist, indicating the presence of additional critical paths within the graph.

The choice is yours, so much so that I will leave this final task as an exercise in imagination and understanding. You may even discover that there are other ways to complete the task than the two outlined. Good luck while path finding!

As you turn inward toward the task, your little internal voice system is broadcasting: "Let's see—if now is the earliest starting time and seven days is the latest finish time and the computer center waiting lines are already overflowing, I better schedule . . . oh, my! What should I do first?"

■ "JUST FOR REFERENCE"

Basic Path Algorithms

To determine path existence by the adjacency array approach, use the inductive method via the boolean product operator—

- for paths of length 2—form ADJ2, the array of path existence, from B×P of ADJ with ADJ, array of edge existence
- for paths of length 3—form ADJ3 from B×P of ADJ2 with ADJ
- for paths of length 4—form ADJ4 = ADJ3 B×P ADJ, and so on

To determine both existence and number of paths, use same inductive method as above with arithmetic matrix product replacing the B×P operator. The shortest path algorithm includes these steps—

- initially MARK all nodes
- using the source node, place all adjacent nodes in the "candidate for next shortest path" list by changing the MARK field
- select the candidate node with the shortest path
- for each adjacent node of the selected node, add the node to the candidate list if it is not currently present; or update the data if the new path distance is less than the current path distance; or ignore node since a shorter path already exists

Task Scheduling and Critical Path Analysis

Steps in establishing the graph of tasks—

- list all activities (NODES)
- list all precedence pairs (EDGES)
- list estimated activity times (WEIGHTS)

Quantities to assist task scheduling (LFT, EFT, and slack time assume a projected completion time for the project)—

- earliest start time (EST) equals the maximum [EST + activity time] of all predecessor tasks
- earliest finish time (EFT) = EST + activity time
- latest finish time (LFT) equals the minimum LST of all successor tasks
- latest start time (LST) = LFT − activity time
- slack time = LFT − EFT

EST algorithm (assumes a topologically ordered linked list of tasks)—

- initialize the working pointer to the start task.
- while a task exists do
  - survey the predecessors via the IN-LIST to determine the maximum EST + activity time
  - store the maximum value as EST of the task
  - calculate and store the EFT for the task
  - step to the next task

LFT algorithm (assumes a reversed topologically ordered linked list of tasks)—

- initialize the working pointer to finish task
- while a task exists do
  - survey the successors via OUT-LIST to determine the minimum LST
  - store the minimum value as LFT of the task
  - calculate and store the slack time for the task
  - step to the next task

Properties of critical tasks and critical paths are as follows—

- when it is necessary to complete the project by a specified time, certain tasks take on added significance
- critical tasks exist when the slack time of the finish task equals the slack time of the task
- critical paths are those that contain critical tasks

EXERCISES

1. Revise the procedure PATH2 to record the first intermediate node in the path of length 2 between two nodes.

2. Revise the procedure PATH2 to record the intermediate node in each path of length 2 between two nodes.

3. Write the procedure ALLPATH3 and ALLPATH4, patterned after the procedure ALLPATH2.

4. Write a recursive procedure to produce the array that indicates the existence of paths of length N, given the adjacency array ADJ and the path length N.

5. Is the operator B×P commutative—that is, does ADJ B×P ADJ3 = ADJ3 B×P ADJ = ADJ4?

6. Using the linked approach, that is, a list of nodes with adjacency lists of edges, write a procedure that lists all the paths of length 2.

7. Using the linked approach, write a general boolean function that yields the value true if a path of length N exists between two nodes. The arguments passed to the procedure will be the two nodes and the integer N.

8. Write a procedure that produces the shortest path between two given nodes. Use the notation A.B.C to represent paths.

9. Consider what changes are necessary to the above procedure if the additional constraint is placed on the path of finding the shortest path whose length is greater than 4. Explain what changes would be made to the procedure.

10. The procedure SHORTEST _ PATH, which was presented in subsection 6.4.2, used a mark field to distinguish candidate cities from noncandidates. Redesign the procedure so that three linked lists are used: one for the cities currently serviced, another for the candidate cities to be considered for expansion, and the last for all other cities not in either of the first two. Which method do you think is more efficient? On what criteria have you based your judgement and why?

11. Write the procedure EST to calculate the earliest start time for tasks in a task graph. Use the algorithm that assumes a linked list of tasks ordered topologically.

12. Write a procedure TOP _ SORT that accepts a list of tasks and a list of precedent pairs. Its objective is to create a graph information structure and print a topological ordering of the tasks. If the graph contains a cycle and the ordering is not possible then an appropriate message is to be printed. Either provide the start node as an argument or use the property that the start node has no predecessors.

13. Revise the EST procedure of exercise 11 to reverse the links while the tasks are being processed. In this way, the topological ordering is reversed and the information structure is set up for the calculation of the latest finish time.

14. Using the record structures presented in subsection 6.4.3, the procedures EST and LFT, and the house task network, write a program that produces a table of statistics. The table should contain the activity time, the EST and LST, the LFT and EFT, and the slack time for each task. All critical tasks should have an asterisk preceding their task number. The desired completion time will be a necessary argument for the table-producing procedure.

15. Given a graph information structure that has had the EST and LFT calculated and stored as part of each task node, write a procedure that prints, in set notation, the graph consisting only of critical tasks. (Hint: By using the transitive property of the precedence relationship, critical tasks can be connected to other critical tasks, with the noncritical tasks eliminated.)

THE WORKOUT ROOM

PROJECT 1: *Mightier Mouse Returns*

The video game industry has given some lucky programmers a opportunity to exercise their skills and imagination. For their efforts, many have undoubtedly been rewarded (via quarterly royalties in rolls of quarters). In this chapter a video game, Pac Rat, was introduced. In this project you are to imbue the electronic rodent with some human wisdom.

By using the graph found in Figure 6.4 as a basis, develop a rodent routine that successfully selects a safe path to one of the four storage areas. To add some intrigue to the journey, randomly choose two nodes at which two of the three cats are napping. These nodes need to be avoided to maintain a healthy lifestyle for our stylish Pac Rat. Assume that Pac Rat has some paranormal abilities and can sense the location of its cat-napping adversaries before it begins its journey selection. The PASCAL procedure that you design should print the shortest safe path to the storage areas.

For additional intrigue, you can assume a Pac Rat of normal senses that perceives the presence of its sleeping foe only when it is on a node adjacent to the one on which the feline is resting. In this case it will need to adjust its path selection as it goes along. To include more stress, the third cat can meander onto the scene at any randomly selected time during the path selection.

Measure your own intrigue quotient and select the scenario that suits your fancy. In the selection process, tap into your ImQ and enhance the scenario to your heart's content.

PROJECT 2: *Pursuit of Happiness, to a Degree*

When a student enters college, she has various goals to be pursued. Along the path certain tasks will be prerequisites for other tasks. One major goal in the pursuit of happiness and the American Dream is receiving a college degree. The path to this goal consists of a sequence of courses, some of which must be taken in a prescribed order.

To assist the student in her happy pursuit, write a program that answers the following questions about the degree program listed below:

1. Which course(s) follows a given course in the curriculum?

2. Which course(s) is a prerequisite to a given course?

3. Given a list of courses taken by a student, which courses can she register for in the next term?

The course curriculum for Data U is as follows:

Course Number	Prerequisite Courses
CS101	none
CS102	none
CS103	CS101
CS104	CS102
CS205	CS103
CS206	CS103
CS207	CS205
CS208	CS206
CS209	CS104
CS310	CS208, CS209
CS311	CS207, CS310
CS312	CS209
CS413	CS311
CS414	CS413
CS415	CS413
CS416	none
CS417	CS414, CS416
CS418	CS415, CS416

PROJECT 3: *The Group Graph*

In psychology, the study of group problems and processes has led to the development of sociometry. This field of psychology measures the social relationships linking group members together.

By asking each group member the question "Who do you favor working with?" and allowing each person to list up to three other group members, a set of ordered pairs is established. For instance, DAVE says he likes to work with WOODY and ALLEN, so the pairs (DAVE, WOODY) and (DAVE, ALLEN) are included in the set. Next, the sociometrist draws a sociogram—a directed graph—where each node is a group member's name and each edge is an affinity connection as indicated by the ordered pairs.

The sociometrist would then use your soon-to-be written program to analyze the group relationships by analyzing the "group graph." The following relationships have been singled out as important concerns by the sociometrist:

1. Pair—two people who like to work together

2. Star—the person who is favored by the most people

3. Isolate—a person who is not favored by anyone and who favors someone who favors someone who favors the star

4. Chain—a sequence of members who favor the next person in the sequence in a circular way

5. Group cohesion—the number of pairs in the group

6. Group integration—the number of isolates.

The program specifications are to read the people pairs from a file, GROUP.DAT; to list the star; to list the pairs; to list the isolates; to list the chains of length 3, 4, or 5; and to produce a graphic image of the sociogram, highlighting the star, the isolates, and the chains, if the computer system has the capability.

7

Tables

Consistency is the last refuge of the unimaginative.

— Oscar Wilde

7.1 Setting the Stage

7.1.1 GETTING IN TOUCH WITH GRANNY

You have used tables in many aspects of your daily life. When you go to the post office and look up granny's postal zip code for the nth time, when you look in the telephone book to find the long-distance evening rates to Miami, and when you look up the federal tax due for your income on the IRS form 1040, you are using the table information structure. Let's look at how these tables are arranged and used.

One afternoon you write a letter to your granny. You tell her about your latest excitements and that life is playing your tune. While addressing the envelope, you realize that you don't have a clue as to her zip code. Hopping on your bike, you're off to the post office for a bit of Sherlock Holmes—detecting the five magic digits that locate dear old granny. Equipped with the key clue—granny's address in Melbourne, Florida—you tackle the postal zip code book. Where do you start?

Since the book is ordered first by state, you start by looking for Florida. Indiana greets your eyes as you open the book so you try again, this time using the first half of the volume. Intuition is with you, and the second iteration yields Florida. You have successfully navigated the first level of the search. To begin the next level, you use another portion of the original clue—the city name. Scanning through the alphabetical list of Florida cities, you find Melbourne. The search for granny's zip code is complete! But wait—the value given is only three digits: 329. Melbourne is a multizone city with a zip code for each zone. Okay, level 2 search is complete; now to the third and last level.

By turning a few more pages through the alphabetical list of multizone cities, you locate the Melbourne section. What clue is needed to access this part of the table? The ordering is based on street addresses. With this in mind your quest for the missing digits is about to end. You find these digits next to the street name, Sunset Boulevard, and hurriedly jot down the complete code, 32901, below the address. Dropping the letter into the slot, you reflect on your interface with the multilevel zip code system.

Sample rates from MELBOURNE to	DIAL-DIRECT					
	WEEKDAY FULL RATE		EVENING 35% DISCOUNT		NIGHT & WEEKEND 60% DISCOUNT	
	First minute	Each additional minute	First minute	Approx. each additional minute	First minute	Approx. each additional minute
Clearwater	.57	.39	.37	.26	.22	.16
Daytona B.	.50	.37	.32	.25	.20	.15
Ft. Ldle	.57	.39	.37	.26	.22	.16
Gainesville	.57	.39	.37	.26	.22	.16
Hollywood	.57	.39	.37	.26	.22	.16
Jacksonville	.57	.39	.37	.26	.22	.16
Chipley	.63	.43	.40	.28	.25	.18
Miami	.57	.39	.37	.26	.22	.16
Orlando	.44	.34	.28	.23	.17	.14
Pensacola	.66	.44	.42	.29	.27	.18
Tampa	.50	.37	.32	.25	.20	.15
W.P.B.	.50	.37	.32	.25	.20	.15

While you are biking home, your imagination clicks into gear, and you envision a computer terminal replacing the zip code book. The following fantasy floats through your consciousness. As you enter the post office looking for granny's zip code for the $(n + 1)$th time, the computer interface begins. When you press the START button, an official electronic voice says:

"Hi, I am Clutron—the postal service's zip code wizard. You provide the clue and with the speed of an electron, I'll provide the magic. Let's start with the first clue from you. Type the postal abbreviation for the state."

You type in "FL."

"Thanks, it is a great state to watch pelicans. Now type in the name of the city in Florida."

You type in "Melbourne."

"For this city Clutron needs another clue. Please type the address in Melbourne."

You type "310 Sunset Blvd."

"Thank you, the number is 32901." *(The number is displayed in large digits on the screen.)*

"It's a real charge helping you. Electronically yours, Clutron. Have a zip—padee—do da day."

Suddenly, the sound of a car's horn pulls you back to the reality of riding your bike as cars zip by, but the fantasy lingers on subconsciously. For the rest of the day your mind toys with the design of the information structures and software procedures that could bring Clutron to life. How shall you implement a multilevel search, faster than a speeding electron, through the many pages of zip code data? It's an exciting challenge. With a few days of creative mulling, you hope a solution will emerge.

A couple of days later your granny receives your letter. Your thoughtfulness inspires her to pass on the kindness. Deciding to "let her fingers do the walking," she plans to call her own granny in Miami. Being a frugal sort, granny checks the sample phone rate table in the front of the phone book. She uses a different access method since the table has a different organization. The clue that granny uses is similar to yours—a city name.

The first difference is that the list of city names is not sorted. Since there are only a few names, this does not pose a problem. The access method is affected since the entire list may have to be searched to find the name or determine that it is not in the list. Can you imagine looking for a zip code in a table with the same organization? Even Clutron would perspire during that search.

The second difference is that the table has a single organizational level and only one clue is needed. When granny finds the "Miami" entry, another difference presents itself. Associated with the key clue, Miami, are three values—the weekday, evening, and night phone rates. These data give granny the input she needs for a decision. After perusing the choices, she dials directory assistance and asks for her granny's phone number for the $(n + 1)$th time.

7.1.2   TABLES IN YOUR OWN BACKYARD

In the everyday life of a computer programmer, the table information structure is a common tool, found at multiple levels. The assembly level uses a **symbol table** of variable names to assist in the assembly process. In its two-phase processing of your assembly program, it creates a table of attributes associated with each variable name. During the second phase, it accesses the table each time a variable name is encountered. Upon completion a copy of the symbol table is printed with the assembly listing. (A compiler operates in a similar way.) Organizing the table structure to efficiently accomplish this task is an important concern of this chapter.

Menu-driven system or application programs use jump tables to facilitate flexible design. The **jump table** is like an information desk at an airport that is being remodeled. As passengers arrive seeking a specific airline, they stop at the information desk. A list is checked, and the passenger is directed to the current location of the airline. When a remodeled section of the airport is completed and the airlines are shuffled about, the information desk receives a new jump table. Passengers are not inconvenienced since the changes are transparent to them. In the context of computer science, the user's menu selection is the passenger and the module handling the selection is the airline. As modules are relocated in the main memory, the jump table is updated and the changes are transparent to the user. Each entry in the menu table is associated with the physical memory address of the section of code used to handle the request—the jump table in your own backyard.

The computer professional frequently uses data files. Some data files exhibit the characteristics of tables. There are three main types of data files—sequential, indexed sequential, and random-access files. Sequential files do not depend on the table information structure for their organization, but the others do.

The indexed sequential file consists of an index table and a collection of records, each with a unique key value. The index table contains key values and a physical address used to locate the record containing the key value. Thus it is analogous to the jump table: a value is used to locate the address of the information desired. Usually the physical address directs you to a block of records on an external storage device, such as a disk. This block of records is read into main memory and searched sequentially until the desired record is found. The table information structure is an integral part of this file organization.

When the number of records in each block equals one, we have the equivalent of a random-access file. This file is used to immediately locate a record given the key value of the record. In this method, the key values do not have to be ordered. The table structure that facilitates this file organization can either be (1) a densely packed index table structure (an entry for every possible key value), sometimes called a random-access directory, or (2) a hash table. The latter table will occupy much of our attention in Section 7.3.

Since the table structures that support file organizations work behind the scenes, you are probably unaware of their presence. Now that your awareness is germinated with the idea, what remains is for your imagination to fertilize the soil of implementation. From this groundbreaking, let us move to the model of the table information structure.

▪ "JUST FOR REFERENCE"

The table information structure consists of pairs of associated entities with these properties—

- one entity is used to provide access to the other
- the primary entities may be ordered for easier access
- the primary entity may be associated with a number of secondary entities

Examples include—

- zip code tables ordered by city name
- zip code tables ordered by street name
- tax tables ordered by taxable income
- long-distance telephone rates
- assembler and compiler symbol tables

- system and application program jump tables
- tables used by indexed sequential and random-access files

EXERCISES

1. List four examples of tables that are encountered in everyday life that were not mentioned in the text.
2. List four examples of tables in the computer science environment that were not mentioned in the text.
3. Describe a situation when a table of zip codes ordered by zip code instead of city name would be helpful.
4. Describe two tables that a teacher might use administratively.

7.2 Formalizing the Structure

Using the examples of Section 7.1 as a basis, we can begin to characterize the table information structure. The postal zip code table has two components—the address and the zip code associated with it. The phone rate table also has two parts—city names and the associated rates (notice that all three phone rates are grouped into one entity).

By abstracting the essential features, a definition is developed: **The table information structure is a set of ordered pairs (K, V) possessing the following property: if (K, V_1) and (K, V_2) are members of the set, then V_1 and V_2 are identical.** The first component of the pair is referred to as the **key** and the second is the table **value.**

In the table set, the above property means that all keys are unique. No two distinct pairs will have the same key; however, two distinct pairs can have the same value, for distinct K_1 and K_2 the pairs (K_1, V) and (K_2, V) can be in the table.

It is important to recognize that the value component V may have separately identifiable subfields. This was illustrated by having three phone rates (weekday, evening, and night) associated with each city. During the implementation a record structure can be used to accommodate such cases.

 IMAGINATION CHALLENGE

Locate a scarf or handkerchief and prepare yourself for some spatial visualization. Take hold of the scarf at opposite corners with your hands. Visualize the scarf as connected to your body—you now have one circular appendage, not two arms. Using only body movements tie a knot in the scarf without letting go.

The primitive operations that are applied to the table information structure are similar to those applied to other structures. Inserting and deleting table pairs are basic operations for a table. Not all applications will require these operations; for the abstract model, however, they are essential. Another operation is updating the value component of a table pair.

Important to each of these operations is the table access strategy used. For instance, locating the pair to be deleted or updated requires that the table be systematically searched. The strategy for accessing the table for this purpose depends on the organization of the table structure. In each application a specialized Clutron software package must be designed. The access strategy for the postal zip code table requires a multistep access strategy because of the multilevel organization. While the phone rate table had only one level, the lack of ordering among the keys affected the access strategy. For this application Clutron would be taught a new way of searching for the table pair. This important connection between the table organization and the access strategy will be a main concern of Section 7.3.

One way to enhance the efficiency of an access strategy depends on the set of keys. If the keys can be sorted then the table pairs can be organized based on the ordering. We will see that some table organizations depend upon this characteristic of the keys. Since the sorting of the keys can enhance the table information structure, this auxiliary operation deserves special attention. For this reason and as an important topic in its own right, Chapter 8 is devoted to presenting various sorting algorithms and the information structures that support them.

Another feature of the table information structure that merits mention is its sometimes static, sometimes dynamic nature. In some applications, the table remains fixed for the duration of its use. Such applications normally possess a known set of keys and values. In other applications, the table's contents are dynamic, such as an on-line data base application for an airline. In such cases, the set of keys can change during the course of the application. Tables also exist between these two poles. For example, the compiler symbol table is created from an unknown set of identifier names. It then remains static during the second pass of the compiler, being accessed only. Therefore, a table's capacity for change is an important factor in planning its organization.

The data file fits the definition of a table information structure, even though it resides on an external storage device. The data file is a collection of records, where each record is uniquely identified by a key field. The record itself consists of a key field and a number of associated data fields. The records in the file may be sequentially ordered or stored randomly on the disk. Records may be updated, added, or deleted, and a specific access strategy based on the file's organization is used. Hence, the file fits the model. Because of its size, its implementation is different than the tables we have seen in the examples. The general access strategy for a data file is to read from the disk into main memory a block of records from the data file. This group of records is then accessed as an internal table structure. If the desired record is not found then it is possible that another block of records is read. The organization of the blocks in the data file adds a new consideration for efficient access to the file as a table structure. We will not cover this important topic in this chapter, as we will be interested in tables that are available in main memory only.

With the footwork done, let's sprint across to the land of implementation. Don't forget to bring along our friendly wizard, Clutron—faster than a speeding electron, wiser than Sherlock Holmes when given a key clue in search of an associated value.

■ "JUST FOR REFERENCE"

The table structure is modeled as a collection of ordered pairs (key, value) where—

- each key is unique to only one pair
- keys may be ordered
- the value component may be multivalued
- the table may be static or dynamic in nature

Operations include—

- table inserting—inserting a new table pair into the organization
- table deleting—removing a table pair from the organization
- table updating—changing fields within the value component
- table access—given a key, locating its associated value; uniqueness of key makes this operation well defined and the organization of the table affects the access strategy

Data files are tables because—

- they are a collection of records identified by a key field
- each record contains key and value fields
- records may be physically or logically ordered or randomly stored on the secondary storage device
- the organization of the blocks of records affects the access strategy

EXERCISES

1. Describe the table information structure in terms of components and relationships.
2. State three differences between the ordered pairs of a table and the edges of a graph.
3. Describe the table access algorithm for an unordered table structure.
4. What auxiliary operation can be applied to a table in order to improve the efficiency of the access operation?
5. Explain how the efficiency of the access operation is improved by the above auxiliary operation.
6. For each of the following tables, specify which entity is the key of the table:
   a) Index of a book.
   b) The nutritional composition of your multivitamin.

c) The card files in the library.

d) The menu at the local natural foods cafe.

7. Explain how a file of students enrolled in a class can be considered a table structure.

7.3 Implementing the Structure

The reasons for presenting the following divergent implementation methods stem from two features a table structure can possess. The first and most important concern is the changeability of the table. How much change to the number of elements is expected? Some methods will not handle changes efficiently, while others can add new table entries in as little time as it takes to locate the proper storage location. So for each method presented, keep this question on the tip of your tongue: how easy is it to add or delete a new element from the table?

The second concern focuses on the set of keys and whether they need to be sorted for the method to be used. One method requires sorted keys, one can have the keys either way (though the efficiency is affected), and one is quite efficient regardless of the arrangement of the keys.

Well, lean back and get ready for this variety pack of table implementation methods.

7.3.1 A LINEAR APPROACH

The simplest way to implement a table structure is as a linear structure, using an array of records to store the table keys and values. This approach begins with the PAS-CAL declarations :

```
type PAIRS = record
               KEY:KEY_TYPE ;
               VALU:VALUE_TYPE
               end;
var TABLE:array[0..50] of PAIRS;
```

In order to retrieve a value associated with a particular key, it is necessary to find the key's position in the array and then reference the subfield VALU. This access strategy is called a **linear search** since we must start at the beginning of the array and perform a comparison until we either find a match or reach the end of the array. The Clutron-type procedure to retrieve the value associated with a particular search key is left as an exercise for the reader.

The ability to add or delete keys and their values is limited by the linear nature of the array. Shifting of table pairs would be required, adding a large overhead cost to the operation. This method is best used with a static table of known keys and values. This organization becomes quite inefficient for large tables with unsorted table pairs.

If the keys are sorted within the array, the efficiency of the access algorithm can be improved in two ways. First, with a sorted table it is unnecessary to search the entire table. When the search has progressed to a point that indicates that the search key is not in the table, the linear search can end. For example, if the above table has an alphabetized table of city names for the keys and if

```
SEARCHKEY  :=  'MIAMI'
```

and for some K,

```
TABLE[K].KEY equals 'NAPLES'
```

then the search can be suspended. The remainder of the table does not need to be accessed since it is clear that the search key is not among the sorted keys.

As a simple measure of performance, if the table has 1024 entries and it is accessed 100 times, then on the average, each linear search will require 512 comparisons, yielding a total of 51,200 comparisons. As a rough comparison between methods, this benchmark example will be used in later sections.

The second way to improve the efficiency of accessing a table with sorted keys requires teaching Clutron a new strategy. The closest analogy to this new strategy is when you access a dictionary to find the definition (value) of a desired word (search key). Rather than starting with the first page and looking sequentially, page by page, you turn to the approximate area of the dictionary and see if you have gone too far or not far enough. You then make another step in the appropriate direction until you have narrowed your search to a single page.

With our table of 1024 entries, we can go to the middle of the table and determine whether the search key is in the first or second half of the table (since the table is ordered we can make this judgement). In this way, we have eliminated 512 potential comparisons, a large number. What worked once will work twice, so, whichever half is likely to hold the search key can also be halved, with 256 keys eliminated in this step. With two steps and two comparisons, 768 table entries have been removed as potential matches for the search key. Continuing in this way, the groups that are eliminated from the search include 512, 256, 128, 64, 32, 16, 8, 4, 2, and 1 keys. At the last and worst case we are left with one candidate key, which is simply tested to see whether it equals the search key. With a maximum of 11 comparisons, we have either found the table entry or proved that it is not present in the table.

Therefore, with this access strategy, called a **binary search,** 100 accesses to a table with 1024 entries will cost our table wizard, Clutron, only 1100 comparisons. This is a considerable improvement over our first approach with 51,200 comparisons, yielding more than a 90% improvement in performance—quite a large reward for a fresh outlook on the problem at hand. Do we lose some of this grandeur by complicating the procedure to implement the strategy? Not at all. The binary search procedure is given below. The VALPOINTER will point to the subscript of the record matching the search key or equals −1 if no match is found.

```
procedure BINARY_SEARCH(var VALPOINTER:integer;SEARCHKEY:KEY_TYPE);
(*  This procedure searches a linear table with sorted keys
    for a given SEARCHKEY using a binary access method    *)
(*  The return argument is the subscript of the table pair
    if found  otherwise  -1 is returned                   *)
(*  Globals are the TABLE array and the table size, TAB_SIZE*)
var MATCH:boolean;
    LOWPOINT,MIDPOINT,HIGHPOINT:0...TAB_SIZE;
begin
LOWPOINT := 0;                (* Initial values for whole table *)
```

```
HIGHPOINT := TAB_SIZE;
MATCH := false;              (* Flag to suspend search when match occurs *)
VALPOINTER := -1;            (* and default value if no match occurs *)
while(LOWPOINT <= HIGHPOINT) and (MATCH = false) do
    begin
    MIDPOINT :=  (LOWPOINT + HIGHPOINT)  div 2 ;     (* Integer division *)
    if SEARCHKEY = TABLE[MIDPOINT].KEY then
                              begin
                              VALPOINTER := MIDPOINT;
                              MATCH := true
                              end
        (* Determine which half to look in *)
    else if SEARCHKEY < TABLE[MIDPOINT].KEY then
                    (* Bottom half is set up *)
                    HIGHPOINT := MIDPOINT - 1
                    else
                    (* Upper half is set up *)
                    LOWPOINT := MIDPOINT + 1;
    end
end;
```

The binary search procedure provides a very efficient way of accessing a table with sorted keys that is implemented as a linear structure. For unsorted keys or implementations with different structures we will find that another fresh approach is waiting for us.

7.3.2 A LAYERED APPROACH

Another organization of the table structure is called **indexed sequential** organization. The zip code book found at the post office gives an example of this method. The first index that you use is the index of states. This index directs you to the zip codes of a single state. The next subdivision of the table is the list of cities. For small cities with only a single zip code, this is the last layer. The single-zone section of the zip code book is organized as a linearly ordered table, alphabetized by the key, city name. But for larger cities with multiple zip code areas within their boundaries, another layer ordered by street address is involved. Thus by following the indexes, a small portion of the table can be located that can then be searched by either a linear or a binary search algorithm.

The indexed sequential organization provides for two types of access. The index part is designed to facilitate access to individual table pairs, by directing the search to successively smaller sections of the table.

The second type of access is to the entire table of pairs—the sequential processing of all table entries. This can be accomplished in two ways. The table pairs may be stored physically in contiguous locations, such as in an array. The sequential access is then simply a linear traversal of the array. In this case, the index table is an array of keys and subscripts, which denote the bounds of smaller sections of the array.

The alternate way of organizing the table pairs is a linked list. Here, the sequential access is simply a logical traversal of the linked list. The index table becomes an array of keys and associated pointer variables. The pointer variables indicate the first node in a designated section of the table.

The index is itself a table, with the index keys being either keys from the original table or part of the key of the original table and the value being a pointer to a section of the original table. Figure 7.1 illustrates this concept for the zip code book. There are three layers to the table organization with two index tables—the table of states and the table of large cities.

The access strategies that we would teach our table wizard, Clutron, for the indexed sequential organization are simple. First, the index table is searched either with a binary or a linear search until a section match is made. By a section match, I mean that the keys in the index table indicate the lowest (or highest) key in a specific section of the table. Using this convention, the search can be narrowed down to one particular section. Next, from the index table, the pointer leads us to a sorted section of the table. The search on this linearly ordered mini-table is performed with either a binary or linear search algorithm. Thus Clutron would receive these two instructions: (1) search index table to located the section the key may be in; (2) search the section for the key.

The general flavor of this organization is depicted in Figure 7.2, using a dictionary as an example. One trade-off is that extra storage space is needed for the index table. Once the correct pointer is procured from the index table then you are assured of looking in the section that is most likely to contain the key if it is present in the table. Actually, you will need two pointers from the index table. Thus the strategy would be: starting at the key pointed to by the A index (AARDVARK), perform a linear or binary search until the key pointed to by the B index (BABBLE) is encountered. The special case of a key beginning with a Z is handled by having an extra entry at the end of index table that points to the end of the table of definitions.

How does this method compare to the linear organization, under the assumptions of 1024 table entries and 100 accesses? First, an assumption of how many keys are in each section is needed. If you assume an equal distribution of all 1024 entries among 26 sections (one for each letter of the alphabet), approximately 40 keys are in each section. If you assume that no comparisons are needed to determine the section that the key is likely to appear in, the number of comparisons needed to search the section is the primary measure of performance. Therefore Clutron can access 100 different keys using 2000 comparisons (with a linear search of the small section of the table) or 800 comparisons (using a binary search). The latter approach yields an increase in performance over the previous best binary search on the linear implementation, which you recall required an average of 1100 comparisons for the same 100 accesses. Just how fast can this table wizard perform? More dazzling demonstrations await.

As was stated before, what worked once will work twice. How about adding another layer of indexing? If you let each pointer of the index table point to another index table that points to even smaller sections of the actual table then you can reduce the number of comparisons even further (see Figure 7.3). But be careful—now you are considerably increasing the storage requirements of the implementation, and the time to search each index table starts to contribute to the total search time. Your extra layer can be more expensive than the savings recovered. Therefore, a careful analysis should be made for each application before considering how many layers of indexes you use to improve efficiency.

The insertion and deletion of new elements from an index sequential table can involve some difficulties. It requires some shifting of data elements if the table is con-

Figure 7.1

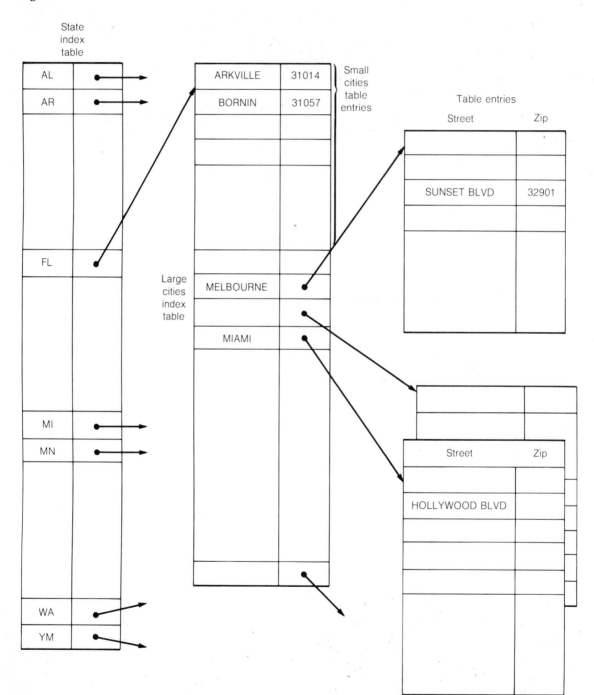

Figure 7.2

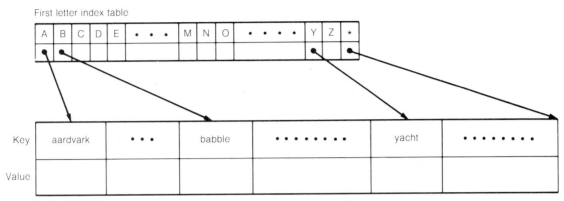

First letter index table

Table of definitions

The last entry in the index table is a special value which points to the end of the table of values.

Figure 7.3

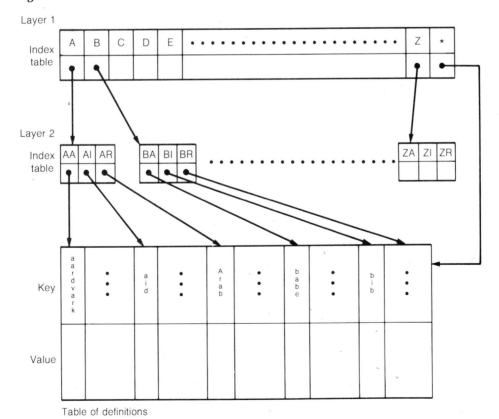

Table of definitions

tiguously stored. If the elements are linked together then this concern does not apply. One question that must be faced is whether the change affects the pointer values in the index table. When the answer is yes then an update of the index table is involved.

This approach is used frequently by operating systems to manage the file system. At layer 1 is an index of all accounts that have file capabilities. This index indicates where the information about the user's files is stored. The second layer is an index of the files owned by a user. Each part of this index points to a block of information about a particular file, which includes the sequence of tracks and cylinders on the magnetic disk where the file's contents are actually stored. As an exercise draw a diagram similar to Figure 7.3 that illustrates this structure. State all assumptions necessary to complete the diagram.

7.3.3   A SCATTER STORAGE APPROACH

The previous two approaches perform well with sorted tables. Can we develop an approach that works well with unsorted tables? Let's take a hint from arrays. We can think of the array as a table information structure. The key is the array subscript and the associated value is the value stored in the corresponding array location. The access strategy is different than those previously presented. The memory address of an array location is the result of a mathematical function whose parameters are the starting address of the array, the subscript, and the length of each array element:

$$\text{address of location} = \text{start address} + \text{subscript} * \text{length}$$

The access strategy simply takes the argument, the array subscript (the key for the array table), applies the function, and uses the address (a pointer to the value) to retrieve the associated value.

No comparisons are required; instead access to the table value is replaced by a function that directs us to the desired value. This method depends on the subscripts being an ascending sequence of integers. The **scatter storage** approach generalizes the above algorithm and removes the limitation concerning the sorted keys.

The objective of the scatter storage technique is to provide direct access to a value, using keys that are of any data type and are not sorted. The idea is to scatter the key-value pairs around memory in a controlled way, based on the key. Given any key, controlled scattering can be repeated to retrieve the stored pair.

The control is accomplished by developing a special function that operates on the keys of a table and produces an integer value between 0 and some upper bound. This integer is then used as an address (in an array, main memory, or auxiliary memory) and the key-value pair is stored in the "neighborhood" of this address. The function is called a scatter storage or **hash function,** the process is referred to as **hashing,** and tables implemented in this way are called **hash tables.**

The development of a hash function that uniformly scatters the key-value pairs throughout memory is a very difficult problem, because the distribution of keys is not usually known or if known, is irregular.

Because of the difficulty in spreading the pairs around memory, it is possible for two keys to be hashed to the same address. When this event occurs, some arbitration

IMAGINATION CHALLENGE

Goal Attending

1. Envision a goal: a desired behavior, a resolution to a current problem, or perhaps the completion of a task.

2. Set aside ten minutes before and after sleeping to experience this goal in your imagination.

3. Relax comfortably in your favorite chair with your eyes closed.

4. Imagine yourself having attained your goal here and now. Experience the behavior, resolution, or task as already attained. For example, if you wish to lose ten pounds, envision yourself *being* ten pounds lighter *now*.

5. Create a vivid and detailed image, adding something for all the senses. "If the imagination is vivid enough and detailed enough, your imagination practice is equivalent to an actual experience, insofar as your nervous system is concerned". *

6. Along with an intense sense of being in your image, imagine the positive feelings evoked by the realized accomplishment.

7. That's all there is. Don't dwell on the goal, don't make a time-table for achieving it, and don't constantly evaluate how you are progressing. Outside of your daily experience of goal-setting, stay in the here-and-now.

*Quote from *Psychocybernetics* by M. Maltz, Prentice-Hall, Englewood Cliffs, NJ, 1960. Activity taken from *Experiences in Visual Thinking*, 2nd ed, by R. McKim, Brooks/Cole Publishers, Monterey, CA, 1980.

policy is invoked to resolve what is commonly called a **hash clash** or **collision.** This is why I said earlier that the pair is stored in the "neighborhood" of the address, if not at the address itself. Ways of defining a neighborhood will be covered in detail later. In order to detect when a clash has occurred, we need to know whether a location in the table is available or occupied by a table pair. To accomplish this, the entire table is initialized with a special value. When a table entry is inserted into an available location this value is changed. If the table insertion operation is being performed, the location associated with a key's hash address is checked. When the special value is not found, another key pair has already occupied the location. This condition indicates the presence of a hash clash. It is very important to remember this hash table initialization step.

To illustrate this concept, let's assume that we are involved in a project of developing a PASCAL compiler for a new microcomputer system. One project task is keeping track of the information on each identifier. This information includes the data type and the physical address for each identifier name. We decide to accomplish this task through a hash table. Two reasons for this choice are the random order of the identifiers within the procedure body and the need for fast access to the information on request. We can construct the table before it is accessed because all the information is contained in the argument list of the procedure and in the variable declaration block directly after the *procedure* statement. This is a very convenient feature for the designer of a PASCAL compiler, if you ever wondered why you must declare all variables before you use them. For the purpose of translating your program to machine language, the identifier name serves as a key into the hash table and the table values are the data type and the actual memory address.

The first step is to decide on the size of the hash table and then to come up with a hash function that produces integers between 0 and the maximum for the table. It is a fair assumption that the procedure will not contain more than 200 identifiers, so let's reserve 200 locations for the hash table.

Now, how can we convert any identifier into an integer between 0 and 199 inclusive, repeatedly and reliably? Each identifier is a string of characters, and each character is represented by a special integer code. The standard codes for the ASCII (American Standard Code for Information Interchange) coding system used on many minicomputers and microcomputers is given in Figure 7.4. Each identifier can be transformed into an integer between 0 and 199 if we add the ASCII numeric code for the first four characters of the identifier together and then consider the sum modulo 200 (i.e., divide the sum by 200 and save only the remainder).

Thus the identifier SUM has the ASCII codes 83 85 77, which totals 245, which equals 45 modulo 200. So we can consider the identifier SUM to hash into the 45th location of the hash table. Figure 7.5 shows the table after a sample declaration block is processed.

So far everything looks great. The nine identifiers are sufficiently scattered around the 200 memory locations, and the same hash function can be used to retrieve the information without comparisons. We can be pretty proud of ourselves to have achieved such success on our first try, but you know that there must be more to the approach than this. Where can difficulties occur? Earlier in this section mention was made of an event called a hash clash—two keys having the same address. With the hash function that we developed, which two keys result in the same hash address?

Since we are only using the first four characters of the identifier, it should be easy to create a hash clash. The identifiers GROUP1, GROUP2, GROUP3, and GROUP4 all produce the hash address of 117 (71 + 82 + 79 + 85 MOD 200). Likewise, identifier R clashes with identifier FLAG, since they both have the hash address 82. If the

Figure 7.4

A	B	C	D	E	F	G	H	I	J	K	L	M
65	66	67	68	69	70	71	72	73	74	75	76	77
N	O	P	Q	R	S	T	U	V	W	X	Y	Z
78	79	80	81	82	83	84	85	86	87	88	89	90

Figure 7.5

```
procedure SAMPLE:
(* The identifiers in the declaration block
            will be placed in the hash table *)

var SUM , PAT , TOTAL : real ;
    I , J , IVAL , COUNTER : integer ;
  FLAG , MATCH : boolean ;
```

Identifier	Hash address
SUM	45
PAT	29
TOTAL	112
I	73
J	74
IVAL	100
COUNTER	109
FLAG	82
MATCH	93

Hash table array

	ID	Type	Memory address
0			
29	PAT	real	406
45	SUM	real	402
73	I	integer	414
74	J	integer	416
82	FLAG	boolean	422
93	MATCH	boolean	423
100	IVAL	integer	418
109	COUNTER	integer	420
112	TOTAL	real	410
199			

programmer adds these five new identifiers to the declaration block, our easy times are soon forgotten and the two terms *arbitration* and *neighborhood* come to the forefront.

Let's investigate three approaches to arbitrating a hash clash. One requires the use of more space and the other two require the use of more computer time while utilizing the unused space in the hash table. Each approach has its place in your toolbox of programming skills.

Arbitration through an Overflow Area

The first way that the clash can be handled is to set aside an overflow area, a separate array, or an extra 20 locations at the end of the array that holds the table entries. The overflow neighborhood is used for all keys that hash to a location that is already occupied by a different key. If a key and its value are being inserted in the table and the location in the table is empty, then the key-value pair can move right in. But if another key already occupies the indicated location in memory, the arbitration procedure must find an empty location in the overflow area. Thus, the neighborhood of an address can be defined as **the location associated with the address plus the overflow area.** When the value of a key is retrieved, its hash address is calculated and the neighborhood is searched for a key that matches.

This approach has the advantage of a simple arbitration policy and can work well if the number of hash clashes is small. It does require extra time for accessing the overflow area because the search will be restricted to either a linear or binary search algorithm. Another problem that requires special attention is the case when the overflow area itself overflows from too many clashes. In Figure 7.6, the five new identifiers have been added to the hash table, using the overflow arbitration method.

Arbitration through Rehashing

The next approach is based on reusing a good thing. If the hash function produces a hash clash, then another hash function is used to produce an alternate hash address. In this way the as-yet unused space in the hash table is used, since the alternate hash address provides an empty location in the hash table. The arbitration algorithm produces a sequence of alternate hash addresses until an empty location is found. (This is like having a sequence of forwarding addresses for someone who has moved five times in three months: "No, they don't live here but try this forwarding address.") In this case, the neighborhood is defined as **the sequence of hash addresses produced by the hash functions.** The number of hash functions that will be needed will be determined by the characteristics of the problem and the effectiveness of the functions chosen. A procedure to access the value associated with a key using three hash functions is given below; it assumes the existence of a procedure HASHSEQ that calculates the various hash functions given the search key and the hash function number to be used.

```
procedure SEARCH(var VALPOINTER:integer;SEARCHKEY:KEY_TYPE);
const MAX=3;
var HASH_ADD,HASH_FUNC:integer;
    FOUND : boolean;
```

```
begin
  FOUND := false;
  VALPOINTER := -1;
  HASH_FUNC := 1;
(* Calculate a sequence of hash addresses until
   the maximum number of addresses is calculated
   or the search key is found *)
  while (HASH_FUNC <= MAX) and not FOUND do
          begin
            HASH_ADD := HASHSEQ(HASH_FUNC,SEARCHKEY);
            if SEARCHKEY = TABLE[HASH_ADD].KEY then
                    begin
                      VALPOINTER := HASH_ADD;
                      FOUND := true
                    end
                    else
                    HASH_FUNC := HASH_FUNC + 1;
          end
end;
```

This approach requires more computation time to arbitrate clashes but utilizes the memory space more efficiently. We can now apply this approach to the compiler hash table problem. As an exercise, devise two additional hash functions to be used in the sequence and draw the hash table after the five additional identifiers have been added.

Arbitration through Probing

The third approach involves a technique called probing. When a hash clash occurs, the idea is to start at the hash address where it occurred and probe the area "around" this address in a systematic way until an available location is found. The probe must be systematic so that when the key needs to be accessed later, the same neighborhood around the original hash address is probed. During the probing operation, the contents of the neighborhood locations must be investigated to determine their status—occupied or available—which implies that the table was initialized as described earlier.

The three main probing styles are presented in Figure 7.7. Each style is described by enumerating the locations contained in a neighborhood of a given hash address. In all three cases, the table is to be considered circular, so that all neighborhood addresses are to be considered modulo the table size.

The three styles have different advantages and disadvantages. The linear style is simple to implement and guarantees that all locations in the array are investigated. It also causes keys with the same original hash address to cluster around this address in a densely populated neighborhood. To return to our compiler, the identifiers GROUP1, GROUP2, GROUP3, and GROUP4 would be placed in locations 117, 118, 116, and 119, respectively. If an identifier with a hash address of 118 is now encountered, it must be placed at the end of the newly created cluster. This becomes a serious problem as the number of table entries grows.

The quadratic style has a better spreading property and avoids clusters because each step is farther away from the last location probed. But it does not guarantee that

Figure 7.6

```
procedure SAMPLE ;
(* Identifiers R, GROUP1,GROUP2,GROUP3 and GROUP4
have been added to the block *)
var SUM , PAT , TOTAL : real ;
    I , J , IVAL , COUNTER : integer ;
    FLAG , MATCH : boolean ;
    GROUP1,GROUP2,GROUP3,GROUP4 : integer
    R : real ;
```

Identifier	Hash address
SUM	45
PAT	29
TOTAL	112
I	73
J	74
IVAL	100
COUNTER	109
FLAG	82
MATCH	93
GROUP1	117
GROUP2	117
GROUP3	117
GROUP4	117
R	82

Overflow area

	ID	Type	Memory address
GROUP2	integer	426
GROUP3	integer	428
GROUP4	integer	430
R	real	432

Hash table array

	ID	Type	Memory address
0			
29	PAT	real	406
45	SUM	real	402
73	I	integer	414
74	J	integer	416
82	FLAG	boolean	422
93	MATCH	boolean	423
100	IVAL	integer	418
109	COUNTER	integer	420
112	TOTAL	real	410
117	GROUP1	integer	424
119			

Figure 7.7

Probe style	Hash address	Neighborhood locations
Linear	a	$a + 1, a + 2, a + 3, \ldots$ $a - 1, a - 2, a - 3, \ldots$
Quadratic	a	$a + 1, a + 4, a + 9, \ldots$ $a - 1, a - 4, a - 9, \ldots$
Permutation	a	$a + P_0, a + P_1, a + P_2, \ldots$ where $P_0, P_1, P_2 \ldots, P_S$ is a permutation of the integers 0 to S, where S is the table size. Example: $P_0 = 4, P_1 = 8, P_2 = 9, P_3 = 6 \ldots, P_{10} = 3$

all locations in the table will be investigated during the probing process, so it is possible for all locations probed to be occupied while available locations exist. With this probing style, the four new identifiers in the compiler example would have been placed in locations 117 (GROUP1), 118 (GROUP2), 116 (GROUP3), and 121 (GROUP4).

The permutation style (also called random probing) ensures that all table locations are checked in searching for an available location after a hash clash. It requires either the storage of the permutation values or their recomputation each time a key that experienced a hash clash is accessed. It also has good spreading properties and eliminates the concern of clustering. With this style, the neighborhood concept loses any topological description.

In addition to these methods of handling hash clashes, methods exist for avoiding them by changing the organization of the table. We will now turn our attention to these methods.

Arbitration through Fixed-Size Buckets

Our first table organization was analogous to an apartment complex with single-family dwellings managed by a person (the arbitrator) who would find an empty apartment in the neighborhood of the one that you were assigned (hashed to) if it was already occupied. What if we build a new apartment complex, where each address is associated with a multifamily dwelling so that more than one family can use the same address though they each have different keys?

This new approach is called a hash table with **buckets.** Each bucket has a fixed number of slots (single-family apartments within the multifamily dwelling) with each slot holding one key-value pair. The hash address produced by the hash function refers to the bucket number. In this way, a fixed number of keys can hash to the same bucket without a need for any hash clash arbitration. Another advantage is that the neighborhood is sure to contain only key-value pairs that share the same hash address, something that cannot be said about the other methods of organization. One disadvantage that you may have noticed is that a number of slots within the buckets may stay unoccupied, hence constituting wasted space. This organization compensates for a hash function that results in numerous hash clashes. Figure 7.8 shows this organization for the declaration block of Figure 7.6. It uses three slots per bucket and can be implemented with a two-dimensional array of records.

Figure 7.8

Bucket number (hash address)	Slot 1			Slot 2			Slot 3		
0									
29	PAT	real	406						
45	SUM	real	402						
73	I	integer	414						
74	J	integer	416						
82	FLAG	boolean	422	R	real	432			
93	MATCH	boolean	423						
100	IVAL	integer	418						
109	COUNTER	integer	420						
112	TOTAL	real	410						
117	GROUP1	integer	424	GROUP2	integer	426	GROUP3	integer	428
199									

Bucket overflow area		
GROUP4	integer	430

In this example, identifiers FLAG and R share bucket 82 and have individual slots of their own. Also, identifiers GROUP1, GROUP2, and GROUP3 have filled bucket 117 and have produced a bucket overflow event for identifier GROUP4. The figure suggests a solution for this event by setting aside an overflow area for all key-value pairs that came too late to squeeze into a popular and populated bucket. This solution is similar to the one used for our original table organization, and the arbitration and access policies are the same.

The two other techniques for handling hash clashes, a sequence of hash functions and probing, can also be used to handle bucket overflow events with the same advantage of utilizing space that is already reserved for the table anyway. The possibility of key-value pairs that have different hash addresses sharing the same bucket would then have to be considered as an acceptable characteristic of this organization.

Using the bucket organization depicted in Figure 7.8, let's look at a procedure that enters a new key-value pair into the table. The input arguments to the procedure will be the key and its value, and the output argument will be an error flag in case the key is already in the table. I will assume that two functions exist, HASHFUNC to calculate the bucket number given the key and EMPTY to test whether a table location is unoccupied. I also assume that there is a procedure that will enter the key-value pair in the overflow area.

```
procedure ENTERPAIR (KEY:KEY_TYPE; VAL:VALUE_TYPE;var ERROR:boolean);
(* This procedure inserts a new table pair into a hash table
   with a bucket organization.
   GLOBALS : the array that holds the table *)
const NUMBEROFSLOT=3;
var BUCKET, SLOT:integer;
    FOUND:boolean;
begin      (* Calculate hash address=bucket number *)
    BUCKET := HASHFUNC(KEY);
(* Initialize slot number and flag for successful insert *)
    SLOT := 1;
    FOUND := false;
(* Until all slots are searched or until empty slot is found *)
    while (SLOT <= NUMBEROFSLOTS) and (FOUND = false) do
      if EMPTY (TABLE[BUCKET,SLOT]) then
              (* Empty slot found, insert pair *)
              begin
                TABLE[BUCKET,SLOT].KEY := KEY;
                TABLE[BUCKET,SLOT].VALU := VAL;
                FOUND := true;
                ERROR := false
              end
          (* Occupied slot,check for duplicate key *)
          else if TABLE[BUCKET,SLOT].KEY = KEY then
                  (* Duplicate key found-error *)
                  begin
                    ERROR := true;
                    FOUND := true
                  end
                  (* Prepare to look at next slot *)
                  else SLOT := SLOT + 1;
      (* CHECK FOR BUCKET OVERFLOW *)
      if not FOUND then OVERFLOWINSERT (KEY,VAL,ERROR);
end;
```

As you can see from Figure 7.8, many buckets went unused because no key-value pair was hashed to them or only one key-value pair was present. At the same time, one bucket, number 117, encountered an overflow event. Both of these conditions are a consequence of having fixed-size buckets. The next table organization removes this constraint and provides a bonus that is difficult to obtain with the previous two organizations.

Arbitration through Linked List of Buckets

If instead of having fixed-size buckets, the number of slots is determined by demand, then some buckets can have no slots while others have four, and all buckets can have another slot if a new key hashes to the bucket. To accomplish this new organization, an available pool of slots will be needed, and some maintenance routines (à la Bruce) to manage the available pool must be available. As before, we can use the linked list concept and consider each bucket to be a singly linked list. This enables a bucket to have from zero to many slots and allows easy insertion or deletion of a key-value pair into a bucket. With this organization we are assured that only keys with the same hash address are present in the hash address neighborhood (the linked list) and therefore no unnecessary comparisons will be made. Each hash address will need a list header to point to the first slot in the linked bucket or to indicate that no key-value pairs have been entered in the bucket. An illustration of this organization using the declaration block of previous examples is given in Figure 7.9.

This organization produces considerable advantages for accessing a table structure. First, only the relevant key-value pairs are investigated when looking for a particular pair, that is, the keys that share the same hash address. No real arbitration policy is needed when a hash clash occurs; it is necessary only to take an empty slot from the available pool and add it to the linked bucket pointed to by the hash address header. Insertions can be made to either the front or the end of the linked list or, if the list is ordered (by frequency of accesses, for example), in the proper position in the list. The table has little unused space in itself (though the available pool constitutes an expense traded for the extra flexibility).

One problem that was not mentioned previously is table overflow, when all locations in the table are occupied with key-value pairs and a new pair needs to be entered. In this situation, the first two organizations are pretty much at a stalemate. If the operating system allows dynamic reallocation of space then the table size could be enlarged by adding additional buckets, but then a new hash function would have to be used and all pairs would have to be rehashed. With the variably sized bucket organization, more space can be added to the available pool of slots and the process continued with no additional changes.

An important advantage that can also be realized if the need arises is the ability to easily delete a key-value pair from the table. In our example of keeping a table of identifiers for the compiler, this operation does not occur. In other applications, though, it could become a possibility. Since the ease of deletion is a characteristic of the linked list, the variably sized bucket organization inherits this advantage.

There are two drawbacks to using this organization. One is the extra storage space required for each link field. This is usually offset by having few unused slots in the table. Another is the extra routines needed to maintain the available pool of slots. These increase the expense of the implementation in program development time,

Figure 7.9

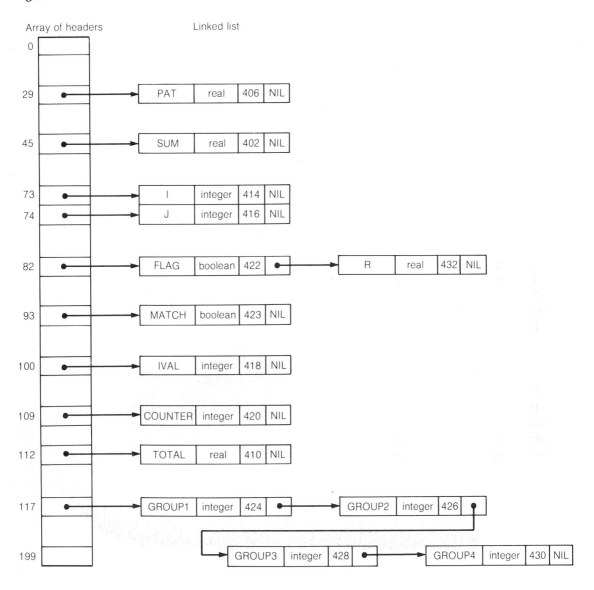

storage space for the routines, and execution time. The main drawback involves the access process of looking for a particular value of a given key. Once the hash function produces the hash address and the pointer to the first slot is retrieved, the efficiency of the access depends on the size of the bucket (i.e., the length of the linked list). Since the only search algorithm for a linked list is the linear search, if the lists are long then the efficiency of direct access—one of the main goals of hashing—is seriously impaired. It thus becomes particularly important to select a hash function that generates a minimal number of hash clashes.

TRADE-OFFS

Leaving the Neighborhood

The deletion of a table entry from a hash table can affect the reliability of the access strategy. The determining factor is the arbitration method. Let's compare the effect of a deletion operation for each of the following arbitration methods. An integral part of each comparison is whether or not the neighborhood concept is corrupted for keys with the same hash address and other keys.

Arbitration through an Overflow Area
If the deletion is made from an overflow area then the neighborhood concept is preserved by shifting the entries in the overflow area forward one location. However, if the deletion is from the hash table itself and the location is flagged as available, then a corruption may occur. Any access to a key that previously clashed with the deleted key is lost. A solution is to recalculate all the hash addresses in the overflow area. If a table pair is found with the same address then it takes the deleted table pair's place. Otherwise, the location is flagged as available.

Arbitration through Rehashing
The deletion of a key when rehashing is used also results in a corrupted neighborhood. In fact, more than one neighborhood may be corrupted, since one location can be a part of different rehashing sequences with different original hash addresses. Therefore, flagging the location as available can result in multiple misinterpretations during table access. The solution is to establish another flag as a part of the location. This new flag indicates that the location is unoccupied and available, but was previously occupied. During an access operation, the flag directs continued searching. During an insertion operation, the flag means that a table pair can be inserted in the location.

Arbitration through Probing
With probing, deletion of a table pair is similar to the case of rehashing. Multiple probe-ways may be corrupted if the location is flagged as available. The solution is the same—a flag that says the location was previously occupied but is now available.

Arbitration through Fixed-Size Buckets
The deletion operation has an effect similar to the first technique presented, the overflow area. If the deletion occurs in the bucket overflow area then a shifting process will resolve the problem. If, however, the deletion is made from one of the slots in the bucket then a different solution is needed. By shifting the succeeding slot entries forward, checking the overflow area for a table pair to fill the newly vacated last slot, and shifting the overflow area if necessary, the bucket neighborhood is preserved. Hence only one flag is needed to indicate the available or occupied state.

Arbitration through Linked Buckets
This method requires no adjustment other than deleting the table pair from the linked bucket with standard linked-list routines. The neighborhood—the linked list of tables pairs—remains intact. This method is therefore the preferred approach for tables that experience frequent deletions and insertions and can afford the extra space for the link field.

Hash Function Considerations and Selection

The choice of a hash function should take two factors into consideration. First, the function should possess the quality of computational efficiency—it should be easy to execute on the hardware available. This is important because the speed of accessing the hash table is the prime goal of the hashing technique. The hash function's second and most difficult requirement is the ability to provide a normal, unbiased distribution of hash addresses, given an unknown and possibly biased collection of keys. The degree to which this characteristic is realized, and the hash clash handling techniques used when it is not realized, are prime determinants of the effectiveness of the implementation.

Two features of the structure of keys must also be taken into account before selecting a hash function. First, the data type of the key is important. If the key is numeric, designing a function to produce an integer value (the hash address) is an easy task. If the key is of character type, some conventions must be developed to interpret the character string as a numeric value before the function is applied. This idea was demonstrated in our example where the identifiers of the declaration block being used as keys were converted to numeric values by way of the ASCII code.

The second feature is the way in which keys are represented in the computer's memory. If we consider the word to be the unit of storage for numeric data types and the byte to be the unit for character data types, a distinction should be made between multiword (multibyte) and single-word (single-byte) keys. With most hash functions the hash address is produced from a single word, and therefore multiword keys must in some way be coalesced into a single word before the function can be applied. In our example, this was done by adding the individual ASCII codes for the first four bytes of the multibyte key to produce a numeric value. For numeric keys a popular method is called **sum-of-digits,** where the digits are summed and this single value becomes the argument for the hash function. Use your improved imagination to design other techniques to combine the multiple parts of a key into a more convenient unit.

Another word (actually, multiword) of advice is to select a function that is not based on only one part of the key. For instance, the lower digits of a number are less random than the rest, so a hash function that depends only on the lower digits is likely to produce more clashes. Also, similarities among a number of keys can result in a larger number of hash clashes. This is highlighted by what happened with identifiers GROUP1, GROUP2, GROUP3, and GROUP4 in our example. By focusing on only one part of the key, our objective of an even distribution of hash addresses is impaired. A hash function should try to reflect the influence of all parts of the key equally.

Figure 7.10

Modulo division	Equals	Word modulo table size
		Example: 0011001010101101 mod prime number
Midsquare	Equals	Word times word anded with mask
		Example: 00100100 × 00100100 yields
		0010100010000 anded with
		0000111111110 yields
		10001000 equaling
		136 (base 10).
Folding	Equals	Divide word into sections
		and add or exclusive OR sections
		Example: 0110101110001100 divided into
		01101 011100 01100 XORed yields
		011101 equaling
		29 (base 10).

With this advice, let's look at some hash functions in Figure 7.10.

Modulo Division. Our previous example showed how the technique of **modulo division** works. With this approach, the single-word value of the key is divided by a constant, and the remainder is used as the hash address. This method gives very good results for different key collection profiles ranging from randomly distributed to slightly related. Experience has shown that selecting a prime number close to the desired table size as the divisor produces the best distribution and the fewest hash clashes, on the average.

Midsquare. The **midsquare** approach multiplies the single word key value by a constant value or by its own value. When the word is multiplied by itself, all parts of the word contribute to the result, thereby reducing any bias toward one part of the key. The resulting product, interpreted as a hash address, is usually larger than the needed table size (a 16-bit word would allow 65,536 possible hash addresses). So a midsection of the result is snipped out and used as the hash address. For example, the calculations below show the single-word key 642 squared; the overflow outside of 16 bits is ignored and a midsection of eight bits is removed to derive a hash address of 120.

```
       642          0 0 0 0 0 0 1 0 1 0 0 0 0 0 1 0
    ×  642          0 0 0 0 0 0 1 0 1 0 0 0 0 0 1 0
   ──────          ─────────────────────────────────
   412164          1 1 0 0 1 0 0 0 1 1 1 1 0 0 0 0 1 0 0
                     └─overflow        └─midsection
```

$$0\ 1\ 1\ 1\ 1\ 0\ 0\ 0_2 = 120 = \text{hash address}$$

Calculate the hash addresses for 641 and 643. How close are they to the hash address of 642?

The size of the midsection will determine the range of hash addresses available, so with this technique the table size is usually selected as a power of two. One word of caution! Some languages check for overflow and terminate execution when it occurs. Thus assembly language–level hash functions may be necessary.

Folding.   For single or multiword keys, the **folding** technique can be used. In this procedure the key is partitioned into separate parts, the parts are combined, and the result is used as the hash address. The parts may be added together with any over-flow ignored or they can be exclusive-ORed, a faster operation for the hardware to perform. Once again, assembly language will be the appropriate level on which to develop this type of hash function.

Hybrids.   Hybrid hash functions can be designed to suit the needs of the application. In our compiler hash table example, we used sum-of-digits to reduce the mul-tibyte character key to a single byte and then we performed modulo 200 division to produce a hash address within range. This is a standard method to scale down the larger range produced by other technique.

Another hybrid operation is performing a shift-and-rotate operation on the single-word key value before applying either the midsquare or modulo division technique. This ensures that all parts of the key contribute to the randomizing character of the hash function.

Well, the choice is yours, to be tailored to the needs of the application and the capa-bilities of the language and the hardware used. I hope all these words have helped to thoroughly mix up your keys without mixing you up in the process.

■ **"JUST FOR REFERENCE"**

In the linear approach to table implementation—

- a linear array is used to store table pairs
- keys may be ordered or unordered in the array
- the access algorithm is either linear search (unordered keys) or binary search (ordered keys)
- addition/deletion of keys is not practical

In the layered approach—

- the table is divided into specific sections
- an index table contains keys and pointers to sections of the table
- the keys indicate the bounds of the section of table entries
- the approach requires the keys to be ordered
- the access algorithm involves searching the index table and then searching the indicated section; both search operations can be binary searches

TRADE-OFFS

The performance trade-offs between the three arbitration techniques—linear probing, rehashing, and linked buckets—have been studied by numerous researchers. Results obtained by D. Knuth and Severance/Duhne are illustrated below. The independent variable is the hash table's loading factor. This quantity is the ratio of table pairs in the table to the number of locations in the table. A loading factor of 0.5 means that half of the available locations are occupied.

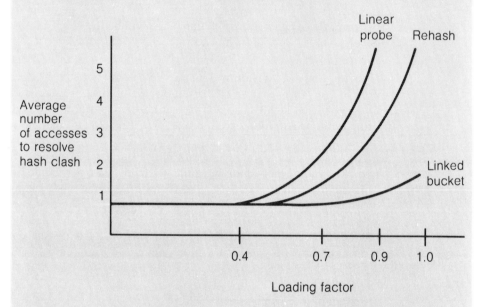

The diagram illustrates some important points. All arbitration methods perform equally well for low loading factors. Therefore, if you can afford to allocate a lot of space relative to the number of keys then any of the three methods is a valid choice.

The increase in accesses required by the linear approach between 0.4 and 0.7 is a result of clustering beginning to occur. As the loading factor approaches 1.0, the linear probe technique behaves like a linear search in an array of table pairs.

The smaller increase in accesses of the rehashing technique between 0.4 and 0.7 indicates that it avoids clustering by accessing the table further from the collision location. However, in the range of 0.9 to 1.0, the rehash technique becomes like a "stab in the dark", a pseudorandom search for a free location. This technique is a valid choice for loading factors less than 0.8 when you want to avoid the linked bucket approach because of the extra storage for the link fields.

The linked list technique performs well across the entire range of loading factors. This makes sense since the "search" for an available location only requires an access of the linked list of available records.

- the number of layers of index tables can be increased to reduce the size of the sections

In the scatter storage approach—

- hash functions use keys to generate an address
- key-value pairs are stored in the neighborhood of the address
- hash clashes occur when two keys have the same hash address

Arbitration techniques for hash clashes include—

- establishing overflow area for all keys that clash
- probing a neighborhood for the nearest empty location
- Using a sequence of hash functions for alternate addresses
- Using buckets with a fixed number of slots
- Using buckets with a linked list of slots

Hash functions should—

- exhibit speed of execution and good distribution of keys
- use all parts of the key to generate the address

Sample hash functions include—

- modulo division using a prime number close to table size
- midsquare technique using bit representation
- folding to include all parts of the key
- hybrid combinations of the above

EXERCISES

1. Using the record description given in subsection 7.3.1, write a linear search procedure on a table of ordered keys. State the condition that indicates that the search has failed although more keys are available for consideration.

2. Assume that a table is organized as an index table with 26 entries, with each of the 26 sections containing 40 table pairs. Calculate the number of comparisons involved in a single access to the table for the following combinations of search techniques.

Search technique on table section

	Linear	Binary
Linear		
Binary		

Search technique on index table

3. The indexed sequential method in subsection 7.3.2 identified the limits of the table sections by using two pointers from the index table. Discuss the ramifications of having the index table point to the first entry in the table section and

   a) The first entry contain the number of entries in the section.

   b) The first entry contain a pointer to the last entry in the section.

4. Draw a diagram of the index sequential organization of a typical operating system file system.

5. Assume that a dictionary table is organized as in Figure 7.3. Write a procedure that accesses the definition of a given word. Create all declarations and state all conventions.

6. Explain how the hash table implementation is a generalization of the array information structure. What are their similarities? In what ways is the hash table a more flexible structure?

7. Write the access algorithm for a hash table that arbitrates a collision by using:

   a) an overflow area

   b) rehashing using three functions

   c) buckets with four slots

   d) linked buckets

8. Assume that a hash table is implemented using an overflow area for hash clashes. How would deletion be implemented?

9. Develop the algorithm for adding an element to a hash table in which clashes are handled by probing the neighborhood in a quadratic way.

10. Using a linear probe arbitration yields one definite advantage that is not present with the quadratic probe style. What is this advantage for the linear probe? Is there a way to add this advantage to the quadratic probe?

11. Assume the definitions below for two additional hash functions. Place the keys of Figure 7.6 in the hash table using the rehashing arbitration technique. Draw a diagram of the new arrangement in the hash table.

   Function 1—Add the ASCII codes of the characters of the identifier and interpret the sum as a modulo 200 value.

   Function 2—Add the ASCII codes of the odd-numbered characters, subtract the ASCII code of the even characters, and interpret the absolute value of the result as a modulo 200 value.

   Function 3—Multiply the ASCII code of the first and last character of the identifier and interpret as a modulo 200 value.

12. For each of the following implementation approaches, describe the impact of deleting a table entry. How is the access operation affected? Is it still valid? What changes are necessary to ensure reliable access? The arbitration approaches are as follow:

   a) sequence of hash functions

   b) quadratic probe

   c) buckets with five slots

   d) buckets with linked slots

13. What two characteristics of hash functions are important to consider to ensure an efficient implementation of the hash table?

14. To aid the scattering of keys, a hash function should include all parts of the key in the calculation of the hash address. Describe a general method to incorporate this feature into a hash function.

15. Given that each key is expressed as two bytes in ASCII code, calculate the hash address of each of the following BASIC language identifiers by using the midsquare technique presented in subsection 7.3.3: DB, C2, AQ, ZU.

7.4 Applications

"Apleekayshuns"—A Spelling Checker

Let's consider an application in which the table information structure is used in two different ways. We have all used word processors to create text files—files of words separated by punctuation delimiters. We have also scanned these files word by word looking for the misspelt (oops!) misspelled word. Let's design a spelling checking system that uses a file of correctly spelled words as a source for checking the spelling of each word in our text file. A number of design considerations will present themselves and the selection of appropriate information structures will be necessary.

The design will be presented in stages. The first stage is to specify the objectives of the system. Our system will:

1. Compare the words in a text file to the words in a a file of correctly spelled words.

2. Create a list of words that do not match any word in the file of correctly spelled words.

3. Allow users to review the list of words that did not match and indicate which are misspelled.

4. Locate the misspelled words in the text file and allow users to change the spelling.

An ambitious set of objectives, indeed.

A number of information structures will support these objectives. Let's begin with the first objective—comparing the text file to a list of correctly spelled words. We must be careful in order to accomplish this task efficiently. We do not need to check the spelling of words that have already been checked. To ensure this we can build a word tree, a binary tree of words that occur in the text file. As we build the tree duplicate text words can be ignored. Why do we use a binary tree? We need a structure that offers easy insertions and a fast access time; deletions are not of concern. All of these features lead us to choose the binary tree. As a further enhancement, we can implement it as a height-balanced tree to ensure the fast access time predicted for binary trees. We can also include threads to facilitate processing all the nodes by a nonrecursive traversal. These are some options to weigh.

Therefore, as a part of objective 1 we will process the text file word by word and add words not yet encountered to the word tree. Words that are already in the tree will be ignored.

The second part of the objective involves the use of a table structure. How do we efficiently check a text word against all the words in a file of correctly spelled words?

Let's refer to this file as the correct word file. We will set up a hash table containing all the correctly spelled words. When we want to check a text word for spelling, we calculate its hash address and see if it is in the hash table. If it is, then it's correctly spelled. If it is not, then we can suspect it is misspelled. (We are not sure, though, since it could be a correctly spelled word that is not in our correct word file.)

Why is a hash table a good selection? First, the words do not have to be sorted in order to access the table quickly. Second, once the table is set up, it is not changed—it is only accessed. Third, the hash table provides the fastest access time of any structure (if good decisions are made concerning the hash function, the arbitration method, and the loading factor for the table.)

Therefore, objective 1 can be expanded to the following steps:

1. Input text file and build binary tree of text words—word tree.
2. Input correct word file and build a hash table—correct word table.
3. Traverse word tree and hash text word into the correct word table.
4. If word is not in the correct word table then add it to a list of suspected misspelled words.

Step 4 links the first objective to the second, generating a list of possible misspelled words. By repeated executions of step 4, the list of words that may be misspelled is created. The information structure to support this objective also supports the last two objectives, allowing the user to review the suspect list and changing misspelled words in the text file. Thus we want an information structure that we can insert data elements into easily (objective 2), that can be processed sequentially (objective 3), and that helps us locate these words in the original text file (objective 4).

To satisfy these requirements we will set up an indexed sequential table structure. Why? A bit more detail may clear up the question. The words will be linked together in a doubly linked list to allow for sequential access and easy insertion. The index table will be used to facilitate quicker access to the linked list. Now for the magic: the linked list will be ordered by the page and line numbers where the word appears in the text file. These data can be captured when the word tree is built and can be included in its node structure. Such an ordering will help with objective 4. Thus our index table will consist of page numbers and pointers to the nodes in the linked list. The pointer will indicate the first word on a given page that is suspected of being misspelled. Figure 7.11 shows a sample of the index sequential structure. Let us refer to this structure as the suspect table.

Step 4—generating the list of suspected misspelled words—can be expanded to:

i. Use page number of suspected word to access the suspect table.
ii. Use the pointer in the index table to locate the first word suspected of being misspelled on the page.
iii. Use the line number of suspected word to locate the correct position in the doubly linked list.
iv. Insert the new node into the doubly linked list.

Figure 7.11

Node structure for linked list of words

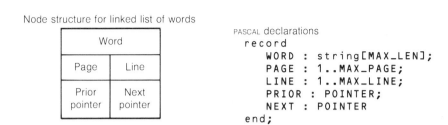

PASCAL declarations
```
record
    WORD : string[MAX_LEN];
    PAGE : 1..MAX_PAGE;
    LINE : 1..MAX_LINE;
    PRIOR : POINTER;
    NEXT : POINTER
end;
```

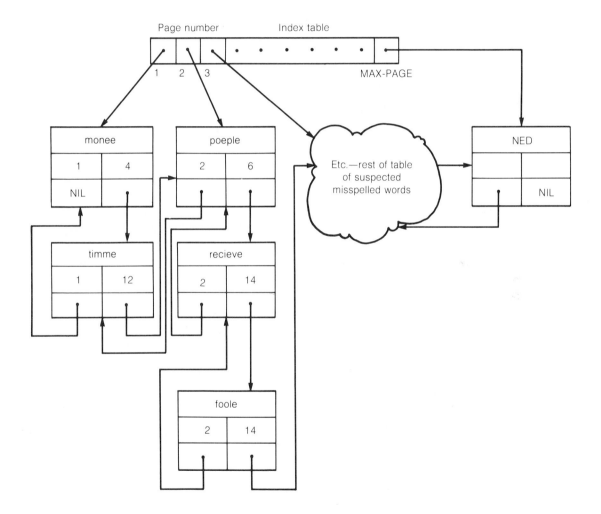

Objective 1 uses three information structures—a binary tree, a hash table, and an indexed sequential table. Figure 7.12 presents the node structures for each of these.

The third objective (user review) involves an interactive interface with the user. The indexed sequential table will be processed sequentially and some words will be deleted from the table—those that are correctly spelled but are not present in the correct word table. This will almost always happen, since the correct word file cannot be comprehensive for all text files.

An enhancement to our system would be to allow the user to add these words to the correct word file. This is not a difficult task. As we delete them from the suspect table we can insert them into another information structure. We can later ask the user if he wants to add them to the correct word file.

What information structure is appropriate for this purpose? There is no need to order the words, and there is no need to delete a word from the structure. In fact, the only operations are inserting into the structure and sequentially processing all the words when adding them to the file. Either a linear array or a singly linked list (actually a linked stack) will suit our purposes—a simple structure to support an attractive enhancement. Let's refer to this as the correct word list.

At the completion of objective 3 we will have an indexed sequential table, ordered by page and line number, of user-specified misspelled words. The last objective—correcting the original text file—can then be tackled. The text file can be read one page at a time. The index for the page directs us to a linked list of misspelled words. A field in each node directs us to a line on the page. The word in the linked list being processed is then compared to each word in the line. When a match is found, the user is queried for the correct spelling. This continues for all misspelled words on the given page. When this is done, the next page is read. The process continues until the last page is corrected. At this time the last objective is fulfilled.

The spelling checker system therefore depends upon the following information structures:

- *Word tree*—A binary tree of text file words. The tree is built using an alphabetic ordering (optionally in-threaded and/or height-balanced).
- *Correct word table*—A main memory hash table using a sum-of-characters method to coalesce the text word into a single integer. A midsquare hash function is used to generate the hash address. Arbitration of hash clashes is through a linked bucket technique.
- *Suspect table*—An indexed sequential table of words that are either misspelled or not in the correct word file. The table entries are ordered by the page and line number of the text word. The suspected words are sequentially stored in a doubly linked list. The index table contains page numbers (maximum of 40) and pointers to the first word suspected of being misspelled on the page.
- Correct word list—A list of suspect words that are judged by the user to be correctly spelled.

    Using these newly defined terms, the spelling checker system design can be summarized as follows:

1. Input text file and build word tree.
2. Input correct word file and create correct word table.

Figure 7.12

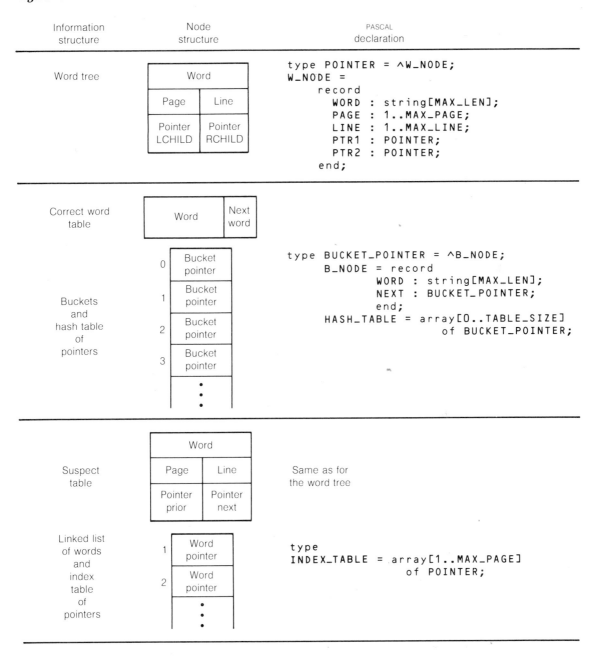

Information structure	Node structure	PASCAL declaration

Word tree	Word / Page / Line / Pointer LCHILD / Pointer RCHILD	`type POINTER = ^W_NODE;`
		`W_NODE =`
		`    record`
		`        WORD : string[MAX_LEN];`
		`        PAGE : 1..MAX_PAGE;`
		`        LINE : 1..MAX_LINE;`
		`        PTR1 : POINTER;`
		`        PTR2 : POINTER;`
		`    end;`

Correct word table	Word / Next word	

Buckets and hash table of pointers	0 Bucket pointer / 1 Bucket pointer / 2 Bucket pointer / 3 Bucket pointer	`type BUCKET_POINTER = ^B_NODE;`
		`    B_NODE = record`
		`            WORD : string[MAX_LEN];`
		`            NEXT : BUCKET_POINTER;`
		`            end;`
		`    HASH_TABLE = array[0..TABLE_SIZE]`
		`                of BUCKET_POINTER;`

Suspect table	Word / Page / Line / Pointer prior / Pointer next	Same as for the word tree

Linked list of words and index table of pointers	1 Word pointer / 2 Word pointer	`type`
		`INDEX_TABLE = array[1..MAX_PAGE]`
		`                of POINTER;`

3. Traverse word tree and
    if text word is not in correct word table then
    insert text word into the suspect table.
4. Allow user to interactively review all the words in
the suspect table and indicate if words are
correctly spelled.
    If the suspected word is correctly spelled
    then delete word from the suspect table and
      insert it in the correct word list.
5. Ask user if the correct word list is to be added to
the correct word file.
    If yes then update file.
6. Sequentially traverse the suspect table and locate
misspelled word on the corresponding page and line of
the text file. Allow user to correct the spelling of
the text word.

We have completed three phases of the development of our system:

1. Listing of objectives.

2. Selection of information structures.

3. Top-level design of the system in terms of the information structures and the objectives.

What is our next step? Stepwise refinement of the top-level design. The expansion of step 1—building a word tree—is an adaptation of building an alphabetically sorted tree. Since we have done this before, this is left as an exercise for the reader. A new feature of this task is determining the limits of the individual words in the text file. By defining a word as the characters between punctuation delimiters, you will be able to parse the text file, extracting the text words. Your next decision involves enumerating the punctuation delimiters. Period, comma, and space are obvious ones; tabs and carriage returns are more subtle—take some time composing the set.

The refinement of the second step in the system design involves building a hash table of correctly spelled words. The following pseudocode is our next refinement.

Algorithm to Build the Hash Table—Correct Word Table

Initialize locations in hash table to available status.
Read word from correct word file.
Repeat until end-of-file on correct word file:
    Coalesce characters of word into an integer value
      by summing their ACSII numeric codes;
    Calculate hash address of the integer value
      using the midsquare technique;
    If location associated with hash address is available
    then store WORD in location and change status to occupied
    else add word to linked bucket neighborhood;
    Read word from correct word file.

Within this pseudocode, three steps will be expanded—coalescing, calculating midsquare, and adding word to neighborhood list. These are left as exercises. Upon their completion we can move to the third step. The following pseudocode brings us a step closer to our goal.

Algorithm to Traverse Word Tree, Check Spelling, and Create the Suspect Table

Initialize pointer P to the root of the word tree.
If P is not nil then
        Traverse left subtree of root P;
        Check spelling of text word pointed to by P and return a SUCCESS flag;
        If not SUCCESS then
            Add text word to suspect table;
        Traverse right subtree of root P.

This algorithm needs two refinements. Checking the spelling of the text word will necessitate accessing the correct word table. Using the two modules developed when the hash table was built, the spelling check step is expanded to:

Algorithm to Check Spelling of a Text Word in the Correct Word Table

Let TEXT _ WORD equal the word field of the node pointed to by P.
Let WORD _ AS _ NUMBER equal the sum of the ASCII codes of TEXT _ WORD.
Let HASH _ ADDRESS equal the midsquare of the WORD _ AS _ NUMBER.
If the location associated with the HASH _ ADDRESS is available
    then set SUCCESS flag to false
    else if word at the HASH _ ADDRESS equals TEXT _ WORD
        then set SUCCESS flag to true
        else search the linked bucket attached to the HASH _ ADDRESS location
            and set SUCCESS flag accordingly.

This algorithm follows the conventions of the table organization and either succeeds or fails in finding a match. Failure does not mean that the word is misspelled, only that it is not in the correct word table. We now add it as a suspected misspelled word to the suspect table—the second refinement to the algorithm for checking the spelling of the text word.

We want to add the text word to the indexed sequential table. Recall that the index table is ordered by page number and contains pointers to the first suspected word on the page. These words are ordered by line number within page number and contained in a doubly linked list. The algorithm for adding a text word to the suspect table follows:

Let P equal the page number of the TEXT _ WORD.
Let L equal the line number of the TEXT _ WORD.
Let LOWER _ PTR equal the pointer associated with the Pth
    entry in the index table.
Let UPPER _ PTR equal the pointer associated with the next
    entry in the index table.
If LOWER _ PTR equals nil then
        Find first non-nil pointer, FIRST _ PTR, in the index table after the Pth entry.
        If successful then

Add TEXT _ WORD before node pointed to by FIRST _ PTR
else Find first non-nil pointer, FIRST _ PTR, before Pth entry
If successful then
Add TEXT _ WORD at end of list
else Add TEXT _ WORD as only word in the linked list;
else
Using the LOWER _ PTR as the beginning of the list
and the UPPER _ PTR as the end of the list of words for page P,
locate the correct position in the list based on the line number;
insert TEXT _ WORD into the doubly linked list at the
correct position.

These two refinement algorithms—checking the spelling and adding the text word to the suspect table—combined with the traversal algorithm for step 3 bring us close to the detail step of coding procedures in PASCAL (or whatever language is selected). This detailed work is left to you, the junior programmer of the project.

The next operation in the system design is to allow the user to indicate which text words in the suspect table (processed sequentially as a linked list) are actually misspelled and which were simply unknown to the correct word file. The steps for performing this operation are standard linked list processing algorithms. The design and implementation of the next level is a challenging assignment for the diligent junior programmer. As exercises, design the next level of refinement and develop the code to implement the algorithm.

The fifth step in the top-level system design is the optional expansion of the correct word file by adding the correct word list. This is a simple operation and as such is another assignment that the system designer would farm out to others in the project group.

The final step in our system design is an exercise in string processing. It will involve reading into main memory a page at a time. Each line is then considered. Each word in the line can be compared to the misspelled words in the suspect table for that line or each word in the suspect table can be compared to the words in the corresponding line. Which approach is more efficient? Consider the two options and choose the one that seems to give the fastest average performance. The algorithm for this final step is left as another assignment to a now overcommitted junior programmer. At this point I will end the presentation of the application involving the table information structure. Much work and detail design are left to produce a software product in which we can place our confidence.

This apleekayshun (oops!) application provided an excellent vehicle for presenting the two most important table information structures. The hash table provided a structure with a fast access strategy. The indexed sequential table contributed its ability to access individual table elements relatively quickly, and its ability to access the entire table sequentially. By storing the table as a linked list we were able to perform the insertion and deletion operations efficiently. It also gave us the opportunity to see the enormous advantage of the top-down design strategem and the working of the stepwise refinement tool.

Well, being the system designer was fun for me. Your help as junior programmer was invaluable. With some years of experience and twists of fate, perhaps someday the tables will turn and you will be assigning others tasks that you have designed.

■ "JUST FOR REFERENCE"

Information structures for the spelling checking system included—

- word tree—a binary tree of text file words built using an alphabetic ordering (optionally in-threaded or height-balanced)
- correct word table—a main memory hash table using a sum-of-characters method to coalesce the text word into a single integer. A midsquare hash function was used to generate the hash address and arbitration of hash clashes was through a linked bucket technique
- suspect table—an indexed sequential table of words that are not in the correct word file. The table entries are ordered by the page and line number of the text word and the suspected words are sequentially stored in a doubly linked list. The index table contains page numbers (maximum of 40) and pointers to the first word suspected of being misspelled on the page
- correct word list—a list of suspected words that are judged by the user to be correctly spelled

Top-level system design for the spelling checking system—

- input text file and build word tree
- input correct word file and create correct word table
- traverse word tree and if text word is not in correct word table then insert text word into the suspect table
- allow user to interactively review all the words in the suspect table and indicate if words are correctly spelled. If the suspected word is correctly spelled then delete word from the suspect table and insert it in the correct word list
- ask user if the correct word list is to be added to the correct word file if yes then update file
- sequentially traverse the suspect table and locate misspelled word on the corresponding page and line of the text file. Allow user to correct the spelling of the text word

EXERCISES

1. Write a procedure that inputs a text file and builds a word tree with each node containing the word, the page number, and the line number of the word's appearance in the text.
2. Write a procedure that coalesces the characters in a text word into a single integer value by adding the sum of the ASCII codes.
3. Write a hash function that uses the midsquare technique. Assume that the table will have 16K locations.
4. Write a procedure to implement the algorithm for adding a text word to the suspect table.
5. Develop an algorithm that allows a user to correct the spelling of the words remaining in the suspect table.

6. After the word tree is used to check the spelling it is no longer needed. Write a procedure to return all the nodes to the available pool.

7. Write the algorithm to traverse the word tree and check the spelling by using the correct word table, assuming that the binary tree is in-threaded.

8. The spelling checker has a flaw! If a user consistently misspelled a word throughout the text (such as "recieve"), what happens? Since duplicate words are ignored, only the first occurrence of misspelled words is recorded. Now that you have been promoted from junior programmer to system designer, alter the design so that all occurrences of suspected words are recorded.

THE WORKOUT ROOM

PROJECT 1: *ISAM Minisystem*

Assume that you have a file of 1000 records stored on a disk. The records contain student information and are ordered by a five-digit student identification number. The file occupies a number of cylinders on the disk. The first track of the first cylinder contains a cylinder index table that indicates the highest student ID number contained on a cylinder. The student records on a cylinder are stored on various tracks of the cylinder, with more than one record per track. Each cylinder contains a track index table. This table indicates the highest student ID number contained on a particular track. The records are stored sequentially on the individual tracks. Thus each record is retrievable through a cylinder number–track number pair. By way of the two-layer index tables the section of records that contains the desired one can be investigated. This organization is referred to as the indexed sequential access method (ISAM).

Write and test a small ISAM system that provides a user-friendly interface for these file operations:

1. Access a student record.

2. Insert a student record.

3. Delete a student record.

To simulate the disk file, you can use a two-dimensional array.

PROJECT 2: *What Is Your Cosmic Hash Address?*

Yes, another information structure project has just arrived and has been decoded by the inverse message mucker. It seems to say that we don't know where the @!$* we are, there seems to be a strange smoke hovering all around us, and we have lost our orientation in both time and space. So, cosmic kid here's hoping that you can find the cosmic traveller's hash address.

In an input file you will find 100 names that have been delivered by a cosmic messenger, Ray. You are to read the names in this file and calculate their hash address using the four methods specified below:

1. Modular division—divide word by 4096.

2. Midsquare—multiply the word by itself and use bits 15 through 4 for the address.

3. Folding—partition the word into three parts, bits 31–21, bits 20–10, and bits 9–0, and add the three parts for the address.

4. Hybrid—set $h = 37$ and repeat for each character in the name: $h = h * \text{ASCII (character)}$ MOD 4096.

On an output file print the 4 hash addresses. Calculate the number of hash clashes produced by each function and include this information in the output file.

    A final message from our messenger, cosmic RAY: *"Life's end is just a change in your cosmic address."*

INSIGHTS WITH DR. DIGITAL

Scene: *Outside of Dr. D's office, Waldo and Wilma are waiting for him. Waldo is paging through the book* Learn to Think. Experiences in Visual Thinking *rests on top of Wilma's information structures notebook.*

Waldo: What does your time watching machine say, Wilma?

Wilma: That Dr. D is late by 8¾ minutes. He's probably answering a load of questions before tomorrow's test.

Waldo: I hope that he has a few answers left. After looking at this book, I feel like a Trivial Pursuit addict: each question manufactures more.

Wilma: Are the questions about info structures?

Waldo: No, Dr. D lent me this book on a thinking method. It consists of a collection of thinking skills or operations which can be used in problem solving. They're pretty PIE.

Wilma: What! Pretty pie? Have you lost your crackers, Waldo? Or has Moon Zappa zapped your mind?

Waldo: Awesomely not! It's my acronym for the thinking method: Penetrating—Interesting—Expansive. You see, Wilma, all the skills have acronyms, like

CAF, AGO and C&S. For instance, CAF means "consider all factors." When faced with a situation, you apply the CAF operation first. The outlook is on discovery—you examine the situation and list as many factors as you can think of, without regard to their importance or to your likes and dislikes. The operation is expansive—you see the situation in a larger frame of reference.

Wilma: Sounds like CAF involves the fluency concept that we learned about in Experiences in Visual Thinking. The quantity of factors is important. Let's see . . . the key was, "Let the judge go on vacation," à la Dr. D.

Waldo: Right on! Let's give CAF a go. Remember last week when we covered critical path analysis? What were the factors involved in the implementation?

Wilma: Each task had various measurements to be calculated. Access to both predecessors and successors was important. The mark field was needed. No changes in the graph structure were made during the analysis. The storage for all the pointers was considered. Certain parameters, like the completion time of the project, influenced the calculation of other measurements. Some algorithms progressed from start to finish, others moved from finish to start task.

Waldo: Good—you've got the CAF by the staff, so to speak. The more factors you see, the more clearly you see.

Wilma: How about the other acronyms? Knowing what S&M is, I'm a little hesitant to ask what C&S is.

Waldo: Oh, how tempted I am to pull your arm and twist your leg on that one! This operation is similar to CAF, except for the time frame. "Consequences and sequels" are factors that may develop in the future as a result of an anticipated action. The objective of this skill is to list the future impact of an action or idea.

Wilma: Oh, like—what would happen if all high schools required students to take a sequence of thinking courses?

Waldo: Exactly and more expansively. What are the immediate consequences? Where would the teachers come from? What thinking methods would be taught? What about long-range effects? In 20 years, would the public be equipped with sufficient thinking power to vote on every piece of legislation through the home computer information utility? Would our society approach the idea of Plato's utopian state? So in C&S, we expand the factors time-wise and effect-wise.

Wilma: Combining CAF and C&S covers a lot of ground, especially since quantity is the criterion.

Waldo: And once the ground is covered, you can apply PMI to the results of both operations. You take one of the factors or consequences and list the Plus points, the Minus points, and the Interesting points. The advantage of this operation is that you force yourself to see both sides and the middle of the road, rather than looking only at what you like.

Wilma: Sounds like you examine an idea rather than judge it—like a conceptual

surgeon friend of ours does when considering an information structures implementation. Can we do a PMI on an idea?

Waldo: Sure! Consider the last factor you mentioned: Some critical path algorithms progress from finish to start, others from start to finish. Give a P point!

Wilma: The structure of the algorithms were similar. I found this positive because it helped me understand the algorithms.

Waldo: Okay, now an interesting point.

Wilma: It was neat how the mark field was used to determine when all the successors were processed.

Waldo: That's a great one! Focus on an M point.

Wilma: Hmm . . . The need to go both directions required a lot of link fields and a linked lists of tasks. That was an expensive factor.

Waldo: As Dr. D would say, "you have PMI well in hand, in mind, and in your tool kit."

Wilma: GFM!

Waldo: What's that?

Wilma: Good for me! Okay, Dr. Waldo, teach me another tool.

Waldo: Let's see—oh yeah, along with factors and consequences, you can also consider the purpose of the action, idea, or solution. The skill that involves purpose is called AGO—aims, goals, and objectives. Its purpose is to penetrate the idea and list the varied purposes behind it. For example, list some objectives of this action: the Department of Education requires all school districts to provide thinking courses to high school students.

Wilma: Obviously to improve the abilities of the students. To procure government funds for innovative programs. To bolster the sagging academic performance of high school students. To provide the prerequisite skills for students entering the computer age. To increase the . . .

Waldo: You've passed that assignment with flying collars. Once you've added AGO to CAF and C&S, you have a broad picture. The next thinking skill begins to refine the picture, to produce a finer focus. FIP can be applied after any of these operations. It is a general-purpose tool like PMI. What's important is *importance*. Given a list of factors, which ones are important, which are trivial? So you rank the items in the list on a scale of 0 to 10 and consider the first five, or whatever, first.

Wilma: So FIP stands for *f*ive *i*mportant *p*arts?

Waldo: How about *f*irst *i*mportant *p*riorities? Good try, though. One point to remember is that there are no absolute choices, since this is a judgement activity. We could change the important AGO and the important factors and consequences would change. Do you understand that?

Wilma: Sure—when I stream into the Artic Ice Cream Station, mocha fudge can win out even with four other favorite flavors teasing my taster, but tomorrow mocha fudge could be a second stringer. This method is pretty PIE, as you acronymed: you expand the picture with the AGO, CAF and C&S skills, you pinpoint interesting and important aspects with PMI and FIP, and combining them, you penetrate the situation to a new level of understanding.

You know, Waldo, these skills seem pretty LB—left-brain analytical activities. Are there any thinking operations that use the right hemisphere functions, like the ones presented in Experiences in Visual Thinking?

Waldo: You've perceived correctly, Wilma. This method is predominantly a left-brain strategy. If I recall correctly, in the diagram of strategic choice given by McKim, either a left-brain or right-brain strategy can be selected. This method is definitely one of the former. However, it does include some right-brain functions. The operations of APC and OPV both benefit from an active imagination. The APC skill is designed to explore *a*lternatives, *p*ossibilities, and *c*hoices. So you exercise the imagination to come up with the not-so-obvious choices. Equally apt to the use of imagination is OPV—*o*ther *p*oints of *v*iew—"Imagine yourself in my socks and shoes." By shifting points of view, new factors, consequences and objectives spring from nowhere. The focus is changed from self-view to we-view and the awareness of the network of life's relationships is awakened.

[Dr. D's image emerges around the corner.]

Dr. D: Well, hello—sorry I'm late. Hopefully, you have used the time to some advantage.

Wilma: With such a scholar as Waldo, it was a piece of pie filling the . . . 36.4 minutes. [As they enter the office -]

Dr. D: So, how can I help you two? Waldo, what's your query?

Waldo: Earlier I had quite a few but actually they've seemed to have answered themselves before you arrived. Here's the Learn to Think book. Thanks and BBYB. [Waldo turns to leave.]

Dr. D: BBYB?

Wilma: "Buddha be your Buddy!"

8

Sorting Structures

*The most magical word
in one's vocabulary is **if**.
It tickles the imagination.*
—Dave Clay

8.1 Assorted Comments

The operation of arranging items into an ordered array or in an orderly way is frequently performed in our homes, our offices, and our minds. The dishes in the cupboard are organized for easy access. The megalibrary of computer manuals in our bookcase alphabetically await our questioned search. Our minds sort and pigeonhole the day's experiences so that we can retrieve the thoughts and feelings associated with a key event. All of these activities share the motives behind the sorting process—the need to arrange related items to facilitate speedy access.

Chapter 7 discussed table organization and access. Two approaches required that the keys be sorted—the linear approach using a binary search and the indexed sequential approach. In these cases, the sort operation can be used as a preprocessing step to prepare for table access operations. Another reason for having a sort utility is that a list must sometimes be ordered using a different field than the original key. For example, a list of students names may be reordered by student number. Such situations occur frequently in information management systems. Since the sort operation is applicable to such varied situations, it is a common utility program in many operating systems.

With such a potentially active role, the selected sort algorithm can affect the efficiency of access to the table, of information management, or of the operating system. To evaluate sorting algorithms, the three areas to consider are the same as for all algorithmic choices: (1) the time required to program the algorithm, (2) the amount of space used by the procedure, and (3) most important, the amount of time required to execute the procedure on a given data set. Threading these three factors together are the related ideas of the anticipated size of the data set and the frequency of execution of the procedure. When the efficiency function of these five variables is applied to two sort algorithms, the results may be surprising. In some cases, your elegant algorithm will shine, but in others, the Cinderella version wins the prize.

What advice can I offer you in the sort algorithm sweepstakes? Let the brain co-op share the load. Know the features of each algorithm with your left brain—know your tools! Know the potpouri of interrelated factors with your right brain—know the environment in which the tools are to be used! Use your imagination to weigh the advantages and disadvantages of each tool. And then, . . . use your judgment to select the appropriate algorithm for the present challenge.

In this case, knowing your tools means knowing the steps in the algorithm, obviously, and having a measure of its performance. Two methods are used to evaluate the performance of sort algorithms. In fact, these two methods are used more generally to rate algorithms of various types. They reflect the left brain/right brain dichotomy. The first method prepares a number of sample data sets and then runs the program using each set. Performance is measured either in the number of instructions executed or in the actual time required to perform the task. Other algorithms can be evaluated in the same way and the measurements compared. In this way, the files serve as **benchmarks** and each algorithm is rated in terms of its performance with the benchmark data. This experiential, right-brain approach doesn't guarantee that the relative ratings are preserved when a new nonstandard data set is used. It also places a large emphasis on the creation of benchmarks in order to instill us with some degree of confidence in the performance measures. For instance, a collection of data sets for the sort algorithm would include a perfectly sorted list (best case), a completely unsorted list (worst case), and a random list (typical case).

The other method relies on analysis, a left-brain function. By studying the algorithm mathematically, independently of a computer language or computer system, a measure of its response to increasing amounts of data can be derived. This measure is called the **computational complexity** of the algorithm. The analysis yields a proportionality operator, reflecting the ratio between the number of data elements processed and the number of steps required to process them. For example, the PASCAL code below has a linear proportionality operator:

```
for I:=1 to N do
      writeln (A[I]);
```

As the number of array elements increases, the number of operations increases linearly. If the array increases from three to six elements, the number of *writeln* operations also doubles. An increase from three to nine elements yields three times as many operations. By contrast, the PASCAL code

```
for I:=1 to N do
   for J:=1 to N do
         writeln (Z[I,J]);
```

has a different proportionality operator. As N doubles, say from three to six, the number of operations increase from nine to 36, a factor of four. An increase of three, from three to nine, yields 81 instead of nine operations—a factor of nine. Here the proportionality operator is the square of the increase in the number of data elements.

Algorithms of more complexity are analyzed in this manner as the data size continues to grow. At some point the asymptotic proportion is reached. (This process is similar to the limit process of integral calculus and convergent series.) A formal treatment can be found in the book, *The Design and Analysis of Computer Algorithms* by Aho, Hopcraft, and Ullman.* For our purposes, we will use the proportional operators to rate the various sort algorithms without justifying why an algorithm merits its rating. Others before us have done the hard work, so we can now appreciatively use their results.

A special notation is used to indicate the proportionality operators. The linear operator is expressed $O(n)$, read as *"of order n,"* while $O(n^2)$ refers to the proportionality operator that demonstrated a squared relationship, expressed as *"of order n^2."* Hence an algorithm that is of order n^2 may experience a 25-fold increase in execution time for a fivefold increase in the number of data elements. Other proportionality operators exist. For our purposes, the important ones will be $O(n^2)$ and $O(n \log n)$, where the base of the log function is two.

All the algorithms that we shall see are designed to run on a single computer system. With the gigantic leaps made in multiprocessor systems, new algorithms are constantly being developed, tested, and evaluated. The evaluation method will also need to develop an improved strategy for keeping pace with new technology and new algorithms. Sort algorithms will have a new dimension (or two), with multiple operations occurring simultaneously in different parts of the multiprocessor. Questions of how to measure the performance of such algorithms will challenge someone's imagination—maybe yours.

*Addison-Wesley, Menlo Park, CA, 1974.

INSIGHTS WITH DR. DIGITAL

Scene: *Dr. D is walking back to his office with Wilma after a test on sorting structures.*

Wilma: My sights were set for a good performance and I feel pretty right-on about the experience, Dr. D.

Dr. D: I see that you've been using your powers of visualizing to achieve goals—that's good mind programming. It's good to see you getting in touch with the mind's power.

Wilma: Thanks, Dr. D. Oh, you just reminded me of something—actually your words "mind programming" did. I recently saw a flyer for a workshop on neurolinguistic programming. Do you have any feel for this? Is it a software technique?

Dr. D: Actually, I do have a sense of the NLP model. My neighbor is a clinical psychologist, Dr. Susan Porter. One day at her home, I saw a book with "programming" in the title and it tickled my interest. We talked about NLP at length. Software it is not—more like headware. She supplied some fascinating information for my biocomputer to process.

Wilma: What does it deal with? I'd like to grasp the basic concept, to see what it's about.

Dr. D: One basic idea is concerned with the representational systems that people use to think and communicate. For instance, your statement just illustrated two of them. Your language (linguistic) implies the thinking system (neuro) that you prefer (programming). You used the phrase "to see what it's about." This means that your perspective was the visual system—you easily access information in images.

Wilma: Oh, that's interesting. What other ways do humans represent their thinking process?

Dr. D: Okay, let's see. [He pauses, looking up and to the left.] As I recall, auditory representation is another primary way of expressing our experiences.

(Suddenly, a couple of taps on the open door are heard—Waldo is standing comfortably in the doorway.)

Dr. D: Well hello, Waldo. How goes it with you?

Waldo: Life is playing my tune. Sorry about the eavesdropping but this NLP stuff sounds intriguing. Can I join the human interface that you two have set up?

Dr. D: Sure. In fact, your timing is near-perfect. Wilma, do you recall what Waldo just said?

(Looking straight ahead—Wilma's eyes drift to the left.)

Wilma: Yes, I remember most of the sentences—why?

Dr. D: What representational system is Waldo's biocomputer running under?

Wilma: Oh, wow—he was auditory: "playing my tune" and "sounds interesting." I see the connection—my language indicates a visual perspective and his says that he's auditory.

Waldo: Is that good? Who's better? I didn't like her tone.

Dr. D: It is not a matter of who's better but a matter of difference. The difference is especially important when you are involved in a communication—a "human interface" as you call it. Similarly in computer communications—two computers may operate using different representational systems, ASCII versus EBCDIC.* To facilitate the communication, both systems are supplied with communication interfaces. The

same is true with you and Wilma. If you two are working on a group software project and she "sees the big picture" while you "hear the actors in the play," then you may not both be able to discuss changes in the "project picture" or the "project script" unless you adjust to each others representational system.

(Wilma and Waldo look at each other and then glance down to the right.)

Dr. D: So you both feel the impact of the difference?

Waldo: How did you know that I was feeling guilty about not relating to Wilma lately?

Wilma: Wow, Dr. D, I was imagining what it would be like to get in touch with Waldo's thoughts.

Dr. D: The NLP model says that your eyes indicate how you are accessing your experience database. You both entered into the kinesthetic system—the third primary system.

Waldo: That's when we get in touch with how we felt about an event?

Wilma: Or how we might feel about an imagined event?

Dr. D: Clear as a bell or a cloudless day! Both of you are right on! You both switched from visual or auditory to the kinesthetic model of accessing your data base. The goal is to achieve an integrated data base in which all three channels are available for communicating with people effectively.

(Wilma's eyes drift down and to the left and Waldo is looking skyward and to the right.)

Waldo: Dr. D, imagine if we had necklaces that light up when we are generating visual images. Oh, how easy communication would be.

Dr. D: [smiling] I see your point. Body language is already broadcasting the message. Trained observers can read your mental processing and tell with which system your biocomputer is on-line. For instance, look at Wilma [a pause]. She is having an internal auditory experience—a dialog with herself. Her eyes speak!

Waldo: She looks like she's in a trance.
Dr. D: As the developers of NLP might say, a trance-formation. She may be reprogramming a past experience by saying what she wishes she had said. Now her mind, which doesn't care whether an imagined or real mental image is recalled, will have a

choice if a similar event should occur.
Waldo: Sounds like a powerful system, this NLP. ** I can see myself using it to enhance my communications with others and with myself. Feels like a perfect fit, this headware. (*Dr. D taps Wilma on the arm and she looks at them with a magical smile.*)

*Extended binary-coded decimal interchange code.

**Neurolinguistic programming books: *Frogs into Princes*, John Stevens ed. Real People Press, Moab, UT, 1979; *Structure of Magic I, II*, by Bandler and Grinder. Science and Behavior Books, Palo Alto, CA 1975; *Trance-Formation*, Connirae Andreas ed. Real People Press, Moab, UT, 1981; *Reframing*, by Bandler and Grinder. Real People Press, Moab, UT, 1982.

8.2 Assorted Algorithms

The collection of algorithms presented in this section cover a large spectrum of approaches. They range from the easily programmed to the recursively programmed, from the slow to the fast, from the brute force to the clever. Each algorithm's purpose is to sort a collection of records into an ascending sequence based on the key value.

Each algorithm will be presented via pseudocode with accompanying explanation and comments. Some will include a PASCAL procedure to implement the algorithm using appropriate information structures. Algorithms for which procedures are not presented are left as exercise challenges to the reader.

8.2.1 SORT ALGORITHMS OF $O(n^2)$ PERFORMANCE

The first three algorithms present the selection, insertion, and bubble sort techniques. They share a common measure of performance, $O(n^2)$, and are straightforward programming activities. For tables with 200 elements or fewer, these algorithms provide sufficient power to accomplish the task.

Selection Sort Algorithm

The principle used in the selection sort is similar to the playground game King of the Mountain, in which the best player is selected from the group and occupies the highest spot in the field.

The algorithm refines this process by applying the principle to the remaining group of $n - 1$ elements until there are no elements left to play the game. So the selection sort algorithm involves two phases: a search for the smallest element in the group and an exchange between the smallest element and the current element in its appropriate position. The pseudocode is given below. The notation *R[i]* indicates the *i*th record, with the record containing the key value upon which the ordering is based.

for $i = 1$ to $n - 1$ do
    1. Search for the smallest key among the
        keys $R[i], \ldots, R[n]$.
    2. Exchange the smallest key with $R[i]$.

The following sequence of interchanges would be experienced by the six keys:

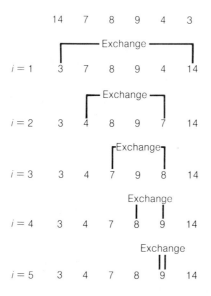

An important point to notice is the amount of record movement. There are $n - 1$ pairs of records exchanged. If the size of each record is large, the time needed to perform the exchanges can become prohibitive. At that point, an option can be considered. Instead of a table of records, you could create a table of pointers to the records. When an exchange occurs, only the pointers are moved and the records remain unaffected. Therefore, the table of pointers is rearranged to produce an ascending sequence of keys and their associated records. This adaptation can be applied to all the sort algorithms presented. You can stash it in your programmer's tool kit for later use. Throughout the remainder of this section, I will assume that the record size does not merit the use of our newly acquired tool. But I feel confident that it will not go unused when you begin applying your skills in your career.

Insertion Sort Algorithm

If you have ever played card games such as bridge, canasta, pinochle, or gin rummy then you have applied the insertion sort algorithm. When you arrange the cards by suit and then by values, you select a card, say the six of hearts, and insert it into its correct position among the already sorted hearts. You then select the next card in the unsorted group and insert it into its correct position. This process continues until the last card is placed in sequence. The algorithm is easily expressed below:

```
for i = 2 to n do
        Shift R[i] forward (toward R[1])
        until  R[j] < R[i] for some j, 1 ≤ j < i.
```

This algorithm divides the table into two groups—the sorted portion (the first i elements) and the unsorted $n - i$ elements. The shifting process is accomplished by repeated exchanges of adjacent pairs of elements. The PASCAL procedure to implement this algorithm is presented below. A few simple declarations set the scene.

```
type KEY_TYPE : (* as required by the application  *)
     RECORD_TYPE :    (*    ditto    *)
     RANGE : 1..N;
RECORD_NODE = record
                KEY : KEY_TYPE;
                REC_VAL : RECORD_TYPE;
                end ;
var    R : array [RANGE] of RECORD_NODE;
procedure INSERTION_SORT;
var I,J; RANGE;
    T : RECORD_NODE;
begin
for I:=2 to N do
      begin
        J:=I;
        while (R[J - 1].KEY > R[J].KEY) and (J > 1)  do
              begin
                T := R[J];
                R[J] := R[J-1];
                R[J - 1] := T;
                J := J - 1
              end
      end
end;
```

An improvement that can be added to this technique is to apply a binary search method to the task of locating the correct position of the record to be inserted. This is possible since the first i elements are already ordered, a prerequisite for the binary search. The exchange process is the same; the improvement comes in the number of comparisons needed to locate the correct spot for the next key.

Bubble Sort Algorithm

The last sort algorithm of $O(n^2)$ uses a feature of the the previous algorithm. By repeatedly comparing and, if necessary, exchanging adjacent pairs, the keys slowly "bubble" forward to their correct positions. Repeated passes through the list of keys will eventually produce the sorted sequence. Two features improve the performance of the algorithm. First, after any pass the list may go flat. By this I mean that no more bubbling occurs—no exchanges happen. This implies that all pairs are sorted and therefore the list is also sorted. The second point is that after the first pass the smallest element (or the largest, depending on the direction of flow) has bubbled to the top and henceforth need not be considered. Thus the second pass need only check

IMAGINATION CHALLENGE

Counting Your Vitamins

Take an opened bottle of vitamins and estimate the number of tablets present. Repeat the following process four times. Pour some vitamins in your hand without looking. Glance very briefly at the vitamins arranged in your hand. Do not count them—only capture the image. Now look at your other hand and reproduce the image of the vitamins. Now count them. Write down the count each time. When you are done, compare the sum of the four "sightings" with the original estimate and with the number determined by actually counting all the tablets. Take a vitamin while you think about the process and how you can improve your performance.

---

the second key through the last key. This property applies to each successive pass.

As an exercise, write a bubble sort algorithm that incorporates the above-mentioned features. Develop a formula that predicts the maximum number of comparisons used by the algorithm to sort n keys into ascending order. Compare the formula and the order of the algorithm.

8.2.2   SORT ALGORITHMS OF O (n log n) PERFORMANCE

The next algorithms provide better performance measures, are more complicated to express, and involve more interesting information structures. Some of them also exhibit some peculiar responses to either worst- or best-case data sets. We will see the tree sort, heapsort and quicksort.

Tree Sort Algorithm

We have already seen this algorithm in the discussion of trees in Chapter 5. This algorithm was used to build a binary tree based on the principle "less than—go left, greater than—go right." In this way, all elements in the left subtree are less than the root element and the elements in the right subtree are greater than the root element. The algorithm for creating a sorted tree from a list of elements is given below.

```
      for each list element do
   1.    if tree is empty then make list element the root
            else
            while a tree element exists do
                if list element is less than tree element
                    then move to the left child of tree element
                    else move to the right child of tree element
   2.    attach list element to last tree element encountered
```

TRADE-OFFS

A most intriguing sorting algorithm was developed by D. L. Shell in 1959, called Shellsort. Its other label, based on how it operates, is the diminishing increment sort.

The idea of this sort is to perceive a list as a group of sublists based on a given increment. For example, a list of 50 elements using an increment of ten would be seen as:

Sublist 1   {1st, 11th, 21th, 31th, 41th element}
Sublist 2   {2nd, 12th, 22nd, 32rd, 42nd element}
.
.
.
Sublist 5   {10th, 20th, 30th, 40th, 50th element}

These five sublists are then each sorted by using the insertion sort algorithm. The same array is used; the sublists exist only in how they are processed.

Next, the selected increment is diminished. The amount of decrease involves some trade-offs. If you decrease rapidly, such as choosing an increment of three, there will be fewer passes (since an increment of one is used for the last pass), but each pass requires more time (more sublists). Selecting an increment of seven means that more passes are made overall but the number of sublists are smaller and the insertion sort finishes more quickly.

Once a selection is made, the sublists are again sorted by the insertion sort. Eventually, the increment diminishes to one and the total list is compared by the insertion sort. By this time, most of the list elements are in their final resting position; few if any interchanges occur.

Determining the computational complexity of the Shell sort is difficult. No absolute formula has been accepted. Various estimates for different sequences of increments have been published. One important result was D. Knuth's finding that using a sequence of relatively prime increments produces a performance that is $O(n(\log n)^2)$.

By using various benchmark files the Shell sort has exhibited a performance that is of $O(n^{1.25})$. Using either method of measurement, the Shell sort outperforms its inspiration, the insertion sort.

Also intriguing is the adapting of the insertion sort to the sublist idea. Are you up to the challenge? Go for it!

Two aids are available to improve the efficiency of this sort algorithm. The shape of the tree structure affects the operation. For instance, if the list to be sorted is by chance already in order, the tree structure is equivalent to a linked list. It can be shown that sorting n elements using a linked list yields an algorithm that is $O(n^2)$. Therefore, for the tree sort the best-case data set produces $O(n^2)$ performance instead of the average $O(n \log n)$.

Does Bruce's magic come to our aid here? No, it is the AVL (height-balanced) property. By building a height balanced tree (depth of subtrees differs by at most one), the shape of the sort tree ensures the desired $0(n \log n)$ performance. This is easy to illustrate. How many comparisons are needed to sort n elements using the tree sort algorithm? The discussion goes something like this: n elements times the average number of comparisons to position one element is equivalent to n elements times the depth of the balanced tree, which in turn is equivalent to n times ($\log [n + 1] - 1$), since the depth of the full binary tree is the log base two of the number of tree elements plus one less one (since depth counting begins at zero).

As n grows larger the constants loss their significance and the number of comparisons is on the order of $n \log n$. By preserving the AVL property, the sort algorithm gains consistent performance throughout the spectrum of possible data sets.

During the sorting process the second performance aid can be included. Once the elements are sorted and stored in the tree information structure, a tree traversal is needed to produce the ordered list. What can you find in your programmer's tool kit to facilitate this operation? Is your mind a mass of cobwebs or do you remember a friendly spider? Correct! Pull out a spool of silver threads and create an in-threaded, height-balanced tree to implement the tree sort algorithm. By attaching the threads as you build the tree, you get the benefits of a height-balanced tree structure for the sort operation and the benefits of a linked list (through the threads and link fields) during the traversal operation. An imaginative collaboration, indeed!

An interesting enhancement to this approach is to generalize the AVL binary tree structure. The generalization of a binary tree is a **multiway search tree.** The m-ary search tree (as it is called) has the property that each node has at most m children and the elements of each sibling subtree pair are relatively ordered. By this I mean that all the elements in the leftmost subtree are less than the elements in the next rightmost subtree. Each nonleaf node contains the pointers to its children and the key values that segregate the elements of its subtrees. Refer to Figure 8.1 to impress this idea on your right hemisphere. The extension of the AVL property to the m-ary search tree yields the B-tree. The B-tree of order m is an m-ary search tree which satisfies the conditions:

1. The root has at least two children, or it is the only node in the tree.

2. Each node has between m DIV 2 and m children, except for the root and the leaf nodes.

3. All leaf nodes are at the same level.

Figure 8.1 depicts a B-tree of order 4.

With this setup, each nonleaf node has a set of pointers and key values that segregate the elements of the subtrees into disjoint, relatively ordered sets. This arrangement is reminiscent of the index table for the indexed sequential table organization. By preserving condition 3 above, the sorting and access operations on a B-tree have a stable and efficient performance.

The alternatives for implementing the tree sort algorithm are varied and interesting. As an exercise, select the alternative that stimulates your adventurous nature and develop a PASCAL procedure to implement the adventure.

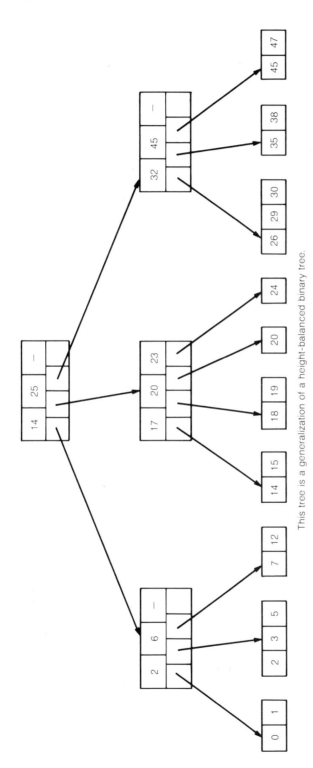

This tree is a generalization of a height-balanced binary tree.

Figure 8.1

HEAPSORT Algorithm

The next $O(n \log n)$ sort algorithm is also based on the tree information structure. The idea behind the heapsort algorithm is to have a "very balanced" binary tree that exhibits a "partial ordering" property. Let's look at this structure one step at a time. What does a "very balanced" binary tree look like? Figure 8.2 presents two versions.

When every possible child at the maximum level is present then the tree is termed **full.** When only children on the right side of the maximum level are missing then the tree is called **complete.** We will be working with complete binary trees for this algorithm.

When the node value of each parent node is greater than or equal to the node value of its children then the tree nodes are **partially ordered.** This produces a transitive relationship among direct descendants but does not indicate any ordering between siblings of a parent node. The complete tree of Figure 8.2 is partially ordered, while the full tree does not possess this property.

The important consequence of using a partially ordered tree is that the largest element is the root of the tree. Combine this with the fact that removing the rightmost leaf node from a complete binary tree yields a smaller but still complete binary tree and you have the secret of the heapsort's success. With the magical ingredients exposed, let's get on with the potion.

We begin by designating a **heap of size n** to be a partially ordered, complete binary tree with *n* elements. Assuming that we are given a list of elements to sort then our first step is to create a heap. The algorithm to accomplish this task will be presented shortly. Once this step is accomplished the following algorithm produces a descending sequence of key values:

Figure 8.2

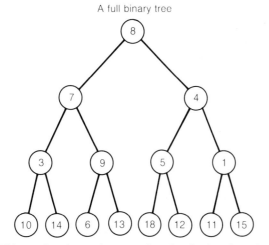

A full binary tree

This tree has the maximum number of nodes for a tree of level 3. No ordering among the nodes is present.

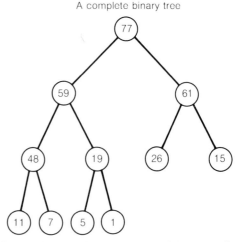

A complete binary tree

This tree is almost full, except for the right most nodes. This tree is partially ordered and is therefore a heap.

```
while a tree exists do
        Remove key value from root of heap (store or print it).
        Copy key value of rightmost leaf node to root of heap.
        Delete rightmost leaf node.
        Adjust the tree to become a heap.
```

The sequence of key values that are removed provides the desired ordering. The largest key value is removed first (since the heap is partially ordered). The next largest becomes the root in the process of returning the smaller and still complete tree to heap status. Continuation of these steps ensures that all key values become the root at the appropriate time. You should note that by storing the key values, either a descending or ascending sequence can then be printed.

To complete the algorithm, let us determine how the last step is accomplished. The partial ordering property may no longer be valid. What is necessary to reestablish it? Let's look at an example.

The tree of Figure 8.3a has just been changed, with the value of 6 moved to the root position. By checking the children of the root, the validity of the partially ordered principle can be checked. Since the parent node is less than one of its children, a change is necessary. By determining the larger-valued child, the parent and the left child are exchanged (Figure 8.3b). Don't stop here without checking the node's new children. If the new children are both of lesser value than the parent, the heap is restored. In this example, one more exchange is required, (Figure 8.3c). Since the node has no children to check after the second interchange, the adjustment is complete.

Therefore, if we start with a heap and apply the algorithm then we end up with a sorted list. How do we get to the starting point? With an unsorted list in our hands, what transformation produces the original heap? Let's give the following algorithm some inspection.

```
if the tree is empty then
        make the first list element the root of the tree.
while list elements exist do
        1. Add next list element to rightmost leaf position.
        2. While added list element is greater than its parent
                and added list element is not the root do
                        exchange position of added list element and its parent.
```

This algorithm adds each list element in a position that ensures the completeness property of the tree. After the tree insertion, it moves the newly added key value up the tree until its parent has a larger key value. This ensures the partially ordered property. Each iteration results in a heap structure, so each insertion simply adjusts the ordering as needed. You may be a bit uneasy with the algorithm, since it moves up the tree from child to parent. All the tree implementations that we have seen are designed to go from parent to child. Do not fear, this is about to change!

As you begin to visualize an implementation scheme for the heapsort algorithm, you see that a special tree structure has been used—the complete binary tree. You also notice that a specific location on the tree has a crucial role—the rightmost leaf node. During the entire algorithm, you are working with a complete binary tree to which additions and deletions revolve around the rightmost leaf node position.

Figure 8.3

a.

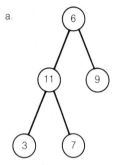

A new root node value changes
the partial ordering.

b.

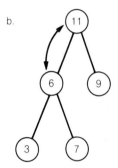

Parent/child relationship
interchanged: larger of the two
sons is used.

c.

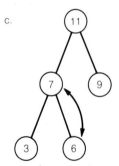

Interchange continues until the
ordering is reestablished or a leaf
node is interchanged.

Is there an implementation of a complete binary tree that provides easy access to this crucial location, in addition to providing the standard access to the left and right child from a parent and the nonstandard access from a child to its parent? The answer to this question is as simple as counting 1, 2, 3. If the nodes of a complete binary tree are numbered as shown in Figure 8.4, then the tree can be stored as a sequence of nodes in an array. The number assigned to each node is its subscript value for the array.

With the sequential representation of a complete tree, the desired accesses are achieved through the use of the following formulas:

Figure 8.4

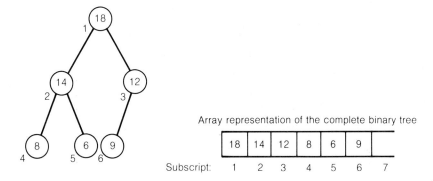

Array representation of the complete binary tree

18	14	12	8	6	9	

Subscript: 1   2   3   4   5   6   7

The nodes of the complete tree are numbered from left to right and from level 0 to the highest level. This number is the subscript in the array representation.

Access:	From	To	Formula
	Parent	Left child	2 * I where I is subscript of parent
	Parent	Right child	2 * I + 1 where I is subscript of parent
	Left child	Parent	J/2 where J is subscript of left child
	Right child	Parent	(J − 1)/2 where J is subscript of right child
		Rightmost leaf	NIT where NIT is the number of elements in the tree
		Next available rightmost leaf position	NIT + 1

With this scheme, which depends on the completeness attribute of the tree, and the algorithm presented earlier, we are ready to tackle the heapsort procedure. Let's assume that the original list has been transformed into a heap and stored in an array TREE. The array and the number of elements in the list, N, are globally available. TREE is an array of records where each record is declared as follows:

```
NODE = record
        KEY:KEY_TYPE;
        DATA_VALUE:RECORD_TYPE;
      end;
```

With these preliminaries established, the HEAPSORT procedure debuts.

```
procedure HEAPSORT;
var I,J,MAX,NIT:integer;
    ORDER:boolean;
    T:NODE;
begin
                (* Set up number-in-tree counter  *)
     NIT := N;
  (* While tree exists       *)
     while NIT <> 0 do
            begin
            (* Remove key and value from root node of heap *)
            T := TREE[1];
            (* Copy rightmost leaf node to root node of heap *)
            TREE[1] := TREE[NIT];
            (* Delete rightmost leaf node from the heap*)
            NIT := NIT - 1;
            (* Store largest key and value in array after the
               new rightmost leaf node*)
            TREE [NIT + 1] := T;
            (* Adjust tree to heap status *)
            (* I represents parent node,
               J represents left child, J + 1 right child,
               MAX is the maximum key value of the left and
               right child *)
            (* Initialize parent to root of heap *)
            (* Determine maximum key value of child *)
            (* Switch parent and child until no children *)
            (*     exist or parent and children are ordered *)
            I := 1;
            ORDER := false;
            (* While a left child exists and partial order
            does not exist *)
            while (I * 2 <= NIT) and (not ORDER) do
                    begin
                    J := I * 2 ;
                    (* Determine maximum key value *)
                    (* Check if a right child exists *)
                    if J + 1 <= NIT then
                        (* Left child less than right child?*)
                        if TREE [J].KEY < TREE[J+1].KEY then
                                        MAX := TREE[J+1].KEY
                                                else
                                        MAX := TREE[J].KEY
                          else
                          (* The only left child is maximum *)
                          MAX := TREE[J].KEY;
                    (* Check if partial ordering exists *)
                    if TREE[I].KEY > MAX then
                                (* ORDER is restored *)
                                ORDER := true
                        else
                        (*    Switch parent and child
                        nodes *)
                        if MAX = TREE[J].KEY then
```

```
                              (* Switch with left child *)
                              begin
                                T := TREE[I];
                                TREE[I] := TREE[J];
                                TREE[J] := T;
                                (* Change pointers *)
                                I := J
                              end
                   else
                              (* Switch with right
                              child *)
                              begin
                                T := TREE[I];
                                TREE[I] := TREE[J+1];
                                TREE[J+1] := T;
                                I := J + 1
                              end
                 end
end;
```

The procedure follows the algorithm to a "T," and as a side effect, the array TREE contains the original list in ascending order. When you combine HEAPSORT with procedure CREATEHEAP (which you can tackle as an exercise) then you have a sorting system that requires very little additional storage space and that provides 0(n log n) performance in both the average and worst cases. Just imagine, all of this derived from the partially ordered property, the complete binary tree, and a clever implementation strategy. Just imagine!

 # IMAGINATION CHALLENGE

Vanishing Parabolic Pictures

Recall an event that took place in the past in which you experienced uncomfortable feelings. Recall the experience in its various details—sights, sounds, feelings. Freeze this recollection into a multisensory picture in your mind.

Now imagine the event occurring again. This time you feel comfortable, even happy, with the experience. Imagine the experience in its various details—sights, sounds, feelings. Take a snapshot picture of the scene in your mind.

Perform the following parabolic transformation. On the left side of a parabolic pathway, visualize the old memory picture at a distance. Have the picture move towards you on the pathway, decreasing in size as it nears you until it vanishes right before your eyes. Immediately, the new imagined picture appears, small and clear before your eyes. This picture begins moving away and gets larger as it glides along the right side of the parabolic pathway. Repeat the process five times.

Now, whenever you are in a similar event, you can consciously (or even unconsciously) focus on whichever side of the parabolic pathway you choose to affect you. Choose wisely and live happily.

Quicksort Algorithm

The last O(n log n) algorithm to be presented is special in a different way. It achieves its lush performance from its problem-solving approach rather than from the tree information structure. The problem solving outlook that is adopted is called "divide and conquer." As it applies to our sorting challenge, we divide the array into two subarrays and sort each of them. So the original task is conquered by creating two smaller tasks and performing them. How do you think the subarrays are sorted? "Divide and conquer," of course. The subarray is divided into two subarrays and each of these is sorted. Eventually, the division process produces a subarray of two elements that can be sorted by a single comparison.

By now, recollections of Madam Azza, the palindrome princess of Chapter 2, should be crystallizing and thoughts of recursion recurring. Yes, the quicksort is a recursive algorithm based on the divide-and-conquer strategy. The method of dividing the array is the important aspect of the algorithm, with recursion providing the conquest.

The strategy for dividing the array is to select an element of the array and, based on the value of the selected element, to divide the remaining elements into two subarrays. The criterion used? The elements in one subarray should be less than the selected element and the elements in the other subarray greater than or equal to the selected element. This approach partitions the elements into two groups relative to a pivotal element. The sorting of either subarray does not depend upon or affect the ordering of the other.

The recursive quicksort algorithm is given below:

if array size is greater than 1 do
    1. Select pivotal key in the array.
    2. Partition array into two subarrays around pivotal key.
    3. Quicksort first subarray.
    4. Quicksort second subarray.

As we analyze the implementation requirements of quicksort, two factors demand our attention. Recursion requires the use of a stack, either a system stack through a procedure's calls to itself or a user-designed stack in the procedure. The additional space requirements can influence the usefulness of the quicksort procedure for tables and files with a large number of elements. This is a cost of quicksort that must be considered. The other factor involves the overhead costs in execution time for handling the sequence of recursive procedure calls. For instance, a list of 128 elements requires 254 procedure calls to QUICKSORT before the sorted list emerges.

What improvements are possible? By writing a nonrecursive version of the quicksort algorithm, we can reduce the execution time. A user-implemented stack that holds the bounds of the subarrays that have not been sorted replaces the system stack. Another saving in stack space is realized if the smaller of the subarrays is sorted first. Since the larger subarray will experience more divisions, and therefore more push operations will occur, the depth of the stack is larger. If the smaller subarray is processed first, its bounds are not on the stack when the larger subarray is being processed.

The selection of the pivotal key in a subarray can influence the performance of quicksort. The optimal choice is a key value that causes the subarrays to have an equal number of elements (or a difference of one). If this happens, the minimum number of calls to QUICKSORT is experienced. The worst choice is the minimum or maximum value in the subarray. One selection method is to look at three key values in the subarray and to select the one whose value is between the other two (and hope for the best from the rest!).

The next improvement is rather surprising. The performance measure 0 is based on the algorithm's performance when n, the number of list elements, grows large. However, for small n, the actual performance of some $0(n^2)$ sort algorithms is better than $0(n \log n)$ algorithms. With the overhead involved in recursion and the stack, quicksort suffers from this drawback. So we choose a threshold value for the size of the array. QUICKSORT is applied whenever the array size is above the threshold and, let's say, the selection sort is used when it is below the threshold. It has been suggested by Dr. D. Knuth, author of the classic book, The Art of Computer Programming, Vol. III: Sorting and Searching,* that a threshold value of nine elements is appropriate.

Technology may provide the last improvement for the quicksort algorithm. In quicksort, the subarrays are disjoint and their ordering is independent of each other. It we had two CPUs with two copies of the quicksort program and a shared memory unit, then the list would be sorted in about half the time. And if we had a multiprocessor system . . . ? The effects of such new computer architecture on algorithm design and performance is only beginning to be felt. You are the computer professionals who will be leading us through its adolescence.

With these suggestions, let's look at a revised version of the quicksort algorithm:

```
if the array size is greater than nine then
    1. Select pivotal key using the medium of three keys;
    2. Partition array into two subarrays around pivotal key;
    3. If first subarray is smaller than second subarray
            then quicksort first subarray,
                    quicksort second subarray
            else  quicksort second subarray,
                    quicksort first subarray
else use selection sort on the array.
```

This approach incorporates three of the improvements into the algorithm. You can include another by writing the PASCAL procedure for quicksort without using recursion. This challenge is included as one of the exercises.

One step in the algorithm remains the major challenge to the implementation process—partitioning of the array around the pivotal key. In what ways can we approach this task? Two stacks could be used to separate the array elements, based on the value of the pivotal element. After the partition is completed, the stacks are emptied and stored sequentially in the array on both sides of the pivotal key. The big disadvantages are the extra memory space and the movement of all the records. So maybe this isn't a good idea for large lists.

The next approach involves some movement of records but does not require more memory space (besides a few local identifiers). It resembles a tennis match with the focus alternating from one end of the array to the other. The algorithm to perform the partitioning is given below:

Initialize lower pointer to lower bound of the array.

*Addison-Wesley, Reading, MA, 1973.

Initialize upper pointer to upper bound of the array plus one.
Interchange the first key and the pivotal key.
while lower pointer is less than upper pointer do
    1. Shift lower pointer to the right
        until the pivotal key is less than or equal to the key pointed to by lower pointer.
    2. Shift higher pointer to the left
        until the pivotal key is greater than or equal to the key pointed to by upper pointer.
    3. If lower pointer is less than upper pointer
        then interchange the two keys pointed to by the lower and the upper pointers.
Interchange the pivotal key in the first position and the key pointed to by the upper pointer.
Shift upper pointer to the left one position.

After this process, the first subarray is delimited by the first position of the array
through the upper pointer and the second subarray is found in the positions indicated by the lower pointer through the maximum subscript. The pivotal key is between
the subarrays and occupies its correct position in the soon-to-be sorted array.

The following table demonstrates the sequence of shifts and interchanges on an
array of seven elements. Assume that the pivotal key equals six, and is pointed to by
k.

The quicksort algorithm produces the best average performance, both in the analytical measure of $O(n \log n)$ and in actual benchmark testing, of all the sort algo-

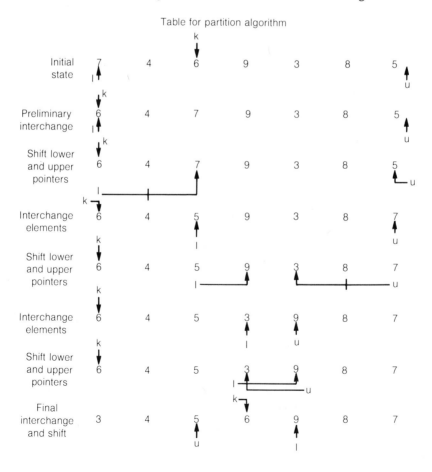

Table for partition algorithm

rithms presented. The algorithm was presented in 1962 by C. Hoare, during the dawn of the recursion concept. It is a tribute to this concept that quicksort has retained its primacy. An unusual feature of quicksort is that an ordered list results in $O(n^2)$ performance. So even the quickest can be quirky, though perky.

■ "JUST FOR REFERENCE"

The objective of sort algorithms is to arrange n *records into ascending order based on the value of the key field.*

Performance measures include—

- benchmark testing
- algorithm analysis—$O(n \log n)$, $O(n^2)$

Options for key/record arrangements are—

- sorting and exchanging entire records
- sorting and exchanging pointers to records

Selection algorithm—$O(n^2)$

for i = 1 to n − 1 do
    1. search for the smallest key among the
       keys k_i through k_n
    2. exchange the record with the smallest
       key with the record with the key k_i

Insertion algorithm—$O(n^2)$

for i = 2 to n do
    shift the record with key k_i forward until
    the record with key k_j is less than the
    record with key k_i

Bubble algorithm—$O(n^2)$

while the number of passes is less than n and some exchanges occur do
    1. set exchange flag to false
    2. increment number of passes by 1
    3. for i = the number of passes to n − 1 do
        if the record with key k_i is greater than the record with key k_{i+1} then
           1. exchange records
           2. set exchange flag to true

Tree sort algorithm—$O(n \log n)$

for each list element do
    1. if tree is empty then
             make list element the root of the tree
      else
        while a tree element exists to investigate do
        if the list element is less than the tree element then

move to the left child of the tree element
else
     move to the right child of the tree element
  2. attach list element to the last tree element investigated

Heapsort algorithm—0(n log n)

while a tree exists do
  1. remove record from the top of the heap
  2. copy record from rightmost leaf node to
      the root node
  3. delete rightmost leaf node
  4. adjust tree to become a heap

Recall that a heap of size n is a partially ordered, complete binary tree with n elements.

Quicksort algorithm—0(n log n)

if array size is greater than 1 do
  1. select pivotal key from the array
  2. partition array into two subarrays around
      pivotal key
  3. quicksort first subarray
  4. quicksort second subarray

Quicksort provides the best overall performance.

EXERCISES

1. Describe three situations not mentioned in this chapter in which items are ordered physically.

2. Describe three situations not mentioned in this chapter in which items are ordered mentally but not physically.

3. Describe three occasions when the operating system sort utility would be required by a user.

4. What are the three areas of concern in selecting a sort algorithm?

5. Explain the two methods of evaluating the performance of algorithms.

6. Describe three benchmark data sets for the sort algorithm.

7. Explain what the measures $0(n)$, $0(n \log n)$, and $0(n^2)$ mean in terms of data set size and algorithm performance.

8. Show that an algorithm to add a node to an AVL tree is an $0(\log n)$ algorithm.

9. Suggest a way to measure performance of a recursive algorithm.

10. Write a selection sort procedure. Are there any improvements to the algorithm that you can suggest?

11. Write an insertion sort procedure by sorting pointers to records.

12. Design and write an insertion sort procedure to arrange a bridge hand. Arrange the hand by suits—clubs then diamonds then hearts then spades—and then by card value within each suit.

13. Write the insertion sort procedure using a binary search to find the correct position.

14. Write the selection sort procedure using a linked list to facilitate the exchange process.

15. Write the bubble sort procedure using the improvements mentioned in the text.

16. Develop a tree sort procedure based on an in-threaded, height-balanced tree.

17. Develop a tree sort procedure based on a 3-ary tree.

18. Assume that you have 50 elements in a list. Draw three versions of m-ary tree structures that are balanced. Discuss the best, average, and worst cases for accessing a typical element in the tree.

19. Develop a tree sort procedure based on a B-tree of order 4.

20. The heapsort depends on two properties for its operation. What are they? How do they contribute to the algorithm's operation and efficiency?

21. Revise the heapsort procedure to reduce the number of exchanges. By waiting until its final position is determined, the child can be shifted up the tree and the parent can occupy the node of the last shifted child. Implement this improvement.

22. Write the CREATEHEAP procedure to implement the heap sort algorithm presented in the text.

23. Write the quicksort procedure using recursion.

24. Write the quicksort procedure without using recursion.

25. Design three benchmark data sets and perform an analysis of the recursive and nonrecursive quicksort procedures.

THE WORKOUT ROOM

PROJECT 1:   *MO_SORT: A Fine-Tuning Sort*

The quicksort algorithm was presented with some suggested improvements. One important change was to use a different sort when the number of elements reached a specific threshold.

Develop a program called MO_SORT, a Measure Optimizing sort system, which allows you to test different threshold levels in order to fine-tune the performance of procedure quicksort. The program accepts the threshold level to be tested and sorts three benchmark files, producing statistics that are useful for the comparison of the threshold levels. The number of comparisons, the number of procedure calls, the actual execution time, and anything else you select are appropriate measures to include in the evaluation.

The three benchmark files should include one that is almost ordered, one that is almost in reverse order, and one that is a potpourri of values. A file with approximately 100 values is desirable.

Determine the optimal threshold value when the insertion and the selection sort are used as the alternate algorithms.

PROJECT 2:   *The Law of Diminishing Returns*

In a recent legal battle between two fictitious software firms, the judge issued an interesting ruling. The contest was over a sort of software paternity suit. One firm, Dessert, Insert, and Flirt, claimed that the other firm, Sea, Shell, and Shore, used a copyrighted sorting algorithm in the production of the software package entitled SEASHELLSORT. The counterclaim by

Sea, Shell, and Shore was that their sorting method came first and that the competitors' package—INSERTSORT—is just a degenerate case of their method with a diminished increment equal to one.

The judge, who soon after went on vacation to a dessert island with carob seashells, has ruled that you should write a PASCAL program to be sold by both firms.

The specifications are that if the number of data elements to be sorted is less than 123 then the INSERTSORT method is to be used. When the number of data elements is larger than this threshold then the SEASHELLSORT method is chosen. For this method described in this chapter's TRADE-OFFS section the sequence of increments must be relatively prime. A function will be used to find the integer that is relatively prime to the last increment and close to half its size. The sorted list of numbers is to be printed in five columns with a summary of the number of comparisons and interchanges.

Flirting with the challenge for a fleeting moment, you "sea" clearly the merging of the insert and shell sort algorithms. With dedicated effort, you are "shore" to get your just desserts.

APPENDIX A

Syntax Diagrams and Samples of Pascal Statements

Interpreting Syntax Diagrams

The syntax of a PASCAL statement can be checked by tracing through the following syntax diagrams. You begin at the leftmost arrow and follow it to a bounded phrase or word or to an intersection point.

BOUNDED WORDS FALL INTO TWO CATEGORIES:

1. Pascal keywords and punctuation symbols
These are bounded by rectangles and represent a class of entities defined by another syntax diagram. When these are encountered in a diagram, the new diagram is to be consulted to

2. Additional syntax entities
These are bounded by rectangles and represent a class of entities defined by another syntax diagram. When these are encountered in a diagram, the new diagram is to be consulted to analyze the correctness of the entity. If the entity is syntactically correct, the original syntax diagram is returned to.*

When you reach an intersection point, you must decide which path to take based on the next entity to be encountered. An important aspect of intersection points is that they can produce loops. In terms of PASCAL, this means, for example, that the number of statements in a *repeat* statement is indefinite.

You have completely and correctly analyzed a PASCAL statement (or a syntax entity for that matter) when you reach the rightmost arrowhead.

*Not all additional syntax entities are presented in this appendix. For a complete set consult a PASCAL text.

449

Statement

SYNTAX DIAGRAM

Figure AP.1

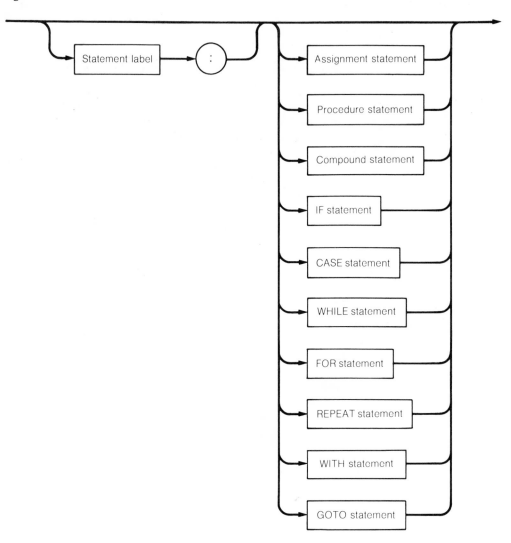

SAMPLES

```
1.                          (* the empty statement *)
2.  40 : X := 0             (* a labelled statement *)
3.  GET_NEXT (NODE_PTR)     (* a procedure call   *)
4.  begin
      .
      .
      .
    end                     (* a compound statement *)
```

Assignment Statement

SYNTAX DIAGRAM

Figure AP.2

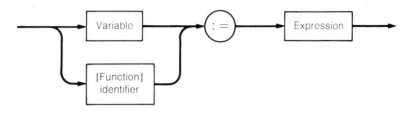

SAMPLES

1. `X := 41.6`
2. `TR := MX_TERM`
3. `I_VAL := MATCH and RIGHT`
4. `COST := 3.4 * PRICE + OVER`

Boolean or Algebraic Expression

SYNTAX DIAGRAM

Figure AP.3A **Expression**

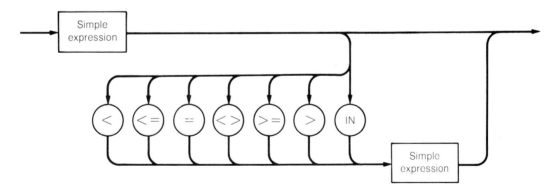

Figure AP.3B **Simple expression**

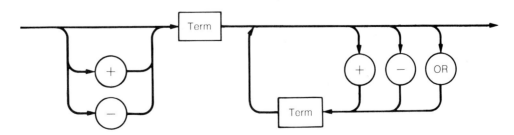

Figure AP.3C **Term**

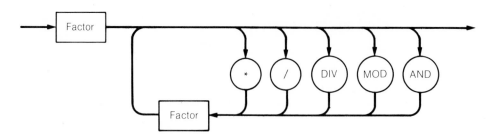

Figure AP.3D **Factor**

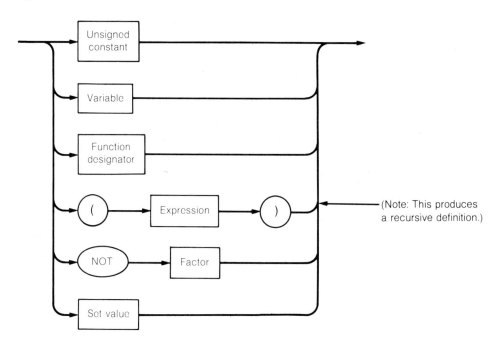

(Note: This produces a recursive definition.)

SAMPLES

1. X <= 14.5
2. X + 2 <> MAX
3. B * B - 4 * A * C
4. X > 5 or X < 0
5. (B - A) * (A - C) + (C - B)
        (NOTE: 3 recursive uses of the syntax diagram)

procedure Statement

SYNTAX DIAGRAM

Figure AP.4

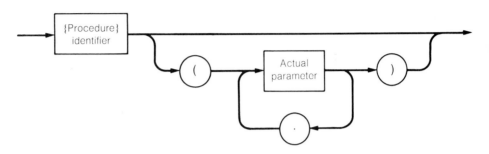

SAMPLES

1. `SHIFT_QUEUE`
2. `PUSH(16.3,STACK)`
3. `POP ( VAL, STACK, SUCCESS_FLAG)`

Compound Statement

SYNTAX DIAGRAM

Figure AP.5

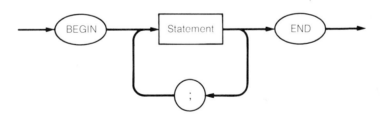

SAMPLES

1. ```
   begin
   end                              (* the empty block *)
   ```
2. ```
   begin
      if X > 0 then POS := true
                else POS := false
   end
   ```
3. ```
   begin
   A := A  + FISH[I];
   I := I + 1
      end
   ```
   ```

if Statement

SYNTAX DIAGRAM

Figure AP.6

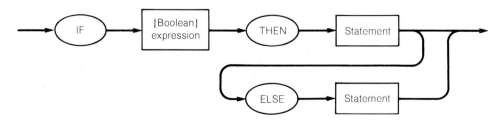

SAMPLES

```
1.  if X < 0 then T:= 0
2.  if P + 2 < 0 then E_VAL := P + 2
                  else E_VAL := D
3.  if A[I] > A[I + 2] then begin
                            T := A[I];
                            A[I] := A[I+2];
                            A[I+2] := T
                            end
4.  if A < B then
            if B < C then MAX := C
                     else MAX := B
            else
            if A < C then MAX := C
                     else MAX := A
```

case Statement

SYNTAX DIAGRAM

Figure AP.7

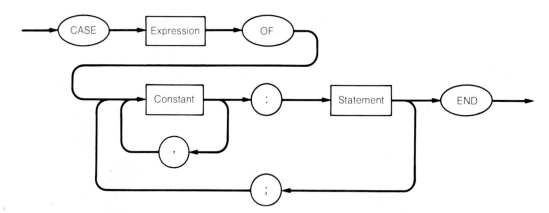

SAMPLES

```
1.  case RESPONSE of
            1 :   WAGE := 4.50 ;
            2 :   WAGE := 6.50 ;
         3, 4 : WAGE := SALARY/52.0
    end
2.  case  FLAG of
      true : begin
                SORT_ARRAY(X);
                SORT_ARRAY(Y);
                MERGE(X,Y,BIG_ARRAY)
             end
      false : begin
                SORT_ARRAY(Y);
                SORT_ARRAY(Z);
                MERGE(Y,Z,BIG_ARRAY)
              end
```

while Statement

SYNTAX DIAGRAM

Figure AP.8

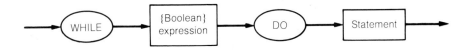

SAMPLES

```
1.  while X[I] > 0 do I := I + 1
2.  while I < 15 do begin
                    T := T + A[I];
                    I := I + 1
                 end
3.  while (PTR <> nil) and (MATCH <> true) do
                  if PTR^.VAL <> MATCH_VAL then
                          PTR := PTR^.NEXT
                              else
                      MATCH := true
```

for Statement

SYNTAX DIAGRAM

Figure AP.9

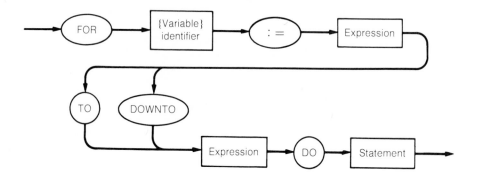

SAMPLES

```
1.  for K := 1 to MAX do A_TOTAL := A_TOTAL + A[K]
2.  for K := UP_BOUND downto LOW_BOUND do
           F_VAL[K] := F_VAL[K-1]
3.  for K := L_BOUND to U_BOUND do
             begin
             if A[K] > 0 then
                           K_POS := K_POS + 1;
             if A[K] < 0 then
                           K_NEG := K_NEG + 1
             end
4.  for R := 1 to MAX do
         for C := R to MAX do
             T := T + X_ARRAY[R,C]
```

repeat Statement

SYNTAX DIAGRAM

Figure AP.10

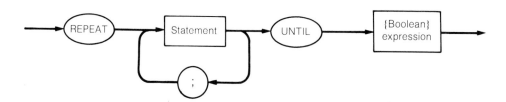

SAMPLES

```
1.  repeat I := I + 1
    until X[I] <= 0
2.  repeat
      T := T + A[I];
      I := I + 1
    until I >= 15
3.  repeat
      I := 1 ;
      repeat
          T := T + A[I,J];
          I := I + 1
      until I >= 15 ;
      J := J + 1
    until J >= 15
```

with Statement

SYNTAX DIAGRAM

Figure AP.11

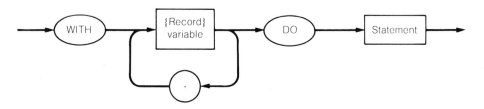

SAMPLES

```
1.  with STUDENT do begin
                NAME := 'BRUCE' ;
                NUMBER := 43210 ;
                CLASS := 7107 ;
             end
2.  with PTR^ do begin
                AFTER := RIGHT_LINK ;
                BEFORE := LEFT_LINK ;
                dispose ( PTR )
             end
```

INDEX